RETROLAND

RETROLAND

A READER'S GUIDE TO THE
DAZZLING DIVERSITY OF
MODERN FICTION

PETER KEMP

YALE UNIVERSITY PRESS
NEW HAVEN AND LONDON

To David and Tricia
Friends of a Lifetime

The past is made of paper
Margaret Atwood

For information about this and other Yale University Press publications, please contact:
U.S. Office: sales.press@yale.edu   yalebooks.com
Europe Office: sales@yaleup.co.uk   yalebooks.co.uk

Set in Adobe Caslon Pro by IDSUK (DataConnection) Ltd
Printed in Great Britain by TJ Books Limited, Padstow, Cornwall

Library of Congress Control Number: 2023937596

ISBN 978-0-300-26962-8

A catalogue record for this book is available from the British Library.

10 9 8 7 6 5 4 3 2 1

CONTENTS

CONTENTS

Part IV   Post-scripts: The Literary Past and Its Afterlife

CONTENTS

Part V Back to the Future: The Impending Past

ACKNOWLEDGEMENTS

In the course of writing *Retroland*, I have run up many debts of gratitude.

The first is to my editor, Julian Loose, who suggested that I write the book and has been a paragon of patience in awaiting its completion and a model of expertise throughout the publication process. It has been a pleasure to work with him and his colleagues at Yale University Press: Frazer Martin, Rachael Lonsdale and Lucy Buchan.

Warm thanks must also go to successive literary editors of the *Sunday Times* for whom, over forty years, I have written as a reviewer and who sent me many of the novels I have drawn upon for *Retroland*: Claire Tomalin, Penny Perrick, John Walsh, Harry Richie, Geordie Greig, Caroline Gascoigne, Susannah Herbert and Johanna Thomas-Corr. Andrew Holgate, the longest-serving literary editor I have worked with – not only as a reviewer but as the paper's fiction editor – couldn't have been a more congenial office companion as well as a continuing highly-valued friend. I would like to thank him and other former colleagues on the paper – David Mills, Helen Hawkins, Cheryl Younson, Jo Duckworth, Mia Ogden, Alex Clark, Robert Collins, Caroline Mansfield and Christina Borg – for years of enjoyable camaraderie in spreading the word about new books. I would also like to express my thanks to Blake Morrison for first inviting me to be a reviewer for the *Times Literary Supplement*, and to Alan Hollinghurst and Lindsay Duguid, editors it was a joy to write for.

Producers and presenters of BBC radio programmes such as *Open Book*, *Kaleidoscope*, *Front Row* and *Critics' Forum* have been of help in frequently inviting me to talk about present-day fiction. Especial gratitude in this regard is due to Tom Sutcliffe and Di Speirs.

I am grateful to novelists, too numerous to name, for insights into their writing given during platform interviews with me at literary festivals, and to festival organisers – especially Sally Dunsmore of the Oxford Literary Festival and Jo James and associates at Cheltenham – for providing such opportunities.

Great gratitude is due to Geoffrey Thomas for inviting me to be a visiting fellow of Kellogg College, Oxford, of which he was then president. His wit, conviviality and verve made academic and social occasions there exhilarating. The English Literature Summer School at Exeter College, Oxford, where, for a number of years, I conducted seminars on contemporary fiction with international graduate students, were invaluable in sharpening my thoughts about current fiction in English and, through lively group discussion, opening up fresh perspectives. Thanks to all who attended them, and to the Summer School's present director, Sandie Byrne, who has been an unflagging encourager of *Retroland*.

So have many other friends: most notably, Mark Lawson, Hilary and John Spurling, Derek Johns, Beatrice Groves, Eddie Gaynor, Judith Stinton, David Brown, Gill King, Tricia Feeney, Gail Cunningham and Joe Bailey. Their much-appreciated support and suggestions continually buoyed me up during the writing of this book.

Two friends must receive special mention.

John Carey, whose books and reviews have shone out as examples of the heights literary criticism can achieve, and who was kind enough to read my typescript, has long been a matchless inspiration.

ACKNOWLEDGEMENTS

David Grylls, whose friendship I have been fortunate indeed to have enjoyed for many years, has in numerous conversations about this book been tirelessly generous in giving it the benefit of his keen critical alertness, stylistic sensitivity, shrewd advice and heartening enthusiasm. I owe him boundless gratitude.

PREFACE

This book aims to be both a map and a display case.

Charting what I see as the salient feature of fiction in English during the last half-century or so – a widespread and diverse enthralment with the past – it also highlights novels that stand out as particularly significant, accomplished, and appealing. As I argue, fictional engagement with the past in various forms expanded massively from around 1970, becoming an unprecedented phenomenon. Combining an overview of novelists' predominant concerns and techniques during this period with frequent close-ups and analyses of especially notable novels, *Retroland* traces interactions between individual imaginations and fictional trends. This approach will, I hope, prove useful both to readers wishing for a survey of the vast terrain of modern fiction and those looking for rewarding and pleasurable novels they may have missed.

Although this book focuses on British fiction, it also draws on works from North America, the Indian subcontinent, Africa, Australasia and the Far East whenever, in an age of literary internationalism, they seem relevant to the argument. The last fifty years have been a rich period for fiction in English all around the world. As *Retroland* seeks to demonstrate – and celebrate – it has displayed both dazzling diversity and remarkable consistency.

INTRODUCTION
Retroland: The Pervading Past

Fiction in English has never looked more various. In style and subject, it is strikingly diverse. Books bulkier than Victorian three-deckers appear alongside slivers of minimalist brevity. There are novels written in blank verse, in three-line stanzas and *ottava rima* sonnets; novels published in serial form, as strip-cartoons, as podcasts or on Twitter; novels interleaved with photographs, maps and recipes; novels composed of texts and emails; novels with chapters printed in different colours or which can be read from back to front or front to back. Bookshops bulge with fantastic fables and fiction barely distinguishable from reportage. Parody, pastiche and other forms of literary ventriloquism are on offer next to novels of raw confessional candour. Magic realism and dirty realism share shelves. Niche appeal 'meta-fiction' rubs jackets with mega-sale blockbusters. Fiction has come from many quarters, among them politicians, stand-up comedians, chefs and food columnists, foreign correspondents, a catwalk model, a celebrity ballroom dancer, a jockey, a tennis champion, a concert pianist, a TV gardener, a quiz show host and a South London vicar who passed himself off as a Muslim schoolgirl to achieve publication. There are novels with variant endings or in which things happen backwards, novels written

1

in the second-person singular or the first-person plural, novels consisting entirely of questions or largely made up of lines 'sourced word for word' from a hundred other books. There's a novel that uses only the 483 words spoken by Ophelia in *Hamlet*, and another that includes a sentence 13,955 words long. One novel excludes the verb 'to have' and makes its prose wander around the page because its subject is dispossessed vagrants. In another, a tapeworm lodged in a Glaswegian policeman's gut intermittently extrudes its say in a wavy-edged tract of prose undulating through the middle of his narrative.

Other out-of-the-way narrators range from a 6,500-year-old Sumerian pot to a supermarket trolley, a fig tree, a bottle of wine (a 'pert, garrulous' Fleurie 1962), and a book (a first edition of Joseph Roth's 1924 novel, *Rebellion*). In a first for French letters, a condom narrates a short story. One thriller's villain is a homicidal high-rise building; another's is a hedge-fund algorithm that goes lethally berserk. Protagonists stretch from dwarves to giants, from a fiddle-playing foetus (and other embryos, including a budding Hamlet) to a 139-year-old Australian conman and a bear that plays jazz on a saxophone. Characters with unorthodox physical fitments – wings, webbed feet, horns, cloven hoofs – appear. Flippered and furred human mutants misshapen by the after-effects of nuclear disaster lurch into view. Psychological abnormality is even more rampant: Jacobean drama and the Gothic novel pale alongside the cannibals, murderous psychotics, serial killers, necrophiliacs, baroque sadists and tattooed sociopaths prowling the pages of fiction in the decades leading up to and after the turn of the millennium.

Clones and other bio-engineered humanoid species have been given fictional voice. Forensic pathologists, paedophiles, bankers, biographers, addicts, alcoholics, archaeologists, abused children, amnesiacs, historians, imperialists and immigrants have proved particularly recurrent character types. One novel is narrated by a man who believes he is a bird. In others, the animal kingdom becomes vocal itself. A novel sequence featuring rabbits, and another chronicling fierce power struggles and palpitating passion among moles have voluminously unrolled. Apes, chimpanzees and monkeys have chattered for attention from some branches of fiction. Dogs – a black Labrador, Marilyn Monroe's Maltese terrier – tell tales. One book's protagonist is a Plantagenet pig. In another, a woodworm stowed away on Noah's Ark gives its version of events. Vampires, revenants and zombies have made a spectacular comeback and deceased real-life personages have been imaginatively exhumed in teeming profusion.

Some books (one commandeering H.G. Wells's Time Machine for its purposes) have journeyed into the future (most usually the further reaches of the twenty-first century, though sometimes far more distantly ahead). Others have sidestepped into alternative worlds where Britain languishes as a Chekhovian colony of the Soviet Empire, an outpost of the victorious Third Reich or a subject territory of the Papacy in a Europe where the Reformation never happened.

To attempt an overview of fiction in English since 1970 is, at first, to be dazzled by a shimmer of miscellaneousness. Can patterns – significant preoccupations, shared motives and motifs, revealingly recurrent character types or narrative strategies – be discerned amid it all? This book will argue that they can, and that by far the most widespread and important of them is an obsession with the past.

Aftermath, repercussions and consequences are the key features of modern fiction in English. Characteristically, it is haunted by consciousness of what has gone before. Looking back is the favoured authorial stance. Storylines are heavily reliant on the rear-view mirror. Nemesis – especially when uncoiling over a long period of time – is a habitual plot device. Where the typifying concern of the Victorian novel was to demonstrate connections between one sector of society and another, the typifying concern of late twentieth- and early twenty-first-century fiction is to demonstrate connections between the present and the past. In an era when the heritage industry burgeoned, heritage (of various kinds, from the most intimately personal to the global) became the dominant fictional preoccupation. Since the 1970s, when the prefix 'retro' first came into vogue, novelists and short story writers have been overwhelmingly drawn into an imaginative territory that constitutes a vast retroland, extensively and inventively concerned with retrospect and recall.

Even structurally, links between the present and the past have been given prominence. A pervasive type of fiction has been the dual-narrative, double time-scheme novel which juxtaposes a contemporary story with one set in an earlier era – most usually the Victorian age – in order to display continuities and parallels. Some novels were composed of even more chronological strata. Ranging from 1650 to 1988, the twelve chapters of Adam Thorpe's debut novel, *Ulverton* (1992), stack up into a history of a Wessex village from its starting-point to its disintegration. E. Annie Proulx's *Accordion Crimes* (1996) charts a century of American immigrant life by recording what occurs as a small button accordion brought to the New World from Sicily gets passed, across eight chapters, through different ethnic groups and different epochs.

'The present,' Vladimir Nabokov observed, 'is only the top of the past.' Constantly, in modern fiction, there's an acute sense of underlying layers – cultural, political, ancestral, personal, literary – on which present-day lives are based. In its eagerness to reveal them, fiction regularly becomes a kind of excavation – sometimes literally so. Numerous novels resound to the clink of spades and trowels as historic sites – prehistoric barrows, tumuli, ancient tombs – are delved into. Archaeology is a prospering fictional profession. So are associated activities such as researching into local or family history, retrieving manuscripts from archives or picture restoration, in which later accretions are peeled away to disclose original outlines beneath. In parallel mode, psychotherapists have been kept busy uncovering the abused child behind the impaired adult or locating early trauma from which malformed maturity has stemmed. Edward St Aubyn likens his Patrick Melrose novels – in which he deals with his father's sexual abuse of him as a child – to 'an archaeological dig'. Cormoran Strike, the private investigator in the detective novels J.K. Rowling publishes under the name Robert Galbraith, thinks of himself as 'playing archaeologist among the ruins of people's traumatised memories'. Memory is of crucial concern in novel after novel. In thrillers, amnesia regularly puts characters in deadly jeopardy. Elsewhere, suppressed or distorted memories are tellingly re-awakened.

The impulse to rewind back to warping starting points has sometimes taken idiosyncratic forms: attempting to unravel the making of a Nazi, Martin Amis's *Time's Arrow* (1991) opens at the moment of his death, then re-spools the events of his life in reverse, concluding with his birth cry. In more conventional ways, consciousness of being at the end of processes whose beginnings need to be discovered and explored has pervaded novels. Some authors have looked ahead but, in doing so, depicted future catastrophes as the consequences of past neglect. 'Sadly, at some point in the 1960s, our sense of the future seemed to atrophy and die', J.G. Ballard remarked. 'Over-population and the threat of nuclear war, environmentalist concerns for our ravaged planet and unease at an increasingly wayward science together made everyone fearful of the future.' The optimistic confidence with which writers such as H.G. Wells (switching off the electrifying pessimism of his 1890s science fiction) greeted the dawn of the twentieth century was nowhere in evidence at the dawn of the twenty-first and the new millennium. Instead, novelists specialised in scenarios of apocalyptic alarm, in which ecological fecklessness is punitively scourged by climate calamity (scorching drought, devastating floods or the rigours of a new ice age) or plagued by indestructible pests, technological collapse and incurable diseases. A notable cluster of novels foresee sterility for our species. In 'speculative fiction' such as Margaret Atwood's *Oryx and Crake* trilogy, present apprehensions about past negligence become future nightmares.

It is to the past, however, that authors' imaginations have most often turned. Historical fiction has thrived. In her 2017 Reith Lectures about the genre, Hilary Mantel – who appreciably boosted its prestige by twice winning the Man Booker Prize with her Tudor novels, *Wolf Hall* (2009) and *Bring Up the Bodies* (2012) – recalled how, when she began writing in the 1970s, historical fiction 'wasn't respectable or respected. It meant historical romance.' From the 1970s onwards, though, fancy-dress escapism dwindled as a significant component of the genre. Stressing that the past is something whose presence can't be escaped, historical novelists saw themselves as writing books that very much pertain to the here and now. 'I don't want to live in the past, but I want to live in a present which is rooted in the past. Only as an extension of the past does the present cease to be a chaos of unmeaning', declared Philip Glazebrook, author of engaging adventure novels set in the twilight years of the Ottoman Empire. 'Only continuity gives coherence.' The aphorism by the German Romantic writer Novalis – 'Novels arise out of the shortcomings of history' – which Penelope Fitzgerald used as an epigraph to her 1995 novel about his early life, *The Blue Flower* (and which Andrew Taylor approvingly quoted in a historical note to his 2003 'Gothic mystery novel' about Edgar Allan Poe, *The American Boy*), is widely applicable to ones published since 1970. Recuperation, restitution, filling gaps, exhuming buried heritages, giving stifled voices a hearing and overlooked groups a presence have been major concerns.

As the year 2000 neared, Helen Dunmore (a novelist who excelled at silhouetting figures against turbulent past eras: the First World War, the siege of Leningrad, the French Revolution) noted that 'the status of historical fiction has changed greatly over the past few years. It has escaped from the corral of genre and now dominates the mainstream literary lists.' One reason for this 'longing to capture the past for our own purposes', she suggested, was the looming of the new millennium: 'We are alarmed by the blank, silent sheet of years around the corner we will turn 18 months from now. While we are still in our home century, we want to imagine again the events that have shaped it.' Certainly, this seems a factor in the great swivel of fictional interest back to the past. But it is only one. After the move into the new millennium, the phenomenon continued, indeed escalated. The pivotal date for this shift was not just before the new millennium but three decades earlier around 1970 or so. It was then that an increasingly extending and intensifying preoccupation with the past got under way.

It was a preoccupation that fell into four categories. First, as the British Empire drew to a close, came an engrossment with the political past: imperialism and its aftermath widely colonised fiction. Second, there was growing engagement with the personal past: novels uncovered buried trauma, childhood damage, traumatic war experience and suppressed lives. Third, historical fiction – the hoisting of bygone worlds back into light – flourished as never before. Fourth, the literary past inspired fiction on an unprecedented scale: novelists plundered the cultural heritage for re-workings, updatings, subvertings, imitations and extensions of classic texts; sequels and prequels proliferated.

In December 2017, Reuters reported that a Belgian man in Ostend, who had chained himself to a block of marble for a live-streamed online performance designed 'to show the "burden of history" from which artists cannot escape', found he was unable to free himself and had to be cut loose after 19 days. 'This block was symbolic of history, the history of art, which I am trying to free myself from. I discovered that this is not possible', he explained. It's a realisation that, in less concrete ways, has been central to fiction in English since 1970.

The rich diversity and often mixed cultural backgrounds of authors writing during this period have rightly received much attention. But, wherever they originated from or came to be located, novelists have had far more in common than separates them. Foremost in this is an alertness less to geographical links than to historical ones. Late twentieth- and early twenty-first-century novelists, whether from Britain, America, India, Africa or Australasia, are never more united than in their enthralment with the past. And the aspect of the past that most extensively engages them is the one that, among other things, gave them their common language: the British Empire. At the start of the 1970s, the after-effects of its splintering apart opened up half a century and more of a remarkable fictional fixation on the past.

Part I

Ends of Empire: The Imperial Past and Its Aftermath

The Ubiquity of Empire

The closing decades of the twentieth century witnessed an unprecedented fictional scramble for empire. Imperialism was the overriding novelistic concern. Almost as fast as history furled up the British Empire, novelists unrolled it again and sent their imaginations out across the great swathe of the map once coloured pink. Many other imperial territories were revisited too: the Venetian and Ottoman empires, the Austro-Hungarian and Russian empires, France's Second Empire under Napoleon III and China's Celestial Empire at the time of the Opium Wars. To delineate salient aspects of colonialism, some authors harked back as far as ancient Britain or imperial Rome. Others projected empires into outer space and fanned them out across the galaxies. Hypothetical empires – England as an outpost of the Holy Roman Empire or under Nazi or Soviet domination; Voorstand, an empire parodically embodying American cultural colonialism – were envisioned as well.

Attitudes to these exhumed or invented empires varied considerably. Imperialism was romanticised, splashed with the gaudy pigments of swashbuckling adventure or suffused in sepia washes of nostalgia.

It was denounced, derided, documented with detailed actuality and burlesqued with surreal farce. Empires became venues for exotic extravaganza, stages for period drama, arenas of violent racial and cultural confrontation. They served as allegories and object lessons, as gorgeously mouldering reminders of inevitable decay and the inexorable erosions of time, as crumbled monuments to the futility of human vaingloriousness and as fierce battlegrounds of political and economic forces. All phases of the phenomenon of imperialism were inspected – from brutal annexations to elegiac lowerings of the flag. With especial frequency, pastiche was deployed to evoke and irony to deflate Victorian and Edwardian imperial swank. Increasingly, from all corners of the English-speaking world, postcolonial voices gave new accents to the epic of empire. Moods in these novels – ranging from angry indignation to cynicism, shame, wistfulness and grudging respect – were diverse. Novelists highlighted different facets of empire to conform with their own psychological, emotional or imaginative configurations, personal, national or racial experience, or political predilections. But, for more than half a century, fascination with the subject proved strikingly persistent.

What is surprising about this fascination is that, by the middle of the twentieth century, empire seemed to have lost its potency as a fictional theme. Writing in 1969 about that stretch of the British Empire which was to show itself of particular allure to novelists in the later twentieth century, Paul Scott wryly observed, 'To the British at home, India has always been high on the list of subjects that fail to arouse their curiosity.' It was not long to remain so. Two authors – Scott himself and J.G. Farrell – inaugurated a decisive reversal of this state of affairs. Already, in 1966, the first of Scott's *Raj Quartet* novels, *The Jewel in the Crown*, had staked out purposeful claim to the territory. Seven years later, with *The Siege of Krishnapur*, Farrell moved into it from a different direction. Together, the two writers initiated a fictional era: one in which empire, under all its aspects, from its origins to its aftermath – and with particular emphasis on the antagonisms it fomented, the displacements it caused and the voices it stifled – would engage the attentions of a phenomenally wide range of novelists.

J.G. Farrell

Throughout the 1970s, the most prominent motifs in novels about empire were disillusion and dissolution. A book that did much to establish them was J.G. Farrell's first historical novel, *Troubles* (1970). Located in a crumbling residential hotel in the turbulent Ireland of 1919–1921, it also registers imperial turmoil further afield by inter-leaving its narrative with newspaper reports of unrest in more far-flung colonies: from Amritsar in India, Mesopotamia, South Africa. Symbolic resonances reverberate from its setting, the Majestic Hotel, an imposingly named but dilapidated edifice incorporating such allegorical amenities as a mildewed Imperial Bar and a Palm Court where unruly tropic growths are taking over. Indigenous roots and branches bursting with flamboyant energy through an imperial overlay really start to come into their own in the 1980s. In the 1970s, as *Troubles* exorbitantly exhibits, it was the disintegration of empire that most stirred imaginations.

Behind its stately façade, the Majestic, a battlemented building populated by superannuated old colonials, is extravagantly ramshackle. Even amid formidable competition in Anglo-Irish fiction, where the decrepit mansion is a stock property, it stands out as spectacularly precarious, echoing with ominous creaks and falling apart at an alarming rate. Finally going up in flames, it is for years under threat from internal decay and external hostility. In this, it resembles the settings of Farrell's subsequent books: the battered and beleaguered British Residency in *The Siege of Krishnapur* (1973) and the flaccid colonial community engulfed by Japanese troops in *The Singapore Grip* (1978).

Each spotlighting an episode of British imperial calamity – the Irish Troubles, the 1857 'Indian Mutiny', the fall of Singapore – these novels send mockery flickering over the incongruities of empire. The bizarre out-of-placeness of the colonists and their cultural baggage keeps attracting Farrell's satiric attention. In *The Siege of Krishnapur*, *objets d'art* high-mindedly imported to afford an improving spectacle to 'the natives' ultimately are deployed as desperate, last-ditch weaponry against them: fired from a cannon, an electro-metal bust of Shakespeare scythes through a platoon of insurgent sepoys who are also peppered with marble chippings from a bas-relief entitled *The Spirit of Science Conquers Ignorance and Prejudice*. The brittle charade of Anglicised enclaves overseas is repeatedly ridiculed in Farrell's pages. In Singapore, the ersatz England the colonists have fabricated around themselves looks like 'a suburb ready to burst at the seams with a dreadful tropic energy'. Nineteenth-century Simla in *The Hill Station* (1981), the novel Farrell left unfinished when he died in 1979, seems 'a make-believe England hanging almost high enough above to escape the reality of India'; its inhabitants' attempts to impose the etiquettes and habits of Victorian England – croquet tea parties, tweed garments, High and Low church rivalries – on to a foreign subcontinent are quizzically observed. But even in this tale of the Raj in its heyday, the farce of imperial pretension is overcast – in a manner distinctive of Farrell – by intimations of imperial malaise and moribundity.

Symptoms of degeneration were something Farrell had personal cause to be alert to. Polio contracted during his first term at Oxford left him – once a rugby-playing athlete – with prematurely grey hair and cruelly wasted muscles (his shoulders and right arm were permanently affected and his diaphragm was so impaired that he had to learn new breathing techniques). In his historical novels, consciousness of physical infirmity shades into panoramas of imperial debility. Mortification of various kinds is the keynote. In a way that would markedly influence subsequent writers about empire, moribundity coexists with mordant humour. The hero of *Troubles*, Major Archer, traumatised by carnage he has witnessed on the Western Front, not only moves into an establishment that is in terminal disrepair but also

14

encounters reminders of mortality everywhere in it. A sheep's head crawling with maggots is discovered in his bedroom cupboard. A dead rabbit, a dead mouse, a dead dog, a dead frog, a dead hen, a stuffed pike, a strangled peacock, butchered piglets and mounds of culled cats swell the novel's tally of deceased creatures. Humans expire in profusion too. Archer's fiancée perishes of leukaemia. Wholesale bloodshed (including a shooting in a theatre called the Empire where a pantomime, *The House that Jack Built*, is playing) bespatters the neighbourhood. Intensifying the *memento mori* atmosphere, the Anglo-Irish gentry soldiering on inside the collapsing Majestic are awesomely geriatric, teetering on the brink of extinction.

Casualties of war and cholera strew the pages of *The Siege of Krishnapur*. True to Farrell's fondness for terminal-looking starting points, its opening scene focuses on what is at first taken to be a town but turns out to be a cemetery. By the end of the book, the Residency at Krishnapur has been virtually reduced to a cemetery: amid the remains of the slain, survivors resemble 'boil-covered skeletons'. Also beginning in sepulchral mode – with a flashback to Sir Thomas Raffles raising the Union Jack over a deserted island littered with 'a great many human skulls and bones, the droppings of local pirates' – *The Singapore Grip* becomes increasingly heaped with civilian and military massacre as colonial hedonism collapses into colonial rout. Its most macabre chapter visits a Chinese 'dying house' where 'skeletons and moribunds' swathed in 'shrouds and bandages' lie on tiered shelves awaiting extinction. Another chapter reports on the thousands of corpses annually found on the streets of Shanghai (a city whose grisly extremities are inspected in a later work that seems much influenced by Farrell, J.G. Ballard's 1984 novel about colonial catastrophe in South-East Asia during the Second World War, *Empire of the Sun*). *The Hill Station* converts Simla into a near-mortuary. Its four graveyards, we're told, are overflowing. Several characters are in the final stages of consumption. A young boy was destined to die of rabies, Farrell's notes for the book reveal. Sounding a funeral knell from the start, it begins with a description of a *tonga* driver who 'ferries' gravely ill British invalids ('poor ghosts' and 'fair skeletons') up to Simla from the railway station on the scorching plains where they arrive. This Charon-like character has, unknown to himself, a potentially fatal heart defect.

One moment in the novel connects all this deathliness with the eventual end of empire by briefly darting across the globe to the London of 1871 where Karl Marx, at work in the British Museum Reading Room, is reflecting 'Soon it will be closing time.' Consistent with this glimpse, an economic perspective on imperialism is adopted (sometimes rather ponderously) in *The Singapore Grip*. Administrative and military perspectives feature in *Troubles* and *The Siege of Krishnapur*. But what gives Farrell's attitude to empire its most characteristic slant – manifesting itself in protagonists paralysingly caught in what they perceive as a grotesque and deadly plight – is a combination of irony and sombreness, the one sharpened by his intellectual acuteness, the other deepened by emotions welling from his personal awareness of perishability.

Paul Scott

Private stresses accentuate aspects of empire in Paul Scott's fiction too. But the initial impetus for his masterpiece, *The Raj Quartet*, was a literary recollection. The opening book in the sequence, *The Jewel in the Crown*, originated, Scott said, with the image of 'a girl running', though where to or from what he at first had no idea. As regards his novel's storyline, this may be so. But what the running girl propelled herself out of – and into the forefront of Scott's imagination – is surely one of the archetypal texts for novels about Anglo-India: E.M. Forster's *A Passage to India* (1924). After the incident in the Marabar Caves where she believes she is being assaulted in the darkness, Adela Quested is seen 'running straight down the face of a precipice'. Forster's novel, which Scott read in 1947 on returning from his first visit to India and again after his second in 1964 – gives *The Raj Quartet* one of its central incidents. Daphne Manners' rape by a gang of unknown Indians during the riots of 1942 intensifies and makes rawly physical Adela Quested's more nebulous nightmare. Salman Rushdie has taken issue with this: 'if rape must be used as the metaphor of the Indo-British connection, then surely, in the interests of accuracy, it should be the rape of an Indian woman by one or more Englishmen'. In fact, *The Raj Quartet* does metaphorically make this point about imperial violation by means of another symbolic assault: the sexual molestation of the Anglicised Indian, Hari Kumar, by Ronald Merrick, the homosexual police officer.

On the first page of *The Jewel in the Crown*, Scott states that his book is about two nations 'locked in an imperial embrace of such long standing and subtlety that it was no longer possible for them to know whether they hated or loved one another, or what it was that held them together'. As Hilary Spurling's biography of Scott documents, ambivalent embraces and marital antipathy were things he was no stranger to. His parents – father from the artistic middle class, mother South London working class – were ill-matched and increasingly alienated from each other. After twenty-five years of married life, Scott's own wife fled from him into a women's refuge. The class rift that helped to prise his parents apart gave Scott a sensitivity to snobbery and its Geiger-counter twitchiness which was invaluable when it came to portraying the prejudices and starchy protocols of Anglo-India. The suppressed homosexuality that impaired his own marriage is also imaginatively channelled into *The Raj Quartet*, where his sense of dissociation manifests itself in the high proportion of characters who are misfits, orphans, *émigrés*, exiles and loners.

Starting with a death during the Quit India riots of 1942 and ending (if *Staying On*, his 1978 coda to *The Raj Quartet*, is included) with a 'notice to quit' giving an old India hand a fatal coronary, Scott's novel sequence massively chronicles imperialism's last throes in India. The titles of its four volumes chart a process of grim deterioration.

After the ambiguous glitter of *The Jewel in the Crown* comes *The Day of the Scorpion* (1968), in which noxious forces emerge self-destructively into the open. Taking its name from the Parsi funeral towers where corpses are laid out to be devoured by vultures, *The Towers of Silence* (1971) gruesomely highlights mortality and predation. The latter is also suggested, along with ruination and partition, by the title of the *Quartet*'s concluding book, *A Division of the Spoils* (1975).

For his panoramic survey of the final years of what he sees as a corroded and corrosive system, Scott employs a kaleidoscope of viewpoints. Journals, letters, memoirs, interview transcripts and streams of consciousness put the reader inside the minds of missionaries, memsahibs, worried liberals, true-blue imperialists (such as Brigadier 'Tubby' Reid with his horror-comic reminiscences, *A Simple Life*), troubled Indians, civil servants, an Albanian nun, a Rajput princess, a Russian count and a Muslim politician (the only major mentality kept opaque is that of the one significant figure to appear in all four books: Ronald Merrick). Throughout this huge accumulation of responses to the tottering Raj, two themes predominate: transition and uncertainty. Crucial events in *The Raj Quartet* tend to occur during journeys. The opening murder – that of an Indian teacher battered to death while safeguarding an elderly missionary, Edwina Crane – takes place on a road after he has been dragged from a car. The *Quartet* ends with a massacre on a train where, after Partition, Hindus butcher Muslims. The blood-spattered British liberal staring aghast at the hacked corpses embodies Scott's sickened awareness of the Raj's lethal bequest to the subcontinent.

Even before this final tableau of shocked helplessness and hopelessness, disorientation has been a frequent sight in *The Raj Quartet*. Its most rebarbative characters – Merrick, the noxious police officer, and Mildred Layton, the poisonous memsahib – move with glazed fixity through the rituals of a once-ossified, now disintegrating society. But, as things fall apart in India, the best and second-best of the British colonists find they lack all conviction about their official role. Missionaries lose their faith; administrators their nerve. Disillusion drives some to suicide (appalled that persisting reflexes of racial superiority on her part have caused the death of an Indian colleague, Miss Crane burns herself alive in a kind of surrogate suttee). Breakdowns are rife. After a lifetime's chin-up dedication to missionary work in India, Barbie Bachelor declines from garrulous decency into dumb despair. Susan Layton, the pretty daughter of an archetypal Raj family, succumbs to screaming schizophrenic collapse.

Stressing its characters' dislocation, the *Quartet* keeps them constantly on the move, just as its narrative, unsettledly and unsettlingly, shifts around in time. Roaming across the books' immense landscapes, as India heaves itself through a transfer of power and a world war pitches people around Europe and Asia, are hordes of dispossessed persons. But, though Scott's characters travel, they never reach satisfactory conclusions. Racial, cultural and social splits entrenched across India (and first put on the British fictional map by E.M. Forster) hamper or engulf them. Division slices through all the main settings of the *Quartet*. Mayapore, bisected by a river that demarcates the British cantonment from the Indian city, displays this at its starkest. In the hill station, Pankot, class snobberies send (often hairline) fissures through the colonial coterie. Mirat, the Princely State in the sequence, is perilously lopsided, with a Muslim ruling over a largely Hindu population. While some damagingly try to reinforce gulfs and hold them in place, others – most notably, Daphne Manners and Hari Kumar – find (as Forster's Adela Quested and Dr Aziz did before them) that attempting to span them can be disastrous.

Paralysis or catastrophe seem the bleak alternatives during this terminal phase of British rule in India. Codes formerly respected have become meaningless. People hitherto occupying clearly defined social niches lose their bearings. And the mounting atmosphere of uncertainty is heightened by Scott's strategies as a novelist. Switching unpredictably from character to character, *The Raj Quartet* provides an almost dizzying variety of viewpoints, none of them authoritative.

19

Apparently familiar narrative patterns are subverted and readers' expectations overturned. Figures assumed to be of central importance, such as Daphne Manners, abruptly disappear. Relationships seemingly destined for centre-stage fulfilment – that of Sarah Layton and Guy Perron, for instance – stay unresolved and slip into the background (that the two eventually marry is just passingly mentioned in *Staying On*). Narrative climaxes are studiedly anti-climactic: as when Perron, in the closing pages, fails to meet Kumar.

Anglicised Hari Kumar – with his Indian looks but pukka accent and alternative 'English' name and persona, Harry Coomer – is the most extreme instance of the divided and uprooted individual. Aptly, he is first seen sprawled in a paralytic stupor on the edge of the river that separates the British cantonment at Mayapore from the Indian city. What has driven him to drink himself unconscious, we later learn, is that a British friend's failure to recognise him in his native environment has cruelly brought home to him the irreversibility of his slide from Chillingborough, the English public school they both attended, to Chillianwallah Bagh, the reeking Indian cul-de-sac he has had to return to after his father's bankruptcy (its name, in a further taunting echo, half-chimes with Jallianwalla Bagh, the scene of General Dyer's infamous massacre of unarmed Indians in 1919). Towards Hari, the tormented cultural hybrid caught between antagonistic worlds, two other outsiders are drawn: Daphne Manners, an upper-class English girl uneasy in the Raj community because of her sensitivity, and Ronald Merrick, a lower-class Englishman uneasy because of his sensitiveness.

Ranklings of shame and exclusion throb as powerfully in Scott's novels as they did in his life. India – 'the metaphor I have presently chosen to illustrate my view of life', he said in 1972 – provided him with a fictional environment in which long-repressed emotions could be imaginatively released (significantly, his image for creativity was of something deformed and imprisoned: 'I think of the artist's *duende* [demon] as a little black hunchback chained to the wall of his dungeon, whose job it is to draw pictures on the walls, pictures that have to be interpreted in words'). His bitterness at having the world of culture barred to him when his father insisted he leave school at fourteen gives him acute sympathy with Kumar's plight. Homosexual urges battened down after they brought him frighteningly close to scandal and jail when in the army (within months of this crisis he married for 'protection and safety', he said) unleash their energies in his personification of Merrick: a man goaded into sadism by sexual guilt, viciously humiliating males who arouse in him responses that he finds humiliating.

Merrick also seeks to exorcise a sense of social inferiority by exercising a sense of racial superiority. In this, he is far from alone. Raj racism is often presented by Scott as an ugly displacement of white anxieties about status. Curling the lip at the Hindu caste system, colonists bend the knee to the British class system. The latter – early stamped on Scott's awareness by the snubs and condescensions his working-class mother received from her genteel in-laws – is something he saw as parallel to the racial segregations set up by imperialism: 'My father's family looked down on my mother's, who all lived in South London.' 'Half close your eyes here,' he said of the Southgate where he spent his early life, 'and you're in Mayapore.' His last novel, a study of the near-dead marriage of a couple who have 'stayed on' in independent India, takes as its heroine a working-class woman, unhappily married to an upper-class man, who has had to endure a lifetime of snooty put-downs in the snobbish hothouse of the Raj.

Looking back at the prejudices of the Raj, Staying On also looks around at the new India and the dwindling space in it for Scott's emblematically named couple, the Smalleys, who have opted to remain there. With the expiry of their lease on the bungalow annexe of Smith's Hotel (now absorbed into the rapidly expanding Shiraz consortium), Lucy Smalley's elephantine spouse, 'Tusker', expires of a heart attack and she is left alone 'here, as I feared, amid the alien corn'.

Earlier in the novel, Lucy has recalled the ceremony of the transfer of power:

> that terrible, lovely moment when the Jack was hauled down inch by inch in utter, utter silence. The only sounds you could hear were the jackals hunting in the hills and the strange little rustles when a gust of wind sent papers and programmes scattering. There was no sound otherwise until on the stroke of midnight the Indian flag began to go up, again very slowly, and then the band began to play the new Indian national anthem and all the crowds out there in the dark began to sing the words and when the flag was up there flying and the anthem was finished you never heard such cheering and clapping.

It's a moment that was to be the starting point of a new fictional regime as well. *Midnight's Children* (1981), written by an author born in Bombay two months before independence, opens on the stroke of 12 a.m., on 15 August 1947. With it, Salman Rushdie set about ousting what he regarded as the pernicious literary staying on of the Raj. In an essay on this subject, 'Outside the Whale', he excoriates Scott for applying 'fictional glamour' to the Raj – though anything less glamorising than Scott's painstaking insistence on the savageries and pettinesses, muddle, evasions, panic, greed, irresponsibility and obtuseness prevalent in the Raj would be hard to imagine. With its political intelligence, social alertness and psychological acumen, *The Raj Quartet* surely constitutes the finest work of fiction in English about imperial disillusion – immeasurably more informed, actual and subtle than *A Passage to India*, for instance. Rushdie's wider and more sustainable indictment in his 1984 essay is that India has been the victim of 'a very long line of fake portraits inflicted by the West on the East' in novels such as M.M. Kaye's Raj blockbuster, *The Far Pavilions* (1978), which crudely and sentimentally re-hashed the plot device in Rudyard Kipling's *Kim* (1900) of an English orphan unknowingly raised as a native Indian boy.

An associated infliction – the domination of Indian novelists' portrayals of their nation by British fictional conventions and precedents – is evident even in the works of so impressive and accomplished an author as the Mysore-born novelist, Kamala Markandaya. Though written from an Indian viewpoint, her books deploy motifs derived from E.M. Forster, Paul Scott and J.G. Farrell. The results can be paradoxical, as with her historical novel, *The Golden Honeycomb* (1977), which uses an elegantly Anglicised literary mode to deplore the elegant Anglicising of a young Maharajah. In an imitative homage to Scott, Markandaya's chronicle of a Princely State during the Victorian and Edwardian eras begins with a quotation from a speech in the British parliament about 'Hindustan, that most truly bright and precious gem in the crown of the Queen' (the acquisitiveness lurking in this glittering image later becomes glaringly apparent when we hear that a fabulous diamond from the Maharajah's throne room 'now adorns the Imperial Crown'). The inability of the British governor to 'conceive that the foul connotations of *caste* can possibly attach to *class*' brings forward another motif from Scott (and Farrell, who mockingly spoke of 'the rigid caste system among the British in Simla'). But it is Forster whom Markandaya most extensively emulates. As in *A Passage to India*, two men of liberal ideals and good will but different racial origin are held apart by the imperial status quo. Recalling Forster's novel even more emphatically, when a young Indian makes amorous advances to the governor's daughter, 'it took him some time to realise that he was, in her view, attempting rape'.

Subliminally re-materialising in that scene, Adela Quested (a phantom presence in many novels about Anglo-India) is more overtly conjured up in Markandaya's 1982 book, *Shalimar* (published in the UK as *Pleasure City*). On a picnic excursion to some local caves, Europeans and Indians jokily hark back to Forster. 'I'm sure none of us ... would even contemplate indulging in rape on this outing', chortles a Muslim hotelier. Remembering 'that awful case of that

English girl', an ex-memsahib hazily comments 'Whatsisname put it in a book, didn't he?'

Pleasure City depicts an updated kind of colonising: international tourism. Economic exploitation and sultry hedonism are coupled in it (as they are in the title of Farrell's *The Singapore Grip*, which punningly straddles both the British commercial hold on the colony and a much sought-after erotic speciality of its Asian prostitutes). But, even as Markandaya describes the concrete tidal wave of a 1980s leisure complex submerging an Indian fishing village, Forsterian motifs irrepressibly surface. Again, two men from opposite sides of a racial and cultural divide are drawn together by mutual affection but kept apart by circumstances: a British executive (descended from the Raj governor in *The Golden Honeycomb*) fails to sustain a friendship with Rikki, a young Indian fisherman who has become a casual employee in the new Shalimar hotel.

At one point, Rikki protests about being put in a novel by an American author resident in the Shalimar, who 'wrote books about India which were admired everywhere, except in India'. She would, he complains, make him seem 'a funny object'. It's to wrest portrayals of India away from such distorting Western workmanship that Salman Rushdie's fiction is designed. Eschewing not only Raj writing but also Anglicised Indian fiction, which he sees as slavishly imitative in its taste for irony and understatement, formal prose, realistic social documentary and alertness to emotional and psychological nuance, he covers his literary canvases with imaginative material that is emphatically indigenous.

Salman Rushdie

Like many modern novelists, Salman Rushdie found his way forward by looking back. Much acclaimed as a postcolonial trailblazer, he has often stressed that what guided him was *The Thousand and One Nights*. Homage to that great accumulation of Persian, Arabic and

Indian tales told by Scheherazade features in all his work after his critically derided and virtually disowned first novel, *Grimus,* in 1975 (modelled on the twelfth-century Sufi poem, *The Conference of Birds*). Scheherazade is mentioned on the first page of *Midnight's Children,* whose narrative set-up (impotent, grotesque Saleem Sinai telling nightly stories to a woman from a pickle factory) burlesques the voluptuous glamour of her nocturnal narrations to her royal spouse. The death threat hanging over her – beheading if she loses her listener's interest – is reactivated in *The Moor's Last Sigh* (1995), whose narrator fends off execution by telling suspense stories to a madman who 'had made a Scheherazade of me'.

In additional tribute, the digits 1001 repeatedly figure in Rushdie's pages. The number of births during the first hour of Indian independence, *Midnight's Children* computes, was a thousand and one ('the resonances . . . are strangely literary'). In *Shame* (1983) 'a thousand and one stories' of a husband's infidelities are embroidered on a shawl. In *The Moor's Last Sigh* (1995) a 'thousand-and-one' anecdotes about a scandal are painted on an artist's canvas. In *The Satanic Verses* (1988), there's an actor known as 'the Man of a Thousand Voices and a Voice'.

Though Rushdie's engaging children's-book-cum-fictional-manifesto, *Haroun and the Sea of Stories* (1990), derives its title and pervasive imagery from a different set of tales (the eleventh-century Hindu anthology, *The Ocean of the Streams of Story*), it also advertises its affiliations with his more usual source. The names of its heroes, Haroun and Rashid Khalifa, are a jokey spin-off from Haroun al-Rashid, the Caliph who roams Baghdad incognito in *The Thousand and One Nights*. From a houseboat decorated with images from Scheherazade's tales and called *Arabian Nights Plus One,* the boy Haroun is air-lifted on a giant bird's back to a fabulous city fanned out across a thousand and one islands. In *The Ground Beneath Her Feet* (1999), precognition enables its musician-hero to hear Presley and Beatles songs 'two years, eight months and twenty-eight days' before they are released on disc: a period 'which adds up (except in a leap year) to one thousand and one nights'.

In addition to these arithmetical squiggles of deference, all Rushdie's novels after *Grimus* imitate *The Thousand and One Nights'* arabesques in and out of different sorts of writing. What attracts Rushdie to Scheherazade's labyrinth of tales isn't just its non-Western provenance, Eastern settings and subject matter, unabashed fantasy and spellbinding display of the power of a storyteller's voice. Above all, he prizes its miscellaneousness. Eager to emulate its baggy hospitality to everything from magical extravaganza to earthy anecdote, his own fiction exuberantly jumbles together fable, autobiography, political polemic, theological vaudeville, satire, the supernatural, whimsy, farce and melodrama.

The Thousand and One Nights isn't the only thing to exert a talismanic hold on Rushdie's imagination. Bombay, his birthplace, does so too. Seen as an urban equivalent to Scheherazade's marvellous miscellany, this 'metropolis of many narratives' gleams from his fictional landscapes as an image of ebullient vitality spawned by a 'multiplicity of commingled faiths and cultures'. For Rushdie, the teeming, tolerant, multicultural Bombay that he knew in his youth (and whose renaming as Mumbai he rejects as Hindu Nationalist bigotry) was the 'most cosmopolitan, most hybrid, most hotchpotch of Indian cities', the place where 'all Indias met and merged'. For him it manifests the jostling, animated, multifarious spirit of the subcontinent, just as the prodigiously various *Thousand and One Nights* exemplifies the most authentic way to convey it.

Midnight's Children, his first attempt to interfuse the two, cascades out like a multi-coloured tidal wave aimed at smashing aside the orderly Anglo-Saxon mode of writing about India. From the start, difference is asserted. Where Scott's *Staying On* took as its image of Indian independence the slow hauling down of the Union Jack, Rushdie's opening paragraph focuses on the hands of the clock joining together at midnight like palms in the traditional Indian *namaste* greeting. Where Lucy Smalley was struck by 'utter, utter silence', Saleem Sinai revels in 'the din of independence'. Hubbub, as his subsequent novels make very audible, is Rushdie's preferred fictional idiom. Multi-ethnic hullaballoo invariably clamours from his pages.

For Rushdie, multiplicity equates with authentic Indianness – the tang in which even the most basic elements of *Midnight's Children* are steeped. Saleem, its Bombay-born narrator who manages a pickle factory, writes his tale on paper that smells of turmeric. Stored in pickle jars, his chapters emit 'the unmistakable whiff of chutney'. His saga is itself a kind of chutney (just as *The Moor's Last Sigh* is, its narrator feels, another indigenous literary commodity: a '*masala* narrative'). In it, chunks of Hindu myth and Islamic lore, bits of Indian history, shreds of autobiography are zestily intermixed with pepperings of political satire. What Rushdie calls Bombay's 'highly-spiced nonconformity' is complemented by his novel's technique.

Pick-and-mix pungency infuses all Rushdie's fiction. To purvey India's cultural diversity, he gives his characters names that incorporate Urdu puns or Islamic allusions, steeps them in Parsi theology or fits them out with features suggestive of Hindu deities (Saleem's large nose, for instance, points to his affinities with Ganesh, the elephant-trunked god of writing and new enterprises). Inhabiting addresses meaningful in Sanskrit or Farsi, they step into streets raucous with 'Coca Cola American' and Indian-English advertising placards.

Ranging far beyond the subcontinent, Rushdie's eclecticism also favours pickings from European fabular fiction and Latin American magic realism. The weird perspectives of Italo Calvino's *Invisible Cities* gave him prototypes for surreal locations such as Jahilia, the city of sand with its silicon gardens and braziers of glowing grit in *The Satanic Verses*. From Gabriel García Márquez and Günter Grass (echoes of whose *The Tin Drum* reverberate through *Midnight's Children*) he learned how to invest characters with uncanny powers, strange metabolisms and symbolic ailments (always a high risk in Rushdie's pages, whose inhabitants are susceptible to a formidable range of weirdly symptomatic maladies from 'the dreadful pustules and cankers of forbidden love' to 'excessive sensitivity to the bacilli of humiliation', chauvinistic sinusitis, rage-induced rupture of internal organs, psychosomatic female hirsuteness, allegorical halitosis, a mystic squint and satiric albinism which causes Western-inclined Indians to start 'going white in blotches'). Inveterately magpie-like, his fiction even picks up hints from British novels about India: George MacDonald Fraser and J.G. Farrell supply blueprints for symbolic properties such as the Hotel Flashman with its cracked golden dome and the 'fleapit' Empire Cinema with its disastrous Hindu-Muslim double bill in *Shame*.

Cinema itself contributes lavishly to Rushdie's pages. A keen fan of this medium 'in which peculiar fusions have always been legitimate', he shares its enthusiasm for dissolves and cross-cuttings. Bombay's film industry plays on his imagination as colourfully as the city itself. The swapped-babies scenario in *Midnight's Children*, in which Saleem and his deadly opposite, Shiva, have identity tags switched at birth, is, Rushdie explains, 'a genuine kind of Bombay-talkie, B-movie notion . . . I thought a book which grew out of a movie city ought to contain such notions.' Adding Hollywood to Bollywood, the model for his horror-cartoon version of Mrs Gandhi as the evil Widow in this novel (which aims 'to restore the past . . . in Cinemascope and glorious Technicolor') was the Wicked Witch of the West from one of his favourite films, *The Wizard of Oz*.

Rushdie's eclectic aesthetic is devised to do justice to India's teeming diversity ('what I was trying to do in *Midnight's Children*', he has said, 'was to make a plural form, since it seemed to me that I was writing about a world that was about as manifold as it's possible for a world to be. If you were to reflect that plurality, you would have to use as many different forms as were available to you – fable, political novel, surrealism, kitchen sink, anything'). But it also has an ideological rationale. Humane as well as artistic gains achieved by giving free rein to variety and merging are repeatedly spotlit in his fiction.

Besides knocking down stylistic barriers, his novels always wage battles between the open- and closed-minded, the tolerant and the dogmatic, the healthily sceptical and the septically doctrinaire.

Tunnel-vision racial or religious bigots – fundamentalist ayatollahs, sectarian politicians and terrorists, National Front thugs, Creationist cranks and similar devotees of ethnic or doctrinal untaintedness – are regularly seen in Rushdie's pages, trying to impose 'the absolutism of the Pure'. Against this, he pits the creatively hybrid. Flaunting their literary 'impurity', his novels present themselves as carnivals of diversity and cross-cultural coupling. Exuberant intermingling and shape-shiftings make segregation and rigidity look arthritic and unnatural. Even in tiny typographical ways, his books signal their allegiance to combining and connecting. Tightening the sense of inextricably linked diverseness, commas are plucked out ('intertwined lives events miracles places rumours') and words coalesce ('angelicdevilish', 'strangebuttrue').

Midnight's Children stages the first of Rushdie's fictional clashes between multiplicity and divisiveness. Like most of his heroes, Saleem Sinai is of mixed, ambiguous birth (raised as the legitimate child of affluent Muslims, he is actually the illegitimate son of a Hindu pauper and an Englishman). Extending his emblematic diversity, telepathic powers Saleem acquires turn him into 'a sort of radio'. Mysteriously attuned to the thoughts of others born in the first hour of Indian independence, his mind buzzes with 'multitudes . . . jostling and shoving inside me'.

But though Saleem initially hums with the multitudinous energies of the new India, he succumbs (as the novel shows his nation doing) to a ruinous falling apart. Fears that his body is starting to split torment him – as well they might. Around him, scenes are crackle-glazed with instances of fragmentation. At one extreme, his grandfather dies of disintegration. At another, Partition bloodily sunders India and Pakistan. As the narrative travels from the jubilant midnight of independence to the nightmarish 'six-hundred-and-thirty-five-day-long midnight' of the Emergency, India splinters. Beginning with euphoria about national integration, Saleem's story of his, and India's, attempt to 'rise above fissures' ends with his shattering into smithereens.

Fracture is even more widespread in *Shame*. Moving from India to Pakistan (as Rushdie's parents and sister did in the mid-1990s), it surveys a bisected nation – carved out by Partition, then torn by civil war – which bizarrely consists of 'two chunks of land a thousand miles apart'. Divisiveness cleaves through the story. Where *Midnight's Children* set Saleem against his destructive opposite, Shiva, *Shame* chronicles the clash between two antagonistic political dynasties (fictional avatars of the Bhutto and Zia clans): one upper-class, secular and cosmopolitan; the other from the peasantry, fundamentalist and nationalist.

Stylistic antitheses are also to the fore, with the book alternating between contrasting genres. Disquisitions on the Pakistan of actuality and Rushdie's family links with it intersperse a Gothic melodrama bristling with blood feuds, murderous stiletto blades and immurings behind massively barred and padlocked doors. Prowling this grand guignol vision of a savagely divided Pakistan is a luridly macabre specimen of insane divisiveness: Sofiya Zinobia, 'disorder's avatar', a crazed, murderous girl – morbidly sensitive to shame but monstrous in all other ways – who rips heads from shoulders in maddened fits of uncanny strength.

Prominently peopled with characters violently uprooted from India to Pakistan, *Shame* also highlights another kind of pulling apart (one which would later run through countless postcolonial novels): migration. The migrant, Rushdie has claimed, is 'perhaps, the central or defining figure of the twentieth century'. He is, he stresses, one himself: 'I am an emigrant from one country (India) and a newcomer in two (England, where I live, and Pakistan, to which my family moved against my will).' Being sent from Bombay to English public school at Rugby and then to King's College, Cambridge, gave him, he considers, 'a migrant's-eye view of the world'. It's one projected into *The Satanic*

Verses, a novel written, he said, 'from the very experience of uprooting, disjuncture and metamorphosis'. With cruel irony, its publication drastically increased his experience of uprooting and disjuncture. Ferociously endorsing his fictional warnings about the dangers of intolerance, Ayatollah Khomeini's *fatwa* against him for blasphemy thrust Rushdie into an existence of extreme dislocation. Book burnings and other inflamed reactions after the declaration of the death sentence from Tehran raged around a situation harsh with paradox: not least that, for a novel deploring the demonising of Asian immigrants in Britain, Rushdie was demonised by Asian immigrants in Britain.

At the book's start, two men – 'conjoined opposites' in the familiar Rushdie mode – tumble from an Air India jet blown up by Sikh fanatics, in which they were travelling from East to West. It's a journey both have already made psychologically. Saladin Chamcha, an Indian radio actor, has rejected his cultural background and become Anglicised. Gibreel Farishta, an Indian film star, has lost his Muslim faith and become secularised. Peering into the rifts this has opened up in them, the novel is 'the story of two pitifully divided selves'.

Floating miraculously unscathed down to earth from 29,002 feet, these two selves meet different fates. After years of striving to pass as a pukka Englishman (his surname is Urdu slang for sycophant), Chamcha – sprouting horns, hoofs, a shaggy pelt and a fearsome phallus – mutates (in accord with racist stereotypes of immigrants) into a half-bestial, half-devilish figure. In this guise, he encounters the ugly underside of the England he has adulated. Redemption comes with return to his native Bombay and reunion with his Indian lover, a physician and art critic who preaches a Rushdie-like 'ethic of historically validated eclecticism'. Gibreel meanwhile, tortured by hallucinatory dreams that travesty the Islamic theology he has tried to discard, succumbs to schizophrenia and shoots himself.

Around these two figures roils the customary Rushdie welter of mutation and mobility. '*The Satanic Verses*,' he has said, 'celebrates hybridity, impurity, intermingling.' But, though multiple instances of them are heaped into the book, the effect is far from celebratory. Fuming with derisive energies, *The Satanic Verses* exudes a febrile, oppressive atmosphere.

Curiously, *The Moor's Last Sigh*, the first novel Rushdie wrote during his years in enforced hiding, has a much more buoyant feel – though it isn't without allusion to its author's grim plight. Moraes Zogoiby, its narrator, is a man on the run, scribbling his story 'with death at my heels'. Chest-squeezing spasms of asthma afflict him. And, by one of those bizarre maladies Rushdie's characters are susceptible to, he finds himself condemned to use up his lifespan at twice the normal speed: at thirty-six, he looks like a seventy-two-year-old. Menaced, stifled and outlandishly denied ordinary existence, Moraes is, it's evident, a surrogate for Rushdie, similarly hounded by would-be assassins after the Islamic theocrats put a £2.5 million price on his head. Reminders of the *fatwa's* bloody after-effects also leave their traces on the story: just as Rushdie's Japanese translator was shot by Islamist fanatics, so a Japanese art expert who helps Moraes is gunned down by a psychotic.

Mostly, though, the tone is genial. Far less clenched and savage than either *Shame* (with its scarifying parables about Pakistan) or *The Satanic Verses* (with its sulphurous sarcasms about Middle Eastern and Western bigotries), *The Moor's Last Sigh*, which largely returns to India, also largely returns to the more relaxed mode of *Midnight's Children*. As Moraes recounts the extravagant ups and downs of his South Indian merchant family, farce outpaces atrocity, unenchanting actuality gets gaudily spray-painted with magic realism.

Radiant images of two far-away Indian worlds shimmer in Moraes' mind's eye: the spice plantations of Cochin, aromatic with cloves, ginger, cinnamon and pepper (the fabled 'black gold' that gave the Zogoibys their wealth) and the clifftop Bombay home of his celebrated painter mother. What's alluring about these places isn't just their heady sensuousness but the ethnic and cultural intermingling they harbour. Amid Cochin's fecund lushness, Christians, Jews and Hindus, Portuguese, British and Indians fruitfully coexist. Bombay again offers a vision of a thriving cosmopolitan community which is also a fertile hotbed of artistic creativity. Behind these two interracial idylls – both of which, it's lamented, have now had their day – hovers the phantom presence of another. Telling his story as he flees across the Spanish sierra, Moraes wistfully recalls the golden age of Moorish Andalusia with its 'fabulous multiple culture'.

In contrast to that civilisation of high tolerance, fundamentalist ferocity of a new kind in Rushdie's pages – virulent Hindu nationalism – erupts. Moraes gets caught up in the militant cult of Lord Ram, which is ominously replacing the 'many-headed beauty' of Hinduism's multiple deities in 1990s India. Dismayed at this latest instance of sectarian belligerence spreading across the subcontinent, *The Moor's Last Sigh* is another of Rushdie's hymns to the hybrid. Reputed to be illegitimately descended from Vasco da Gama, Moraes is 'a high-born cross-breed', part Catholic, part Jew or, as he puts it (with Rushdie's usual enthusiasm for unorthodox coalescing even of a verbal kind), 'a jewholic-anonymous, a cathjew nut'. His mother's paintings, an artistic equivalent to her son's jumbled heredity, conform to the regulation Rushdie recipe of fruitful 'impurity, cultural admixture and melange'. Like earlier figures such as Rani Harappa, the allegorical embroiderer in *Shame*, she seems a stand-in for 'those other freakish, hybrid, mutant exceptional beings – novelists – those creators of the most freakish, hybrid and metamorphic of forms'.

Rushdie's Influence

Rushdie's impact upon fellow practitioners of the novel form was immense. Before being thrust into prominence as an extreme instance of the persecuted writer (still grimly the case, as a stabbing attack he suffered in 2022 appallingly displayed), he held emblematic status as a postcolonial pioneer, the initiator of a liberating new literary idiom. 'For the first time an Indian writer had found the language to say things which we had all been through but had still not found the words for', the novelist Anita Desai enthused of *Midnight's Children*. 'After that, I think every young Indian writer tried to write like Salman. The whole next generation of Indian writers started off by writing their own *Midnight's Children*. The effect his writing had on Indian writers was somehow to loosen their tongues.' Another Indian novelist and short story writer, Calcutta-born Bharati Mukherjee, eagerly concurred:

> Before *Midnight's Children*, writers of Indian origin writing in English were encouraged by convention to write of their world with detachment and irony . . . With *Midnight's Children*, Rushdie breaks down these conventions. He aggrandizes, and that's marvellously healthy . . . Many of the writers before him tried, very unfortunately, to 'tame' India for foreign readers . . . Colonialism forced generations of Indian writers to value British models and to look down on the native. The British managed to convince Indians that British literature was rational, realistic, and superior, and that Indian literature with its magical qualities was childish.

Rushdie, she declares, 'discards British models' and sets up an exemplary alternative model. More than four decades on from the publication of *Midnight's Children*, Shehan Karunatilaka, Sri Lankan author of the 2022 Booker-winning novel *The Seven Moons of Maali Almeida*, stressed its influence and significance, praising it as an achievement that 'gave us permission as South Asians to write in a language that was our own', and explaining 'It inspired us to write in our own voices, our own type of English. We didn't have to emulate anyone else – that was liberating.'

Rushdie's stylistic declaration of independence – his insistence that fiction 'needs to be decolonised' – had a seismic effect on the late twentieth-century fictional scene. In his wake, novelists sharing his concern with postcolonial shifts and mergings energetically shucked off deference to British literary precedents and took their lead from literature closer to home. Shashi Tharoor's *The Great Indian Novel* (1989) – which boisterously lampoons Raj writing (chapter titles include 'The Duel with the Crown' and 'The Bungle Book'; comic butts such as 'Colonel Rudyard' and a caricatured Ronnie Heaslop from *A Passage to India* are on display) – retells twentieth-century Indian history by recasting situations from the Hindu epic, the Mahabharata, and salutes *Midnight's Children* in being supposedly dictated by a narrator of bastard birth to an 'elephantine' secretary 'with a big nose' (whose name Ganapathi is a variant of Ganesh). Similarly acknowledging Rushdie's achievement in imposing his fictional signature on material previously held to be the preserve of Raj writers, Mukul Kesavan's *Looking Through Glass* (1995) shows a Muslim-born author magically transforming the name of Aziz to Salman wherever it occurs in a copy of *A Passage to India*.

Rushdie's widespread (and not always helpful) influence saturated postcolonial fiction. What *The Moor's Last Sigh* calls 'Epico-Mythico-Tragico-Comico-Super-Sexy-High-Masala-Art' interlaced with a 'Technicolor-Story-Line' became a standard genre. Florid family sagas spanning several generations and peopled with preternaturally beautiful or grotesquely freakish figures (routinely endowed with paranormal powers and set against a background of luscious natural scenery but social and political dilapidation) were produced on a copious scale. Plausibility-free zones generously hospitable to the larger-than-life (torrid passions, monstrous crimes, outlandish aberrations), they are generally embellished with indigenous mythology and written in prose gaudy with metaphor and patois. Frequently near-clones of Rushdie's fiction, they often come close to caricaturing his literary traits with their lookalike lineaments.

Arundhati Roy's *The God of Small Things*, which won the 1997 Booker Prize for fiction, is sizeably fabricated from components patented by Rushdie. As in *Midnight's Children*, a pickle factory provides characters with employment and the author with imagery. Like Saleem, Roy's protagonists have telepathic powers. As in *The Moor's Last Sigh*, the setting is lush green Cochin. Catastrophe comes from savagely bigoted hostility to unorthodox couplings.

Sharing Rushdie's world view, Roy also replicates his style. His liking for what he calls 'concertinaed words' is mimicked ('Littleangels', 'Littledemons'); his use of comic-strip imagery is imitated in a way that verges on parody ('silence gathered its skirts and slid, like Spiderwoman, up the slippery bathroom wall'). Jejune emulation ('Prer NUN sea ayshun', 'a Bar Nowl') reminds you of Rushdie's taste for facetious puns and comic orthography ('djinns-and-tonics').

A desire to follow Rushdie's lead motivated not only Indian novelists. *Salt and Saffron* (2000), by the Pakistan-born author Kamila Shamsie, sometimes reads like a near-parody of *Midnight's Children*. Three of its central characters are born around midnight, one just before, one just after, and the other on the cusp, 'his head emerging on 28 February, the rest of his body following the next day'. Unusual ailments afflict characters: a woman who trekked to Pakistan from India in 1947 kisses the ground so repeatedly that its dust lodges permanently in her throat and for the rest of her life she can't breathe deeply without coughing. There are arch domestic nicknames of a kind similar to those in Rushdie's pages ('the Starched Aunts', 'Hibiscus-Eating Ayah'). As her novel's title intimates, Shamsie rehashes Rushdie's use of food imagery (pickles, masala) as a symbol for fiction.

Rushdie imitators turned up well beyond the subcontinent. *White Teeth* (2000), by Zadie Smith, an author with a West Indian immigrant family background, copiously recycles his fictional mannerisms and preoccupations. Pluralism and fundamentalism collide in its storyline (which includes a visit to Bradford at the time of the public burning of *The Satanic Verses* there). Migrations and cultural mergings provide the main subject matter. Characters are two-dimensional fabrications. Uncanny events (someone weeps red tears, identical twins who are continents apart each break their nose around the same time) are routine. Smith's authorial voice has the revved-up, slangy garrulity Rushdie favours. His stylistic tics are mimicked. Words coalesce ('borntherebornhere', 'greenandpleasantlibertarian-landofthefree'). Facetious orthography (the Indian dish Lamb Dhansak implausibly becomes 'Lamb Dawn Sock') is favoured. There are Rushdie-like appositional stackings-up of synonyms and near-synonyms ('immigrants, 'fugees, émigrés, travellers', 'bumming, cadging, begging'). Jokey sound-effects ('*Eeeesh ... Oaooow ...jii ... ka-toof ... Boof*') echo his. As in *The Satanic Verses* ('Gibreelsaladin Farishtachamcha'), characters' names meld together ('Millat and Magid. Majlat. Milljud').

Midnight's Children's fictional offspring widely populated the postcolonial literary scene. Ben Okri's novels, particularly those featuring Azaro, the *abiku* or 'spirit-child' – *The Famished Road* (1991), *Songs of Enchantment* (1993) and *Infinite Riches* (1998) – attempt to adapt Rushdie's fictional procedures to Nigerian settings. Though a far more simplistic creation than Saleem Sinai, Okri's spirit-child narrator who alternates between the impoverished actual world and a visionary transcendental realm, has much in common with him: telepathic powers, regular experience of peculiar physio-logical states (cataleptic trances, uncanny illnesses) and frequent encounters with unusual entities (glass-breasted women, leopards with the feet of white men, a bodiless stomach bowling purposefully along a path). Some of these oddballs are especially reminiscent of Rushdie. Prostitutes with 'legs of goats' and politicians with cloven hoofs recall Chamcha's bestial mutation in *The Satanic Verses*; an eerie descent of butterflies reminds you of an eerie swarm of them in Rushdie's novel.

More expansively, Okri emulates Rushdie's combination of surreal fable and scathing political satire. Like Saleem, Azaro (whose name is a diminutive of Lazarus) is a fantasticated symbol of his nation ('Our country is an *abiku* country', a character spells out. 'Like the spirit-child, it keeps coming and going.') Nigerian power struggles are heavily caricatured in continuing clashes between 'the Party of the Rich' and 'the Party of the Poor'.

The ponderousness of such episodes typifies Okri's approach. Touching in effects with a deft hand isn't his metier. Local colour is applied in thick dabs ('aquamarine beginnings ... indigo sky ... cobalt sky ... ultramarine air'). Rushdie's call for imperial speech to be replaced by suppressed voices is responded to on no mean scale. 'In the English class my spirit-companions sang polyphonic chorales at me in a blending of seven traditional languages', Azaro declares.

The need to drown out the language of the colonisers is a Rushdie theme that is loudly re-delivered in Okri's pages. What Okri calls 'World dominators' are also seen as word-dominators. In *Infinite Riches*, Azaro complains that, by suppressing African history and culture, the British Governor-General has 'effaced us from creation'.

> He rewrote the long silences of the country which were really passionate dreams ... He rewrote the seasons, and made them limited and unlyrical ... He redrew the continent's size on the world map, made it smaller, made it odder. He changed the names of places which were older than the places themselves. He redesigned the phonality of African names, softened the consonants, flattened the vowels. In altering the sound of the names he altered their meaning and affected the destiny of the named ... The renamed things lost their ancient weight in our memory. The renamed things lost their old reality. They became lighter and stranger. They became divorced from their old selves.

Azaro further contends that 'in his rewriting of our history', the Governor-General 'deprived us of language, of poetry, of stories, of architecture, of civic laws, of social organisation, of art, science, mathematics, sculpture, abstract conception, and philosophy. He deprived us of history, of civilisation and, unintentionally deprived us of humanity too.' The credibility of this encyclopaedic indictment isn't helped, though, by Okri's own mode of writing about Africa. Azaro's grumble that the Governor-General 'rewrote our night-spaces, made them weirder, peopled them with monsters and stupid fetishes ... rewrote our daylight, made it cruder' rings oddly in a novel whose own night spaces weirdly feature six-eyed spirits and crustacean-legged monsters, and whose daylight scenes crudely pit the Party of the Poor against the Party of the Rich. But, while never finding a persuasive fictional voice of his own, Okri tirelessly proclaims the urgent need to escape the discourse of the colonial dominators. In an essay paying tribute to his fellow-Nigerian novelist, Chinua Achebe, he stresses the necessity of attending to 'the silences of strangled nations' and 'the age-old warnings that have always lurked in the oral fables of storytellers and shamans'.

Rushdie's Limitations

Even without the off-key renditions of a Roy or an Okri, dissonances are discernible in the postcolonial idiom initiated by Rushdie. Rushdie's preferred fictional voice, whether a novel is narrated by him or one of his characters, is hyper-loquacity. Chatter, patter, talky digressions, buttonholing of the reader and rhetorical spiels rattle out. The prose can be alive with quick cartoonish verbal deftnesses (splashing on to a foot, boiling gravy fries it 'like a five-toed egg'; a disgraced daughter is thrown into the street 'like a bucket of dirty water') but, behind the volubility and animation, paradoxes muffle his fiction's impact. For an author who attaches such significance to storytelling, Rushdie is curiously inept at telling stories. Narrative momentum in his novels is minimal: thickets of verbosity, side-steppings into sub-plots, and veerings back and forth in time continually hamper it (if Scheherazade had attempted to narrate

The Satanic Verses to her restive bedfellow, you feel, she would have been lucky to have kept her head on her shoulders for even one night).

Another obstacle to involvement is that, while ceaselessly acclaiming diversity and 'newness', Rushdie's fiction has increasingly lacked these qualities. Over the years, his excitement about pluralism has taken on the narrowing qualities of a monomania. Thematic fixatedness – his unvarying stress on the virtues of change and mobility – is compounded by artistic repetitiveness. Plot patterns, narrative incidents, character types and stylistic mannerisms recur like compulsive tics. His characters are, for instance, repeatedly grouped into threes: the three sisters (Saleem's mother and her two siblings) in *Midnight's Children*, the three sisters (Chhunni, Munnee, Bunny) in *Shame*, the three sisters (Ina, Minnie, Mynah) in *The Moor's Last Sigh*, the three Cama brothers in *The Ground Beneath Her Feet*, the three male hijackers, three immigration officers and three pagan goddesses in *The Satanic Verses*. A corresponding taste for trios manifests itself in his prose which has a prolix habit of stacking up triplets of synonyms or near-synonyms ('eternal, undying, immortal', 'walls, boundaries, restraints', 'poisonous, degrading, defiling').

Special effects are recycled with dulling frequency. Premature whitening of the hair afflicts a high proportion of Rushdie's figures: among them Saleem's mother, Moraes' mother, Moraes' great-uncle, Moraes himself, Iskander and Ijizz in *Shame*, the charismatic Ayesha and Chamcha's wife Pamela in *The Satanic Verses*, and Ormus Cama in *The Ground Beneath Her Feet*. Plot devices are repetitively re-triggered too. *Midnight's Children* and *Shame* each end with an explosion. *The Satanic Verses* begins with one. The main narrative of *The Moor's Last Sigh* concludes with a bomb blast (the book's tacked-on-looking coda in Andalusia ends as *Midnight's Children* did, with a man bursting apart). True to this penchant for opening or closing with a bang, *The Ground Beneath Her Feet* – in which Rushdie's favourite techniques are exaggerated to the point of self-parody – gets under way with an earthquake.

Rushdie's reliance on recycling means that, despite his proclaimed agenda of giving voice to the human variousness of the postcolonial world, his fiction tends more to monotony than polyphony. The garrulous, digressive narrators of *Midnight's Children*, *The Moor's Last Sigh*, and *The Ground Beneath Her Feet* all sound the same, and all sound like Rushdie's own authorial voice in his other books. There is little sense of his being a novelist who has ever really listened to other people. Distinctive individuality is something he finds it hard to catch the timbre of. Despite his insistence on the need to shun stereotypes, he largely peoples his pages with them (stereotypes, moreover, that he redeploys from novel to novel). Some qualities, it has become more and more apparent, are limitingly excluded from the capaciousness Rushdie's fiction professes. There are marked gaps in the literary 'pluralism' he preaches, the most notable being his closed-door policy against psychological subtlety. Lavishing baroque inventiveness on his characters' frequently outlandish physiques, Rushdie rarely bothers to complicate their personalities beyond cliché. His plots are sensationally but unstirringly stocked with evil beauties, cartoon-strip termagants, ogreish tycoons and warped celibates. Flimsy in characterisation though swarmingly populated, his novels seem simultaneously crammed to bursting-point and depthless.

As we have seen, Rushdie (not unlike his *bête noire*, Paul Scott), has a notable enthusiasm for imagery of splits. 'We live on a broken mirror, and fresh cracks appear in its surface every day', it's asserted in *The Ground Beneath Her Feet*. Fresh cracks certainly keep appearing in Rushdie's fiction. Disintegrating bodies, split personalities, fractured families, partitioned nations, earthquake-torn landscapes all receive attention. But he seems oblivious to a major fault line running through his work: the mismatch between his subject matter and his style. All Rushdie's novels focus on pain and atrocity. All trivialise the horrors and agonies they depict into satiric farce or Gothic melodrama.

Rohinton Mistry

The novels of an Indian author of less literary wizardry but more sober purpose, Rohinton Mistry, throw into relief the flashy emptiness Rushdie's fiction can be content with. Like Rushdie, Mistry (who moved to Canada but was born into a Parsi community in India) is a native of Bombay. Like him, he writes large novels whose characters are silhouetted against events of traumatic momentousness in India's recent history. *Such a Long Journey* (1991) takes place during the 1971 war with Pakistan and the bloody secession of Bangladesh. *A Fine Balance* (1996) sets its darkest episodes during the internal Emergency of 1975.

Located within the same time span as *Midnight's Children*, Mistry's novels also share its physical setting: Bombay. But the fictional world they take you into is very different from Rushdie's. Unlike the effervescent idyll of intercultural tolerance on view in *Midnight's Children*, *The Satanic Verses*, *The Moor's Last Sigh* and *The Ground Beneath Her Feet*, Mistry's Bombay is filthy, ramshackle and dangerous – a nightmare metropolis that mangles and maims its inhabitants in ways that Mistry, a writer acutely responsive to injury, conveys with feeling immediacy. In *Such a Long Journey*, victims of workshop accidents sit stoically in a dispensary, clutching severed digits wrapped in newspaper. A bonesetter's clinic is packed with patients with fractured femurs and splintered tibias. The father at the heart of the story has a damaged hip incurred when rescuing his young son from Bombay's deadly traffic. Another of his children has an intestinal disease from the city's polluted water. Their neighbour is crippled and brain-damaged from a childhood fall. Even greater tribulations – humiliation, exploitation, violent abuse culminating in castration and amputation – beset the 'untouchables' who are the central figures in *A Fine Balance*, as Mistry displays in scenes wincing with furious compassion.

Excellent on the small, sapping harassments of poverty as well as its larger calamities, Mistry lacks Rushdie's flamboyant repertoire of literary resources. His fiction can be ponderous in its ironies (when a vicious extortioner is murdered while unable to defend himself because one of his hands is weighed down by a bag of coins he has chained to it, it is rather clankingly pointed out that 'He who had lived by the beggings of helpless cripples died by those beggings, rooted by their heaviness'). Ghastly turns of fate occur with an inexorableness even Thomas Hardy might have baulked at. But, with their exacerbated intensity, Mistry's novels make you aware of imaginative numbnesses in Rushdie's work. Where *Midnight's Children* tricks out its section on the Emergency and its compulsory sterilisation campaign with abstract witticisms about 'sperectomy' and the excision of hope, *A Fine Balance* makes you see the mutilations that ensued and feel the victims' physical and emotional wretchedness.

Another infamous episode in Indian history – the massacre of unarmed civilians at Jallianwalla Bagh – likewise receives fantastical treatment from Rushdie. Caught amid the protesters, Saleem's grandfather survives because a lucky giant sneeze ('Yaaaakh-*thoooo!*') pitches him forward onto his face out of the range of rifle fire; his only injury is a 'mysterious' bruise on his chest that 'will not fade until his death, years later'. Again, a comparison with a novelist of less extravagant techniques – Abdullah Hussein who translated his Urdu bestseller about India's struggle for independence, *The Weary Generations* (1963) into English in 1999 – exhibits what Rushdie's approach sacrifices. Hussein's pages about the slaughter in Amritsar's Jallianwalla Bagh communicate the terror of the protesters, as bullets volley into them, with far greater human directness. Ugly debasements inflicted in retaliation for the disturbances are given sickening vividness: forced at rifle point to crawl on their bellies, men are seen 'squirming and slithering like a herd of pythons with their heads buried in the earth and faces bleeding'.

To re-enter Rushdie's fictional world after spending time in Hussein's or Mistry's is to experience a contraction in emotional span. Atrocity is slicked over by gamesomeness. Even when the tone darkens, the prevailing narrative voice of jokey loquacity merely shifts into the stagey accents of melodrama – to whose clichés Rushdie is exceptionally partial ('she had planned her terrible revenge', 'the first lady of Jahilia will wait years to take her terrible revenge', 'Alia Aziz had begun to wreak her awful spinster's revenge'). Postmodern knowingness ('Melodrama piling upon melodrama; life acquiring the colouring of a Bombay talkie') applies a smart-seeming gloss to this but adds nothing deeper. *Shame* – a novel which takes its title from an emotion, and purports to explore its different manifestations in a degraded, postcolonial society – actually evades emotion in order to indulge, almost camply, in mock Gothic. Sufiya, the damaged girl who personifies shame, starts as a fantastic freak (her blushes are so hot that her clothes smell of scorching and her bathwater scalds the nanny who washes her), then degenerates into a Hammer Horror ghoul. 'Lurking inside Sufiya Zinobia Shakil there was a Beast', the book shrills like a lurid movie poster. Daubed with technicolour menace, she has 'appalling eyes, whose deadly yellow fire blows like a wind through the lattice-work of the veil'; when she becomes murderously enraged, 'purple bubbles' form on her protruding tongue. Her escape from her attic prison is depicted in an image straight out of a comic-strip or cinema cartoon ('there was a hole in the bricked-up window. It had a head, arms, legs').

Garishly rendered, Rushdie's scenes of horror are emotionally wan and psychologically colourless. Staking out humiliation and disgust as its subject, *Shame* conveys nothing of the feel of either. Semi-sardonic Gothic dehumanises and diminishes its characters and happenings every bit as much as Rushdie's associated appetite for facetiousness does (despite painful misfortunes meted out to them, it's hard to take seriously figures such as Nadia Wadia and her parents, Fadia Wadia and Kapadia Wadia in *The Moor's Last Sigh*).

What's particularly surprising about this willingness to play with caricature, cliché, sensationalism and stereotype is that it is at such flat variance with Rushdie's stated desire to free Indian life from dehumanising and diminishing fictional portrayals of it. It would be extraordinary for anyone to care what happens to a Rushdie character – and, given his literary intentions, it's extraordinary that this should be so. Gaining access to other people's inner worlds by his telepathic powers, Saleem Sinai possessed, we're told, 'the greatest talent of all': 'the ability to look into the hearts and minds of men'. It's the talent his creator most limitingly lacks.

Vikram Seth

'Magic realism, at least as practised by Marquez . . . expresses a genuinely "Third World" consciousness', Rushdie has maintained. 'It deals with what Naipaul has called "half-made societies", in which the impossibly old struggles against the appallingly new, in which public corruptions and private anguishes are somehow more garish and extreme than they ever get in the so-called "North".' This belief, which he has done so much to put into literary circulation, has been enormously influential among postcolonial writers. But even in India there have been significant dissenters from it – most notably Vikram Seth who, with *A Suitable Boy* (1993), produced a prodigious feat of naturalistic fiction which stands as one of the most remarkable late twentieth-century novels. Like *Midnight's Children*, Seth's book aims to put the subcontinent between hard covers. Under India's vast sky, across its huge plains and from every quarter of its teeming cities – temples and mosques, court rooms and courtyards, factories, fields, lecture halls, nightclubs, hovels, palaces, parliament, hospitals, jails, bookshops, bedrooms, purdah quarters and polo grounds – hundreds of people stream into view, each illuminated by the warm lucidity of Seth's regard. From a gross bejewelled rajah and a devout old nawab to dispossessed peasants and near-destitute slum-dwellers, India's human profusion – its imams and gurus, government ministers, scarred refugees from Pakistan, doctors, musicians, courtesans, civil servants, playboys, pious matrons, police, poets, pedants and caste-obsessed fanatics – pours out across the pages.

Struck by the novel's amplitude (at 1,439 pages, it is one of the longest works of fiction in the English language), its publishers invoked comparisons with Tolstoy and George Eliot. Instead of seeming, as you might expect, embarrassingly over-large, these come to look more and more relevant as the book unrolls. Conceived on the grand scale of the great nineteenth-century novels – *War and Peace*, *Middlemarch* – *A Suitable Boy* resembles them in breadth and depth as well as length. Spreading spaciously outwards to encompass an entire society, it simultaneously sinks inwards into the private worlds of its multifarious inhabitants.

The time is the early 1950s. Post-independence India is approaching its first general election (the largest ever held on earth, involving a sixth of the planet's population). Concurrently, a bill is being argued through parliament to wrest feudal power from land-owners by breaking up their estates. Against this double test of Indian democracy, Seth silhouettes an immense range of minutely depicted domestic and emotional circumstances. Four large groupings of characters – extended families with their lovers, friends and associates – dominate the foreground. Three locations are prominent: Brahmpur, a city in India's heartland; Debaria, a village on the plains; and Calcutta, seen as a Westernised metropolis of 'brown sahibs' who still emulate the departed British.

As the novel shifts between these settings, it at first appears discursive. But, gradually, its shuttlings back and forth interweave strands of narrative and intertwine existences. Opening and closing with a wedding, *A Suitable Boy* is as fascinated as Rushdie (and Paul Scott) by the processes that draw people together, often across tradi-tional dividing lines. Its main plot presents a high-caste Hindu girl, Lata, with a group of suitors (a handsome Muslim fellow-student, a clever Bengali writer and a jauntily resourceful worker in the shoe trade), then watches as differing factors determine her choice of partner. Alongside this runs the story of a jeopardised friendship between a Hindu politician's son and a young Muslim lawyer, and of the former's ill-fated affair with a prostitute. Around these central situations stretches a huge web of emotional, sexual and social affiliations. Caught in its mesh of tragic, comic, humdrum or intense entanglements, people send repercussions by their actions and decisions through even distant lives of which they are unaware.

Though Seth's novel has a humane enthusiasm for amity, gregariousness and cooperation, he is as alert as Rushdie (and again Scott) to the damage divisiveness wreaks. Riven by differing religions, cultures and gaping social inequities, India affords formidable evidence of this. From family discord and academic infighting, through political hostilities, sectarian suspicions and squabbles between traditionalists and progressives, the book finally bursts open into butchery when a procession of ululating Muslim flagellants fatally converges with a Hindu jamboree of drums and fireworks.

Seth conveys his relish for human diversity and invites respect for it in a contrasting way to Rushdie. Even figures who appear for just a paragraph or so are stamped with the lineaments of unique individuality. There's a seemingly endless outpouring of characters alive with credibility and seen from ever-altering angles. *A Suitable Boy* modulates unawkwardly between moments of delicate emotional and psychological accuracy and scenes of panoramic turbulence. One of its most unforgettable set-pieces – a nightmare sequence in which hundreds of people are crushed to death when a swarming festival on the banks of the Ganges surges out of control – first gives you an appalled spectator's view of the horrific mêlée, then thrusts you into the suffocating heart of it, alongside a mother vainly struggling to hold onto her child's hand as, finger by finger, it slips from her grasp.

Not – though it also features rioting mobs, suicide, and a murder trial – that Seth's novel mainly deals with extremity. Its predominant tone is balanced, tolerant, often amused. Its territory of choice is the middle ground. As if to highlight this (and its likeness to *Middlemarch*) it opens in the capital of a state 'which lay in the centre of the Gangetic plain, which is itself the heartland of India'. By far the largest part of its narrative is spent shrewdly and humorously observing lives that revolve around fixtures such as the Shady Ladies local canasta club, visits to the zoo, tea parties, Brahmpur University's syllabus committee or its student production of *Twelfth Night*. The book's most pervasive presence – Lata's widowed mother, Mrs Rupa Mehra – is a muddled, sentimental, fretful, warm-hearted, and averagely biased devotee of decent sociableness and family ties.

Written in the mode of classic nineteenth-century British and European novels, *A Suitable Boy* capaciously displays a diametrically alternative way of fictionalising postcolonial subject matter to that initiated by Rushdie. So, on a smaller scale (and with affinities to Thomas Hardy), do the novels of Rohinton Mistry. But the writer whose work is most emphatically at variance with it was V.S. Naipaul.

V.S. Naipaul

In his autobiographical book, *Finding the Centre* (1984), Naipaul recounts that, one day, his father looked in a mirror and saw no one there. Behind this shock, which heralded a nervous breakdown, lay an earlier traumatic loss of face: an irreverent campaigning journalist vehemently contemptuous of superstitions, Naipaul senior had been humiliatingly terrorised by fanatically orthodox fellow Hindus into publicly beheading a goat as a sacrifice to the goddess Kali. The work of his son reflects a similar fear of losing identity, of becoming like the casualties of postcolonialism who populate his significantly named novel *The Mimic Men* (1967) and most of his other books. Where Rushdie celebrates post-imperial migration as vitalising and creative, Naipaul deplores it as deadening and destructive. For him, rootlessness withers.

Postcolonial dislocation is Naipaul's great – essentially, his only – subject. Born into the detritus of a disintegrating empire as a member of a colonial minority (Indians shipped to Trinidad generations earlier as indentured labour for its sugar plantations), he left it behind for England and a nomadic literary career that lasted more than half a century. But beneath the sharply observed surface diversity of the works he produced in the course of his global travels, the contours of his Trinidadian background remain discernible. Society after society that he visits is presented as a similar postcolonial wasteland, despoiled, disorientated, lacking any real centre. Large tracts of the Northern and Southern hemispheres are seen as rotting and discarded by-products of colonialism. Caribbean islands moulder in a meaning-less independence in which 'they will forever consume; they will never create'. South American nations such as Argentina ('an artificial frag-mented colonial society') or Uruguay ('profoundly a colonial people, educated but intellectually null, consumers, parasitic on the culture and technology of others') are equally dire. India is just 'the fragmen-tation of a country without even the idea of a graded but linked society'. Much of Africa is another postcolonial disaster area: touring Zaire, with its 'nonsense name', Naipaul observes its natives reeling round in 'red-eyed vacancy'. Across his postcolonial landscapes, confusion and riots swarm. Mobility – hailed by Rushdie as vivifying – is seen as menace by Naipaul. Travel brings discomfort and danger. In his fiction, West Indians who journey to England come to grief; an English visitor to the West Indies is hideously murdered.

Naipaul's travelogues typically present him as a harassed misfit in disorderly, often over-populated postcolonial societies. Where Rushdie revels in multitudinous diversity, he recoils from it. Even his jaunty first work of fiction, *Miguel Street* (1959), conveys a sense of apartness. At first sight, its Trinidad street community is extrovert, warm, noisy and nosy. But links in the ramshackle society portrayed are loose: at the end of almost every chapter, someone drifts away. Feuds and resentments fracture the rumbustious togetherness. Finally, the narrator, always on the periphery of things, departs alone for England.

In the Naipaul novel most packed with people, *A House for Mr Biswas* (1961), the hero – a fictionalised version of his father – is rarely alone but almost always lonely. Marriage into an extended, almost tribal, and devoutly reactionary Hindu family shuts this progressive, rationalistic man in on himself. Irately expressed irony and intelligence distance him from those around him until he seems a foreigner in his own home and often absents himself from it.

Elsewhere, a string of exiles, expatriates and outsiders trail their solitary way through Naipaul's narratives. Some of his most striking shorter pieces are monologues by displaced persons: a Hindu convert to Presbyterianism, a Bombay domestic transported to Washington, a West Indian adrift in England. Two are included in his collection, *In a Free State* (1971), whose title novella works bleak variations on the theme of lack of rapport, as a couple of casual acquaintances, Bobby and Linda, are flung together on a risky journey through a newly independent African country riven by civil war. Penned together in a car hemmed in by thick forest and torrential rain, they remain worlds apart. Bobby, a comfily paternalistic homosexual keen on African boys, quivers with antipathy at evidence of Linda's sexual hungriness; she shrinks in embarrassment from his attempted confidences. Outside, the tribal violence they are trying to escape highlights the frailness and artificiality of their colonial connections with the country. By the time of Naipaul's next novel, *A Bend in the River* (1979), located in the Congo, the picture has darkened further: here it's an African who is dispossessed and on the run from his fellow Africans.

The starting point for *A Bend in the River* was an account of Mobutu's Zaire, 'A New King for the Congo', which Naipaul wrote for the *New York Review of Books*. Likewise, articles he published in *The Sunday Times* about Michael X and the Black Power killings in Trinidad grew into *Guerrillas* (1975), his savage novel about a murderous West Indian revolutionary. The divide between fact and fiction was always porous for Naipaul. Reportage and autobiography seep into his fictional scenarios. Authorial surrogates – rootless, unillusioned figures, melancholy, noticing – feature regularly.

'Glamoured' is a favourite word of Naipaul's. One of his favourite procedures is de-glamorisation. Travelling during his far-reaching literary career, through lands colourfully portrayed in imperial romance – India, Africa, South America, the Middle and Far East – he strips them bare of beguilement. Wheeling back to the Caribbean in one of his hybrid books, *A Way in the World* (1994), his undazzled gaze scans a region lavishly overlaid with legend – the Spanish Main, galleons, sugar and spice islands shimmering in the sun-gilded gulf – and contemplates its decrepit present-day actuality. Nothing could be further from Rushdie's vibrant beglamourings of postcolonial worlds.

An earlier hybrid work, *The Enigma of Arrival* (1987), subtitled 'a novel in five sections' but frequently reading more as autobiography than fiction, focuses on a West Indian writer closely resembling Naipaul who has left behind his stultifying colonial birthplace and sought revitalisation in travel, only to find that years of journeying have taken a gruelling toll. Worn down, he finds refuge (as Naipaul did) in a house on what was once a great Edwardian estate in Wiltshire.

Houses are always significant in Naipaul's fiction. Epitomising his view of colonial existence, when Mr Biswas at last acquires a house of his own after a transient's life in other people's premises, it is a precarious, jerry-built emulation of European properties. In *The Enigma of Arrival*, the landed mansion at the centre of the estate where the narrator recuperates stands as an image of Edwardian spaciousness and security. Having scrutinised what he regards as hastily flung up and now tumbledown postcolonial societies – West Indian islands subsiding into mob violence, South American nations succumbing to bankruptcy and anarchy, bloody African upheaval, Middle and Far Eastern countries in ugly ferment – the writer situates himself at what he deems the heart of the old empire.

Impermanence and lack of tradition tormented him on his travels; fixity and inherited responses provide solace here.

Ironically, Naipaul's pilgrimage in *An Area of Darkness* to what he thought of as his true cultural home, 'ancestral' India, dealt him his greatest shock of dislocation. Hoping to find a society endowed with a meaningful shape lacking in Trinidad's squalid muddle, he encountered chaos on a subcontinental scale and the spectacle of a nation ('the great dereliction of India') still ravaged, he believed, by the ruinous after-effects of its twelfth-century subjugation into the Muslim Mughal Empire. In *The Enigma of Arrival* the narrator finds himself feeling most at home where he might least have expected to. In contrast to the crude, unmellowed colonial societies he has described in book after book, he encounters an environment where everything rests on a rich substratum of antiquity. Here, almost uniquely in Naipaul's writings, people 'still have the idea of being successors and inheritors'. The landscape is as much a matter of history as geography. Ancient barrows and tumuli gently obtrude. The old wagon and coach roads are still open. A Victorian church looms from a pre-medieval foundation. Everything is encrusted with a patina of cultural associations. The water meadows outside the narrator's windows are reminiscent of Constable's paintings; riverbank scenery recalls illustrations to *The Wind in the Willows*. Thoughts of Gray's 'Elegy' and Goldsmith's 'The Deserted Village' superimpose themselves on the rural prospects. A local labourer is 'Wordsworthian'.

Rootlessness unceasingly nagged at Naipaul's imagination, as he repeatedly reveals in this book about putting down roots in an unexpected place. Arriving in Wiltshire feeling 'unanchored', his fictional alter ego burrows therapeutically into life there while simultaneously delving into the basis of his creativity. His global journeys, he comes to recognise, have paralleled his 'writer's journey' around the configurations of his psyche.

The notion of a journey being at once real and metaphorical recalls *Heart of Darkness*, a work that very evidently contributed to

Naipaul's sombre, distinguished Congo novel, *A Bend in the River*. True to his belief that colonials are 'mimic men', emulating European models, several of his books seem ingenious reworkings of Western novels. In *The Overcrowded Barracoon* (1972), he reveals that he mentally 'set in Trinidad, accepting, rejecting, adapting, and peopling in my own way' books by Dickens, Wells or Conrad that he'd read or had read to him as a boy. *A House for Mr Biswas* – located in a hybrid society where schoolchildren peruse the *King George V Hindi Reader* – takingly demonstrates the result of such cross-fertilisation. Dyspeptic, irascible, stuck in a profitless shop and uncongenial domestic circumstances, Mr Biswas is a Trinidadian Mr Polly. Both frequently denounce the existence they're trapped in as 'a hole'; both escape being stuck in a bankrupt shop by burning it down.

The Enigma of Arrival mocks this imitative urge in a neophyte writer. Naïve and bewildered on his first foray out of Trinidad, its narrator recalls, he struggled to produce an account of his experiences that would sound as 'elegant, knowing, unsurprised' as something by Somerset Maugham or Aldous Huxley: it took travel, time, and 'how much writing!' for him to achieve a successful synthesis of colonial and author. It's a synthesis that could hardly differ more from that exhibited by Rushdie: denunciatory and regretful rather than approving and jubilatory; introverted rather than extrovert; near-documentary rather than fantastical; favouring grainy newsreel actuality over lush technicolour extravagance.

Toni Morrison

Diametrically contrasting postcolonial prominences, Naipaul and Rushdie stand at opposite poles of imaginative territory into which the creative energies of multitudes of writers have been drawn since 1970. The mountainous range of fiction this has given rise to is a phenomenon unparalleled in literary history for its vastness, surface variety and underlying cohesiveness. Hundreds of authors from widely different backgrounds have converged, for more than half a century, on similar themes, occurrences, upheavals, dominations and liberations. Overwhelmingly, the central preoccupation has been with loss: loss of faith in an imperial ideal of bestowing betterment, loss of heritage, of land, status and dignity, loss of indigenous culture, voice and identity. Significant titles – *The Inheritance of Loss*, *The Migration of Ghosts* – have highlighted this. With its intimation of being called to account, *Something to Answer For*, the name of the novel with which P.H. Newby won the first Booker Prize in 1969, struck a note that would reverberate through English fiction for decades, just as its subject – a shaming colonial debacle, the 1956 Suez Crisis – typified much that would follow.

Narratives of territorial dispossession and its consequences – especially in North America, Australia and South Africa – proliferated. *The People*, the novel that Bernard Malamud (like Saul Bellow and Philip Roth, an acclaimed chronicler of Jewish immigrant experience in America) was working on when he died in 1986, takes as its hero a Jewish peddler in 1870 Idaho who tries to prevent Native Americans being evicted from their ancestral land and shunted off to a distant reservation almost certain to prove their death sentence. Grim after-effects of similar forced diasporas in North Dakota are chronicled in the novels of Louise Erdrich, a writer who, like many of her characters, has Chippewa Indian ancestry. With a title echoing Gertrude Stein's lament about the obliteration of her childhood home in Oakland, California ('there is no there there'), *There There* (2018), an angry fictional debut by Tommy Orange, a novelist of part-Cheyenne descent, portrays scattered and damaged Native American Indians congregating for what becomes a traumatic tribal reunion in present-day California. Exemplifying the way postcolonial concerns surface in modern crime fiction, Tony Hillerman's eighteen-book sequence of detective stories about Joe Leaphorn and Jim Chee of the Navajo Tribal Police investigates not just murder mysteries but Native American experience – rather as Walter Mosley's fifteen-book Easy Rawlins private investigator series does with Black American experience from the 1940s to the 1960s.

Black American experience was of course powerfully portrayed in fiction well before 1970. But it found its unsurpassed chronicler in Toni Morrison who, throughout more than four decades, unrolled a fictional chart of it. Her most celebrated novel, *Beloved* (1987), laid bare the ferocities and atrocities of black slavery in 1850s Kentucky. In subsequent works she traced slavery's long, cruel repercussions, depicting racial and cultural trauma with intense empathy, and shifting her attention to the trials of freedom. The malign after-effects of Black oppression become graphically apparent as very different and widely dispersed characters fail to shake off the shackles of the past.

Black arrivals from the South responding to the liberations of city life in 1920s Harlem gave *Jazz* (1992) its theme. Its opening pages hark back to a dramatic scene. Shot by her lover, a Black girl lies in her coffin. The man who fired the fatal bullet sobs and shakes with shock and remorse. Pushing her way through the mourners, his wife draws a knife and tries to slash her dead rival's face. It's a tale that might have been given throaty rendition on some crackly old Victrola blues record. With virtuoso artistry, *Jazz* takes it as the base material for a sequence of variations – forlorn, jaunty, tender – on the theme of Black experience in early twentieth-century America.

The year is 1926, the place Harlem. Smart young dudes strut the streets in yellow shoes and fancy tic-pins. Silk stockings whisper on girls' legs. Hair is fixed into marcelled waves. Through windows and doors, phonographs scratchily transmit the national anthem of the district: jazz with its growling urgencies, raw-voiced grievings, sauntering insouciance, sexy riffs and sudden wellings-out of mellow harmony. Catching all this with high fidelity, Morrison's novel attunes itself not just to the sound but the soul of jazz. As interludes swerve back to slavery and its aftermath, she brings out what it was that gave the music its inherent ability to modulate from aching desolation to sassy defiance and back again.

Links of all kinds connect Morrison's Black characters to their past. Even their names, reminders of what some slave-owner's joke or bene- factor's whim imposed on their forebears, can seem like vestigial verbal brands. Finding out about the past or being unable to escape it are central situations in her fiction. The spirit of a destroyed child haunted characters in *Beloved*. In *Jazz* the memory of the shot girl hangs para- lysingly over people's lives until a kind of exorcism is affected.

Many Black characters in Morrison's novels bear physical scars of their suffering: at the core of *Beloved*'s scenes from 1850s Kentucky is a woman whose back is welted with scars from a slaver's whip. The migrants from the South to Harlem whose lives are charted in *Jazz* have been mutilated in less immediately evident ways by racist brutalisings and abrasions. As her narrative opens up the background behind each of the characters trapped in its lethal love triangle, Morrison quietly and appallingly lays bare the emotional and psycho- logical damage wreaked by cruelty, oppression and want. Dorcas, the dead girl, was an orphan whose parents horribly perished in race riots. Violet, the skinny, hard-working hairdresser driven to jealous frenzy by her husband's first infidelity, comes from a dirt-poor family who scraped subsistence among the cotton and cane fields of Vesper County, Virginia. Joe, who she met and married there, was aban- doned at birth by his mother who lived wild in the woods.

As Morrison tracks the fatal convergence of these three, the winding paths her narrative takes are crowded with instances of the outrages that Blacks encounter even after leaving the South on segregated trains and alighting in the supposedly emancipated North. Spasmodic flarings-out of racist agitation leave characters burnt or battered to death. Those who don't end up in the mortuary face vicious mortifica- tion as routine. Dorcas's decent, carefully turned out, churchgoing aunt accepts as a fact of her life that, when she travels on a New York trolley car, 'women who spoke English said "Don't sit there, honey, you never know what they have." And women who knew no English at all and would never own a pair of silk stockings moved away from her.'

But, though uglinesses, great and small, afflict its characters, *Jazz* is a heartening as well as a sometimes harrowing read. Partly, this comes from its euphoric responsiveness to 'the City': a world where Black arrivals fleeing violence and destitution still encounter bigotry and barbarism, but have at least a chance of an independent and fulfilled life. Along with excitement at the bright-lit, broad streets of 1920s New York goes a relish for the diverse opportunities the metropolis offers. One way in which Morrison's fiction attacks racism's crude rigidities and hulking generalisations is by eloquently underscoring individual uniqueness and unpredictability. *Jazz* celebrates these liberating qualities even in its form. Initially, its narrator, seeing another girl move into the orbit of Joe and Violet, anticipates that the earlier pattern will be bleakly reprised. But events exultantly send the characters spinning off in a new direction. A jazz-like ability to change key, escape dragging rhythms and lift sombre strains into something fresh and upbeat carries a novel that opens in funeral discord to a vibrantly humane finale.

After following slavery's continuing consequences into an all-Black settlement in 1950s Georgia in *Home* (2012), a small 1970s Midwest town in *Paradise* (1998), and a 1980s East Coast resort in *Love* (2003), Morrison went back, in what is arguably her finest novel, *A Mercy* (2008), to the start of it all: the period when the 'peculiar institution' was just beginning to spread its stain across the patchwork of young colonies precariously surviving along America's Atlantic seaboard.

Ranging from the sultry plantations of the South to the rigours of the Puritan North, the story opens in 1682 with a merchant, Jacob Vaark, travelling through a Virginia convulsed by civil unrest into Catholic Maryland. Although this province is more stable, the staunchly Protestant Jacob is repelled by its Romish atmosphere – a revulsion that increases when he reaches his destination: the grandiose home of a Portuguese plantation owner, D'Ortega, who, revealing that he can't pay debts owed to Jacob, offers him slaves instead. Angrily rejecting the proposal at first ('flesh was not his commodity'), Jacob changes his mind when the mother of a little Black girl he has seen tottering quaintly around in cast-off grown-up shoes begs him to rescue her daughter from D'Ortega. From this act of mercy, harsh after-effects unroll.

Before heading back north to his not-very-thriving farm, Jacob hears of large, easy profits to be made from two sought-after new commodities, sugar and rum. Already infected by a desire for a house as grand as D'Ortega's, he invests in this lucrative business and becomes (at a conscience-sparing distance) a beneficiary of the slave labour on which the sugar cane plantations depend. With veteran subtlety, Morrison then shows how yielding to this sweet temptation corrodes his decency and leaves him in thrall to acquisitiveness and display.

Enslavement of numerous kinds dominates the novel. Occasionally visible in ugly glimpses of rape and maimings, the ever-growing slave trade gives the story its grim hinterland. Not only Black Africans are reduced to merchandise. The sole survivor of a tribe wiped out by smallpox, a Native American adopted by Presbyterian settlers is put up for sale ('Hardy female, Christianised'), Jacob's wife Rebekka was packed off to him by her parents as a commercial transaction.

Subserviences of other sorts play a key part in events, too. The delusion that her mother rejected her leaves Florens, the child Jacob saved, with an over-mastering need for love. When a handsome freed slave arrives to make ornate iron work in the mansion Jacob is having built, this impulsion drives her towards disaster. Other characters are also subject to repercussions of damage done in their past.

Religious bigotries hold sway over individuals and communities. Riskily journeying through the backwoods of Massachusetts, Florens almost falls foul of witch-hunters. Even Rebekka – whose fulfilling marriage to Jacob is conveyed with warm credibility – surrenders to sour piety as bereavements take their toll.

As with all Morrison's best work, *A Mercy* compellingly combines immediacy and obliquity. Its evocation of pioneer existence in America surrounds you with sensuous intensity. In arduous northern winters, where 'ice-coated starlings clung to branches dripping with snow', characters chomp on pigeon and turnips or forage for dead salmon under frozen waters. An attack by a bear ('the smell washed over them at the same moment the sow crashed through the laurel clicking her teeth') is described with thrilling power. In the swampy South, Jacob washes away the cloying aftertaste of a plantation meal of sugared rice and fried hog-cuts dripping in molasses with the 'bitter, clear' tang of ale gulped down in a tavern. Idioms have potent directness, too. 'Hunger wobbles me,' a girl faint with famine says. 'Mistress passed her days with the joy of a clock', it's remarked of a depressed woman's mechanical proceedings.

Rich knowledgeability about seventeenth-century America is put to telling effect. Voices speak to you as if you were there. As episodes told by Florens alternate with ones that take you into the consciousnesses of other characters, the book keeps you vividly aware of the vital human individuality that racism is brutally trying to iron out.

From this diversity of viewpoints, a stark story of the evils of possessiveness and the perils of dispossession emerges slantwise. Hints, suspicions, secrets, ambivalences, scarcely acknowledged motives and barely noticeable nuances serve as signposts to enormities and desperation. Around slavery's large-scale uprootings, Morrison spotlights individual instances of loss (orphans and outcasts are, as often in her fiction, much in evidence; compensatory alliances they form are feelingly presented).

Colonial Consequences: Chimamanda Ngozi Adichie

Morrison's status as the pre-eminent portrayer of African American experience matched that of Chinua Achebe as the pre-eminent portrayer of colonial and postcolonial experience in Nigeria – most celebratedly in his trilogy, *Things Fall Apart* (1958), *No Longer at Ease* (1960), and *Arrow of God* (1964). His memoir, *There Was a Country* (2012), published shortly before his death, gave a stark account of Nigeria's 1967–69 Civil War and the brutal crushing of the breakaway state of Biafra by massacre and starvation. It was a calamity Achebe's fellow-Igbo writer, Chimamanda Ngozi Adichie, depicted in her novel, *Half of a Yellow Sun* (2006), and saw as the ruinous legacy of colonial rule. 'Empire was crumbling ...', one of her characters observes, 'But the British had to preserve Nigeria as it was, their prized creation, their large market.' At independence in 1960, with its potentially disastrous regional, cultural, economic and ethnic splits still unhealed, the country was, it's said, 'a collection of fragments held in a fragile clasp'. As its narrative swings between 'The Early Sixties', throughout which tension builds, and 'The Late Sixties', when carnage erupts, *Half of a Yellow Sun* harrowingly records the bloody breaking apart of that fragile clasp.

Postcolonial disjunction of another kind – migration, with its disorientations, alienations, and humiliations – was the subject of Adichie's next novel, *Americanah* (2013). Again setting a pair of jeopardised lovers at the centre of a widespread, vividly populated story, she here juxtaposes not periods but places: Nigeria, North America and England. At a self-congratulatorily *bien pensant* dinner party in Islington, when talk turns to immigration, a Nigerian who, unknown to the others, is an illegal immigrant, silently reflects that they 'all understood the fleeing from war, from the kind of poverty that crushed human souls, but they would not understand the need to escape from the oppressive lethargy of choicelessness. They would not understand why people like him ... conditioned from birth to look towards somewhere else, eternally convinced that real lives happened in that somewhere else, were now resolved to do dangerous things, illegal things, so as to leave ... hungry for choice and certainty.' *Americanah* explores this postcolonial impulse and the culture clashes that ensue.

In these two outstanding novels – companion-volume displays of what colonialism has left in its wake – Adichie brings an acutely informed, fiercely felt and intelligently nuanced sense and sensibility to empire's aftermath. Ranging from bleak contemplation of devastating upheaval and slaughter to suave satire of earnest smugness, their tonal scope is as wide as their social and geographical span. One speciality in these books that quiver with alertness is attentiveness to voice. In *Half of a Yellow Sun*, this can become a matter of life or death: a give-away Igbo accent proves fatal during interrogation by Yoruba militia in the Civil War. In the less lethal world of *Americanah*, its Igbo heroine, Ifemelu, who has a fellowship at Princeton, eventually decides 'to stop faking an American accent ... the blurring of the *t*, the creamy roll of the *r*, the sentences starting with "So" and the sliding response of "Oh really".' The importance of authenticity of voice – a prevailing concern in postcolonial fiction – is stressed in *Half of a Yellow Sun* by the device of having an Igbo houseboy embroiled in the Civil War ultimately take over the project of recounting the tragedy of Biafra from his employer, an English academic historian. In *Americanah*, a blog by Ifemelu – 'Raceteenth or Various Observations by a Non-American Black on the subject of Blackness in America' – provides keen-eared, sharp-eyed outsider social commentary.

Colonial Collisions and Their Aftermath

The repercussions of American Black slavery were shown by Toni Morrison as wide and long-persisting. The dark hinterland of the slave South from which their forebears escaped still cast shadows over the industrious citizens of the God-fearing, law-abiding, prosperous little town amid the tall grasslands and windswept horizons of mid-1970s Oklahoma that gave her novel *Paradise* its setting. The ironic resonances in its title resound in books by other authors too. Harking back to the German colony of Muslim East Africa in 1910, *Paradise* (1996) by the Zanzibar-born novelist, Abdulrazak Gurnah, resurrects a world where slavery at its crudest (the blatant trafficking in fettered human beings) is officially over but more subtle forms of subservience – economic bonds, not leg-irons – are replacing it. Colonially ravaged paradises haunt the imagination of Romesh Gunesekera. Located in 1825 Mauritius, his novel *The Prisoner of Paradise* (2012) journeyed back in time to observe one example. Set on an unnamed, once-lovely island, his near-future fable, *Heaven's Edge* (2002), gave an allegorical twist to his concern with shattered idylls. Where the concern originated is evident in his collections of short stories, *Monkfish Moon* (1993) and *Noontide Toll* (2014), which depict with quiet finesse how decades of postcolonial civil war reduced his native Sri Lanka from an Eden to an abattoir.

Another small island, Tasmania – the extermination of whose Aboriginal inhabitants by European colonists incited H.G. Wells to write *The War of the Worlds*, his 1898 tale about Martian invaders mercilessly subjugating England – has also been the site of later novels about lethal colonial despoliation. Imperial greed and indigenous deprivation were headlined in the punning title of Richard Flanagan's novel, *Wanting* (2008), about the island in the early nineteenth century. Travelling to its sun-baked dustlands in the 1860s, Robert Edric's bitterly titled *Elysium* (1995) focused on the plight of its supposedly last pure-blooded Aborigine, William Lanné. In Matthew Kneale's sometimes harrowing, sometimes tartly funny *English Passengers* (2000), one storyline takes you aboard the emphatically misnamed *Sincerity*, a ship on which a clergyman, outraged at godless assaults on the literal truth of the Bible, is en route to Tasmania to further his claim that the Garden of Eden was located there. Far from being an Eden, the novel's other storyline reveals, the island is a hell. Through the eyes of Peevay, the fair-haired, dark-skinned son of an Aborigine woman raped by a convict, Tasmania is seen to be a killing ground where genocide rages almost unimpeded. Overt slaughter – massacres conducted by stockmen who mow down Aborigines ('shooting crows' is their term for it) – gives way to more insidious extermination as colonial society begins to pride itself on being more enlightened. Promised better territory and a safe haven, Tasmania's surviving Aborigines are misled into fatal resettlement where sickness, loss of cultural identity and physical scope cause them to waste away. As Peevay's mixed parentage reminds you, Tasmania – Van Diemen's Land – was a two-tier hell: a place of imperial genocide and a dreaded penal colony. Amid the variegated pages (printed in different colours of ink) of *Gould's Book of Fish* (2001), a semi-surreal fictional hodge-podge by Flanagan, who was born and raised in Tasmania, nightmare scenes from the island's convict past stand out starkly.

Convicts – like slaves, hideously maltreated victims of colonialism – are frequent presences in Australian fiction. Kate Grenville's *The Secret River* (2005) followed the progress of one of them based on her great-great-great grandfather, a Thames boatman transported to the penal colony, 'a prison whose bars were ten thousand miles of water', at the start of the nineteenth century. Peter Carey resurrected fiction's most famous deportee to Botany Bay, Abel Magwitch from Charles Dickens's *Great Expectations*, in *Jack Maggs* (1997). In a nineteenth-century London of pea-souper fogs and flaring gaslights, literature's best-known 'bolter from New South Wales' encounters Ma Britten, an emblematically named purveyor of miscarriage pills who aborts potential in many ways. Also set in the mid-nineteenth century, Carey's next novel, *True History of the Kelly Gang* (2001), provided a companion volume to his inventive spin-off from Dickens. Again, sympathetic response to outsiders combined with Carey's other abiding concern: the cruelties of colonialism. The earlier novel – making you aware of the lash-seamed back under Maggs's swagger clothes and the lacerated decency beneath his bruiser demeanour – forcefully attested to the iniquities a barbarous penal regime had inflicted. Its successor lets another casualty of colonial injustice, Australia's legendary outlaw, Ned Kelly, purportedly penning his journal, put his case with demotic vigour. In the background looms 'the Demon', Van Diemen's Land, the penal colony to which his father was transported from Tipperary. Persecuted as a former convict's son, Kelly is driven to become a hounded bushranger, presented by Carey as a goaded-beyond-endurance victim of a 'colony made specifically to have poor men bow down to their gaolers'. 'They were Australians,' Kelly declares in his journal, 'the historic memory of UNFAIRNESS were in their blood'.

The other historic atrocity Australia was stained by – the massacres of its indigenous people by European settlers – also pervades Carey's fiction. His storylines make their way back to it in calculatedly unexpected ways. *A Long Way from Home* (2018), which reconstructs a 1950s car-race-cum-endurance-test around the continent, starts as what seems an ebullient comic caper. As peppy little Irene Bobs and her equally diminutive and bursting with get-up-and-go husband Titch take on the 10,000-mile challenge, setbacks are at first jauntily steered past. But, before long, things darken as the novel changes track. A turning point comes with the discovery of the remains (most affectingly a small child's skull, 'fragile and powdery as an emu egg', punctured with a bullet hole) of an Aboriginal graveyard broken open by a storm. After this, location begins to quiver with significance. 'If this was our country's heart, I never saw anything so stony, so empty, so endless, devoid of life other than predatory kites', a character reflects. By a devious route, *A Long Way from Home* (its title taking on multiple meanings) closes in on the dispossession of Australia's Aboriginals. What opened as a story about a race ends as one about race. Grenville's *The Secret River*, which starts with focus on the atrocities of forcible transportation, closes in on the atrocities of forcible dispossession as her initially maltreated convict-settlers respond with genocidal savagery to the indigenous inhabitants of territory they seize.

Colonial collisions between races shudder through Australian fiction. Encounter-shock is conveyed with raw palpability in *A Fringe of Leaves* (1976), Patrick White's novel (based on the real-life experiences of Eliza Fraser in the 1830s) about a shipwrecked Englishwoman thrown into gruelling subsistence with an Aboriginal tribe before being rescued by an escaped convict. Similarly based on a true story (that of James 'Gemmy' Mitchell in the 1850s), David Malouf's

Remembering Babylon (1993) portrays what happens when a cast-away cabin boy, Gemmy Fairley, who has spent sixteen years with an Aboriginal tribe, bursts into a small settler community whose frail homesteads are strung out under the alien glare of Australia's eastern coast, stammering 'Do not shoot. I am a B-b-british object!' Fair-haired but burnt tar-black by the sun, speaking only vestigial English, he first comes under suspicion as a spy, then stirs even more unsettling fears as colonists see his hybrid state as a threat to their racial assurance.

Likewise fictionalising actuality, in this case that of Australia's first Aboriginal outlaw, Jimmie Governor, Thomas Keneally's *The Chant of Jimmie Blacksmith* (1972) charts how abuse and humiliation goad another 'hybrid' – son of a Black woman and a white man – into a bloody killing spree. Retaliation narratives of this kind have become widespread in postcolonial fiction. When a white woman is raped by two Black men and a Black boy in J.M. Coetzee's comfortless picture of post-apartheid South Africa, *Disgrace* (1999), her father suggests that 'It was history speaking through them ... A history of wrong.' In response, she wonders if her attackers see themselves as 'debt collectors', and the assault was 'the price one has to pay for staying on'. Few writers would push things to this extreme. But narratives of cruel postcolonial nemesis abound. Towards the end of her more-than-fifty-year fictional career of chronicling the evils and absurdities of apartheid with steady integrity and scrutinising with sharp-eyed understanding the mixed motives and ideals tinged with compromise that it generated, Nadine Gordimer published a notable postcolonial novel, *The House Gun* (1998). Where an earlier book by her, *July's People* (1991), imagined a bloody revolution in which Black South Africans rise up against the apartheid government and hunt down and murder white South Africans, *The House Gun*, written after the end of apartheid in 1994, trains its sights on the actual aftermath which Gordimer was now witnessing around her. With old hostilities unquenched, the new South Africa seethes with aggression. The transition from the barbarities of the apartheid era to something more civilised hasn't lacked casualties. Even in a more enlightened climate, after-effects of former atrocities cause disruption. With the 'daily tally of deaths as routine as a weather report', the crime rate soars. Hit-squads previously in the pay of the state now work for drug dealers. Knifings, stranglings, and burnings are rife. Taxi drivers compete for customers with gunfire. Tiffs in discotheques are resolved with bullets. Violence is so entrenched in everyday life that a lethal weapon can be seen as a routine domestic appliance, like 'the house gun' with which a young man fatally shoots a friend. As political and social factors that played a role in fomenting the shooting come to light, the killer's parents – always cautiously muted in their opposition to the apartheid regime – are confronted with the consequences of their past passivity.

Northern Ireland matched South Africa in being grimly fertile in fiction of violent postcolonial repercussions. Its long-persisting sectarian strife, especially in the Belfast which degenerated into an urban battlefield between the IRA and the UDA, has spawned a plethora of gory thrillers as well as novels and stories of sombre distinction. With *Cal* (1983), his novel about a young Catholic complicit in the killing of a Protestant policeman who falls guiltily in love with the man's widow, Bernard MacLaverty began a fictional exploration of Ulster's ugly, entangled traumas which he continued in two piercingly perceptive collections of stories, *Walking the Dog* (1994) and *Matters of Life and Death* (2006). Where James Joyce's *Dubliners*, clearly a model for him, offered stories portraying the deadening torpor of the Irish metropolis at the start of the twentieth century, MacLaverty captures the deadly turmoil of the Northern Irish metropolis in more recent times. Urgent with reportage-like immediacy, his stories pitch you into the fearfulness of 1970s Belfast. One character declares that the fall of the Roman Empire was due to the lead in its water pipes. 'Being forced to drink poison helps no one,' it's remarked. The implications of this ramify through stories where the unremitting drip of 'sectarian poison' takes its toll. Toxic rancour simmers beneath the everyday (as when, in one particularly chilling story, a matey-seeming Protestant policeman malevolently puts his trusting Catholic neighbours at risk). The past is shown to scar and warp the present. In *Midwinter Break* (2017), a Northern Irish couple, Stella and Gerry, who (like MacLaverty and his family) moved from Belfast to Scotland in the 1970s to escape Ulster's 'traps and atrocities', are encountered forty years later as they fly out from Glasgow to Amsterdam for a winter weekend break. After-shocks from a graphically recalled terrorist outrage during which the then-pregnant Stella was near-mortally shot, it emerges, still rever-berate through their marriage.

Harkings Back

Near-present-day, close-to-actuality narratives about carnage and havoc wreaked by colonialism's aftermath are outnumbered by ones that – responding to the prevailing pull of the past – looked further back in time. South of the border from MacLaverty's Belfast, Roddy Doyle, whose initial fictional territory was rumbustious working-class Dublin in the 1980s and 1990s, went back in *A Star Called Henry* (1999) to Irish freedom struggles at the start of the twentieth century. Now seeming a period piece in more ways than one, the novel almost parodically conforms to the fictional mode Rushdie pioneered. Born into the Dublin slums of 1901, its hero-narrator is equipped with paranormal qualities. The midwife who delivers him finds that her hands mysteriously tingle ever afterwards. At his birth, his illiterate, black-shawled crone of a grandmother miraculously acquires the ability to read – and devotes the rest of her life to doing so, sometimes perusing two books at once by casting a different eye over each. Around this uncanny granny, other stock fitments of the magic realist postcolonial novel are on view: a fantastically erotic dwarf, a larger-than-life brothel madam, females of supra-normal voluptuousness and availability, telepathically transmitted sexual magnetism.

An urge to burrow back in time – often from near-autobiographical starting points – is evident in the careers of many postcolonial novelists. *The Final Passage* (1985), the first book by Caryl Phillips, who was born in St Kitts, fictionalised his parents' emigration to England from the West Indies in the late 1950s. With *Cambridge* (1991) he travelled back a century or more to focus on a Victorian spinster journeying out to a Caribbean sugar plantation. *Crossing the River* (1993) took Liberia in 1803 as the start of its panorama of Black diaspora. Drawing on *Othello*, one of the linked stories comprising Phillips's *The Nature of Blood* (1997) portrayed a Black African general hired to command the army of fifteenth-century Venice. In similar fashion, *Disappearance* (1993), the first novel by David Dabydeen, born in Guyana, told the story of a young Guyanese man in present-day Britain; his next, *The Counting House* (1996), was set among indentured labourers in early nineteenth-century British Guyana; with *A Harlot's Progress* (1999), he re-cast Hogarth's 1732 print sequence to depict African existence in eighteenth-century London. Buchi Emecheta, who migrated to Britain from Lagos in 1960, began her literary career (writing in what was her fourth language) with sturdily unself-pitying novels, *In the Ditch* (1972) and *Second-Class Citizen* (1974), about the challenges and hard-won triumphs of her life as a single Black mother in run-down and often racist areas of North London, then imaginatively resurrected early twentieth-century Nigeria and its varying kinds of female subjugation in *The Slave Girl* (1977). The fiction of Andrea Levy, daughter of parents who had arrived in Britain from Jamaica in 1948, likewise showed a progress back through time. Strongly autobiographical, her first three novels – *Every Light in the House Burnin'* (1994), *Never Far from Nowhere* (1996) and *Fruit of the Lemon* (1999) – documented the lives of second-generation Caribbean immigrants, children of the *Windrush* generation, in later twentieth-century London. Then, juxtaposing two insular communities – those of Britain and Jamaica – *Small Island* (2004) went back to the Second World War and its immediate aftermath. Her final novel, *The Long Song* (2010), was presented as the memoir of an elderly woman once a slave on a sugar cane plantation in nineteenth-century Jamaica.

Timothy Mo

This pattern of advancing back into the past as a postcolonial literary career unrolls is displayed with particular virtuosity by Timothy Mo. His first novel, *The Monkey King* (1978), was set in the Hong Kong where he lived with his Cantonese father and British mother until the family moved to London when he was ten. *Sour Sweet* (1982) involved itself with gangland vendettas in London's Chinatown. Then, with *An Insular Possession* (1986), Mo sent his imagination back to the South China coast at the start of the Opium Wars. A writer always drawn to pugnacity (he began his literary career writing for *Boxing News*), he found panoramic scope there for his punchy fictional vitality. Large-scale battles a nineteenth-century Royal Academician would have been proud to put his brush to – the storming of the Heights of Canton, the fire-rafts and war-junks of the Celestial Empire routed by British cannonades – erupt in his novel's closing stages. From the beginning of its story, banked-down antagonisms growl. Colonists cooped up in Macau or the thin strip of Canton's waterfront ceded to them by the Celestial Empire are pelted with mud by coolies or smeared by wall posters full of 'revilements' about their sexual tastes. Among the merchants and missionaries of this embattled enclave, prejudices fester: English Protestants look askance at Portuguese Papists, British and Americans periodically clash. Even entertainments are combative. Written up with gory exultation in one of the colony's papers ('Henshaw hit him with a facer, drawing the cork from his nose and making the claret issue copiously'), there's a savage boxing match between two sailors. At a more decorous boat race, passions still run belligerently high. Even when people get together to put on a play, it's Sheridan's *The Rivals* – and rivalry rages both among the leading players and the different nationalities vying for pre-eminence in the audience.

The most rancorous competitiveness, though – eventually triggering an ugly duel – is between the community's two newspapers: *The Lin Tin Bulletin and River Bee* and *The Canton Monitor*. Run by young Americans, Chase and Eastman, the former attacks Britain's rapacious fomenting of the opium trade in China. The latter, a cholerically pro-British broadsheet, thunders against the machinations of the mandarins and bespatters its Yankee rivals with leaden contempt. Arguments of a less aggressive kind – as to the relative merits of painting (practised in the colony by a rubicund, toping old portraitist) and daguerreotype (a photographic innovation enthused over by Eastman) – are also aired. Through the disputes between the two men, Mo brings into focus the rationale behind his own work. Art, it's suggested, can aggrandise and falsify by too great stress on selection and composition; photography is more authentic because more sensitive to reality's random immediacy.

The latter technique is what *An Insular Possession* opts for. Scorning what he calls 'the blatant truth of retrospect', Mo imposes no historical pattern on his material – indeed barely imposes a fictional pattern. What looks set to become a central sexual triangle between Eastman, Chase and a young heiress is deliberately allowed to lapse into something more amorphous. When Eastman's involvement with the girl is broken off, the storyline trails away; it's only among the small print of an appendix to the novel – a fictitious *Gazetteer of Place Names and Biographies Relative to the Early China Coast* by An Old Hand – that we learn of her subsequent life. Historically too, breaking off – as it began – *in medias res*, the book shuns the diagrammatic. Conclusions, in both senses of the word, are eschewed. Instead, contemplating an inflamed area where two empires irritably chafe against each other, Mo colourfully chronicles its seething diversity: mandarins, the brittle length of their fingernails shielded by scabbards, compete in the inditing of elegant, brush-stroked verses;

British traders with Madeira-flushed faces reel out to billiards or balance sheets; peasants huddle round rice straw fires as blindfolded buffalo trundle waterwheels.

With especial brio, the novel conveys not only the look of a time and location but their sound. Dialogue is racy with the idioms of the era. Extracts from journals and letters open up adeptly seized opportunities for period pastiche. Pages from the rival newspapers graphically reproduce early nineteenth-century journalistic prose with its mixture of trenchancy, elegant variations, classical tags, ponderous puns and formally phrased ferocities. With considerable flair, Mo himself often adopts the mannerisms – rhetorical sallies, button-holings and rallyings of the reader, ironic circumlocutions – likely to be the stock-in-trade of a novelist contemporary with the events and characters. This technique, like Mo's taste for thronged panoramas, gives a stronger sense of period than personalities. As cultural, polit-ical, and economic currents stream through the novel, individuals eddy into the background. The book opens with a description of a turbulent Chinese river sweeping along a jumbled freight of boats and effluvia, corpses, livestock, traders, silt and dignitaries. Swirling with people and incidents, Mo's presentation of the flux of history has a similar torrential power, culminating in the founding of Hong Kong as a Crown Colony (which attracted the attention of other novelists as well: its changing fortunes, from the imperial complacency of the 1930s through the savagery of the Japanese occupation to the post-war economic boom, were chronicled in John Lanchester's 2002 novel, *Fragrant Harbour*; also Paul Theroux wove a macabre suspense tale around its hand-over to China in his 1997 novella, *Kowloon Tong*).

In subsequent novels, Mo's engagement with imperialism and its after-effects fanned out across the globe. *The Redundancy of Courage* (1991) depicts what happens when a 400-year-old empire slackens its hold on a far colony and an aggressively expansionist new power seizes it. Danu, a dilapidated tropical fringe of the empire, which Portugal is exhaustedly relinquishing, has one of those arbitrary

71

borders whose contours are the result of distant pen-strokes on mahogany desks in European chancelleries. On the opposite side of it are the militant *malais*. Soon after the Portuguese depart, they invade. In a dramatic opening scene, hundreds of parachutes are seen descending like thistledown. Above them flit what look like tiny silver insects. With eerie gradualness these sharpen into focus as threatening men and machines. Then as the *malais* tear into Danu's capital, normal life is submerged with terrifying suddenness under a welter of slaughter as occupation begins.

Blending actuality and invention, Mo fictionalises Indonesia's brutal shackling of East Timor to its archipelago empire in 1975. Though his novel's annexed nation has an invented name, Danu, details repeatedly clinch the connection between fiction and fact. But the book isn't simply an imaginative recreation of a local atrocity largely ignored by the international community. Adopting a three-section structure – life among the subjugated, life among resistance fighters, life among the conquerors – it opens up wider perspectives on to imperialism. For most of the novel, Mo keeps his story pent up inside a sweltering tropical microcosm of colonial tyranny and national resistance. But, having involved you at close quarters with the life-and-death realities its inhabitants face, he finally pulls back from it. The book's recurrent references to puppetry, the region's distinctive art form, take on taut significance with revelations of cynical political string-twitchers far overseas. Having filled its pages with specimens of impressive bravery – from a dedicated woman doctor to an unswerving guerrilla leader – *The Redundancy of Courage*, as it closes, suavely and shockingly justifies its title.

Moving over to the Philippines – for 300 years a Spanish colony, for 50 an American one – *Brownout on Breadfruit Boulevard* (1995) shines a harsh light on another devastated postcolonial society (whose hellish capital, a city seen as somewhere between Dracula's Transylvania and Capote's Chicago had, a year earlier, generated an excoriating, almost phosphorescently Gothic novel about its mutilated lives and monstrous death-rate, James Hamilton-Paterson's *Ghosts of Manila*). Halfway through Mo's novel, the perspective swivels from vistas of terminal breakdown (politicians and racketeers operating virtually unimpeded as warlords; gun-wielding thugs as routine a feature as warrens of prostitutes and mumbling hordes of drug addicts) to a symposium on multiculturalism and associated ecological issues held for PR purposes in a handsomely appointed new conference centre. As international delegates – some decently motivated, others expense-account blowflies hovering round Third World decay – jet in, the novel modulates from atrocity to acerbity. Chapters witheringly record proceedings as assembled intellectuals, radical celebrities, media pundits and academics verbalise about postcolonial issues. Against a hinterland of postcolonial nightmare, a caustic comedy of international collisions and collusions is played out. With *Renegade or Halo²* (2000) and *Pure* (2012), Mo continued to roam and report on garishly crumbling postcolonial societies in South-East Asia. Exceptional knowledgeability combined with imaginative force, cultural breadth, political acumen, prose crackling with energy and an acutely keen ear for speech made his the most compelling fictional bulletins from the region.

Barry Unsworth

It wasn't only writers personally caught up in colonialism and its consequences who found empire an irresistible subject. Barry Unsworth, born into a mining community in England's industrially depressed north-east in 1930, won acclaim for fiction far-flung in time and place from his starting point. After publishing five novels with present-day settings, he largely devoted himself to fiction about imperial cruelties and imperial collapse. The glamours and rapacities of empire became his continuing theme in books that atmospherically evoked the gaudy sunset of the Ottoman Empire, Venice's resplendent prime and velvety decadence, the feverish turbulence of

Africa's Guinea Coast at the height of the slave trade, twelfth-century Sicily under Norman rule, and 1914 Mesopotamia where, amidst the archaeological remains of long-gone empires, British, German and American imperialists competed for lucrative oil and railway rights. What Unsworth found haunting about Istanbul, where he taught for some years was, he said, that 'It's like Vienna or Madrid, one of those cities where you really feel the decline and the peculiar melancholy of imperial trappings that all the life has gone out of.'

With *Pascali's Island* (1980), he observed the finale of the Ottoman Empire from a vantage point on its outermost limit: an Aegean island in 1908. As the rotten jigsaw of the empire falls jaggedly apart, a man whose own life is falling apart contemplates a panorama of disintegration. Pascali, a paid informer who has for years been sending reports to Constantinople, fears that the local Greeks have discovered what he does. As he waits for them to kill him, he pens his last bulletin, packed with symptoms of approaching doom. Politically, ominous cracks are gaping ever wider. In the garrisons, disaffected Turkish troops barely obey orders; in the hills, Greek freedom fighters become every day more venturesome. Nor are things merely collapsing at the empire's edge; the centre cannot hold either. Clogged with corruption, the administrative channels have seized up. Rumours leak out from the capital, where there are said to be more spies than police, of a paranoid Sultan virtually self-imprisoned in his Yıldız Palace. *The Rage of the Vulture* (1982) plunges you into the imploding core of the Ottoman Empire, the chaotic Constantinople of 1908. This time the central figure isn't a shabby obese Levantine informer frightenedly conscious of being under observation himself but a lean smart British officer and political agent aware that he is stationed in a city riddled with spies. But the novels complement each other as gripping feats of fictional archaeology, exhuming historical scenes with vibrant immediacy and in vivid detail. Both testify to impressive amounts of research. Before beginning a novel, Unsworth revealed, he always amassed 'a plethora of material to strengthen the illusion', then used, he reckoned, about 20 per cent of it.

It was an approach that stood him in good stead with *Stone Virgin* (1985), a three-tier novel dominated by a masterpiece of Venetian Gothic, a sculpted limestone Madonna which casts its shadow over a triptych of stories – one set in the fifteenth century, one in the eighteenth, and one in the 1970s – which chart Venice's descent from imperial vigour to melancholy decline. In the year that it was published, Unsworth ended his career as a peripatetic English teacher in the Eastern Mediterranean to become writer-in-residence at Liverpool University – and, ironically, immediately experienced writer's block. What enabled him to overcome it was writing a novel about a novelist afflicted with writer's block. *Sugar and Rum* (1988) features Clive Benson, the author of a historical novel set in Venice, now unsuccessfully struggling in Liverpool to complete a novel about the port's collusion with the African slave trade. Liverpool, Unsworth felt, had affinities with the two cities his fiction had most recently been contemplating: 'Liverpool, Venice, Istanbul – all to me have similar qualities, imperial connections', he affirmed. There was, though, a significant difference. Where the remnants of imperial prosperity in Istanbul and Venice took picturesque forms, in Liverpool there was only squalid dereliction. Unsworth was 'stricken by the sight of so much stricken around me'. Similarly paralysed with despondency at the unemployment and decay he sees everywhere around him, Benson ekes out a living teaching creative writing. This gives Unsworth entertaining scope for comedy, especially in parody of stagily unreal historical fiction penned by his students ('Nay then, an you list, let us ride into the coverts. I will not gainsay you'). But, amid the exuberant mockery, personal qualms are discernible: anxieties as to whether the historical novels Unsworth himself wrote were not much more than colourful escapism.

One of the ways in which he resolved it was with his next novel, *Sacred Hunger* (1992). Here, Unsworth's research about the 'Triangular

Trade', the immensely profitable maritime shuttling between Liverpool, West Africa and the West Indies, that he had undertaken to give substance to Benson's work in *Sugar and Rum* is complemented by material garnered by a further three years of immersion in eighteenth-century naval and commercial history. The result isn't just a sturdily traditional historical novel, epic in scope and length, that resurrects with tremendous immediacy the horrors of an imperial atrocity. Working on the novel in the 1980s, Unsworth 'began to see more strongly that there were inescapable analogies' between that decade and the period of his story: 'You couldn't really live through the Eighties without feeling how crass and distasteful some of the economic doctrines were. The slave trade is a perfect model for that kind of total devotion to the profit motive [the 'sacred hunger' of his book's title] without reckoning the human consequences.' With empire providing analogy, the novel shows him confidently evoking a distant era and simultaneously airing apprehensions about his own. Bygone imperial barbarity carries persisting pertinence. So – it's emphasised in *Land of Marvels* (2009), Unsworth's novel about Mesopotamia on the brink of the First World War – does past economic imperialism. In a final paragraph that glances ahead to Britain's annexation and renaming of a vast swathe of this territory after the Ottoman Empire was dismembered, the last word of this penultimate novel Unsworth wrote is 'Iraq'.

Foulds and Flashman

British imperial misdeeds, miscalculation and muddle, put on display by Scott and Farrell in the 1970s, have never ceased to stir novelists' imaginations, sometimes in unexpected ways. Particularly remarkable was Adam Foulds's *The Broken Word* (2011) which used the now rarely encountered genre of verse fiction to spotlight a dark chapter of British colonial history. Largely set in 1950s Kenya during the Mau Mau uprising, it focuses on a young man, returned to his family's East

African farm after leaving public school in England and before going up to Cambridge. Rapidly, he finds himself caught up in carnage. Mau Mau rebels butcher the white settlers occupying their land (and the Kikuyu who stay loyal to them). The British retaliate with barbarities of their own: ferocious reprisals, detention camps, beatings, torture, slaughter. With remarkable accomplishment, Foulds moves around territory half a century and thousands of miles away from him. Place and period are conjured up as assuredly as if he had been there. In the East Highlands Country Club, colonists in creaking leather armchairs grumble through drifts of cigar smoke about MMBA ('Miles and miles of bloody Africa'). Outside sprawl dangerous 'lion-coloured slums / with their cattery stink'. Wittily deft metaphor sharpens keen observation: a reactionary colonial cove has a 'tweed moustache: / threads of ginger brown and white'. Speech is captured with similar high fidelity. Hunting and sporting imagery makes the British feel more at home with outrages they are perpetrating. Stiff-upper-lip understatement plays its part, too ('It hasn't been . . . entirely quiet', 'Chaps got a bit worked up, / actually, sort of let them / have it somewhat'). Among the colonials, euphemism reigns. An elderly homosexual couple, whose ghastly hacking to death by their servants' *pangas* is unforgettably rendered, are 'the two old boys who dine together'. Bringing taut power to the portrayal of colonial violence and terror, Foulds's verse tale is a *tour de force* of concise indictment.

A more expansive subversive eye was cast over the swagger of Britain's imperial past by George MacDonald Fraser, who from 1969 onwards published twelve books, purportedly instalments from the memoirs of Sir Harry Flashman VC, KCB, KCIE, which followed the military career of the man who had been the cowardly bully in *Tom Brown's Schooldays*. Usually set against a backdrop of momentous episodes from British imperial history – the First Afghan War, the charge of the Light Brigade, the Indian Mutiny, the Opium Wars, the Siege of Khartoum – the Flashman novels provided an exuberantly deflationary view of renowned episodes in the annals of the empire, energised by Fraser's historical and literary expertise. His prose is constantly perked up by lively use of period slang: people don't knock on doors but 'knuckle the walnut', characters don't die but 'have their gas turned off'. Vitalising substance is given to preposterous scenarios by a wealth of knowledge about nineteenth-century military, political, social and cultural life (solidly backed up by pages of notes at the end of each volume of Flashman's memoirs). Resolutely craven and unswervingly self-interested, Flashman bristles with the racial and sexual prejudices of his era. But coexisting subversively with meticulous recreation of the nineteenth-century scene and Flashman's unreconstructed mores are more modern-sounding tones of cynicism and scabrousness. Rampageously disreputable sentiments and outrageous farce upend myths of gallant imperial derring-do and expose absurdities and monstrosities of empire.

Invented Empires

Enthralment with empire hasn't only concerned itself with what Britain did as an imperial power but with what it might have had done to it, if subjugated by another power. Some alternative history narratives have envisaged Britain as a colony of the Nazi Third Reich. Len Deighton's *SS-GB* (1978) imagines what might have transpired if Hitler's Operation Sea Lion – his plan to invade the United Kingdom during the Battle of Britain – had been victoriously carried out instead of being postponed and then abandoned. Months after British surrender in 1941 – and repercussions including the execution of Churchill, the imprisonment of the King in the Tower of London and the escape of other Royals to New Zealand – a homicide investigation leads a policeman into perilous involvement with the resistance movement. C.J. Sansom's more sophisticated and atmospheric *Dominion* (2012) opted for a variant scenario: the replacing of Neville Chamberlain as prime minister in 1940 not by Churchill but by the appeaser Lord Halifax. In 1952, in an increasingly authoritarian

Britain governed by Lord Beaverbrook and Oswald Mosley and more or less a Nazi satellite state, a growing British Resistance, headed by Churchill and Attlee, provokes a fierce German clampdown. Again, the narrative takes the form of a police chase, though this time amid a range of more involvingly characterised collaborators and resisters. Kingsley Amis's *Russian Hide and Seek* (1980) conjured up another kind of imaginary imperial conquest: a twenty-first-century Britain which has been a Soviet Russian protectorate for fifty years. As in the Nazi Britain novels, the prevailing atmosphere is grey, devitalised, run-down. But, instead of a thriller plot of resistance and fight-back, Amis's novel offers a vision of a nation sunk into the kind of apathy you'd expect to find in some Chekhovian backwater of Russia.

The most extravagantly invented empire came from Peter Carey. His 1994 novel, *The Unusual Life of Tristan Smith*, assembled a fantastic world in which familiar-seeming historical and geographical landmarks were boldly realigned in a narrative of two nations, Efica and Voorstand. An antipodean archipelago of eighteen islands, extending from Nez Noir in the north to the Madeleines in the south, Efica is the humid epitome of tropic colonialism. Palm trees rustle in sultry breezes. Monsoons clatter on corrugated iron roofs. The smell of seaweed wafts along the Boulevard des Indiennes, the capital's main street. Speaking a soft patois of Gallicised English, the Eficans, wryly aware of their global insignificance, are ironic, self-doubting and self-mocking. In contrast, Voorstand – the vast land-mass that now holds Efica in a kind of surreptitious imperial grip – is rich, powerful, confident and, behind a grin of geniality, ruthless in manipulating other nations to serve its ideological and economic ends. Though expert at destabilising un-cooperative regimes, it is less adept at controlling unruliness nearer to home. Violence rips through its social fabric. Saarlim City, its famed metropolis bristling with skyscrapers, is a disaster area of pollution and lawlessness.

Notions as much as nations, Efica and Voorstand are, it quickly becomes apparent, rejigged versions of Australia and the United

States seen as paradigms of the colonised and colonising. The relationship between the two countries, which has intermittently engaged Carey ever since his first novel, *Bliss* (1981), here sparks off a dazzling feat of metamorphosis. In order to make his novel's contrasting countries as emblematic as possible, Carey superimposes several colonial and imperial patterns on them. Efica's progress from penal colony to welfare state sounds Australian, but its Gallicised culture (people nibble '*croix* cakes' and use endearments such as '*mochou*') suggests the French West Indies or the Seychelles. Similarly, Voorstand chiefly resembles America, but an America with origins as deep-rootedly Dutch as those of South Africa: '*bhurgers*' exchange greetings like '*gaaf-morning*', congregate in Demos Platz or read about proceedings in the Guildcourt.

Voorstand's present state exhibits how an ethic of Dutch-Calvinist earnestness has mutated into cut-throat capitalism. Efica exudes the bittersweet atmosphere of an exploited backwater. Voorstand's colony in all but name, it is used as a sump for the superpower's chemical waste. When a government less congenial to Voorstand looks likely to take control, covert electoral manipulation and political assassinations are triggered. Around this scenario are dotted instances of more paradoxical and ambivalent interactions between the two countries. Eficans eager to shake off Voorstand's ideological hold can still be enthralled by its cultural vitality. Voorstanders staying in Efica are seduced by an ambience less harsh and urgent than their own.

The novel's views on colonialism aren't out of the ordinary. What is extraordinary is the detail, scale and gusto with which they are given fabulous actuality. A gorgeous carnival of conjuring up, Carey's book makes two new nations materialise, brimming over with indigenous customs, folklore, scenery, cuisine, idioms, arts and entertainments. Vestiges of old bigotries are shown as still quaintly lingering in unexpected crannies of the contemporary world: a favourite dessert in once-Calvinist Voorstand is 'Pope's Head Pudding', a mound of dough from which strips of grated carrot protrude like hair. There are satiric coinages: cigarettes are 'cancerettes'. Believable bits of popular poeticising are dreamed up: a pint of beer is known as a 'bride' because of its foaming white 'train'.

Carey's most flamboyant fabrication is the Sirkus – an electronics-enhanced spectacular in which the Voorstand way of life is paraded before the world with alluring razzmatazz and thrilling high-tech wizardry. A surreal surrogate for the likes of Disneyland, Hollywood and McDonald's, the Sirkus reminds you how closely Carey's fiction can resemble that of the Victorian circus's great enthusiast, Charles Dickens. There is the same entrancement with grotesques and clowning, risk and dazzle, the same unquenchable-seeming verve. The alternative world Carey creates is laid out upon a ground-plan of opposites: Efica and Voorstand, shruggingly powerless wit and tunnel-vision dominance, small-time humaneness and superpower barbarity. Lifting his novel from the level of two-dimensional parable into a wonderfully filled-out achievement is the inventive detail and imaginative relish with which he populates it.

An even more out-of-this-world response to colonialism came from Doris Lessing, whose literary career began in 1950 with *The Grass Is Singing*, a novel about tensions between Black and white inhabitants of Southern Rhodesia where she grew up. Her five-book science fiction sequence, *Canopus in Argos*, projected concerns awakened there into outer space. Settling into clearest focus in the series' third novel, *The Sirian Experiments* (1980), Lessing's fictional cosmos contains three stellar empires: Canopus (benign, flexible, liberally progressive), Sirius (technological, utilitarian, emotionally arid) and Puttiora (predatory, sadistic, murderous). The most problematical planet to come within their spheres of influence is the Earth or 'Shikasta, the . . . damaged one'.

The Sirian Experiments sends Ambien II, initially a desiccated high-ranking Sirian bureaucrat, on an aeons-long astral aid mission to Shikasta. As this mission, undertaken with a Canopean counterpart, proceeds, a parable about colonisation unfolds. Puttiora, it becomes more and more obvious, represents colonising at its crudest – brutal exploitation. Sirius displays the dangers and double standards of an ostensibly more rational approach. Only Canopus – taking nothing, striving to create the right conditions for growth – genuinely succeeds. And even here there can be backslidings: as when a Canopean colonist, seedy as anything from Somerset Maugham or Graham Greene, cracks beneath the strain of exile ('I've been in this hellhole for . . . ages, ages') and 'goes native' under the seductive influence of a barbarous local beauty. The Shikastans too, as they evolve, start colonising one another: most damage, it's noted, being done by white races from 'the Northwest fringes'. The novel's closing irony is to reveal that Ambien, heading a colonial power, has been colonised as well. Throughout the millennia (like all Sirians, Ambien is virtually immortal, constantly reconditioned by ichor-transfusions and spare-part surgery), the Canopeans have subtly encroached on her thought-processes. Finally, their concepts fully occupy her mind (just as concepts from Sufi mysticism were then occupying Lessing's).

Rather smugly non-directive, Lessing's galactic gurus, the Canopeans, hover about until the less evolved start asking themselves the right questions. Eventually, Ambien gets round to this, though with some effect of anti-climax. Millennia might seem an excessive amount of time for the absorbing of such undemanding notions as the need to respect the ecological balance, to avoid unnecessary interference with other species, and to deplore power-mania, nuclear arms and private property. A curious exercise in Sufi sci-fi, *Canopus in Argos* awkwardly mixes the imaginative and the naïve. Sometimes powerfully inventive, Lessing can be bathetic and even melodramatic – as when frail, blonde Ambien pluckily braves the swarthy bullyboys of Shammat, the pirate planet. And though the exposures of negative behaviour are sharply defined, the novel's positives – for all their endorsement by the Canopean lords of the nebulae – are often nebulous.

Imperial America and Rome: Gore Vidal and Robert Harris

Back on Earth, a seven-novel sequence, Gore Vidal's *Narratives of Empire* (a title he insisted on despite his publisher's preference for the less tendentious *American Chronicles*), fabricated another fanciful imperial set-up. Beginning with *Washington, D.C.* (1967) and proceeding in non-chronological order through *Burr* (1973), *1876* (1976), *Lincoln* (1984), *Empire* (1987) and *Hollywood* (1989) to end with *The Golden Age* (2000), its increasingly adipose books charted what Vidal saw as the rise and fall of the American empire. Always keen on grandiose parallels (his 1948 novel about homosexual embroilment among boyhood buddies, *The City and the Pillar*, was silhouetted against the legend of Sodom and Gomorrah), Vidal lavishly bestowed ancient Roman analogies on his venture.

Vidal wasn't unusual in turning his imagination backwards in this way. Rome – seen as a paradigm of empire – has been a frequent subliminal or overt presence in modern fiction. In particular, the period when the Republic mutated into the Empire seized imaginations. Allan Massie's *Emperors* quartet fictionalised the lives of four of them in *Augustus* (1986), *Tiberius* (1991), *Caesar* (1993) and *Caligula* (2003). The career of Rome's first emperor was brought to life with absorbing accomplishment in John Williams's novel, *Augustus* (1979). Beginning with *Roman Blood* (1991) and concluding with *The Throne of Caesar* (2018), Steven Saylor's engaging and knowledgeable *Roma Sub Rosa* series merged episodes from classical Rome during the final decades of the Republic with motifs from classic detective fiction. *Last Seen in Massilia* (2000), set in a besieged city ringed by Caesar's troops, worked an ingenious variation on the locked-room murder mystery scenario.

Saylor's starting point for *Roman Blood* was an early case of Cicero's, his defence of Sextus Roscius against accusations of parricide. Cicero's slave and secretary, Tiro, who appears with his master in that novel, is the narrator of by far the most astute and compulsive fictional portrayal of Rome's succumbing to the lure of empire: Robert Harris's trilogy, *Imperium* (2006), *Lustrum* (2009) and *Dictator* (2015). A passion for politics has always pulsed through Harris's pages. Initially a shrewd and stylish journalistic commentator on life in and around Westminster, he went on to specialise in thrillers – *Fatherland* (1993), *Enigma* (1995), *Archangel* (1998) – that made nerve-tingling excursions into the world of totalitarian menace. Like his literary role model, George Orwell, he has an imagination put on creative red alert by tyranny and its terrors. Nazi Germany casts shadows over his first two novels, Stalinist Russia over the third. Written, he has said, 'to escape the traps of the modern political novel by going back 2,000 years', *Imperium* and its two successors combine insights Harris acquired through his immersion in politics with high-tension techniques sharpened in his thrillers. Chronicling Cicero's progress from unprepossessing young advocate from the provinces to Rome's most acclaimed and feared orator, they follow an extraordinary individual pursuing an often perilous course as the Roman Republic begins to buckle under autocratic pressures. Looking back in old age over his 36 years as Cicero's confidential secretary, Tiro records his master's rise to fame and power in a society over which the advent of empire sinisterly looms. Around Cicero, more ominous power figures, each brought alive in all their idiosyncratic energy, manoeuvre for political supremacy: Pompey, using his military resources and renown to push for dictatorship; Crassus, deploying his fabulous riches to undermine the Republic; Catalina, spurred on to abet a coup d'état by his aristocratic background and swaggering taste for thuggery; Julius Caesar stealthily positioning himself for the seizure of power; Octavian finally moving in to scoop up the imperial prize. Resurrecting a society two millennia away, Harris contrives to make it appear at once distant and relevant. Electoral predictions in Rome may be based on auguries and entrails rather than focus groups and opinion polls but, beneath surface differences, the prototypes of our own politics are visible. Tiro seems a precursor of the legal

reporter and the lobby correspondent. As he watches political necessity and moral idealism clash, and even Cicero become tainted by
compromise and concession, the trilogy masterfully dramatises issues
pertinent not only to a vanished world but to our own.

Where Harris alertly notes, but doesn't force, parallels, Gore Vidal
cumbersomely imposes them. His thesis – advanced with monumental simplicity in novel after novel – is that there are striking
affinities between America and ancient Rome: both began as repub-
lics, then abandoned their pristine ideals for the corruptions of
empire; like Rome, Washington has a Capitol and a Senate; like
Julius Caesar, some American presidents were assassinated; slavery is
another shared feature.

The role Vidal flatteringly sees himself playing in this milieu is
that of a latter-day Suetonius, a suave patrician observer of the enormities and pettinesses of imperial power figures. Descended from
America's oligarchy of political families and having made some forays
into politics, he assumes the stance of an urbane, imperturbable
contemplator – simultaneously cynic, epicurean and stoic – of the
violences and vulgarities of an arena from which he has disdainfully
withdrawn. Silkily above it all, he remains very much in the know –
as he is keen to let you know – about the chicanery and treacheries
of hardened statesmen. Like the author of *The Lives of the Caesars*, he
particularly aims to record the treacheries and rapacities, opulence
and guilt of empire. A major impediment to this enterprise is that,
although near-obsessed by the notion of an American empire, Vidal
is strangely hazy about its particulars. Wildly inconsistent dates as to
when he deems it began jostle in his pages. He is also muddled as to
when it ended or, indeed, if it ever has. 'On 16 September, 1985 . . .
the American empire died', one of his essays collected in *Armageddon?*
(1987) resoundingly declares. But a flash forward to 2000 in *The
Golden Age* sees 'our global empire' still thriving ('Let TV be our
Colosseum and the third-worlders our gladiators'). As that quote
suggests, Vidal (who divided his time when penning these novels

between his villa overlooking the Sorrentine coast's litter of classic ruins and his Roman apartment in a 2,000-year-old street) has a marked taste for archaic analogies. His imagery drapes Roman trappings over everything. A man with a barber's bib tucked around his neck is likened to a toga-ed senator. 'Shall I pack my toga?' asks someone else. Another character gasps of Roosevelt, 'Teddy's got it all now! Do you realize that he occupies a place greater than Trajan's at the high noon of the Roman empire?' Photographs of film stars are 'reverently arranged like Roman household deities'. Minds turn to Roman resemblances on unexpected occasions: 'His hand strayed towards her groin. The hand froze where it was; she thought of the petrified citizenry of Pompeii.'

By the time Vidal's sequence reached its conclusion, his penchant for classical lookalike imagery had become little more than a reflex – and sometimes a confusing one. One analogy with ancient Rome that he particularly favoured was the crossing of the Rubicon. *Empire* presented America as doing this and taking an irrevocable step into imperialism by entering into the 1898 Spanish-American War; *Hollywood* presented it as doing so by entering into the First World War; in *The Golden Age* it's by entering the Second World War. The sameness of these scenarios typified the near-carbon-copy mode of producing novels for which Vidal increasingly settled. This manifested itself even in minor ways, such as the routine turning up of famous authors in cameo roles. Washington Irving pinched the hero's thigh in *Burr*, Walt Whitman applied for a job in *Lincoln*, Mark Twain drawled wisecracks in *1876*, Henry James pontificated in *Empire*, *The Golden Age* saw Tennessee Williams at a first night. Compromising letters, blackmail and triangular sexual intrigues recur. Characters are repeatedly seen circling round the centre of political power in Washington, portrayed as a glamorous hotbed of Roman orgy-like decadence and ruthlessness. Stalely recycling their fictional techniques and effects, Vidal's *Narratives of Empire* never find anything fresh to offer about imperialism.

South-East Asia: Kazuo Ishiguro, J.G. Ballard and David Mitchell

Whether other authors would be able to is a question that presents itself after more than half a century of comprehensive fictional treatment of the subject. Despite widely varied geographical settings, there can be an identikit look to many novels, sedulously fitted out with indigenous mythology, sprinklings of magic realism and historical harkings back, turned out on what can seem a postcolonial conveyor belt.

Nevertheless, the genre of empire continues to prove capable of generating masterpieces – as was demonstrated by *The Thousand Autumns of Jacob de Zoet* (2010), David Mitchell's novel about imperial encounter between Japanese and Europeans around the start of the nineteenth century. Twentieth-century Japanese imperial aggression had earlier been surveyed in two exceptional novels: Kazuo Ishiguro's *An Artist of the Floating World* (1986) and J.G. Ballard's *Empire of the Sun* (1984). Like the *ukiyo-e* Japanese prints central to its story, Ishiguro's novel is a work of spare elegance: refined, understated, economic. Through his melancholy first-person retrospect, it's revealed that, as 1930s Japan became increasingly militant, Masuji Ono, an artist specialising in the portrayal of kimono-ed courtesans titivating themselves by lantern-light, turned his talents to producing prints designed to stir the nation's 'new manly spirit' by graphic reminders of its warrior past. Geishas prettifying their coiffures gave way to scowling samurai; fans and combs were pushed aside by staves and military banners. Now, amid the post-war wreckage wrought by the belligerent expansionism Ono helped to foment, he contemplates his art's disastrous collaboration with the forces that ruined his country.

One result of Japan's military expansionism is on view in *Empire of the Sun*, set in and around Shanghai in the turbulent years between Pearl Harbor and Hiroshima, and drawing closely on Ballard's own experiences during that period. At first seeming to represent a change of direction in his writing, the novel – with its panoramas of dereliction and its focus on extremity and the dehumanised – increasingly indicates why he had previously found apocalyptic science fiction a compelling a genre.

While remaining naturalistic, *Empire of the Sun* chronicles the outlandish. Before the Japanese invasion, Shanghai is a grotesque conglomeration of squalor and swagger: garden parties and public stranglings, pampered expatriates and starving natives. Chauffeured in Buicks and Cadillacs, European colonials glide through mobs of shiny-suited Chinese gangsters, pimps, touts and peasants, beggars rattling Craven A tins, and misshapen rickshaw coolies with 'veins as thick as fingers clenched into the meat of their swollen calves'. Street scenes sizzle with pungency as pavement vendors fry gobbets of snake in peanut oil. Eurasian prostitutes in ankle-length fur coats whistle through their teeth at men emerging from the hotels. The lopsided extravaganza of the place is epitomised in the mustering of 200 hunchbacks from its slums to stand in medieval costume around the Cathay Theatre – the world's largest cinema – as a publicity stunt for the premiere of *The Hunchback of Notre Dame*.

Ballard's sharpest attention falls on the city's International Settlement where, in the days leading up to Pearl Harbor, colonial life fecklessly and recklessly has its final fling. Amid the limousines and leisure of this still-neutral zone, the struggle in Europe largely features as just another facet of recreation: the war effort is fuelled by bottles of whisky cheerily raffled at dances. Even when catastrophe strikes and the Japanese take over, this playtime mentality persists – apparent in the luggage the prisoners tote into captivity: 'Having spent the years of peace on the tennis courts and cricket fields of the Far East, they confidently expected to pass the years of war in the same way. Dozens of tennis racquets hung from the suitcase handles; there were cricket bats and fishing rods, and even a set of golf clubs.'

These expectations are rapidly bowled over in the camps – as are readers' traditional assumptions. Ballard's account of incarceration brims with the unexpected. As anarchy rages in Shanghai, the Europeans find the Japanese their protectors as well as their oppressors, a military shield between them and the desperate, destitute Chinese. Heightening the book's unfamiliar angle on things is the fact that its narrative viewpoint is that of a young boy – only eleven years old when the action begins. Separated from his parents as the Japanese attack, Jim finds he needs to fend for himself over four arduous years. Initially – in thrall to 'the stern morality of the *Chums Annuals*' – he defies the invaders and leads an outlaw-like existence in the deserted residences of the International Settlement, subsisting on olives and cocktail biscuits as water ebbs from once-gleaming swimming pools and perfectly clipped lawns revert to wilderness. Then, as Shanghai becomes ever more dangerous, he learns that survival necessitates surrender. By considerable effort, he escapes into a camp.

With unsettling steadiness, Ballard recounts the routines here. Enormities are dispassionately retailed: the violence, the diseases and the malnutrition. Tormented by flies and mosquitoes, sick and famished prisoners fumble through their feed for the bonus of a few weevils to provide protein. Developing uncommon sense, Jim discovers 'how important it was to be obsessed by food', that 'it was probably sensible to do anything to survive'. Helping others when possible, he still takes it for granted that, like him, they will always, in extremity, put themselves first. Not that quite all of them do. Though devoid of military heroics, the book does record some civilian heroism: a hard-pressed doctor resourcefully helps Jim stay alive, as does an altruistic Dutch woman. In keeping with the book's emphasis on the self-absorption and the matter-of-fact acceptance of appalling circumstances generated by conditions in the camp, Jim's attention touches only fleetingly on subsequent disasters befalling his benefactors. The doctor, it's revealed in passing, has been blinded in one eye. Mrs Hug, the Dutch woman, is treated with even more jolting casualness: dropping out of sight as Jim has to cope with the rigours of camp life, she re-enters the narrative with stark brevity as a wrist-bone poking out of a makeshift grave.

Like a more luridly lit and eerily affectless version of the colonial debacle J.G. Farrell chronicled in *The Singapore Grip*, the novel is filled with gruesomely emblematic tableaux: skeletal European prisoners expiring in an Olympic stadium whose tiers are heaped with *de luxe* detritus – refrigerators, cocktail cabinets, roulette wheels – looted from their homes; Shanghai's river, the Yangtze, awash with a 'regatta of corpses' as dozens of paper-garlanded coffins, launched by those too poor to buy a burial, swing backwards and forwards on its tides.

In their differing modes, Ishiguro and Ballard identify Japan's ferociously re-awakened martial spirit as the result of a humiliated sense of long subordination to foreign influence. David Mitchell's *The Thousand Autumns of Jacob de Zoet* (2010) travels back more than 200 years to a place where resistance to such influence held sway. Its story starts in 1799 when Jacob de Zoet, a pastor's son from Amsterdam, disembarks at Dejima, a high-walled small artificial island offshore from Nagasaki that the Japanese have made available as a trading post for the Dutch East Indies Company. Beyond its land gate, a bridge stretches towards the Shogun's 'Closed Empire', barricaded against the outer world. Its sea gate, where cargo boats unload sacks of sugar and take aboard Japan's most prized commodity, copper, is the furthest outpost of the Dutch maritime empire.

From this pent-up huddle of warehouses and cramped quarters – a temporary meeting ground for foreigners forbidden to leave the island and Japanese forbidden to leave their native land – Mitchell unfurls a narrative of panoramic span. Populated with Dutch traders, Malay and Ceylonese servants, a Yankee sea captain and a motley flotsam of assorted drifters, the novel's first section is redolent of Joseph Conrad's tales of waterfront life in the Far East. As with Conrad, adventure-yarn excitements – an earthquake, a typhoon, tense confrontations – coexist with an exploration of psychological and moral intricacies and ironic observation of cultural clashes.

Swathed in silky etiquettes, the Japanese wince at the blatancy with which Europeans push for profit. On Dejima, the foreigners fume at cunning Asiatic obliquity.

Within a community bristling with suspicion and shady goings-on, Jacob struggles to keep his bearings. Awkwardly honest, he makes enemies by the outspoken conscientiousness with which, as a junior clerk, he exposes fraud and embezzlement. Initially hoping to work in Dejima for just a year in order to make sufficient money to marry his fiancée in Amsterdam, he finds himself penalised for his integrity and condemned to remain far longer on the fringes of a nation that proudly terms itself the Land of a Thousand Autumns. A further complication is his growing attraction to Orito Abigawa, a young midwife with a burn-scarred face. Having saved the life of a high-ranking official's concubine and baby with her skills, Orito has been granted the rare privilege of regular visits to Dejima for tuition from the company's doctor. Her story becomes central in the novel's second part.

As his other books have exhibited, Mitchell is restless with genre. His first novel, *Ghostwritten* (1999), had nine narrators. *Number9dream* (2001) kept mutating into different kinds of story; *Cloud Atlas* (2004) interlinked six very different narratives, from nineteenth-century historical pastiche to science fiction; *The Bone Clocks* (2014), swirling around notions of mortality and survival, had five narrators. Switching style, mood and tone, while continuing to deal with the same themes is a hallmark of Mitchell's fiction. Although *The Thousand Autumns of Jacob de Zoet* begins as an engrossingly detailed, almost naturalistic novel, when Orito is abducted and removed to a Shinto shrine in the mountainous domain of a sinister abbot, things take on a Gothic shimmer. A smaller-scale prison within the prison nation of Japan, the convent is the subject of scared rumours. Runaways mysteriously expire. Its twelve inmates are always women with physical blemishes. Strange euphemisms – 'Engifters', 'the Solace' – thicken the menacing atmosphere. At an inn near the foot of the mountain there is an ominous graveyard. Orito's experiences in this eerie nunnery, counterpointed by a rescue bid by a Japanese interpreter who has wished to be her husband, are recounted with shuddery finesse. A similar shiveriness ripples through Mitchell's scenes of refined ferocity in eighteenth-century Nagasaki. Public beheadings take place amid ornate ceremonial. Lethal niceties, such as poisoning by venom extracted 'from the glands of a tree-snake found only in a Siamese Delta', are favoured. Curving back to Dejima, the book's final section returns to less *recherché* modes of violence. With the arrival of the British frigate ready to open fire on both the Dutch and Japanese, a third empire belligerently intrudes.

Exploitation and oppression, predation and enslavement – always to the fore in Mitchell's fiction – are nowhere more powerfully presented by him than in this novel of clashing empires. Dejima, Jacob learns to his cost, is a welter of peculation, fraud and scrabbling for advantage. Around the cooped-up island alongside a locked-in nation, imperial antagonisms thunder. What's also telling about the book, though, is another theme that sounds through it. Inspiration for the novel, Mitchell has recalled, came in 1994 when, during his first New Year's holiday in Japan, where he had taken up a teaching post in Hiroshima, he visited Nagasaki and got off a streetcar at the wrong stop. Intrigued by an assemblage of old-looking buildings there, he found that he had stumbled upon the remains of the tiny trading island, Dejima, now reduced to a dingy patch of Nagasaki after the harbour silted up. A day in its museum gave him half a notebook of material about this 'cat flap between Europe and Japan for two hundred and forty years' and was the starting point for a historical novel suffused with subjective involvement.

Historical fiction, Mitchell has said, 'delivers a stereo narrative: from one speaker comes the treble of the novel's own plot while the other speaker plays the bass of history's plot'. Prodigiously researched, his novel powerfully transmits the dramas of imperial interaction and the ironies of history (greedily jockeying for profit on their remote island, the Dutch traders are unaware of having been left redundant by the bankruptcy of the East India Company far away in Amsterdam). Simultaneously, a much more personal note is transmitted. Japan's 'outermost defence', Jacob comes to believe, is 'obscurity'. Unimpeded communication between nations is what he and all the book's most admirable figures strive for. Fictionalising his own early struggles with a severe stammer, Mitchell's autobiographical novel, *Black Swan Green* (2006), was eloquent about impediments to communication and the importance of speaking out. 'What feels like a curse when you're younger', he has said, 'can prove a long-term ally.' The hyper-alertness to difficulties and triumphs of communication that his stammer gave him proved a particularly fruitful ally in his novel about Dejima. Jacob and a Japanese contemporary struggle to acquire each other's language. Interpreters throng the narrative. Dictionaries are much prized. In a tense climactic scene, a scroll bearing a crucial message gets translated in the nick of time. Always adept at capturing the tones and idiolects of differing fictional voices, Mitchell fills his pages with a medley of accents, idioms and speech habits. What is and isn't said is of utmost significance. Translators are flummoxed by 'terms without a ready Japanese equivalent, such as "privacy", "splenetic" or the verb "to deserve"'. Coded jeerings and muted declarations play their part. Lying (the story is riddled with verbal betrayals and traps) is pervasive. Speech can be treacherous or telling in more ways than one.

Mitchell was far from alone, of course, in infusing a novel about imperialism with individual concerns. Scott's sense of disorientation, Farrell's awareness of debility, Naipaul's rootlessness, Mo's appetite for combat, Vidal's vanity and numerous other personal predispositions have tinged, energised and shaped books about empire written during the immense modern fictional engrossment with it. Reflecting in an interview on his fiction's high proportion of orphans, Peter Carey related it to his having been sent away from home to boarding school at the age of eleven. *His Illegal Self* (2008), the novel about drastic relocation which he was writing when he gave that interview, was, he said, a story about an orphan that is 'also the story of Australia, which is a country of orphans': 'Our first fleet was cast out from "home". Nobody really wanted to be there ... Later, the state created orphans among the aboriginal population through racial policies, stealing indigenous kids from their communities and trying to breed out their Blackness. Then there were all these kids sent from England to Dr Barnardo's Homes, which were institutions for homeless and destitute children, some of them run in the most abusive, horrible circumstances.' 'I have the good fortune', he declared, 'that my own personal trauma matches my country's great historical trauma.' It's to fiction about personal trauma – a subject that has received ever-increasing attention in modern novels – that we should now move.

Part II

Scars and Silences: The Personal Past and Its Aftermath

Individual Trauma

It wasn't only crumbling empires whose repercussions resonated through modern fiction. More localised forms of upheaval and damage reverberated too. A spreading and deepening interest in varieties of mental illness – the standard US *Diagnostic and Statistical Manual of Mental Disorders*, 100 pages long in 1952 reached 500 by 1980 – was increasingly reflected in fiction. Psychological and emotional injury and their after-effects were widely and keenly scrutinised; plot lines traced psychic disturbance back to its source. Post-traumatic stress disorder was viewed from many fictional angles. New perspectives on to it opened as novels focused on the aftermaths of the First and Second World Wars, especially their toll of mental and emotional casualties. As awareness of the prevalence of child abuse grew, novels filled with depictions of its persisting harm. Early abuse – not always sexual, sometimes emotional or physical bullying – received widespread fictional attention. Novels exploring it, such as Sally Rooney's *Normal People* (2018) or Elizabeth Strout's 'Lucy Barton' series were much acclaimed. Therapeutic bringings to light of things warpingly suppressed became a prominent fictional aim. In the half century after the passing of the 1967 Sexual Offences Act, advances in LGBT liberation freed marginalised minorities previously stigmatised into muteness to break their silence and tell their stories. Psychotherapists joined archaeologists and historians as significant presences in modern fiction. The novelist particularly influential here was Pat Barker.

Pat Barker

When living with her grandparents as a child in North Yorkshire, Pat Barker was struck by two things. The first was a 'hideous wound' in her grandfather's side that she would see when, stripped to the waist, he washed at the kitchen sink before going out to the British Legion for his weekly pint of beer. The second was the fact that he 'never talked about it at all'. The injury, she later learned, was from a bayonet attack, on the Western Front, which could have proved fatal ('the bayonet was stuck in but it wasn't twisted, because his officer shot the man who was about to twist it. If you twist and withdraw, it's a difficult wound to survive'). Such information – including the statistic that only 3 per cent of total wounds were caused by bayonets as close combat of that kind was relatively rare – was acquired in the course of her becoming an outstanding fictional chronicler of the First World War. Before that career unfolded, she has recalled, 'there was the wound and there was silence'.

Wounds and silence – two themes that have ramified through modern fiction – featured centrally in *Regeneration* (1991), the breakthrough novel with which Barker, previously an observer of present-day female working-class communities in books such as *Union Street* (1982) and *Blow Your House Down* (1984), sent her imagination back in time, up the social scale and across the gender divide. Ever-present in its background is the long abattoir of the Western Front. In the foreground are some of its more insidiously maimed casualties, men with crippling phobias and psychosomatic paralyses: a captain unable to eat after a shell blast has filled his mouth with decomposing flesh, a lieutenant left voiceless by unspeakable things he has witnessed, an army surgeon – once operating at a rate of ten amputations a day – now so terrified by blood that a shaving cut precipitates teeth-chattering collapse. Housing all this trauma is Craiglockhart, an Edinburgh hospital where officers invalided from the front receive treatment for 'war neurosis'. By day, pallid stammerers blink and shuffle down its corridors. Nights are loud with screams, vomiting and choking fits, as scarcely buried horrors resurface in dreams. The slightest stimulus can tip men nightmarishly back into the trenches. Lime blossoms waft suffocating memories of gas attacks. Branches rapping on a window-pane trigger panic about machine-gun fire and bring the distant battlefield smotheringly close.

Subsidiary struggles fought out in the shadow of the First World War are shown. At the core of the novel is a real-life encounter that took place at Craiglockhart in 1917 between W.H.R. Rivers, an army psychologist, and the poet Siegfried Sassoon, dispatched to the hospital by military authorities eager to contain his anti-war protests within a context of mental derangement. As the two meet for psycho-therapy sessions, an unanticipated kind of transference occurs. In response to Sassoon's arguments, Rivers turns against the war himself.

The novel sits in on therapy sessions with others as well. Most resemble verbal skirmishes, given edge by the patients' hostile parry-ings of Rivers' probings. What causes this entrenched resistance, he believes, is an inner conflict within these battle victims between the attempt to blank out their war experience and the need to remember it. Exacerbating the turmoil this generates is the fact that the men's disorders aren't only symptoms of war trauma but the result of social taboos. The belief that 'manliness' entails emotional repression mili-tates against open admission of the harrowing responses that life – and death – in the trenches arouse.

Some of Barker's earlier concerns – vulnerability, injury, strife – reappear in the new areas into which this novel takes her. An affair between a Craiglockhart patient and a munitions girl displays the antagonism Barker always finds entangled with sexual relations. As an officer from humble circumstances encounters sneers for wearing a non-pukka shade of khaki shirt and never having ridden to hounds, class hostilities are shown to be still virulent even in a nation at war. Hostilities crackle between reactionary and progressive assumptions in the medical sphere too, when Rivers witnesses a bullying colleague trying to galvanise men out of their mutism by applying violent electric shocks to their throats.

One of *Regeneration*'s war casualties, a young officer, Billy Prior, has been traumatised into dumbness by a particularly vile experience in the trenches: a shell attack that left him holding a man's eyeball in the palm of his trembling hand. Depicting the psychosomatic choking that ensued, *Regeneration* is preoccupied with nerves and speech, neurotic disturbance and the ways in which communication can relieve or be blocked by it. *The Eye in the Door* – a sequel as keenly intelligent as its predecessor – turns its attention to nerves and sight. Hideous reflections of the glistening eyeball that traumatised Prior glint in a narrative about dreads induced by surveillance and censorship. Social suppression as well as individual repression is shown imposing painful silence.

The year is 1918. The setting has shifted from Scotland to an England suffering drastic shortages. Black-edged cards darken house windows. General Haig has just issued his grim 13 April order of the day: 'there is no other course open to us but to fight it out. Every position must be held to the last man.' In the climate of exhaustion and hysteria amid which the war is wearing to its close, pressures to fall into line become fierce and take ugly forms. At the forefront of her story, Barker places figures especially menaced by this: pacifists, conscientious objectors, homosexuals.

Prior's bisexuality and ambivalent social background involve him with these groups. Early in the novel, he picks up a fellow officer, Charles Manning, in Hyde Park. As with most episodes in the book, dividedness soon becomes apparent. Physical excitement tangles with class antagonism as the two have sex: Manning is an upper-class chum of Churchill and Eddie Marsh; working-class Prior has been promoted by his military rank into a 'temporary gentleman' for the duration of the war. Like Prior, Manning is in a state of nervous instability from ordeals on the Western Front, haunted by having had to watch one of his men sink to a horrible death in the mud. But his stammer and spasms of uncontrollable twitching aren't only caused by this. He is being harried by anonymous letters threatening to expose him as a homosexual. One of these missives encloses a copy of an article (actually published in a magazine of 1917) alleging the existence of a Black Book containing the names of 47,000 British subjects, some extremely highly placed, who have been homosexually debauched by German agents in order to facilitate the Kaiser's victory. Agog with reference to 'Paphian photographs' and 'lascivi-ousness as only German minds could conceive and only German bodies execute', this phobic fantasia provides some splendidly berserk quotes: 'Wives of men in supreme position were entangled. In Lesbian ecstasy the most sacred secrets of State were revealed. The sexual peculiarities of members of the peerage were used as a leverage to open fruitful fields for espionage.' But the novel is alive to the ways in which the nation's embattled circumstances make such stuff frightening as well as fatuous. The trial of an actress who has played Wilde's Salome in a private performance is under way because of the witch-hunt whipped up by the Black Book's claims. In court, the finger of accusation jabs out at other supposed deviants. As pressure mounts, Manning – tormented by fears of being watched – suffers paralysing panic attacks.

Meanwhile, Prior's work for the intelligence unit brings him into contact with scapegoats of another kind. Investigating the case of a northern shopkeeper, Beattie Roper, grotesquely convicted of plot-ting to kill Lloyd George with a curare-tipped dart, he enters the harshly persecuted world of pacifists and 'conchies'. Two factors make this particularly nerve-wrenching. One is that the regulation peephole in Roper's cell door has an eye vividly painted around it – which jolts Prior's mind back to his hideous experience in the trenches at the same time as he is tormented by the doubleness of his role – both spy and friend – towards her. In reaction, he lapses into a Jekyll and Hyde state, his normal consciousness punctuated by amnesiac interludes. What occurs during these blanked-out phases – about which Prior harbours increasingly appalled suspicions – is eventually conjured into the open by the hero of this novel, as of *Regeneration*: Rivers, whose dual interests as neurologist and anthropologist, match Barker's twin fascination with individual psychodramas and communal patterns of behaviour, and the ways in which both can scar and silence.

After the concluding volume of her *Regeneration* trilogy, *The Ghost Road* (1995), which followed these issues up to the war's final days, Barker sought to withdraw her fiction from the Western Front. *Another World* (1998), set in contemporary Newcastle, explored how past domestic violence could seep into late twentieth-century life. But, significantly, the character who most vitalised the book was Geordie, an elderly grandfather and survivor of the First World War.

Fictional sorties into other combat zones – *Double Vision* (2003) focused on a reporter burnt out by experiences in Sarajevo and Afghanistan; a 2007 short story, 'Subsidence', traced aftershocks of the war in Iraq – similarly showed that Barker wasn't finding it easy to demob her creativity. If imaginations had colours, hers, you feel, would be khaki. With *Life Class* (2007) she initiated what would become – along with *Toby's Room* (2012) and *Noonday* (2015) – a second trilogy about the traumas of 1914–18. Where *Regeneration* centred on Rivers, whose psychotherapy sessions aimed to rebuild shattered psyches, *Life Class* centres on Henry Tonks, the art professor at the Slade whose involvement in pioneering plastic surgery helped to rebuild shattered faces. Instead of shell-shocked men stunned into muteness or psychosomatic stuttering, mutilated soldiers with missing eyes and destroyed jaws are brought into view. In keeping with its concentration on verbal communication, the *Regeneration* trilogy was prominently peopled with writers: Siegfried Sassoon, Wilfred Owen, Robert Graves. Surveying visual responses to war damage, *Life Class*, *Toby's Room* and *Noonday* take as their main figures young painters who are fictional composites of the talented pre-war generation of students at the Slade: Paul Nash, Christopher Nevinson, Mark Gertler, Dora Carrington, Stanley Spencer.

After *Noonday*, which follows the repercussions of the First World War up to the Blitz in 1940, Barker's next novel travelled vastly further back in time. Moving beyond history into legend, it re-worked (as did a number of early twenty-first-century novels) a scenario from Greek myth. With *The Silence of the Girls* (2018), a novelist who had established herself with a book populated by men stunned into dumbness by horrors witnessed on the Somme looked back to European literature's archetypal armed conflict: the Trojan War. Again (true to her affirmation, 'all my interest in war comes from what is not said'), her aim was to remedy voicelessness. 'What I took away from my first reading,' she recalled of the *Iliad*, 'was silence, because the girls whose fates are being decided say not a word. I knew I was going to have to write about it one day: about the experience of those silenced girls.' Accordingly, in her novel and its successor, *The Women of Troy* (2021), Briseis, queen of a city on the Trojan plain, who is handed over to Achilles after he has reduced it to corpse-strewn rubble, recounts her story and that of other women dragged off by the victorious Greeks to 'a rape camp'.

It isn't the first time a female perspective has been trained on Homer's epic portrayals of male valour. Jauntily rejigging material from the *Odyssey*, Margaret Atwood's *The Penelopiad* (2005) gave a new slant to events on Ithaca where the emblematically faithful Penelope awaited her husband's belated return. As might be expected from a writer long immersed in the traumas of war, Barker's reworking

103

of episodes from the *Iliad* is more sombre, raw and painful. From opening moments tense with urgency (Achilles' battle-cry ringing round the walls of the doomed city, women and children futilely fleeing to its citadel), menace and fear predominate. Terror rarely slackens its hold. As the Siege of Troy nears its close, Briseis and other female captives become mere spoils of war. Starkly depicting the degradations they are subjected to, Barker also displays their survival strategies. Supportive female resilience is shown to have a gritty vigour reminiscent of the embattled communities of northern working-class women in her first two novels, *Union Street* and *Blow Your House Down*. The book's legendary battlefield similarly recalls territory that Barker had previously made her own. Bogged down among sandbags and duck boards in a muddy wasteland gouged by trenches and occasionally visited by blustering generals, her Greek and Trojan warriors inhabit an Aegean Somme where, viewed through Briseis' disenchanted eyes, deeds familiar from the *Iliad* take on unheroic resonances. Within a mythic combat zone, Barker works further variations on her persisting themes of wounds and silence.

First World War Trauma: Robert Edric and J.L. Carr

Barker wasn't alone, of course, in writing fiction about the after-effects of the First World War: the scars and the silences it inflicted. The title of Robert Graves's 1929 memoir of the Western Front, *Goodbye to All That*, could hardly have proved less prophetic. Literary harkings back to the trauma of the trenches have never ceased. As D.H. Lawrence predicted in *Lady Chatterley's Lover* (1928), it would take many years for 'the bruise of the war' to fade. Fiction of the 1920s and 1930s is packed with casualties of the Great War: physically and psychologically damaged ex-soldiers, jobless demobbed servicemen reduced to begging, selling matches or trundling barrel organs through the streets for pennies, hosts of widowed and unmarried women denied the likelihood of a partner. Resurrections of the conflict itself often surface in modern fiction. Sometimes, as with William Boyd's *An Ice-Cream War* (1982), a novel in J.G. Farrell's mordantly satiric vein about strife between British and German colonists in East Africa, this was part of the persisting consciousness of empire – the First World War seen as a catastrophic consequence of imperial belligerence. But, with striking frequency, it was the ravages the war left behind – physical, psychological and emotional scars – that drew novelists' attention, as in Sebastian Faulks's acclaimed trilogy tracking its repercussions across several decades, *The Girl at the Lion d'Or* (1989), *Birdsong* (1997) and *Charlotte Gray* (1998). In Graham Swift's beautifully atmospheric *Mothering Sunday* (2016), set among the war-bereaved gentry of rural Berkshire, the 'great gust of devastation' unleashed by the First World War is still achingly apparent on an idyllic day in March 1924, casting shadows over a 'sun-bathed, lamb-dotted England' where 'church bells throbbed beneath the birdsong' and hawthorn blossom froths from hedgerows.

Particularly intense scrutiny of post-war trauma came from Robert Edric, an author who has specialised in surveying man-made hells. In his novel about religious cruelty in seventeenth-century East Anglia, *The Earth Made of Glass* (1994), a woman wonders 'how it would be if in some places under the bracken and grass and soil the earth was to be made of glass so that we might see straight through it and into Hell below'. But, in Edric's fictional world, there's no need to go to such lengths to observe the infernal. Devilish behaviour is only too visible on the planet's surface. His historical novels constitute a tour, conducted by an always alert and informed guide, of hell-spots scattered around the globe and across the centuries.

Recreating John Franklin's misbegotten 1845 expedition in search of the Northwest Passage, *The Broken Lands* (1992) opened with talk of the strangeness of thinking of 'Hell as a burning, fiery place' when enduring the glacial rigours of the Arctic. *The Earth Made of Glass* (prefaced by an epigraph from Swedenborg's *Heaven and Hell*) had an ecclesiastical investigator uncovering atrocities in a remote fenland parish in 1691. *Elysium* journeyed to the sun-baked dustlands of mid-nineteenth-century Tasmania, where racist inhumanity cruelly colluded with belief in Aboriginal sub-humanity. *The Book of the Heathen* (2001) plunged into another colonial hell-hole: the Belgian Congo of 1897. Expert at presenting the barbarities of the imperial heyday, Edric also closed in on the consequences of the carnage of the First and Second World Wars.

Hospitals and asylums harbouring war-trauma victims provide settings for a number of his novels. *In Zodiac Light* (2008), a work with many parallels to Barker's *Regeneration*, takes place in the City of London Mental Hospital in 1923. As in Barker's 1916 Craiglockhart, upheaval is caused by the arrival of a war-traumatised writer – here, the Gloucestershire poet (and composer) Ivor Gurney. Again, reactionary and progressive attitudes to combat-induced psychosis clash in a milieu of neurasthenia and mutism. Dr Irvine, who narrates the novel and holds patiently probing conversations with Gurney, has a humane intelligence similar to that of Barker's Rivers.

In Zodiac Light (in which the delicate salvage and repair of damaged beehives in the hospital's grounds provide a metaphor for Irvine's restorative psychoanalytical therapy) wasn't Edric's first fictional engagement with the scars and silences ensuing from war. *Hallowed Ground* (1993) opened not long after VE Day in the hospital of a small southern German town chaotically thronged with refugees and Allied soldiers. *In Desolate Heaven* (1997) – for which *Hallowed Ground* was 'an early dry run', Edric has said – went back to 1919 to explore the First World War's aftermath of trauma and mutilation.

Its setting is a Swiss spa where Elizabeth Mortlake, a young woman from Oxford, is holidaying with her widowed sister-in-law, Mary. Here, they hope to begin to recuperate from their shared loss of a brother and a husband in the war. But it soon becomes apparent that they could hardly have selected a location less favourable to forgetfulness and consolation. Along the lakeside, nurses escort shuffling lines of the walking wounded and men blinded in the war. The blare of a crassly impatient motorist's horn throws shell-shocked survivors into panic-stricken terror. A convent hospital houses ex-soldiers so hideously disfigured that all reflective surfaces have had to be removed and even windowpanes painted over. In the local quarry, plans are afoot to start hewing rock for the headstones the new military cemeteries require by the million.

Shutting herself in her room, Mary dangerously sinks into anorexic depression. In contrast to this private pining, Elizabeth experiences the wider ravages of the war. Through her friendship with Jameson, a crippled former officer now running a dubious photography business in the town, she becomes a visitor to the hospital. Psychologically as well as physically damaged, Jameson also scathingly alerts her to the callous hypocrisies and stupidities attendant on the war. Through him, she becomes aware that, in some quarters, rehabilitation is progressing indecently quickly. The visit of a once-warmongering Habsburg nobleman is greeted with public applause and the town band. A munitions manufacturer complacently guzzles in a well-appointed dining room. Hoteliers and restaurateurs are petitioning the local council to shift war invalids and convalescents elsewhere since they deter tourism.

Alongside these unlovely peacetime grovellings and greeds, the recently defunct war continues to exact casualties. A friend of Jameson's awaits court martial for his role in hindering an obscenely callous military scheme. A disturbed young man goes mad and defaces himself with ghastly literalness. The emotional climate of the novel is as freezing as the late-autumn Switzerland Edric atmospherically evokes. Eerily distanced formal prose – largely devoid of metaphor and entirely devoid of sentiment – communicates an appropriately numbed-seeming lack of warmth. With piercing lucidity, military and civilian, male and female victims of war are viewed against a background normally associated with peaceful neutrality and healthy invigoration.

War-trauma victims were portrayed in a wide variety of settings and from both sides of the conflict by other authors. *Metropolis* (2019), the final book in Philip Kerr's thriller series about the Third Reich, went back to the early days of his tough police detective Bernie Gunther in the garish, bankrupt Berlin of the Weimar Republic. In a city pullulating with emaciated whores and beggars in tattered military uniforms, Gunther's visit to an institute for mutilated ex-soldiers triggers a 'recrudescence of horror' and brings on nightmares bespattered with 'grotesquely vivid images of myself back in the trenches ... my best friend's brains in my hair after a stray bullet from a Lewis gun shattered his skull; a man screaming his last breath into my face, followed by most of his blood and guts; a field surgeon amputating wounded limbs with a guillotine, to save the time a surgical saw would have demanded'.

At the opposite extreme to Kerr's hellish German cityscape, two war-survivors in the tranquil summer depths of the 1920 English countryside are racked by similar traumatic flashbacks in J.L. Carr's *A Month in the Country* (1980). One of the men is uncovering an ancient Doom painting in a church; the other, excavating a tomb outside it. Silhouetted against the medieval Hell meticulously being restored to view, each displays after-effects of the militarised inferno they have endured: severe facial spasms, fits of stammering, a leg lamed by shrapnel, nightmares that make them scream out in terror.

Other novels also juxtaposed war and excavation. A superb chapter portraying the start of the First World War in Adam Thorpe's *Ulverton* is narrated by a colonial official retired home from India after his wife's recent death there. Seeking distraction from his grief by 'delving back into memories safely other than my own', he takes part in the excavation of a Bronze Age barrow near his remote village on the Wessex Downs. As news of the carnage in Flanders gradually filters through, 4,000-year-old bones and buried weaponry simultaneously surface. A similar counterpoint was effected in John Preston's *The Dig* (2007), which skilfully fictionalised the excavation of the Sutton Hoo Anglo-Saxon burial mound, with its shattered warrior helmet, in Suffolk on the eve of the Second World War.

In Barry Unsworth's *Land of Marvels*, an English archaeologist likewise races against time in 1914 to excavate an Assyrian site in Mesopotamia, where the rubble of a once-commanding empire puts British, German and American manoeuvrings for economic and political dominance in the region into withering perspective.

In the early summer of 1914 too, a young English woman in Kamila Shamsie's *A God in Every Stone* (2015) travels out to a dig in Turkey where the outbreak of war separates her from an archaeologist she is in love with. In *Anil's Ghost* (2000), Michael Ondaatje sends a female archaeologist, teamed with a forensics expert, into 1990s Sri Lanka convulsed by civil war. Amid the sixth-century bones on a historical site restricted to government access, they unearth a present-day skeleton. It's a situation – recent remains found intermixed with far older ones – that has proved popular with crime writers (especially Elly Griffiths, who has published a sequence of novels in which her forensic archaeologist heroine, Ruth Galloway, regularly encounters modern corpses criminally stowed in prehistoric or historical sites). Ondaatje makes it the start of a tense narrative of post-mortem detection that lays bare the harrowing actualities of sectarian warfare in Sri Lanka.

Damaged Childhoods: David Cook, Graham Swift and Peter Carey

Exhumation – literal and metaphorical – in modern novels has extended far beyond military contexts. Historical fiction, as we shall see later, has resurrected societies and eras on a panoramic scale. Conversely, novelists have delved into the crannies of an individual's past. 'There was a secret in Nell's life, a thing so buried that she could only unearth it piece by piece, struggling with memories like an archaeologist struggles to make sense of found bones', Rose Tremain remarks of one of her characters. That metaphor (famously used by Freud in his *Studies on Hysteria*: 'I arrived at a procedure which I later developed into a regular method and employed deliberately ... of clearing away the pathogenic psychical material layer by layer ... we liked to compare it with the technique of excavating a buried city') is applicable to numerous other fictional figures of recent years.

By far the most frequent buried secret to be unearthed is an abused childhood. David Cook – a novelist whose imaginative strength was portraying vulnerability: characters with injured person-alities or impaired minds – treated the issue with near-documentary authenticity in *Crying Out Loud* (1988). His preceding novels had shown him to be an affecting chronicler of human forlornness. Vagrants, children in care, the derelict and the disadvantaged attracted his sympathetic but never sentimental attention. Like one of his literary models, George Orwell, he spared no pains in getting at close quarters with his subject matter. To write accurately about down-and-outs, he tramped the country, slept rough or dossed down with the homeless in empty trains at Waterloo station. Psychiatric wards, long-stay mental hospitals and children's homes were visited. Involvement with social work brought further knowledgeability about the field, whose challenges his fiction powerfully dramatised.

Cook's one historical novel, *Sunrising* (1984), took his concern with the way the initially unfortunate can be made even more wretched by society's shortcomings back to 1830. Picaresque in structure like his other books, it made colourfully apparent how greatly he was influenced by Dickens. As its near-destitute central trio trek around England, they encounter amiable grotesques: a big-hearted dwarf, a gentle giant, a benevolent bearded lady. Moral uprightness is located in such outsiders. There's a Dickensian revul-sion from callous officialdom and bumbling petty despots ('homes' and hostels cast shadows across Cook's storylines as starkly as the workhouse and the debtors' prison do in Dickens's). But *Sunrising* adds a dimension denied to Dickens: open presentation not just of physical but sexual menace to children. In the novel's re-creation of gas-lit nineteenth-century London, hapless youngsters are paraded round the discreet establishment of a twinklingly ladylike purveyor of juvenile prey to paedophiles.

Expertly familiar with twentieth-century social work and police procedures, *Crying Out Loud* depicts the present-day actualities of child abuse. The tendency of incest to recur through generations of a family is stressed in its two storylines, which ultimately intertwine. One concerns a father's abuse of his young son; the other a woman abused when a child by her father.

With rare exceptions such as Shelley's verse play about paternal rape, *The Cenci*, or the revealing of what lies behind Nicole Diver's schizophrenia in Scott Fitzgerald's *Tender Is the Night*, sexual abuse of a daughter hasn't featured prominently in earlier literature. In *Pericles*, the 1608 play written by Shakespeare in probable collaboration with George Wilkins, it merely provides a plot device to get the hero's adventures and misadventures under way. Deploring the lack of insight into the mind and personality of the daughter (who is not even given a name and speaks just two lines), Mark Haddon, placed her at the centre of his 2019 updating of the story, *The Porpoise*. Weaving together the novel's disparate material – scenes among jet-setting plutocrats, fragments of myth and legend, flashbacks to Shakespeare and Wilkins in Jacobean London, copious allusions to *Pericles* – is the fraught imagination of a self-harming girl, irreparably damaged by a parent desperate to keep her mute about his molestation of her.

It's a situation numerous modern authors have broached. A sexually abusive father is glimpsed behind an emotionally impaired young woman in Ian McEwan's *On Chesil Beach* (2007). Deborah Moggach's *Porky* (1983) charted how a father's sexual exploitation of his daughter's affection warps her into an affectless adult. Alexander Stuart's controversial *The War Zone* (which won the 1989 Whitbread Award for Fiction, only to have it withdrawn after one of the judges subsequently declared the book 'repellent'), drenched the subject in lurid sensationalism. Edna O'Brien's *Down by the River* (1996) created a furore in her native Ireland with its explicit and fervidly accusatory account not just of a father's rape of his fourteen-year-old daughter but its aftermath of complicit or scared silences and legal battles over abortion in a nation still dominated by the Catholic Church. Focused on a production of *Peter Pan* in 1950s Liverpool, Beryl Bainbridge's *An Awfully Big Adventure* (1989) gave what began as chirpy back-stage comedy a shock ending when a man discovered that a teenage girl he'd seduced was a daughter he had unknowingly fathered. Paternal abuse lurked in the background to the trilogy – *The Clothes in the Wardrobe* (1987), *The Skeleton in the Cupboard* (1988) and *The Fly in the Ointment* (1989) – by Bainbridge's friend and fellow-writer of slim idiosyncratic novels, Alice Thomas Ellis. Elizabeth Jane Howard portrayed it in her *Cazalet Chronicle*. P.D. James, Ruth Rendell and Simon Brett unmasked female murderers as victims of the repercussions of sexual abuse by a father. Buchi Emecheta, earlier an observer of patriarchal pitfalls hindering her African heroines' progress, brought father–daughter incest in a Jamaican immigrant family to the fore in *Gwendolen* (1989). In the 1930s rural Georgia of Alice Walker's massively selling novel, *The Color Purple* (1982), adolescent Celie is repeatedly raped and twice made pregnant by her stepfather. 'Yorkshire', one of the short narratives in Graham Swift's *England and Other Stories* (2014), compressed a clutch of modern fictional preoccupations – post-war trauma, early sexual molestation, the uncertainties of memory – into a taut vignette: a wife lies sleep-less, dreading the coming day when her husband, an airman psycho-logically damaged by the Second World War, is to face police questioning over accusations by their forty-eight-year-old daughter that he sexually abused her as a child.

Bleak repercussions shiver through much of Swift's fiction. Most of his novels are like fictional seismographs tracing the aftershocks of extreme events. The reverberations of war and other kinds of violence are a continuing concern. In *Waterland* (1983) a chain-reaction of disasters is set off by the conversion of a country house into a hospital for 'broken-minded soldiers', casualties of the First World War. Concealment of its (also war-damaged) owner's seduction of his daughter and the birth this leads to has consequences that calamitously resonate through generations of the family.

Father–son incest (a less frequent fictional subject) recurred through three generations in Peter Carey's *The Tax Inspector* (1991). Packed behind a title as drab as a buff envelope, a high-coloured report on irregularities well beyond the scope of the inland revenue unfolded. The Catchprice family, owners of a second-hand car business near Sydney, have, it emerges, long been adept at evasion on more than the financial front. Through the aberrant behaviour of their youngest grandson – a schizoid adolescent with bleached hair and a neurotically scrubbed and waxed body tattooed with angel wings – what has been kept undeclared is becoming increasingly difficult to conceal. When a tax official turns up to audit the firm's accounts, deferred dues of other kinds tumble out. Adding metaphorical resonances to the situation, Carey expands his novel into a dark fable of domestic, civic, national and global pollution.

Edward St Aubyn

The most remarkable portrayal of the consequences of paternal abuse of a son came from Edward St Aubyn in his painfully acute and ferociously funny sequence of autobiographical novels: *Never Mind* (1992), *Bad News* (1992), *Some Hope* (1994), *Mother's Milk* (2006) and *At Last* (2011). The first three follow his fictional alter ego, Patrick Melrose, through an appalling childhood (terrorised and sexually assaulted by his monstrous father, neglected by his alcohol-glazed mother) into years of drink and drug addiction, a suicide bid and other failed attempts to escape the trauma that continued to torment him even after his sadistic father's death. The fourth book, which rejoins Patrick in his forties, shows him struggling to maintain the shaky stability that rehab clinics have given him, while battling (in vain) to stop his mother, Eleanor, from donating Saint-Nazaire, the idyllic family property in Provence that had become his haven, to a New Age charlatan and his followers. Having previously focused on damage done by a viciously cynical father, attention shifts to damage done by a ruinously gullible mother.

Confined like several of its predecessors to the events of a single day, *At Last*, the closing book in the series, focuses on Eleanor's funeral, which St Aubyn turns into a jamboree of jet-black satiric farce. Bringing together supercilious socialites and garish cranks, super-rich members of the American dynasty from which Eleanor inherited the fortune she credulously squandered, resentful relatives who didn't benefit from her eccentric philanthropy and beaming phonies who did, the grotesquely assorted gathering of mourners brims with comic potential. St Aubyn lets it overflow to savagely hilarious effect. A viperish old snob fatefully collides with one of Eleanor's dubious charity cases on a manic rampage after discontinuing her medication. Upper-crust hackles rise in the garrulous presence of Annette, a former member of the Dublin Women's Healing Drum Circle, now ensconced at Saint-Nazaire amid a milieu of mantras, chakras and 'Walking with the Goddess' workshops.

With his acute ear for dialogue and deftness at capturing characters' self-approving thought processes, St Aubyn adroitly impales upper-class vanity, greed, spite and hypocrisy. New Age inanity is scathingly relished too. A comic high-spot in the crematorium is Annette's eulogy to the deceased. After lauding her far-sighted funding of a Croatian inventor purportedly developing a world-saving 'zero-energy fuel cell' and of a Peruvian archaeologist claiming to have evidence that the Incas communicated with their Egyptian 'mother culture' by 'solar language', she reassures her audience: 'But you mustn't think that Eleanor was only concerned with the higher echelons of science and spirituality.'

Ironic contrasts are displayed not only between but within individuals. Patrick's intelligence processes his turmoil into elegantly exact, near-aphoristic formulations ('It was not the end of closeness but the end of the longing for closeness that he had to mourn', he reflects about the loss of his always-distant mother). But emotional ferment still seething from his betrayed boyhood keeps his body – 'a graveyard of buried emotion' – churning with unruly symptoms.

Although retrieving Saint-Nazaire proves impossible, recovery of other kinds is perceptible as the novel ends. Resisting further urges to self-destructiveness, Patrick is last seen heading back to his young sons, whose unspoiled decency is an appealing force for rehabilitation in the novel. Damaged by his parents, it seems he may be saved by his children.

Another kind of healing process had been in operation from the start of St Aubyn's fictional sequence. Where other authors have regarded memory of childhood trauma as something suppressed and in need of excavation, this isn't, he emphasised in an interview, a theory he shares: 'I think trauma, during the period of our lives we can remember, doesn't lead to repression. I never understood that theory. It leads to splitting and fragmentation. I never had any trouble remembering what were the most outstandingly violent and life-threatening events in my childhood.' When, shortly after his father's death, he began to write the first of his novels revisiting the years of rape and other physical and emotional assaults he underwent as child, the main impediment he faced was near-paralysing anxiety as to whether the novel could be published: 'I thought, It's impossible, I can't tell this story'. At that time, he believed, autobiographical exposure of incestuous assault was taboo ('no one else was talking about it. And, for all I knew, it might not have happened since ancient Greece'). But a counter-pressure impelled him to persist: his conviction that 'either I write a novel which I finish and get published, and is authentic, or I'll kill myself', otherwise there would be 'nothing so far in my life that I'm not ashamed of and horrified by'.

The five-book sequence that ensued is masterly in more ways than one: a brilliantly controlled story of a life sent out of control.

Intellectual poise – prose crisp with irony, unwavering perceptiveness – coexists with emotional upheaval. The paranoia, voices in the head, fumbled suicide bid and other near-lethal consequences of the alcohol and drugs with which St Aubyn tried to blot out his nightmare childhood are scrutinised with a kind of sardonic fortitude. Abuse is recalled with bitter wit: as Patrick walks along a New York street carrying a brown-paper bag containing his father's cremated remains in *Bad News*, he reflects that 'it was the first time that he had been alone with his father for more than ten minutes without being buggered, hit, or insulted'. Caustic intelligence is stingingly applied to a lacerated past. Excoriation aids recuperation as, to sanitise, wounds are laid bare.

David Vann

Trauma inflicted on a son by his father is also at the root of fiction by David Vann, a writer of exceptionally raw and inflamed creativity: if it were possible to take the CAT scan of his imagination, it would probably resemble a bruise. The five stories and novella that comprised his first book, *Legend of a Suicide* (2009), each worked a variation (sometimes close to the facts, sometimes twisted into an alternative but still extreme scenario) on a calamity that has reverberated through his life: his father's suicide – by shooting himself in the head – when Vann was thirteen.

Caribou Island (2011), Vann's first novel, extended this preoccupation with parental suicide and its psychological and emotional repercussions. The setting, as before, is his native south-east Alaska, with its lonely islands in glacial lakes and vast, wild hinterland around pockets of tacky tourist development. Again, fraught fiction stems from painful actuality. Behind this book, Vann has said, lies the suicide of one of his stepmother's parents after murdering the other. A witheringly contemptuous portrait of his father features in a subplot.

At the forefront are Gary and Irene, a couple in their fifties whose marriage, long riven with resentments and insecurities, is breaking apart. Trapped in punishing proximity, they struggle, numb with cold and lashed by rain, to complete a log cabin they are building in Alaska before the -30°C winter descends. But the lopsided and uninhabitable-looking structure they are maladroitly assembling seems a more and more obvious symbol for their teetering marriage. With a stark momentum not unlike that in the Anglo-Saxon poetry we're told Gary venerates, things escalate to a ghastly ending.

What had made *Legend of a Suicide* a riveting debut was its coalescing of the lurid and the lucid. Rigorous clarity was applied to turbulent material. Fictionally confronting the traumas in his past, Vann viewed desperation and extremity through prose of icy transparency. In *Caribou Island*, violence and derangement aren't as surely held in place. As Irene, tortured by agonising psychosomatic head pains, spirals through panic and insomnia towards breakdown, and Gary retreats ever further into a delusional saga world echoing with lines from *Beowulf* and *The Seafarer*, the novel feverishly builds to a melodramatically macabre climax in which, after impaling her husband with arrows from her hunting bow, Irene hangs herself above his corpse.

Dirt (2012), which unrolled another deadly family scenario – a deranged son's murder of his suffocatingly possessive mother – shifted from Alaska, whose natural splendours and tourist debasement Vann always evokes in scenes that glint with brilliancies of image and observation, to the cruelly hot Californian desert. Its successor, *Goat Mountain* (2013), seemed designed as an equally torrid companion piece. Again, a homicidal psychopath is surrounded by oedipal tensions. But where *Dirt* concentrated on a malign female family world, *Goat Mountain* concentrates on a malign male one. Its unnamed narrator recalls the havoc that erupted when, as an eleven-year-old, he travelled with his father and grandfather to their Northern California ranch for his first deer hunt. After he shot a trespassing poacher dead with his father's rifle, gruesome consequences ensued, culminating in another fatal shooting.

The novel's high frequency of fast, verbless sentences, and its restriction to a short period of time, suggests that Vann was striving for a streamlined urgency like that of Greek tragedy with its tight focus on abattoir-like family atrocities and their aftermath. But overblown melodrama soon dissipates any intensity. Squandering his talent for portraying landscape, Vann makes this book's setting a garishly symbolic terrain where snakes slither among poison oaks and other 'vicious plants' on a mountainside topped with rocks resembling a devil's horns. Words such as 'atavistic' repeatedly insist on a primal male urge to kill. References to Cain and other biblical figures run amok in prose often so febrile as to verge on gibberish. Despite strenuous efforts to give its carnage archetypal significance, *Goat Mountain* – continuing Vann's compulsion to immerse his imagination in a domestic bloodbath – seems a shambles in both senses of the word: a scene of slaughter and a mess.

As if further attempting to impose a tauter pattern on his scenarios of family excruciation, Vann moved even closer to ancient Greek drama with *Bright Air Black* (2017). Retelling the story of Medea, with its parental bloodshed and sacrificed sons, it further testified to his unremitting urge to find a fictional form to clench around the tragedy that traumatised his early life: an event returned to in near-autobiographical mode with his 2019 novel *Halibut on the Moon*, which imagined, this time with affecting empathy, his depressive father's final days before his suicide.

Toni Morrison

In contrasting ways, the novels of St Aubyn and Vann stem from painful personal experience of early trauma. More usually, it was increasing public awareness of it that drew writers to the subject – not infrequently with ersatz-seeming results. One of modern fiction's more depressing achievements is to have sometimes trivialised child abuse to a facile plot device or a narrative cliché, staled and cheapened by predictability. In Martin Amis's *London Fields* (1989), the identification of an angelic infant's violent abuser (by the belated deciphering of a letter of the alphabet) seems little more than a gimmick. An almost risibly synthetic presentation of paedophilia features in A.N. Wilson's *Dream Children* (1998) where it emerges that an eminent middle-aged philosopher and a pre-teenage girl, 'Bobs', '"did things" for which he could be arrested'. Anything remotely disturbing about this is rendered unreal not just by the book's prissy prose (letters aren't handwritten but 'calligraphed', a relationship doesn't cool but undergoes 'frigorification') but by the remarkably mature demeanour of Bobs. Piquing herself on 'learning to be the most detached and non-participatory observer of the human scene' and voicing acid little *aperçus* ('Aren't diaries meant to be indiscreet? Isn't that their point?'), she is an unusually precocious ten-year-old. Disconcerting visions of Wilson in white knee-socks, grey pleated skirt and school blazer flicker into mind whenever she appears.

The most bizarre fictional treatment of childhood trauma and its aftermath came from Toni Morrison in her 2015 novel, *God Help the Child*. Like her preceding two books, *A Mercy* and *Home*, both of which it resembles in brevity, it mainly consists of what had always been a powerfully effective element in her fiction: interior-monologue-like sections that take you to the core of a character's consciousness. Initially, its subject appears to be a further instance of the malign after-effects of centuries of Black oppression that Morrison's fiction had always compellingly chronicled.

In the opening pages, a light-skinned Black woman recalls her horror at giving birth to a baby 'so black she scared me. Midnight black, Sudanese black.' Although this occurred in the 1990s, fears persisting from the days of open race discrimination, when there were 'coloured only' drinking fountains and courthouses had a Bible 'reserved for Negroes', caused her to rear the child, Lula Ann, with loveless severity.

The next voice heard is that of 'Bride', the glamorous persona with a chic new name that the adult Lula Ann has devised for herself. Now a high-salary executive in a prospering cosmetic company, she has become a formidably cool ebony beauty, elegantly highlighting her colour in 'white-only clothes ... Ivory, oyster, alabaster, paper white, snow.' Smartly going places career-wise and sexily partnered with a handsome Black lover, Booker, she congratulates herself on her liberation from her early background. But, in Morrison's fiction, the past is never easily escaped. When a figure from her childhood re-enters her life and Booker rejects her, Bride weirdly regresses. Her pubic hair mysteriously vanishes, her 'spectacular breasts' deflate and she shrinkingly reverts to a 'too-black little girl'.

Around this surreally literal reminder that the damaged child can resurface through the seemingly assured adult self, Morrison heaps multiple instances of child abuse: a girl traded out for sex by her prostitute mother, a predator lurking near a playground, a toddler screaming in a car as her parents smoke crack. Booker's brother, it emerges, was mutilated and murdered by a paedophile serial killer. As a youngster, Bride spotted a neighbour raping a boy. Her best friend was molested by an uncle. A paedophile scandal convulsed her school.

Rather unnecessarily in view of this plethora of case histories, the novel warns that 'what you do to children matters. And they might never forget.' Modern fiction has widely and often harrowingly concerned itself with this subject. But Morrison, matchless at portraying racial and cultural trauma among Black Americans, operates with far less sureness when exploring childhood trauma. Crudely over-emphatic and even faintly ludicrous (as when Bride rejoices at 'the magical return of her flawless breasts'), *God Help the Child* is an ill-judged deviation from imaginative territory she occupied with power and subtlety into an area that more and more writers have – not always fortunately – found it almost mandatory to explore.

Margaret Drabble

A prodigious example of the unbeneficial pull that the theme of child abuse could exert on an author's imagination was Margaret Drabble's trilogy: *The Radiant Way* (1987), *A Natural Curiosity* (1989) and *The Gates of Ivory* (1991). After making her name in the 1960s with compact, psychologically acute novels each centred on a resourceful young woman, Drabble began, in the 1970s, to be restive with the neatness and conventional nature of such fiction. Her novels grew longer and more amorphous. *The Radiant Way*, which begins with a glittering New Year's Eve party to usher in the 1980s, launched a sprawling fictional sequence that concluded, in *The Gates of Ivory*, with a memorial reception near the decade's end.

The trilogy's first two books, *The Radiant Way* and *A Natural Curiosity*, seem intended as contemporary exercises in State of the Nation fiction, updatings of the Victorian Two Nations novel with its focus on social and economic gulfs, usually between North and South. Storylines shuttle between Northam (a 'figurative Northern city' that resembles Drabble's birthplace, Sheffield) and London (metropolitan life in all its diversity). *The Gates of Ivory*, which opens on a bridge between Thailand and Cambodia where visitors from the 'Good Times' of the affluent West peer across at the 'Bad Times' of Pol Pot's killing fields, vastly broadens out from the earlier North–South national divide to an East–West global divide.

The last word of *The Gates of Ivory* is 'multitudes'. And multitudes – of people, plots, themes – are exorbitantly spilled out in it. Characters come at you in droves: chattering London socialites, international travellers, relief workers, refugees. Figures transitorily brought to the forefront of this surging throng are emphatically various: a bejewelled Bangkok glamour queen, a Booker Prize-winner, an Alzheimer's patient in a Somerset nursing home, a female French spy, a director of deconstructed Shakespearean plays, Khmer Rouge guerrillas, redbrick academics, an amputee, a psychotic decapitator, a Japanese supporter of Pol Pot, and a gay anthropologist with a cannibal boyfriend. As this variegated horde intermingle and shift about, numerous topics are broached. Stories are told of female entrepreneurship in Thailand, nightmare ordeals in Kampuchea and unexpected romance in NW3. Multiple subplots – about everything from tampons to the significance of severed heads – are reeled out, and you're kept aware that many others could be. Potentiality seethes with the same profusion as actuality: a favoured device is to list alternative turns of event that might have propelled characters down different paths.

The reason for this tsunami of multiplicity, Drabble announces, is that 'a queasiness, a moral scruple overcomes the writer at the prospect of selecting individuals from the mass of history'. Such an approach, she explains, would be distastefully irrelevant in an age of 'Big numbers. Mass destructions. Mass graves.' Illustrating this, two characters from her 1972 book *The Needle's Eye* are reintroduced, only to be shooed away as having unacceptably 'wandered into this story from the old-fashioned, Freudian, psychological novel'.

This dismissal of psychological fiction and Freudian thinking comes strangely in a trilogy whose most pervasive character is a psychiatrist and which is much engaged with primal trauma. Despite their superabundance of reportage-like contemporary detail, *The Radiant Way* and *A Natural Curiosity* are heavily fixated on the past. Each has as its narrative climax the revelation of hidden trauma that has bedevilled a character. Throughout both novels, a retrospective inclination tilts things away from the present. *The Radiant Way* takes its title from a 1930s school primer whose cheery cover illustration depicts education as a sunlit path. Some of the novel's best scenes look back with shrewdness, wit and nostalgia to its characters' heady experiences at school and college. Its central figures are three women who met at Cambridge and formed a lasting friendship there: Liz (a psychiatrist with deep-rooted neuroses), Alix (a social worker with problems of her own) and Esther (an art historian unknowingly living near to something very ugly). Initially, Drabble seems to be aiming to interweave their differing perspectives within a fictional-ised documentary of modern lifestyles. But *The Radiant Way* soon deviates in an odder direction. This isn't simply a matter of its narra-tive voice being crankily dismissive of fiction's devices: 'she is concealing something from herself. But what is it? Does she know what it is? Do you know what it is? Do I know what it is? Does anybody know what it is?' What is most striking is the way the novel keeps veering away from its sweeping survey of 1980s life in England to compulsive concentration on a clutch of themes and motifs pertaining to the past.

Abuse during childhood increasingly receives predominant atten-tion. Uncovering documents about a shameful family secret, Liz is confronted with the fact, long buried in her memory, that her father sexually molested her as a young girl. Simultaneously, after-effects of childhood maltreatment of another kind luridly display themselves, as a murderous psychopath, known to the tabloid press as 'The Horror of Harrow Road', terrorises West London. Decapitating at least five women before being caught, he turns out to have lived perilously close to Esther (and leaves one of the heads he's severed on the driving seat of Alix's Renault). Much of *A Natural Curiosity* recounts Alix's prison visits to him and her search for what underlies his derangement, culminating in the discovery that, tormented by an insane mother, he is a casualty of childhood trauma.

The Horror's decapitations aren't by any means the only behead-ings in Drabble's trilogy. Cambodia's pyramids of skulls in *The Gates of Ivory* heap them up in macabre profusion. The pages of *A Natural Curiosity* are lavishly cluttered with reference to severed heads: plaster-cast crania of Louis XVI and Marie Antoinette, King Charles's head, chopped-off heads in *Titus Andronicus* and Tacitus, the skull that Keats's Isabella hid in her pot of basil, the skulls of ritu-ally beheaded Celts and the sorry case of a beheaded mother-in-law reported in the newspapers. There are pigs' heads, horses' heads and a brass door knocker that looks like Medusa. It's no wonder, you feel, that someone admiringly tells Liz, 'I was always impressed by the way you and Shirley kept your heads screwed on.'

The plethora of decapitation in *A Natural Curiosity* is part of its wider concern with the abnormal. Its punning title refers both to 'freaks of nature' and the fascination they exert. Alix's eagerness to get to the root of The Horror's murderous derangement is seen as just an extreme instance of a universal human urge to explore the aberrant. 'Attractive danger. Natural curiosity. Unnatural Curiosity': these things, it's suggested, impel Drabble's swarming cast of characters towards risky undertakings of all kinds, from a journey to Kampuchea in search of Pol Pot to a probably calamitous affair with a cad. Alix's social worker sleuthings into The Horror's past uncover a monster mother who is 'a fury, a harpy, a gorgon'. Happenings in twentieth-century London and Northam, you're constantly reminded, are merely the latest layer of mankind's dark history, encrusted with atavistic malignities and primal crimes. To emphasise this, The Horror is given a passion for archaeology (one shared by Drabble, whose 1975 novel, *The Realms of Gold*, exhaustively dwelt on an archaeologist's excavations in the Sahara, international lecture tours, and relations with her geologist-cousin and her historian-lover). Ancient atrocities – such as the ritually murdered Bog Man of Buller or the mass slaughter perpetrated by the Celtic Queen Cartimandua – are described in the books he's seen perusing in his prison cell.

Where *The Radiant Way* opened up a panorama of regional and social divides, *A Natural Curiosity* narrows such gulfs by implying, often through lists of particularly aberrant crimes reported in newspapers, that life in England has become deranged everywhere. 'Although Liz does not yet know it,' Drabble declares, '1987 is to be the Year of Child Sex Abuse. For some years now the subject has been arousing interest and controversy amongst the professionals, but in 1987 it will catch the press and the popular imagination like a fever. 1987 will be a psychotic year, the year of abnormality, of Abuse.'

Charting this, *A Natural Curiosity* is, we're told, 'a pathological novel. A psychotic novel.' To convince you of this, events in the book wildly chafe against the bounds of the usual: after being mugged in the rose garden in Regent's Park, one character sets out to brave terrorists in the Middle East; another, losing her wits after her husband's suicide, drives to France in a near-comatose state, picking up a lover on the way; Alix's quest to solve the mystery of The Horror's past concludes in a battle with a madwoman, amid a pile of canine corpses, with a can of dog food as a weapon. The novel further parades its 'psychotic' credentials by displaying in even more exaggerated form the eccentricities of narrative met with in *The Radiant Way*. Sentences go into spasms of repetitiveness, reeling out synonyms and near synonyms: it is 'late, late, late', things are 'gloomy, morbid, grisly', 'ghastly, doomed, menacing', 'aberrant, deviant, almost pathological'. Drabble makes disordered-seeming appearances in her narrative ('Sorry about that. It won't happen again. Sorry') and buttonholes the reader with confessions of her difficulty in remembering a character's birthday: 'And anyway, what *is* her age? I must say I have lost track of this a little myself. Is she forty-eight or nine now, as I had thought, or fifty, as others tell me?' But what this novel – not so much 'psychotic' as compulsively retrospective – most notably exhibits is how fictional depiction of the present can by pushed awry by an impulsion to swivel back to the past: through superimposed archetypal patterns, mythic cross-references, unearthings of long-suppressed personal trauma and delvings into archaeological sites.

Iron Age Excavations: Sarah Moss

Modern fiction has been widely hospitable to practitioners of what could be termed the memory professions: historians, biographers, psychiatrists and psychologists, archivists, picture restorers, palaeontologists and, most numerously, archaeologists. With remarkable frequency – as if in conscious or subconscious recollection of Freud's image for psychoanalysis – archaeology in is placed close to trauma: post-war trauma in novels such as *A Month in the Country*; sexual trauma in a wide range of works. Mary, the abused girl in Edna O'Brien's *Down by the River*, is first assaulted by her father next to a stretch of bogland he would like to turn into an archaeological site such as ones he's read about where Iron Age cadavers were discovered. His rapes come to light when mention of them is discovered in his daughter's diary alongside lines she's copied out from a newspaper about a 5,000-year-old 'Ice Man' found preserved in the Alps.

In *A Natural Curiosity*, visitors to a British Museum exhibition, 'New Views of the Past', stare at 'the strangely preserved, smooth, brown, plump, patterned immortal skin of Lindow Man. Bard or Druid, victim or sacrifice. Ageless, timeless, rescued from the bog.' When Elly Griffiths' archaeologist detective, Ruth Galloway, is confronted with a dead priest spreadeagled on an Italian altar in *The Dark Angel* (2018), her immediate thought is that he looks 'like Lindow Man lying face down in the peat bog, like the Iron Age bodies found in Denmark pegged down on the marshes in an attempt to appease the gods'.

Peat-preserved bog corpses keep surfacing in modern literature: most famously in the poems Seamus Heaney wrote after reading about, and seeing pictures of, the 'Tollund Man' and the 'Grauballe Man' in the Danish archaeologist P.V. Glob's book, *The Bog People: Iron Age Man Preserved*, which was published in English translation, to considerable interest, in 1969. Similar photographs of leathery Iron Age cadavers are seen in *Ghost Wall* (2018) by Sarah Moss. Fascinated by archaeology, she has said that she 'planned to be an archaeologist, and spent the summer I was seventeen working on a Roman dig in central France, which was when I noticed how the developing community of archaeological workers mirrored the ancient community we were uncovering and thought that the parallel stories would provide the structure of the novel I intended one day to write'.

Two of her novels – *Bodies of Light* (2014) and *Signs for Lost Children* (2015) – resurrect the Victorian era. After a baby's skeleton is uncovered in a garden on a Hebridean island, *Night Waking* (2011) harks back to the 1870s. *Cold Earth* (2009) focuses on archaeologists excavating a medieval Norse settlement in Greenland.

Moss's *Ghost Wall* takes place in 1990s Northumbria where three vacationing students and their professor are joined in an exercise in 'experiential archaeology' by teenage Sylvie, her downtrodden mother and her overbearing father, a man obsessed with what he sees as the tough authenticity of Iron Age life. In contrast to the chilly locations Moss previously favoured, it is high summer. The sun beats down on a little settlement where – in tents and a reconstructed roundhouse – the group aim to 'have a flavour of Iron Age life'. At first, irony about Iron Age re-enactment is to the fore. Homespun tunics prove itchy. Sleeping on straw-crammed sacks isn't easy. Anachronistic amenities such as toothbrushes are reluctantly permitted on the grounds that probably the only reason Iron Age folk didn't have them was that they never lived long enough to lose their teeth. Pseudo-prehistoric provender – foraged burdock roots and tiny, bony fish cooked over an irritatingly slow turf fire – is furtively supplemented with Mars bars and Hula Hoops, garnered on surreptitious student sorties to a Spar superstore. Gradually, though, things darken. Divides surface between the middle-class southerners from a university milieu and the northern working-class family headed by a surly patriarch whose brutality, misogyny and xenophobia reveal themselves more and more harshly.

A brief prelude to Moss's increasingly tense tale describes the ritual sacrifice of an Iron Age girl buried and preserved in a peat bog. Sylvie's father, it emerges, enjoys poring over photographs of such cadavers. In Heaney's poetry about the 1970s Troubles, they provided images for victims of Ulster's 'tribal' violence. In *Ghost Wall*, they give grim resonance to domestic violence. The novel depicts parenting – a continuing preoccupation in Moss's fiction – taking a monstrous form.

'Sylvie' is a shortened version of the 'proper native British name' Sulevia (an ancient Northumbrian goddess), that her father has inflicted on the girl. It's far from the only instance of his domineering outlandishness. His cantankerous tyranny becomes ever uglier as the story proceeds. There are flesh-creeping moments, as when, scrutinising scars on an Iron Age sacrificial victim, he absorbedly observes: 'see, not enough to kill, just done for the pain like'. It's no surprise that bruises, contusions and other evidence of his violence towards his wife and daughter, become visible as suspense mounts. But Moss resists making the man simply an ogre of sadistic patriarchy. Behind the horribleness there is some pathos. Shamed feelings of self-educated inferiority painfully emerge as he envies those 'who'd passed the eleven-plus and made summat of themselves' or, in conversation with the history professor, blusteringly tries to extricate himself from factual blunders ('aye . . . I knew that, right enough, course I did'). It's writing that – along with keen response to the natural world and acute alertness to class, regional and sexual tensions – recalls the early fiction of D.H. Lawrence and adds enriching complexity to a tale of modern menace within a context of ancient cruelty.

Archaeologists: Penelope Lively and Hilary Mantel

Using archaeology to gratify belligerent and sadistic urges, the autodidact father in Moss's novella is something of an anomaly in modern fiction, where archaeologists tend to be much admired. Seen as analogous to novelists' own procedures, their activities – resurrecting the past, bringing buried things to light – arouse fellow feeling. Penelope Lively (who has called herself 'an archaeologist manquée') described the palaeontologist hero of her novel *Cleopatra's Sister* (1993) as her 'surrogate'. Empathy between author and archaeologists often wells out in her fiction. *Treasures of Time* (1979) – its title taken from lines in Sir Thomas Browne's *Urn Burial* ('The treasures of time lie high, in Urnes, Coynes and Monuments, scarce below the roots of some vegetables') – brims with sympathy in its portrayal of unfulfilled love between two archaeologists, thwarted by a manipulative egotist contemptuous of their vocation. Browne's eerily resonant and earthy lines are quoted again in Lively's memoir, *Ammonites and Leaping Fish* (2013), where she recalls how her enthusiasm for palaeontology was awakened by the fossil-rich cliffs and beaches of her Somerset childhood. Similar enthusiasm is awakened in the hero of *Cleopatra's Sister* after he picks up an ammonite – a Jurassic fossil of an extinct cephalopod – on a Somerset beach as a child. Later, as a geology student peering through a microscope at one of 'those bizarre, unlikely and immaculate animals' embedded in the Cambrian Burgess Shale, he notes that he 'had fallen – not in love but into fascination'. It's a fascination that ultimately brings amorous as well as professional fulfilment. Journeying deep into Africa to inspect unidentified fossils of what were 'almost certainly Burgess Shale fauna', he finds romance there even amid a bloody political uprising.

Lively remarks of her fossil-lover: 'The more spectacular areas of the discipline were not for him, he realized, turning his back on the Jurassic, on dinosaurs, on early mammals. He was drawn to the beginnings, to that ultimate antiquity, in which anything is possible.' In this he differs from another appealing palaeontologist central to a modern novel, Lesje, the young Canadian museum employee in Margaret Atwood's *Life Before Man* (1980) who likes to fantasise that she 'is wandering in prehistory. Under a sun more orange than her own has ever been, in the middle of a swampy plain lush with thick-stalked plants and oversized ferns, a group of bony-plated stegosaurs is grazing . . .'

In 'Stone Mattress' (2014), Atwood's entertaining tale about long-deferred revenge dealt out during an Arctic cruise for well-heeled senior citizens, a stromatolite – a chunky 1.9-billion-year-old fossil of Earth's earliest-known life-forms – comes in handy as a perfect modern murder weapon. Another primeval find – a 150-million-year-old bivalve shell, scientifically termed a gryphaea but more commonly known as a 'devil's toenail' – plays an emblematic role in Hilary Mantel's haunting and subtle *A Change of Climate* (1994).

It's a novel scattered with fossils and relics. From a Norfolk landscape dotted with ruins and tumuli, Roman skeletons and terracotta shards are unearthed. Flint arrowheads jut from the ground. Prehistoric bison bones turn up on a beach at Cromer. Elsewhere, a stroller across the sands finds a 'devil's toenail', a sinister-looking fossil – 'thick, ridged, ogreish' – which goes on to figure in Mantel's novel as a symbol of evil that has maimed the lives of two good people and remained petrifyingly lodged in their past. First scooped up from the seaside by a young man alive with idealism, it is flung away decades later by his harrowed older self. In between, Mantel unfolds a descent into hell.

At the centre of her novel are a couple born into godly circles. Ralph Eldred and Anna who becomes his wife are the offspring of families which subscribe with dour literalness to Bible doctrines. In this milieu, Ralph's announcement that he wishes to read geology at university causes consternation. Inexorably, righteous bigotry thwarts his plans. Silhouetted against a Darwinian background of fossils and fundamentalists, and displaying how theological dogmas and conflicts more usually associated with the late Victorian era lingered on in the rural Norfolk of the 1940s and 1950s, Mantel's account of Ralph's worsting by his parents reads as a chilly domestic shocker. From there, his story moves out to a climate that is warmer meteorologically but in other ways far bleaker.

The first staging post in Ralph's journey with Anna towards their heart of darkness is a South African township to which they travel as a newlyweds, glowing with liberal Christianity and faith in progress. The year is 1956. Before leaving England, they have read Trevor Huddleston's *Nought for Your Comfort*; and in the rebarbative society they encounter, little comfort is in evidence. Frayed and exhausted by their efforts to help oppressed Black people, they reel between the thuggery of the Afrikaner authorities and the desperate lawlessness apartheid foments. Brave but hopeless opposition to the race laws lands them in prison, then results in deportation to Bechuanaland.

It is here – in a benighted teaching mission on the edge of the Kalahari – that the Eldreds fall foul of a barbarity so lacerating that it leaves a permanent scar across their lives. Menacing creatures creep around their mission house. Anna sees a leopard with fresh blood still wet on its chest. Tropic downpours whip snakes hidden in the garden out into the open so that the ground seethes 'like a living carpet'. But horror strikes from a different quarter as, in a heart-thumping sequence, Mantel shows how Ralph is impelled by his fatal trust in human nature to open the door to atrocity.

Set mainly in 1970s Norfolk, where the Eldreds – now fatigued and unillusioned – have become social workers, the novel takes a long time to disclose exactly what has devastated them. In narratives of this kind, there's a high risk that the eventual bringing of the horror to light will be an anti-climax. But, steadily eschewing sensationalism, Mantel confronts you with a happening of such vileness that there's never any doubt about its continuing power to contaminate and appal. Despite the ghastliness at its core, her novel is far from despairing. Recounting how two traumatised but persistingly well-intentioned people struggle on to lead useful, unselfish lives, it is crisp with wintry humour, and pulses with unstaunchable vitality. Astringent wit tingles through the prose. Quick, sharp psychological and social insights glint, whether Mantel is observing sanctimonious sadism in East Anglia or political viciousness in South Africa.

In one African scene, she notes how 'the go-away birds wheeled overhead ... squawking out their single, unvaried message'. Clearly intended also to be give-away birds, they seem a little flight of homage to the author Mantel has always admired and, in this book, follows to brilliant effect. Muriel Spark's story, 'The Go-Away Bird', sent the same warning call echoing over a disillusioning and dangerous South Africa. And similarities between her fiction and Mantel's reverberate in other ways too. Like Spark, Mantel writes imperturbable prose spiked with surprising images and interspersed with snatches of acutely – and often hilariously – caught dialogue. Like Spark, she sets a hellish aura flickering around brittle scenes, is much engaged with good and evil, and deploys flashbacks and flashes forward with crafty flair.

Brisk, unsentimental, unsurprised but uncynical, Mantel had previously written with rueful comedy about social workers and misfits (*Every Day Is Mother's Day*, 1985; *Vacant Possession*, 1986), with barbed fascination about religion (*Fludd*, 1989), and with choking tension about personal and political nightmare (*Eight Months on Ghazzah Street*, 1988; *A Place of Greater Safety*, 1992). *A Change of Climate* clenches all these concerns together in a narrative strewn with baleful imagery from, and admiring approval for, geology.

While archaeology in modern fiction is usually linked with (and often uncovers buried evidence of) human violence, palaeontology opens up deeper, more vertiginous dimensions: unimaginable aeons of humanless existence on our planet, bizarre long-extinct life-forms. Staring at the coil of an ammonite in Tracey Chevalier's *Remarkable Creatures* (2014), a Victorian fossil collector 'felt for a moment that I was being sucked into its spiral, farther and farther back in time until the past was lost in the centre'. It's not only the past that could be lost in contemplation of fossils. Religious faith could disintegrate too. The clink of the palaeontologist's hammer presented far more menace to the Rock of Ages than the scrape of the archaeologist's trowel ever could. Highlighted in Mantel's novel, this is an issue that also features in Chevalier's fictional reconstruction of early nineteenth-century Lyme Regis, where two remarkable creatures of that period – the pioneering palaeontologists, Mary Anning and Elizabeth Philpot – bring to light remains of remarkable prehistoric creatures. Enthrallingly, Chevalier re-assembles the milieu of excitement, puzzlement, hostility and awe within which her amateur 'fossilists' – battling bigotry of various kinds – advance new ways of thinking about the world by their seashore discoveries.

Particularly appreciative fictional attention has been given to the gritty perseverance of Mary Anning who, undaunted by a sparse education, family poverty and the ever-present dangers of collapsing cliff-faces and coastal landslides, collected 'snakestones' and 'verteberries' (ammonites and vertebrae) to sell to visitors to Lyme Regis, before going on to make spectacularly influential finds such as an 18-foot-long ichthyosaurus and a complete skeleton of a plesiosaurus. In Judith Stinton's *Under Black Ven* (1995), Anning relates her life in a tale tangy with Dorset dialect and local knowledge, and recalls in old age her momentous find, on a snowy beach, of what she initially thought was 'a crocodile . . . year upon year old'. Her recovery of that first complete skeleton of an ichthyosaurus provides a high-spot in the many fictionalisations of her career written for children, such as Marie Day's *Dragon in the Rocks* (1992), Laurence Anholt's *Stone Girl Bone Girl* (2006), Jeannine Atkins's *Mary Anning and the Sea Dragon* (2012), Patricia Pierce's *Jurassic Mary* (2015) and Anthea Simmons's *Lightning Mary* (2019), this last title being a reference to her extraordinary survival after being struck by lightning when fifteen months old.

Historians: Julian Barnes

Along with archaeology, history is a discipline that has received a sizeable boost in modern fiction. Near the start of Swift's *Waterland*, its schoolteacher narrator complains that he has been forced into early retirement by his headmaster who informed him, 'We're cutting back on history.' The novel (whose first words are 'And don't forget') is an extended demonstration of the fatuity of that announcement. Set in the porous region of the Fens, where water seeps unstoppably into land, it demonstrates how the present is inextricably interfused with the past. Individual, family, social and political history saturate the novel.

'I'm writing a history of the world . . . And in the process, my own', declares Claudia Hammond, the elderly historian who narrates

Penelope Lively's 1987 novel, *Moon Tiger* (she begins by recalling her childhood fall from a cliff when hunting for ammonites). Counterpointing personal and vaster historical perspectives is a technique much favoured by modern novelists. Julian Barnes worked ingenious variations on it in *A History of the World in 10½ Chapters* (1989). Fascination with history has shown itself throughout his career – most quirkily in his black comic novel, *Before She Met Me* (1982), whose protagonist, an academic historian, murders a novelist. Starting with one of the most eye-catching opening lines in modern fiction – 'The first time Graham Hendrick watched his wife commit adultery he didn't mind at all' (she's a film actress) – it unrolls towards a gory conclusion as, increasingly possessed by jealousy, Hendrick attributes a more and more luridly promiscuous history to his guilt-less wife. But the book by Barnes that most tensely wove together preoccupations with history, memory and consequences was *The Sense of an Ending* (2011).

Tony Webster, who narrates this quietly nightmarish novel (the first words of which are 'I remember'), has had a peaceable life. Contentedly retired after a satisfying career in arts administration, he is on amicable terms with the wife he placidly divorced years ago and their daughter. Apart from one distant period of turbulence – when he was involved at university with a 'bloody difficult young woman', Veronica Ford – his existence has been singularly well regulated. It's a state of affairs that, in fiction, often bodes ill. And dramatic upset duly arrives in the form of a solicitor's letter. Veronica's mother (whom he barely knew) has, Tony is amazed to learn, left him £500 in her will, along with a letter apologising for her family's treatment of him: during his one visit to their home, he was mocked by Veronica's drink-flushed father and insultingly patronised by her brother; only Mrs Ford was welcoming.

This unexpected bequest should also have included, Tony discovers to his further bewilderment, the diary of his one-time school-friend, Adrian Finn, who took up with Veronica after she and Tony parted, and sometime later, while a star philosophy student at Cambridge, committed suicide. Eager to read the diary (and discover how it came into Mrs Ford's hands), Tony tracks down Veronica, who has commandeered it. Even more acridly brusque than before, she grudgingly yields him one photocopied page of it. Another photocopy – of a vindictive letter he wrote to Adrian about Veronica – follows. Trying to unearth what lies behind it all, Tony, a history graduate and keen member of his local history society, finds himself embroiled in history painfully close to home.

A dexterously crafted narrative of unlooked-for consequences, *The Sense of an Ending* increasingly takes on the momentum of a taut horror tale: a twenty-first-century successor to the suspense novellas – quivering not just with tension but with psychological, emotional and moral reverberations – of late Victorian and Edwardian masters such as Joseph Conrad, Henry James and Robert Louis Stevenson. Coincidentally, it shares its title and some of its concerns with a work that Barnes later declared he 'hadn't heard of . . . let alone read': Frank Kermode's classic 1967 literary critical book about 'the play of consciousness over history' and the urge to impose reassuring patterns on it. As Tony's consciousness, stirred by revelations and realisations, plays over his own history, the novel's title acquires a significance of its own. This is a story, it becomes apparent, about making sense of one particular ending – Adrian's slitting of his wrists – and of Tony's lacerated recognition of his contribution to that tragedy and others.

Like much of Barnes's later writing, *The Sense of an Ending* is also about making sense of the ending of life: coming to terms with mortality and its intimations. In 2002, he published the first English translation of Alphonse Daudet's stoically lucid journal of his terminal illness, *In the Land of Pain*. His short stories in *The Lemon Table* (2004) dealt with ageing and death. His 2008 memoir, *Nothing to Be Frightened Of*, offered non-fictional reflections on decease. His short story collection, *Pulse* (2011), focused on failing senses and the inroads of moribundity. Suffused with reference to deteriorating and defective memory, *The Sense of an Ending* continues this concern. Toll taken by the passing years is wryly registered. There's attention to 'learning the new emotions that time brings'.

In Tony, time also awakens belated emotions. His story which begins, like Barnes's first novel *Metroland* (1980), in a milieu of self-consciously bright sixth formers, progresses from that world of subversive flippancy to recognition of the sobering ironies time can effect. Retrospectively, pity for victims of life's cruel complications is felt as Tony recalls the callow inadequacy with which he and his friends responded to a classmate's suicide after getting his girlfriend pregnant, and later to Adrian's killing himself. Persisting Barnes themes – cleverness and its limitations, injury caused by jealousy and rivalry – are again highlighted. As in *Flaubert's Parrot* (1984) and *A History of the World in 10½ Chapters*, and his novels consisting of contrasting monologues of personal justification, *Talking It Over* (1991) and *Love, etc.* (2000), varying viewpoints exhibit the difficulty of interpreting past events. Origins of other things besides the First World War are sought for but usually remain ambiguous. Injury inflicted early in life – 'damage a long way back' – is recurrently mooted, with the strong suspicion that, in Veronica's case, this may have taken the form of paternal sexual abuse. Uncovering, link by link, an appalling chain reaction of briefly wished-for revenge, almost accidental damage, and remorse which agonisingly bites after most of a lifetime, the work is a sombre tale rich in humane resonances.

It's also a tale which intertwines themes that, as we have seen, suffuse modern fiction. Tony isn't the only historian in the book. Its opening scene takes place in a classroom where a history teacher, discussing the origins of the First World War with his sixth formers, outlines problems of historical investigation such as 'the question of subjective versus objective interpretation, the fact that we need to know the history of the historian in order to understand the version that is being put in front of us'. Adrian quotes a definition of history as 'that certainty produced at the point where the imperfections of memory meet the inadequacies of documentation'. Inadequate documentation is central to Tony's quest to make sense of Adrian's suicide, Veronica's behaviour and the mysterious bequest. The imperfections of memory are emphasised throughout the book, which is packed with reminders of it: 'what you end up remembering isn't always the same as what you have witnessed', 'Was this their exact exchange? Almost certainly not. Still, it is my best memory of their exchange', 'Again, I must stress that this is ... my memory now of my reading then of what was happening at the time.'

Failures of Memory: Kazuo Ishiguro and Peter Carey

The fallibility of memory is something that modern fiction never lets you forget. In ways less subtle than those deployed by Barnes, thrillers use it to ratchet up tension. Failures of memory – due to alcoholism (*The Girl on the Train*, 2015), a car accident (*Remember Me?*, 2008), Alzheimer's or senile dementia (*Elizabeth Is Missing*, 2014) – puts characters in deadly jeopardy. Resurgence of repressed memory can be even more perilous, as a wife suffering from retrograde amnesia (which leaves her unable to retain memories for more than a day) finds in S.J. Watson's bestselling novel, *Before I Go to Sleep* (2011), a modish variant on the 'gaslighting' motif of melodrama. Martin Amis's *Other People* (1981) took total amnesia – a young woman awakes in hospital apparently with no recollection of who she is or any knowledge of the world around her – as the basis for an exercise in defamiliarisation that aimed to emulate in prose Craig Raine's 'Martian' poetry techniques: planes are 'crucifixes' in a sky where clouds are 'fat white creatures', an old-fashioned telephone seems a 'bandy, glistening dumb-bell'. But the technique was only intermittently sustained. Margaret Atwood's brief, affecting piece about decayed memory, 'The Labrador Fiasco' (1996), achieved far more resonance in a few pages. As an account of a doomed 1903 expedition into the Canadian wilderness is read to the narrator's stroke-impaired father, once a naturalist skilled at wilderness survival, she is poignantly aware of how the geographical disorientation that led to the explorers' deaths parallels his mental disorientation.

A whole strange landscape of amnesia is brought into view in Kazuo Ishiguro's *The Buried Giant* (2015), a novel in which haze is the norm. Icy fogs and dank mists hang over a Dark Ages Britain from which the Romans have long departed. Vestiges of former civilisation and splendour – sturdy roads reduced to rubble, a ruined villa with wrecked, once-fine mosaic floors – are glimpsed through the prevailing murk. Across this blighted terrain, an elderly couple, Axl and Beatrice, make a journey in search of their lost son. Both are afflicted by a malaise of memory loss that shrouds the nation. Their personal forgetfulness – inability to recollect almost anything about their son or darker episodes in their long years of marriage – merges into a tactically cultivated forgetfulness that holds the country loosely together: Saxons and Britons bank down memories of their near-genocidal battles in earlier times. While this 'buried giant' stays unrecalled, a precarious peace holds. Amid imaginative terrain populated with the personnel of fantasy fiction – ogres, dragons, evil monks, crones, a ferryman to the isle of the dead – and legendary figures such as a triumphant Beowulf brandishing a marsh-monster's head or a superannuated Sir Gawain on his last quest, Ishiguro unrolls a part-fabular, part-allegorical display of the necessities and perils of deliberate forgetfulness within relationships and between previously warring groups.

In similar fantasy fiction mode, Philip Pullman's *La Belle Sauvage* (2017), the first volume of his *The Book of Dust* trilogy, contains an episode that seems a homage to *The Buried Giant*. Swept along the swollen Thames in a canoe after Oxford and its surroundings have been inundated by a flood, a boy and girl encounter a submerged giant who enlightens them about a location they have drifted past. In its glowingly illuminated gardens, elegant evening-dressed figures strolled among flowers and fountains as waltz music beguilingly

wafted from a ballroom. On the opposite bank of a river the immac-
ulately tended lawns sloped down to was thick fog – which, the boy
later discovers, obscures 'a wilderness of broken buildings, burned
houses, heaps of rubble, crude shanties made of shattered plywood
and tar-paper, coils of rusty barbed wire, puddles of filthy water
whose surfaces gleamed with the toxic shimmer of chemical waste,
where children with sores on their arms and legs were throwing
stones at a dog tied to a post'. The paradise-like garden is, the giant
informs the youngsters, 'the place where people go when they forget'.
On the other side, 'That fog's hiding everything they ought to
remember. If it ever cleared away, they'd have to take stock of themselves, and they wouldn't be able to stay in the garden.'

Cultivated obliviousness – suppression of uncomfortable memories and awkward facts – is treated less allegorically in Peter Carey's
Amnesia (2014). In it, his fascination with outsiders – felons, fugi-
tives, misfits – coalesces with another persisting concern: political
skulduggery – in particular, secret American machinations in
Australia. Prior to this book, Carey's most extensive fictional response
to undercover American interference had been *The Unusual Life of
Tristan Smith* (1994), his extravagant fantasia in which Voorstand, a
superpower skilled at manipulating other nations to its own ideological and economic ends, was seen holding antipodean Efica in a
surreptitious imperial grip. *Amnesia* roots its return to the subject in
factuality. Felix, its hero, is a crusading left-wing journalist whose
special subject is the 'traumatic injury' done to Australia 'by our
American allies in 1975'. The CIA-engineered coup that overthrew
Gough Whitlam's popular, progressive Socialist government in that
year has, Felix laments, shamefully 'passed from mind', become part
of Australia's 'Great Amnesia' about its relationship to America.

What re-kindles interest in that relationship, in Carey's novel, is
the release of a virus into computerised security systems in Australian
and American jails, freeing large numbers of prisoners. Unexpectedly,
Felix finds himself pulled into the ensuing firestorm of fury. Charged

with terrorist offences against the US, the hacker turns out to be Gaby Baillieux, the daughter of friends of his from student days – Sando, now a Labour MP, and Celine, his actress wife. To help Gaby, who has gone on the run, a wealthy acquaintance of theirs commissions Felix to write a sympathetic book about her.

This commission provides the starting-point for one of Carey's bravura twisty narratives. Felix is transported by devious routes to a shack hidden in a mangrove swamp. Here, sorting through a jumble of papers, tapes and cassettes, he assembles an account of Gaby and her family history. At its centre is what he sees as long-continuing covert conflict between Australia and America. Celine, he learns, was conceived as a result of happenings during a hushed-up bloody battle between Australian and American troops in Brisbane in 1942. With further neatness, Gaby was born just as the Whitlam government was toppled in 1975. Uncovering a plethora of past and present political and corporate malpractice in Australia, the novel sizzles with accusatory indignation at repression and falsification of memory on a national scale.

Hard-to-maintain communal amnesia in the Balkans, after the bloody fracturing of Yugoslavia in the 1990s, was the subject of *The Hired Man* (2013) by Aminatta Forna, whose previous novel, *The Memory of Love* (2010), had focused on survivors amid the aftermath of civil war in Sierra Leone. As a local handyman restores a semi-derelict house a comfortably-off English family have bought as a holiday home in a Croatian village, a mosaic that has been whitewashed-over returns to view and re-awakens memories of murderous atrocities wreaked by ethnic enmities. Having started as what seemed a comedy of culture clash – pampered well-heeled incomers blundering into a tight-lipped community rife with mystifying animosities – the novel moves into darker, more ambiguous territory. The re-emergence of the mosaic (like the uncovered medieval Doom painting, excavated bog cadavers and exhumed ancient weaponry in other novels about past and present violence) serves as a vivid reminder of the hells that humans can create. Like many modern novelists, Forna (whose father fell victim to political strife in Sierra Leone) explores the after-effects of these hells: post-conflict coexistence among once savagely opposed groups; communities precariously, and resentfully, balanced on latent ethnic hatreds and cruel memories it has been found politic to suppress.

Childhood Harm and Creativity: Margaret Atwood

Memory – 'the great sustaining ballast', as Penelope Lively calls it – can sometimes seem almost tangible in modern fiction ('a new lump of memory detaches itself from the frozen forgotten backward stretches, and bumps downstream into the light', Margaret Drabble reports in one novel). Almost obsessively dwelt on, it is variously presented as liberating, imprisoning, motivating, paralysing, stultifying or invigorating. Often depicted as destructive, it can alternatively – and sometimes simultaneously – nourish creativity, as two novels, Margaret Atwood's *Cat's Eye* (1988) and Ian McEwan's *Atonement* (2001), demonstrate.

In an autobiographical essay, Atwood recounted how accident victims clutching severed bits of themselves – fingers, ears, noses, thumbs – used to turn up at the house of her grandfather, a country doctor. From the anorexic heroine of her first novel, *The Edible Woman* (1969), to the emotionally maimed Elizabeth in *Life Before Man* (1979), the physically and psychologically scarred Rennie in *Bodily Harm* (1981), the traumatised Offred of *The Handmaid's Tale* (1985), the trio of betrayed friends in *The Robber Bride* (1993) and the jailed murderess in *Alias Grace* (1996), a not dissimilar procession of damaged women have filed through her fiction. *Cat's Eye* is no exception to this concern with casualties. Its subject is a woman whose career as a painter stems from harm inflicted during childhood. Elaine Risley recollects that as a girl she thought the word 'gifted' sounded 'like vaccinated, something that is done to you and leaves a mark'.

Endorsing this, the novel uncovers the experience that both scarred her emotionally and inoculated her with the germ of her art.

Returning to Toronto for a retrospective exhibition of her paintings, Elaine, now an acclaimed artist nearing fifty, finds herself simultaneously holding a private retrospective of her life. What stimulates this is the transformation she sees in a city she once knew well but has avoided for many years. The dowdy preserve of provincial puritans when she was a girl, Toronto has metamorphosed into a glitzy metropolis of neon and chic boutiques frequented by pouty androgynes in black leather with gelled haircuts. Flashbacks illuminate tableaux of its former ways of life: post-war living rooms with their maroon upholstery and large, dark-varnished radios; the colonial classrooms of the 1940s where children were taught to draw the Union Jack, 'using a ruler and memorising the various crosses'; 'bachelorette' apartments for 'career girls' in buildings with names like 'The Monte Carlo'; dimly lit 1950s beer parlours segregated into 'men only' and 'ladies and escort' sections.

In the foreground of this cavalcade of social change is the story of Elaine's mutation from cheery outdoor child to tense introspective artist. Swivelling the novel in the opposite direction to that taken by her preceding one, *The Handmaid's Tale*, a futurist fable about social tyranny imposed by political patriarchy, Atwood presents an intensely individual, backwards-looking story in which the oppressors are little girls.

In an early childhood much resembling Atwood's own, Elaine enjoys a happy open-air life, travelling with her family around the Ontario countryside where her naturalist father collects data about insect life. This wandering, bucolic existence means she is inexperienced at making friends with other girls when the family eventually settles in Toronto. With the arrival at her school of Cordelia – precociously self-assured, slightly odd-seeming – awkwardness escalates into nightmare. Like other Atwood heroines before and after, Elaine undergoes trial by ordeal.

142

Backed up by her allies, censorious Grace and giggly Carol, Cordelia inflicts a regime of psychological bullying on Elaine. Remorselessly, this grows from schoolgirl bossiness into sadistic mental torture that leaves its victim miserably gnawing the skin from her lips, vomiting and fainting. Adding to the ugliness is young Elaine's discovery that the persecution is being conducted with the collusion of Grace's fiercely evangelical mother, Mrs Smeath, who self-righteously sees it as God's chastisement for the atheism of Elaine's parents.

Curdled rectitude often wafts its sour odour through Atwood's fiction. In *The Handmaid's Tale* it permeated the atmosphere of an entire society. Largely as a result of it, the young Elaine almost dies after being coerced to climb down into a snowy ravine. It's an incident with chilling after-effects. One of the many folklore and fairy-tale elements worked into the novel has Elaine surviving, but with a splinter of ice in her heart – and her art. Something hard and cold and sharp is left embedded in her personality and painting. She retreats into a life lived mainly through her eyes: stiffly determined to give nothing of herself away while transfixing others with her acute vision.

For Elaine, the painter's eye is often like the evil eye. Her pictures of scenes from her past offer a means of revenging herself on Mrs Smeath and her like. In the middle of the constellation of eye images glinting from the book is that of the 'cat's-eye'. A child's marble which Elaine has kept as a talisman, this glassy orb streaked with webs of colour resembles, she feels, the eye of an alien, gazing with affectless, outsider perceptiveness at the world.

The effects of Elaine's alienation are traced with trenchancy and ruefulness. In some of the more sardonic scenes, where she casts a cold clear eye over present and past styles and assumptions, it can seem a source of strength. At other times, you are made aware of what she has been deprived of. Surprisingly, this turns out to include rapport with Cordelia. After a while, you learn, the two drifted together again and became adolescent allies. As they grow up, the damaged personality behind Cordelia's behaviour (paternal abuse as so often in contemporary fiction is the main suspect) becomes more and more apparent. When last seen, she is a bloated inmate in a mental home, whose appeal for help Elaine is icily ignoring.

Skilfully, *Cat's Eye* keeps altering its field of vision. From peering into the ambiguous recesses of the personality or scrutinising the phases of a woman's life, it expands into surveying the contours of a culture or ominous global patterns. The aesthetic and the scientific elegantly interact. Elaine's training and career fill the narrative with specimens of different types of art and their overt and covert purposes. Zoological references, brought in by her father's profession, never let the book's view of humanity stray far from the natural world and its imperatives. Theories of time and space expatiated on by her scientist brother open dizzying perspectives. Recalling his comments about the galaxies and their gleaming though long-dead stars, Elaine reflects of a moonless, starry night, 'It's old light, and there's not much of it. But it's enough to see by.' It's a moment perfectly in keeping with *Cat's Eye*'s sombre brilliance.

Childhood Harm and Creativity: Ian McEwan

In Atwood's novel, harm done in childhood spurs artistic creativity. In Ian McEwan's *Atonement*, harm is done by an artistically creative child, who subsequently devotes a long literary career to trying to make amends. Taking you into the world of a country house situated amid handsomely landscaped grounds, the novel begins with a leisurely expansiveness unexpected from McEwan. It is the hottest day of the hot summer of 1935. Thirteen-year-old Briony Tallis, feverish with literary ambition, has just written a play for family performance. As she tinkers with this juvenile production, the cast for a grimmer real-life drama (in which Briony will be both author and crucial actor) assemble around her. Prominent among them are her precocious cousin Lola, not yet sixteen; her brother and his guest, a thrustful confectionery tycoon; and, just down from Cambridge, her sister Cecilia, moodily preoccupied with Robbie Turner, the son of one of their domestics, whose brilliant undergraduate career (also at Cambridge) the family has funded. With Mr Tallis absent as usual in Whitehall, control of this fateful house party is in the ineffectual hands of sickly Mrs Tallis.

It might almost be a novel by Elizabeth Bowen. From its mock-Gothic façade to its artificial lake and island with an imitation Greek temple, the big house and its estate are rendered in confident detail. Light effects are luminously captured: the 'filtered orange glow' of the sultry evening sky hanging over the park, the 'soupy yellow glow' seeping through fake-parchment lampshades. In keeping with the 1930s fictional ambience too, the influence of Virginia Woolf is constantly perceptible: the narrative flows in and out of differing consciousnesses; a disastrous roast meat dinner fed to sweltering guests parodies the triumphant serving up of *boeuf en daube* in *To the Lighthouse*.

Instead of the dramatic shock-start to a novel that he had often favoured (the lightning-fast abducting of a child, a death-plunge from a helium balloon), McEwan here opts for a slow, suffocating build-up of tension. Catastrophe approaches like an initially distant thundercloud. Elements notable in his earlier fiction – premature inductions into adulthood, sexual turbulence, ranklings of class resentment – coalesce as it explodes. Engrossed not just by damage but its aftermath, McEwan then gradually lays bare the lifelong repercussions of this traumatic night.

In a way that initially seems surprising, his book's next two sections turn from violence and outrage within a house party to panoramas of wider devastation. Only glancingly anticipated in the 1935 scenes (a casual joke about stroppy Mr Hitler, family boredom at Mr Tallis's work in 'Eventuality Planning' for civilian protection and mass-evacuation), war now becomes central. Often drawn to ravaged landscapes (bomb-shattered Berlin in *The Innocent*, the scarred

Languedoc in *Black Dogs*), the novel follows Robbie, exhausted and with a shrapnel wound festering in his chest, across northern France to the Dunkirk beaches. Then the book jumps back over the Channel to watch Briony, guilt-ridden at her role in earlier events, training as a nurse in London in the eerie lull before the Blitz.

Both sections are immeasurably the most powerful that McEwan, already a master of nerve-tingling suspense and flesh-crawling horror, had so far written. As Robbie limps past surreal tableaux of defeat – Allied troops smashing their vehicles and armaments before retreat, French cavalry ceremonially slaughtering their horses, padres doing their bit by incinerating Bibles – he is rocked by near-miss bomb blasts and strafed by machine-gun fire from diving Stukas. The hospital ward sequences uncover hideous injuries with unflinching, delicate precision. But, modulated and nuanced, the novel doesn't restrict itself to intense emotion. A ghastly account of bone-weary nurses struggling round the clock to staunch the agonies of terribly mutilated refugees from Dunkirk is immediately followed by a preening letter ('there is much to do in this office') from Cyril Connolly to Briony about a novella she has submitted to his magazine. Typifying McEwan's refusal to simplify or caricature, this self-importance goes along with real critical acumen. Connolly's comments on the novella are shrewd.

Subtle as well as powerful, adeptly encompassing comedy as well as atrocity, *Atonement* is richly intricate. Unshowy symmetries and patterns underlie its emotional force and psychological compulsion. A rape takes place outside a mock-Greek temple; later, a wedding occurs in a church resembling one. Briony's childish playlet ironically prefigures later adult scenarios. As a novelist, she shares her father's professional concern with 'Eventuality Planning' and has affinities with her grandfather, a locksmith who made the family fortune by patenting devices that mesh together and enclose.

Literary allusions branch like capillaries through *Atonement*. Cecilia reads *Clarissa*, Samuel Richardson's tale of rape and attempted amends. In a Cambridge production of *Twelfth Night*, Robbie played Malvolio, the man from below stairs whose upwardly mobile aspirations are cruelly thwarted. The novel's epigraph comes from *Northanger Abbey*, Jane Austen's comedy of misplaced suspicions that lead to shame; in a 1999 coda to *Atonement*'s narrative, the country house is now a hotel called Tilney's (the name of Northanger Abbey's owners). Elsewhere, faithful to the 1930s décor, references to T.S. Eliot, D.H. Lawrence and the like proliferate.

All this accords with the book's main subject. Though graphic in its depiction of the horrors of war, it is the dangers of the literary imagination that it scrutinises most piercingly. The instinct for order (so important in the army, Robbie finds; so beneficial in the hospital, Briony discovers) proves of more ambiguous effect when the artistic temperament impinges on life's confusions. Throughout sixty years as a writer, Briony seeks to rectify a 'crime' she perpetrated in 1935 because of the impulses that later made her a distinguished novelist: a desire to tidy up actuality into satisfying forms, a readiness to pry into privacies, a willingness to dramatise, a need for attention and approval. Boldly, McEwan's closing pages (after he has used just three words to pivot everything into a new perspective) leave you unsure whether her final attempt at atonement is an act of restitution or a last instance of self-interested manipulation. Whatever equivocations cling around Briony's behaviour, though, there's no doubt about McEwan's masterly achievement in this book which combines a dazzling display of the powers of the imagination with an acute interrogation of them.

Intelligence enthrals McEwan. No novelist has explored and employed it more keenly. Mindsets of varying kinds fascinate him. *Saturday* (2005), his novel about rationality and unreason, takes its readers into the mind of a neurosurgeon who routinely probes the hemispheres of the brain, scrutinising its lobes and fissures as he excises tumours, extracts blood clots and clears blockages. *Solar* (2010) focuses on the thought processes of a Nobel Prize-winning physicist. The legalistic reasoning of a High Court judge is central to *The Children Act* (2014). *Sweet Tooth* (2012) juxtaposes the – sometimes contrasting, sometimes complementary – casts of mind of the fiction writer and the spy. *Machines Like Me* (2019), one of whose central figures is a robot, explores artificial intelligence. In its alternative world, Alan Turing, who has survived to make trailblazing advances in the possibilities of 'machine consciousness', observes: 'How wondrous a thing the brain is. A one-litre, liquid-cooled, three-dimensional computer. Unbelievable processing power, unbelievably compressed, unbelievable energy efficiency, no overheating. The whole thing running on 25 watts – one dim light bulb.' *Atonement*, arguably the finest of McEwan's fictional explorations of what the brain can do and why, shows how mental predispositions – can form and deform a lifetime.

Damage done by and to children – teenage incest, sexual molestation of pre-pubescents, drownings of youngsters by deranged adults – is copiously on display in the two short story collections, *In Between the Sheets* (1975) and *First Love, Last Rites* (1978), with which McEwan began his literary career. Sometimes bedecked with jauntily callous titles – 'Homemade' (a teenage incest story), 'Dead as They Come' (simultaneous rape and murder) – these early pieces are written with calculatedly disturbing calmness. Nervelessness aims to unnerve. When not being molested, their juvenile protagonists can be hustled into prematurely adult life: as in McEwan's first novel, *The Cement Garden* (1978), where siblings are caught in a ghastly parody of grown-up existence. Weird kinks in the continuum between childhood and maturity enthralled McEwan in the opening phase of his career (and were returned to with far more substantiality and acumen in his 2022 novel *Lessons*, where a boy at boarding school is seduced into an intensely sexual and possessive affair with a disturbed young woman who is his piano teacher). A character in one story is kept as a baby in a cupboard until his late teens by his mad mother. Simile constantly endows the chic couple holidaying in Venice in

The Comfort of Strangers (1981) with childlike attributes. Like most children in McEwan's early fiction, they come to grief: an older pair entrap them and maul the young man to death throughout a night of sexual torture. With his imagination seemingly wedged on an adolescent-like cusp, McEwan's callowly unfeeling first books appeared to be instances of arrested development themselves.

What showed a significant advance from this and marked the start of one of modern British fiction's most impressive careers was *The Child in Time* (1987). Childhood vulnerability was again in evidence. But the loss of a three-year-old daughter at the heart of this narrative isn't just a frisson in a slickly affectless tale. It unleashes a desolation that almost kills a marriage. Notably, too, the novel isn't only about a missing child (though the heart-thumping crescendo of mounting panic as the little girl is searched for after being snatched from a supermarket is one of McEwan's most gripping feats of controlled, high-intensity writing). A missed childhood is part of its pattern too: in an intertwined subplot, a middle-aged man denied a proper child-hood succumbs to a psychosis that has him living in a tree-house, reading books such as *Just William*, and romping like a ten-year-old in short trousers, his pockets crammed with humbugs, marbles, a catapult and a dead newt. In the soulless near-future world the book envisages, a government manual advocates a heavily authoritarian approach to childcare. By the time McEwan came to write his next alternative-future novel, *Machines Like Me*, the need to rescue a young boy at risk, played a decisive role in the conflict between humane and artificial intelligence. Intervening novels – *Atonement*, *On Chesil Beach*, *The Children Act* – variously contemplated the vulnerability of the young to emotional or psychological scarring.

Scars: Keri Hulme and J.K. Rowling

Physical scars have long featured in literature: the scar on Odysseus' thigh from a childhood boar hunt that enabled his old nurse to recognise him on his return to Ithaca after the Trojan War; the livid mark imprinted on the bald forehead of *Vanity Fair*'s lecherous Lord Steyne by the diamond brooch flung at him by Becky Sharp's outraged husband, who had ripped it from her dress after catching them together; Rosa Dartle's scarred lip in *David Copperfield* testimony both to the destructiveness of Steerforth (who inflicted it by throwing a hammer at her in their youth) and to her damaged personality. But where such earlier literary scars have individual significance, those that stand out in modern fiction are more likely to be generic, the result of widespread types of violence, oppression and maltreatment: the war wounds on soldiers mutilated in the First and Second World Wars that numerous novels have focused on; the welts on Black slaves such as the savagely flogged Sethe in Toni Morrison's *Beloved*, or on the soles of tyrannised women in the patriarchal theocracy of Margaret Atwood's *The Handmaid's Tale*; the scar that sectarian shooting in Belfast leaves on Stella in Bernard MacLaverty's *Midwinter Break*; the lash-seamed backs of convicts such as Peter Carey's Jack Maggs, and other victims of colonial and penal injustice; the weals from beatings in abusive childhoods like those left on Carey's protagonists in *A Long Way From Home*, and on Jaxie, the battered teenager whose trek to safety across the sun-baked saltlands of Western Australia Tim Winton's *The Shepherd's Hut* (2018) depicts with searing immediacy.

Hurt children have figured prominently in modern fiction. Large-scale child abuse of a phantasmagoric kind is the nightmarish horror at the centre of one of the most celebrated accomplishments of twentieth-century young adult literature, Philip Pullman's *His Dark Materials* trilogy: *Northern Lights* (1995), *The Subtle Knife* (1997) and *The Amber Spyglass* (2000). In an alternative universe where children are psychically and emotionally linked to external manifestations of their inner selves known as 'daemons', the Magisterium, a malign theocracy representing religion at its most viciously repressive, aims to cut off these connections. 'Intercision', a guillotine-like procedure, severs youngsters from their vitalising spirits. Those who survive this excruciating process (a surreal version of the stultifying educational regimes scathingly satirised by Victorian novelists like Dickens in novels such as *Hard Times*) are left cowed and stunted husks, devoid of curiosity, originality, freedom of thought, humane empathy and capacity for pleasure and affection.

One of the most harrowingly portrayed victims of child abuse in modern fiction appears in the New Zealand novelist Keri Hulme's *The Bone People*. Routinely cited as a prime example of an absurdly unworthy winner of the Booker Prize (which it was awarded in 1985), Hulme's novel is in fact a remarkable achievement, one in which scars and silences are put to powerful effect. Dominating its story are three characters, each in some way cut off from life. Kerewin Holmes, who first comes to the fore, is a part-Maori artist. Estranged from her family and now alienated from her talent, she lives in a tower she has built – with her half-ironic, half-serious relish for symbols – on a lonely seashore of New Zealand's South Island. Exotic bibelots and choice bits of bizarrerie decorate its rooms: an antique crucifix, jade, lacquer, porcelain, curious fungi and bonsai trees. All this is gradually revealed as just an ornate casing for emotional vulnerability. The tower is not, as it first seems, a fairy-tale-like emblem of resplendent self-sufficiency but a protective shell.

Kerewin has another defensive layer too: the jauntily unfeeling manner she has cultivated as a hide for her sensitivity. Much of the book is about the piercing of this by two people she is thrown into contact with: Joe, a Maori workman, and his mute autistic stepson, Simon. One of the novel's many re-workings of literary precedents shows Kerewin's isolation broken when – as in a parody of *Robinson Crusoe* – she finds not a footprint on her deserted shore but a child's sandal, discarded because a large splinter has gouged through its heel. True to the book's concern with the pain and benefit that can follow from the penetrating of protective layers, this launches Kerewin – whose surname Holmes isn't without aptness – on a trail of discovery

151

about herself, the shoeless silent boy who has limped into her life, and the man who is struggling to look after him. Soon, she spots the intelligence banked behind the child's autism, and the vulnerability underlying his tough manner.

Then, she is shocked to discover that Simon hasn't only metaphorically developed a thick skin. Keloid tissue covers much of his body, welted and scarred by repeated belt-blows from Joe. With delicate unflinchingness, the novel brings out what lies behind this abuse. All the disgusting horror of the battering of the child is unsparingly conveyed; simultaneously, Hulme registers the pressures that twist Joe – generally loving and almost neurotically concerned in his attitude to Simon – into fits of frenzy. Physical damage, especially in the form of fractured bones, is widespread in the book. Other kinds of injury are probed as well: the psychological harm Joe's past has dealt out to him, the way Kerewin unleashes the worst violence by flaying Simon with words.

Despite its documenting of breakings-up and breakings-down, *The Bone People* is ultimately a story of integration. As its central trio knit together into a bond of support and dependence, it demonstrates the need for links: with other people, with all aspects of the self, and with the past. Backed by allusion to Maori lore about 'bone people' – the name for kinsfolk and figures of fruitfulness – it stands as a reminder of the creative powers generated by human interconnection and overcoming scars and silences.

In less intense mode, one other fictional wound – of almost stigmata-like significance – should be mentioned. The most famous scar in modern literature is the one on Harry Potter's forehead. Its zig-zag shape has caused controversy among J.K. Rowling fans as to whether it depicts a lightning-bolt or is a representation of the hand movement necessary to transmit the deadly Avada Kedavra Killing Curse. Whatever the case, it has proved a very versatile cicatrice: an early warning system that throbs when danger looms, a mark of specialness, a device that bugs the brain of evil Lord Voldemort, a medium for telepathic communication and, ultimately, the crucial element in resolving the series' intricately complicated plot. Rowling originally intended, she has said, to end the final novel in her sequence, *Harry Potter and the Deathly Hallows* (2007), with the word 'scar'. In the event, in a flash-forward to Harry's adulthood, the closing words became 'The scar had not pained Harry for nineteen years. All was well.' A richly deserved peaceful retirement for a physical feature that had served such a multi-purpose role in her pages.

Unvoiced Lives: Sarah Waters

One of the ugliest archaeological finds in modern fiction surfaces in Stevie Davies' novel, *Impassioned Clay* (1999). Dug up from the garden of a centuries-old Cheshire house, it dates back to the Civil War and wears a 'brank' or 'scold's bridle' – the instrument of punitive reproof designed to cage a recalcitrant woman's head in iron bands and, with its spiked metal 'tongue', mutilate her mutinous mouth and break her teeth and stubborn jaw. Olivia, who as a teenager witnessed the unearthing of this hideously muzzled skeleton, resolves, after becoming an academic historian, to discover who the victim was and give posthumous voice to her horribly silenced story. Herself an outspoken lesbian from a Quaker background, she is excited when research reveals the woman to have been a seventeenth-century kindred spirit, a Quaker rebel who, along with her female lover, boldly and disastrously challenged the forces of reaction.

Restoring presence and giving voice to communities suppressed or occluded in the past has been a widespread mission in modern fiction. Postcolonial literature has extensively recuperated cultures smothered by imperialism and foregrounded those stifled by it. Signalling his aim to rectify this, the Nigerian writer Chigozie Obioma took as an epigraph for his novel, *An Orchestra of Minorities* (2019), an Igbo proverb: 'If the prey do not produce their version of the tale, the predators will always be the heroes in the stories of the hunt.' Toni Morrison, who declared in an interview 'What was driving me to write was the silence – so many stories untold and unexamined', spoke feelingly of a hideous implement, '*the bit* . . . put into the mouth of slaves to punish them and shut them up without preventing them from working'. Slavery's equivalent to the scold's bridle, it features in *Beloved* – like the 'brank' in Davies' novel – as a monstrously stark manifestation of the desire to control and silence.

Suppressed female voices have increasingly been made audible in modern fiction. In parallel, there has been a drive to recover concealed or shunned lives of sexual minorities. Where forgetting has been seen as an affliction to be regretted, being forgotten has been seen as an injustice to be remedied. In a period when wounds and silence have been central fictional concerns, silence on some matters has been regarded as wounding.

A writer who has responded with impressive versatility to this urge to recuperate the excluded and unearth the buried is Sarah Waters (who, like many modern novelists, originally wanted to be an archaeologist). Her first three books looked back from contrasting angles at different decades of the Victorian age. *Tipping the Velvet* (1998) brought a jaunty music-hall swagger to its story of a young lesbian's escapades in the 1880s. *Affinity* (1999) gave resonances reminiscent of Emily Dickinson or Henry James to a haunting tale of spinsters and spiritualists in the 1870s. *Fingersmith* (2002) plunged into the lurid realm of the 1860s sensation novel. Chock-a-block with melodrama – a jeopardised heiress, incarceration in a madhouse, a sinister isolated mansion, false identities, arrant villainy – it paid florid homage to the Wilkie Collins of *The Woman in White*.

With *The Night Watch* (2006), Waters advanced into new historical territory. This time, the setting is the 1940s, and her fascination with what has gone before shows itself even in the novel's structure. Opening in 1947, the narrative moves back through sections set in

1944 and 1941 to uncover what has brought its central characters to their later situations.

Excavation of casualties from bombed buildings features vividly in the story. Excavation of another kind has always been Waters' principal concern as a novelist. Disclosing buried lesbian lives, existences scarcely glimpsed in nineteenth-century fiction, motivates her Victorian novels. In *The Night Watch*, she spotlights covert, mainly homosexual lives in the 1940s, then delves back to expose the happenings that have shaped and intertwined them.

Events start just after the Second World War. London is still a shaky sprawl of wreckage but echoes to the sound of rebuilding. At Lavender Hill, upper-class Kay, a mannish shirt-and-trousers lesbian lodging in grimy rented rooms, watches damaged individuals seeking to be cured by her faith-healer landlord. Off Bond Street, Helen and Viv run a marriage bureau offering repairings of another sort to those the war has deprived of a partner. In White City, Viv's nervy brother Duncan works in a factory set up to rehabilitate the physically and psychologically injured. Everywhere, the atmosphere is one of weariness and wariness shot through with flickers of anticipation about revived opportunities and new directions.

Wheeling back from this fatigued milieu to 1944, the novel erupts into scenes of high-adrenaline intensity: a scary trek across the shattered hinterland of St Paul's under heavy bombing, panic in prison cells during an endless-seeming air raid ('like being trapped in a dustbin while someone beat on it with a bat'), rescue bids among smouldering ruins that suddenly flame up as if riddled by a giant poker. In this environment, Kay, sniggered at as an androgynous freak in peacetime, is in her element. One of the crew at an ambulance station largely staffed by fellow spirits, she routinely performs feats of bravery and resourcefulness. The courage, stamina, expertise and emotional control needed to drive, through hailstorms of shrapnel and debris, down nightmarishly potholed streets into the heart of an inferno where the mutilated and traumatised lie under rubble amid mangled bodies and dangerously teetering walls – all this is conveyed with pulsing immediacy. Simultaneously, the book's other characters face climactic urgencies and crises of their own.

Besides factual research, Waters was much assisted in the reconstruction of her vanished worlds by her habitual technique of pre-immersion in the literature of the period. With its solitaries and misfits trailing through shabby streetscapes, *The Night Watch*'s opening section recalls Patrick Hamilton's down-at-heel chroniclings of London in *Hangover Square* (1941) and *The Slaves of Solitude* (1947). A seedy dentist/abortionist whose botchings are near-fatal could have sidled in from a novel by Graham Greene. Elsewhere in the novel, the influence of Henry Green and Elizabeth Bowen is perceptible. Duncan is clearly modelled on the writer, Denton Welch. Recreating the look and sound and moods of the 1940s with uncanny exactness and only the rarest wobble into anachronism ('checking out the competition'), Waters brings her pages alive with people of a distinct era caught in believable predicaments.

Constraint and escape always play a significant role in her plots. A high proportion of her characters are pent up in jails (in *The Night Watch*, Wormwood Scrubs looms as large as Millbank Prison did in *Affinity*), trapped in locked rooms, asylums, hostile institutions, oppressive relationships and repressive circumstances. In *The Little Stranger* (2009), the imprisoning edifice is a haunted house, within which Waters seeks to revive a type of fiction that has struggled to survive in recent years: the ghost story. It's a genre that, despite its affinity with the currently vigorous literary impulse to conjure up the past, has seemed on its deathbed for some time. After its flesh-creeping prime in the Victorian period – the heyday of spine-chilling apparitions in lonely mansions, ancient inns, dark panelled rooms and gloomy graveyards that gave it an ideal imaginative eco-system – it has dwindled to a shadow of its former self. With religious scepticism stilling qualms about the afterlife, and modern amenities such as the electric lightbulb doing more to dispel the powers of darkness than the clove of garlic ever did, most modern tales of the supernatural are no great shakes at making you shiver. In *The Little Stranger*, Waters attempts to resuscitate the genre.

To do so, she returns to the exhausted England of 1947 when her previous book, *The Night Watch*, began. This time, the setting isn't bomb-shattered London but the depths of rural Warwickshire, where she puts in place traditional components of the ghost story. Increasingly unnerving phenomena manifest themselves in Hundreds Hall, a secluded Georgian gem whose centuries-old way of life is in terminal decay. Struggling to maintain their ancestral home in the inimical climate of austerity Britain, widowed Mrs Ayres and her children, Roderick and Caroline, subsist in surroundings of dilapidated splendour. Plaster sags from ornamental ceilings; watered silk wall coverings in gracefully proportioned rooms are ripped and patched; heirlooms have long gone to auction. These depredations prove as nothing, though, to the eerie ordeals that bedevil the family as the story proceeds.

True to the conventions of the genre, the narrator is that standby of the supernatural horror tale, a man of scientifically disposed bent whose rationality is nerve-tinglingly put to the test by uncanny happenings he witnesses. Faraday, the local doctor who fills this role, isn't only an observer. He is also, you gradually recognise, involved in what occurs. His opening remarks recall how, as a boy, he was taken to an Empire Day fete at Hundreds by his mother, once a nursery maid to its owners, the Ayres family. Marvelling at the handsome house, he was briefly allowed into it by a friendly servant and, when left unattended for a moment, snapped off a plaster acorn from a decorative frieze.

Showing a desire both to possess and damage, it's an act whose repercussions fork out decades later. A summons to the hall to attend to a sick servant girl brings Faraday, now a shabby, balding bachelor nearing forty, not very successful and, like many in his profession,

157

apprehensive about the imminent advent of the National Health Service, into contact with the Ayres family again. When he offers to provide therapy for injuries the severely scarred Roderick has received as a fighter pilot in the RAF, this contact draws closer. Assisting charming Mrs Ayres and plain, down-to-earth Caroline as well, he is soon occupying an ambiguous position somewhere between physician and friend.

Again displaying her flair for period evocation, Waters recreates backwater England just after the Second World War with atmospheric immediacy. Class assumptions, discomforts and resentments are adroitly captured in scenes where the Ayres family mingle with *nouveau riche* neighbours who have taken over properties vacated by bankrupt gentry. The way graciousness can slip to reveal underlying condescension and bred-in-the-bone snobbery is tellingly conveyed – particularly in episodes where the Ayreses are uncertain whether Faraday's frequenting of their home represents social encroachment or genuine helpfulness. As a fictional rendering of post-war disorientations and displacements, *The Little Stranger* is as acute and absorbing as the novels and stories of Elizabeth Taylor.

Where its grip slackens is when it strives to exert a macabre clutch. After ominous preliminaries (a servant girl's nerviness, a pet dog's unaccountable lapse into savagery), the plot escalates through inexplicable harassments (strange smudges on inaccessible stretches of ceiling, odd letters materialising on antique woodwork, dreadful noises gurgling from the speaking tube to the nursery where Mrs Ayres's most beloved child died of diphtheria) into conflagration and nightmarish calamities.

These occult horrors are attributed by Caroline to a poltergeist. Later, one of Faraday's colleagues holds forth in similar vein about a disturbed 'subliminal self' that can, unknown to its owner's conscious mind, 'break loose, detach itself, cross space, become visible to others'. Intimations as to who might be the source of this paranormal malignity intermittently surface in the story, and its final line clinches it.

But it would be an unusually trepidant reader whose blood ran cold at any of this. The book's ghost story apparatus merely seems a surreal heightening of its – much more compelling – naturalistic picture of post-war dislocation and change. Tension palpitates far more hauntingly in its social scenes. Nerves are plucked at to more unsettling effect as Faraday courts Caroline with gauche avidity. It's the conjuring up of a Zeitgeist, not a poltergeist, at which Waters' novel excels.

The Paying Guests (2014) continued her concern with the aftermath of war but, this time, an earlier one. Where *The Little Stranger* focused on a dilapidated Georgian mansion deep in the shires in 1947, this book focuses on a Regency villa in South London not long after the First World War. The year is 1922 and in their once well-to-do home on Champion Hill, a genteel enclave of Camberwell, Frances Wray and her widowed mother are apprehensively awaiting the arrival of lodgers (or 'paying guests' as Mrs Wray prefers to call them). Left in dire financial straits after the death of Mr Wray has revealed that he had squandered the family money, the two women brace themselves to welcome a young couple of 'the clerk class', Lilian and Leonard Barber, as lodgers. As a tradesman's van from Peckham disgorges the Barbers and their belongings, the Wrays flinch at their 'refined' elocution-school accents and watch with politely concealed dismay as worrying items – a gramophone, an ashtray on a chunky stand (Mrs Wray deplores smoking) – are carried into their sedate household.

The stage seems set for a satirical comedy of class collision, not unlike that in George Gissing's 1895 novella about social ructions in suburbia, *The Paying Guest*. Early scenes entertainingly provide this, especially a ripely funny one where Lilian's gaudy sisters and her mother, Mrs Viney, a game old Cockney with a 'jolly, throaty, hop-picker's voice', come over from the Walworth Road to inspect her new living quarters. Congratulating the Wrays on their spacious premises, Mrs Viney warmly assures them 'you could bring in trippers and do them teas'.

But as the novel progresses, emotion intensifies. Trapped into the role of stay-at-home spinster by her father's death and the loss of her two brothers during the war, twenty-six-year-old Frances develops, during shared housework and walks in the local park, a deepening rapport with Lilian. As the relationship gains in confidence, confidences are exchanged. To Lilian's initial shock, Frances tells her of a love affair with a suffragette friend, ended by her mother's discovery of a compromising letter. Lilian discloses that her marriage to Leonard, an insurance clerk full of cocky vitality, has its secrets. Inside the house on Champion Hill, class tremors are increasingly displaced by sexual stirrings.

Always superb at suspense, Waters draws you into a narrative that, while remaining agonisingly credible, is a masterly feat of twists and shifts. As in *Fingersmith*, her pastiche homage to the Victorian virtuoso of high-tension plotting, Wilkie Collins, events swivel into alarming new perspectives, but in this novel with deeper emotional substance. As the story progresses from frightened excitement through risky passion, calamitous mischance, violent death, terrified efforts to evade detection, and a brilliantly done murder trial at the Old Bailey, suspense rises to a pitch of high intensity. There are moments dank with horror: water poured into the mouth of what turns out to be a corpse just 'sat there like water in a vase'. Dramatic surprises keep nerves on edge until the last paragraph.

What adds to the grip of the plot is Waters' flair for involving you with her characters by making them engrossingly believable and complex. Frances's mixture of dutiful frustration and reckless impulsiveness is expertly caught, as is the way Lilian's taste for exotic bric-a-brac – Turkish slippers, a kimono – signals both thwarted artistic instincts and a slightly concubine-like disposition. You're made aware of pathos behind Leonard's almost aggressive jauntiness, of decent concern for her daughter behind Mrs Wray's still-Edwardian conservatism, of good-heartedness and stoicism behind Mrs Viney's vulgar garrulity. From a delinquent youth in Bermondsey to the

Wrays' domineering friend, wealthy Mrs Playfair, proudly mourning her son killed in Mesopotamia, characters are brought alive in all their complicatedness.

Not one of them is unscathed by the war. Its after-effects suffuse the novel. Emotional depletedness casts a pall over most of its figures. So does financial need. An ex-serviceman in a trench coat and Tommy's cap trundles a barrel organ through the streets on pram wheels, playing 'Roses of Picardie' and begging for work. Frances's life is one of ceaseless economy – taking a tram rather than a bus to save a penny, watering down the evening's cocoa, trying to steam the nap back into worn-out suede shoes.

Consciousness of the recently deceased haunts the post-war period Waters resurrects. As in all her novels, almost subliminal reminders of past fiction thicken the atmosphere too. Fleeting references to Dickens recur (a now-wizened flower seller he bought carnations from is seen still at her stall outside St Clement Danes). His novel *Little Dorrit* is mentioned – and appropriately: its concern with constraint and its portrayal of the mutinous Miss Wade passionately entangled with another woman are matched by Waters' concentration on uncovering hidden lesbian lives and exhibiting past female struggles for scope and freedom. A nod towards *Little Dorrit* also seems apparent in the book's quiet ending amid the bustle and clamour of London: an unillusioned but tentatively hopeful conclusion to a novel of ambitious reach and remarkable accomplishment.

Unvoiced Lives: Alan Hollinghurst

Before she became a novelist, Sarah Waters wrote a postgraduate thesis: *Wolfskins and Togas: Lesbian and Gay Historical Fictions, 1870 to the Present*. Before he became a novelist, Alan Hollinghurst wrote a postgraduate thesis: *The Creative Uses of Homosexuality in the Novels of E.M. Forster, Ronald Firbank, and L.P. Hartley*. There is a further similarity. Both writers weren't only prompted to write openly about gay experience after exploring ways in which it had been surreptitiously presented in preceding literature – under draperies of exoticism, in clandestine pornography, by strategic changes of lovers' gender or by coded formulations designed to speak to the initiated. Waters, who has not yet written about lesbian life in modern times, focused on it in novels set in the past, novels which have, as she put it, 'a common agenda in teasing out lesbian stories from parts of history that are regarded as quite heterosexual'. Hollinghurst has said he seized on the way the 1967 Sexual Offences Act 'changed what could be said about the private lives of gay people'. The 'new freedom to talk about these things' with a candour such as other novelists were increasingly bringing to heterosexual relationships was one he welcomed. But, from the start ('I wanted to contrast a homosexual life that had been lived under strong legal and social constraints with one being lived rather thoughtlessly in the present'), he juxtaposed this liberation with the concealments and obliquities of the past. His first two novels, *The Swimming-Pool Library* (1988) and *The Folding Star* (1994), intersperse scenes of post-1967 gay life with episodes from decades earlier. Using the two-tier narrative time scheme so prevalent in modern fiction, Hollinghurst counterpoints newly available scope with closeted ingenuity.

His masterpiece, *The Stranger's Child* (2011), one of modern fiction's outstanding achievements, opens in 1913. Cecil Valance, heir to a 3,000-acre baronial estate and already gilded with something of a reputation as a poet, is amusedly spending a weekend at 'Two Acres', a suburban house where George Sawle, a fellow undergraduate with whom he has started a sexual affair at Cambridge, lives with his widowed mother, older brother and sixteen-year-old sister, Daphne. Erotic and class tensions tingle as Cecil insouciantly disturbs the household. Before leaving, he scrawls a polite version of a poem inspired by his escapades with George at 'Two Acres' into Daphne's autograph album.

The impact of a young man's stay at a university friend's home had been the subject of Hollinghurst's previous novel, *The Line of Beauty* (2004). But where that focused on just four years – the mid-1980s Thatcherite high noon – *The Stranger's Child* follows the consequences of Cecil's visit through an almost century-long cavalcade of changing social, sexual and cultural attitudes, exhibited in sensuously imagined scenes and surveyed with urbanely ironic wit.

Leaping ahead, its narrative moves on to 1926 and the scene shifts to the Valances' Victorian Gothic mansion, Corley Court. Daphne, it's a surprise to find, is now resident here as Lady Valance, wife of Cecil's war-damaged brother Dudley. Cecil, fallen on the Western Front, is present only as an idealised marble effigy in the family chapel. For the nation at large too, he has become an iconic figure: a gallant soldier-poet who laid down his life for the England his verse celebrated. Much anthologised and mythologised, his poem, 'Two Acres', is especially beloved. Work on a suitably adulatory *Life* is under way.

Drastic revisions of Cecil's status are displayed in subsequent leaps forward. By 1967, his inflated stanzas provoke satiric sniggers. In 1980 an opportunist biographer plans to profit from disclosures of his bisexual promiscuity. By 2008, his lines ('Love comes not always in by the front door . . .') are under analysis by Queer Theory.

Opening with furtive, risky encounters in suburban shrubbery and ending after a rather grand memorial service for a gay man's dead husband, the book unrolls a century of changing homosexual lifestyles. Changing literary styles suffuse it too. Hollinghurst, who began his writing career with a book of verse, *Confidential Chats with Boys* (1982), expertly produces pastiche Georgian poetry ('The footings of the fawn among the fern') for Cecil, his amalgam of Rupert Brooke and Julian Grenfell. There are strategic echoes of Henry James, E.M. Forster, Lytton Strachey, Ronald Firbank, Evelyn Waugh and Angus Wilson (whose similarly panoramic family saga and cultural cavalcade, *No Laughing Matter*, is eagerly perused by one character on its publication in 1967 for its frank depiction of gay life).

True to Hollinghurst's keen responsiveness to architecture (it's hard to think of any other novelist who would make a young man entering a Soho porn cinema pause to admire the 'beautiful Caroline fenestration' of its façade), buildings stand out in *The Stranger's Child*, from the Arts and Crafts homeliness of 'Two Acres' to the mock-Gothic ambience of Corley Court. In keeping with the novel's concern with flux, they (like their inhabitants) undergo sometimes severe transformation. Its pseudo-chivalric flamboyances boxed in during the 1920s, Corley eventually becomes a boys' boarding school, the setting for one of the book's funniest scenes, a staff meeting where a hidebound headmaster gruffly enlarges on the Matron's discovery of 'the most revolting publications hidden behind the radiators in the Sixth Form'.

Always relishing the conversational eddies, froth and undercurrents of swirling social occasions, Hollinghurst places one at the centre of each section of his novel. An ill-assorted dinner party, a country house gathering on the eve of the General Strike, a lavish seventieth birthday celebration, an Oxford college conference prickly with malice, and a commemorative assembly in a Pall Mall club in turn provide masterly set pieces, captured in richly textured prose and observed with sardonic humour. Superlatively acute in its attention to idioms and idiosyncrasies, tone and body language, psychological and emotional nuances, the book gives intensely credible life to its swarm of characters – from a footman to a predatory lesbian interior designer, from a Wagner-loving German widow to a vain celebrity don. Upper-class monsters (something of a speciality for Hollinghurst, as *The Line of Beauty* demonstrated) are again unleashed. Outdoing even Cecil's lordly assurance, his brother Dudley, near-psychotically snobbish and derisive, is a mesmerisingly venomous star turn.

But even its most repellent or farcical figures, the novel shows, are partly products of their time. Maimings inflicted by the two world wars (which, like other key events, occur in the intervals between the book's five sections) become evident. Bereavements cripple some lives. Dudley 'doesn't go out at night' after a sniper shot a comrade he was standing next to on the moonlit Western Front. Near-death burial in a collapsed tunnel while attempting to escape from a German POW camp during the Second World War leaves another former soldier with lifelong agoraphobia. Other pressures take their toll too. From a young man giddy with lust and daring, George desiccates into a closeted workaholic married, for appearance's sake, to an unappealing wife. Daphne hardens from vulnerably ardent girl to tough, watchful old age.

Zestfully depicting the torments that bedevil an on-the-make biographer rummaging for scandal about Cecil (bruising snubs, glimpses of infuriatingly withheld documents, tape-recorder batteries that expire at crucial moments, the maddening vagaries of possibly senile interviewees) and riddled with concealments and oblique or ambiguous disclosures, *The Stranger's Child* derives sly comedy from bafflements that frustrate biography. But, as might be expected from a work whose title comes from lines in Tennyson's *In Memoriam* (contemplating how the passing years erode the initial significance of things and overgrow them with new ones), there is also an elegiac aspect to its various illustrations of transience and change.

In Hollinghurst's next novel, *The Sparsholt Affair* (2017) – which similarly consists of five significantly dated sections chronicling shifting social, cultural and sexual attitudes over eight decades – there's apt mention of a play called *The Triumph of Time*. *The Stranger's Child* simultaneously challenges that triumph by recuperating suppressed past lives and acknowledges it by stressing the fragility of memory and the vulnerability of biographical material. At the centre of its beautifully gauged closing scene is a house-clearance bonfire on which a cache of possibly revelatory data – unseen letters, lost poems – may have been incinerated. The last fading traces of Cecil's visit to 'Two Acres' and its ramifying consequences over eight decades could, it's implied in the book's final line, be just 'the smell of smoke' on a man's hands.

Shortly before this, there's a visit to the hi-tech office of a computer wizard who runs a website, 'Poets Alive!', on which he posts 'eerie little videos of long-dead poets reading, authentic sound recordings emerging from the mouths of digitally animated photographs'. In one of them, 'against a rainstorm of hissing and the galloping thump of the cylinder' on which he recorded verses from 'Come into the garden, Maud', Tennyson is synthetically brought back to life ('the bard's beard quivered like a beast in a hedge, as the famous face made repetitive mincing and chewing movements'). It's to the numerous – and usually less grotesque – ways in which historical personages have been re-figured in modern fiction that we should next turn.

Part III

Resurrection Writing: The Historical Past and Its Afterlife

The Resurgence of the Historical Novel

'The journey of the imagination to a remote place is child's play compared to a journey into another time', reported Thornton Wilder, who had undertaken both in his Pulitzer Prize-winning novel about early eighteenth-century Peru, *The Bridge of San Luis Rey* (1927). The latter journey is, however, one that modern novelists have been notably eager to make. Since 1970, historical fiction has boomed. What is remarkable about this is that, prior to it, the genre – once highly esteemed after the prestige and popularity Walter Scott achieved with his early nineteenth-century *Waverley* novels – had slumped in status. Although later nineteenth- and early twentieth-century novelists found it almost mandatory to try to their hand at what was seen as an especially elevated mode of fiction, the results weren't encouraging. Works such as Trollope's *La Vendée* (1850), George Eliot's *Romola* (1863), Hardy's *The Trumpet Major* (1880), Edith Wharton's *The Valley of Decision* (1902) and George Gissing's *Veranilda* (1904) hardly displayed their authors' talents at their most impressive. Reading them, you feel Jane Austen's prompt declining of a regal invitation to write a historical romance about the House of

Saxe-Coburg was prudent. For Henry James, the historical fiction genre was irredeemably inferior. Writing in 1901 to the New England author, Sarah Orne Jewett, he declared 'You may multiply the little facts that can be got from documents, relics and prints, as much as you like – the real thing is almost impossible to do, & in its essence the whole effect is as nought . . . You have to *think* with your modern apparatus a man, a woman, – or rather fifty – whose own thinking was intensely-otherwise conditioned, you have to simplify back by an amazing tour de force – and even then it's all bunkum.' Despite occasional successes such as Robert Graves's *I, Claudius* (1934), the genre had, by the middle of the twentieth century, largely subsided into either flimsy fancy-dress escapism or piously marmoreal reconstruction along the lines of religiose Victorian antecedents – often featuring early Christians, catacombs and martyrdom – like Cardinal Wiseman's *Fabiola* (1854) or John Henry Newman's *Callista* (1855). Fictionalising the quest for relics of the true cross by the Emperor Constantine's sainted mother, Evelyn Waugh's *Helena* (1950) sadly lacks his biting flair.

What boosted the genre to prominence and profuseness (newspapers' books pages found they had to publish frequent round-ups of new historical novels to keep pace with the spate) was the surge in fictional fascination with empire. Paul Scott led the way by fictionalising recent history in his *Raj Quartet* and J.G. Farrell by harking further back in *The Siege of Krishnapur*, his novel about India under nineteenth-century imperial sway. Soon, as we have seen, numerous other novelists were imaginatively reconstructing the last days of the British Empire, resurrecting pre-colonial societies and exhuming long-crumbled empires.

The renewed respectability – and ever-spreading popularity – of historical fiction proved welcome to practitioners such as Patrick O'Brian (who had been indignant to discover that 'to shift the scene of a novel to another age . . . and to cast it in an English some degrees pleasanter than the current, put me in a disreputable genre') and

Hilary Mantel (who felt that 'historical novelists face – as they should – questions about whether their work is legitimate. No other sort of writer has to explain their trade so often'). In keeping with the revived interest in the genre, and seen as its pre-eminent current practitioner, Mantel was invited to deliver a series of talks about it, which she entitled 'Resurrection: The Art and Craft', as the 2017 BBC Reith Lectures.

In them, she broached concerns central not only to the historical novels she herself had written from her first venture into the genre, *A Place of Greater Safety* (1992), onwards but to the fiction produced by fellow authors in the field. 'The task of historical fiction', she contended, 'is to take the past out of the archive and relocate it in a body'; it is a type of writing that 'frees people from the archive and lets them run about, ignorant of their fates, with all their mistakes unmade'; 'your real job as a novelist is not to be an inferior sort of historian, but to re-create the texture of lived experience: to activate the senses, and to deepen the reader's engagement through feeling'. 'It's the novelist's job', she asserted, 'to put the reader in the moment, even if the moment is 500 years ago.' The most noticeable way in which she sought to achieve this was by narrating her much-acclaimed Tudor trilogy, *Wolf Hall* (2009), *Bring Up the Bodies* (2012) and *The Mirror and the Light* (2020), in the present tense (as she had aimed to do with *A Place of Greater Safety*, though, to her annoyance, its publisher opposed her approach). It's a technique she was far from alone in adopting. In his 2017 collection of essays about storytelling, *Daemon Voices*, Philip Pullman observed that 'A quite extraordinary number of novels published these days, for adults as well as for children, use the present tense ... Something has happened to our understanding of fiction, or of the past ... to make the present tense the way in which young people, and adults as well, want to talk about something that can only be in the past, namely the events about which they are writing.' Once used extremely sparingly – Dickens's employment of it for one of his two narrative strands in *Bleak House*

(1853) was regarded as boldly unusual – the technique has become ubiquitous. Events in historical fiction are now far less likely to be recounted in the past tense (as was routinely the case in nineteenth-century fiction) than in the present. In the course of a period during which the past has become an ever more insistent fictional presence, verbs have intensified this. Narratives set in the past are reported as if currently occurring. Heightening the past's vividness and prox-imity, retrospect quivers with immediacy.

Mantel ended her last lecture with a quote from George MacBeth's 1986 poem sequence, *The Cleaver Garden*: 'All crib from skulls and bones who push a pen./Readers crave bodies. We're the resurrection men.' They are lines that had seized her attention before and been used as an epigraph to her novel *The Giant, O'Brien* (1998), which featured eighteenth-century 'resurrection men' – body-snatchers and grave-robbers – lucratively and illegally exhuming corpses for surgeons and anatomists to dissect.

Exhumation both as an actuality (in archaeology and palaeon-tology) and as a metaphor is something we have seen manifesting itself in novels about imperialism, child abuse, post-traumatic damage, and suppressed lives. It has done so on an even larger scale in historical fiction. The past has become an enormous quarry from which novel-ists extract figures to be reinspected, renovated, held up to be viewed from varying angles and in different lights. Ancient Romans (Julius Caesar, Cicero, Augustus, Tiberius, Nero, Vespasian) have received copious attention. The Tudor, Elizabethan, Victorian and Edwardian eras have been exhaustively revisited and the First and Second World Wars surveyed from a wide range of vantage points. Banking on royals to boost royalties, retinues of novels have attended on Henry VIII and his wives, Elizabeth I, the Stuarts, Victoria and Albert, even the Windsors. Gusts of imaginative energy have unfurled the sails of the British Navy in the age of Nelson. Explorers such as Alexander Laing (the first European to enter Timbuctoo), Sir John Franklin or Captain Scott have been sent to their doom again down fictional storylines.

Notorious murderers have been let rip (including Jack the Ripper and the Yorkshire Ripper). Genocidal dictators – Hitler, Stalin, Idi Amin – have inspired novels. Fictional life has been breathed into defunct notables from Cleopatra to Catherine the Great, Oliver Cromwell to Churchill. In 1997 alone, two novels fleshed out Christ's earthly career. The elderly Virgin Mary has given her testament. Mary Magdalene, something of a scriptural star turn, has made repeated return appearances. In a 1984 novel, she told her story as a 'fifth gospel'. Dan Brown's *The Da Vinci Code* (2003) put into circulation the notion that she married Jesus. Scrolls hidden by her in the Pyrenees featured dramatically in a 2006 novel written by 'an ordinary Little League mom' who claimed direct descent from her and Jesus Christ.

Amid the variegated throng of disinterred figures populating modern fiction (Helen of Troy, Sappho, Boudicca, Heloise and Abelard, Saladin, Lucrezia and other Borgias, the printing press pioneer Johannes Gutenberg, Robespierre, Newton, Nelson, Copernicus, Casanova, Kant, Kepler, Lincoln, Mason and Dixon, Cecil Rhodes, Theodore and Eleanor Roosevelt, Machiavelli, Mack Sennett, Fatty Arbuckle, Freud, Alfred Hitchcock, Lee Harvey Oswald, Martin Luther King, Richard Nixon, Marilyn Monroe . . .) one group stands out. Writers (and their works, as we shall see later), have been by far the prime candidates for resuscitation in other writers' fiction. Artists (Leonardo da Vinci, Velázquez, Vermeer, Rembrandt, Canaletto, Géricault, Watts, Van Gogh, Monet, Egon Schiele, Alfred Wallis) and composers (Byrd, J.S. Bach, Beethoven, Berlioz, Elgar, Mahler, Delius, Sibelius, Shostakovich) have received the fictional kiss of life as well. Biblical figures – Adam and Eve, Cain and Abel, Noah, Abraham and Sarah, Saul, David, his daughter Tamar and his son Absalom – have been the subject of revisionist scriptures. Mythical beings such as Perseus, Circe, Sinbad and Merlin have been conjured up afresh.

Why (in addition to the retrospective pull of empire) so much creative energy and industrious research has been channelled into this kind of resurrection writing is a question to which answers vary. David Mitchell, author of a particularly fine example of the genre, *The Thousand Autumns of Jacob de Zoet*, offered a bluntly practical explanation: 'as the zeitgeist begins to outpace aging novelists, the past can make a dignified refuge'. It has provided this most hospitably for writers of whodunnits. 'DNA has changed the crime novel', one of detective fiction's most distinguished practitioners, P.D. James, declared in 2003. Ever more sophisticated forensic techniques, along with other high-tech inconveniences to pleasurable puzzlement and suspense – CCTV, mobile phones, satnav records, instantly accessible databases – have sent many murder mystery writers back into the congenial amateurism of the past. And, faced with dialogue like 'Her PGM's one-plus, one-minus. Her PEP is A-one, EAP's CB, ADA-one and AK-one' in crime novels by forensic pathologists such as Patricia Cornwell or Kathy Reichs, swarms of readers have been eager to accompany them. Historical crime fiction has become a vigorously thriving genre. From Steven Saylor's *Roma Sub Rosa* novels featuring Gordianus, a toga-ed tec who investigates murders perpetrated during the last days of the Roman Republic, to Frank Tallis's novels in which a young disciple of Freud lays bare the truth behind baroquely executed killings in Vienna during the last days of the Habsburg Empire, from C.J. Sansom's crime novels set in an England convulsed by the Reformation to Andrew Taylor's Restoration murder mysteries played out across a London devastated by the Great Fire, from Abir Mukherjee's Raj police novels located in a sultry 1920s Calcutta of cantonments and corruption to Philip Kerr's Bernie Gunther thrillers about Nazi Germany and its aftermath, a high standard has been set for fiction that blends mystery and history, whodunnit suspense with rich period colour and substantial background knowledge. Bibliographies of archive sources consulted are now almost as much a standard feature of crime novels as red herrings, shaky alibis and circles of suspects.

Crime novelists haven't, of course, been the only authors to find historical fiction an inviting genre. The urge to re-create the past has proved widely compulsive. Mantel has claimed that 'Historical fiction comes out of greed for experience.' But, as the huge array of it produced since 1970 displays, it is motivated by many other impulsions too. Prominent among them are political or other ideological incentives, desire to subvert received opinion or rectify omission, celebratory nostalgia, personal obsession, relish for lusher language and gaudier scenarios than modern subject matter usually affords, and not least – since the genre attracts huge readerships – commercial considerations. Feeding into the prevailing literary alertness to what has gone before – antecedents, starting-points and events whose after-effects still resonate – factors such as these have generated a phenomenally wide-ranging body of fiction.

Language Problems: Paul Kingsnorth, James Meek and Barry Unsworth

If, as L.P. Hartley's much-quoted line has it, 'the past is a foreign country; they do things differently there', it's one into which throngs of modern novelists have been keen to seek admittance. Prior to entry, some have reflected on the language problem facing them. 'Wardour Street English' – pseudo-period parlance sprinkled with *mayhaps* and *methinks*, *haply*s and *quoth*s (as furniture for sale in London's Wardour Street was once notoriously tricked out with fake antiqueness) – is something no serious historical novelist would want to fall back on. But what to replace it with could be a quandary. In an afternote to his engaging novel *Pilgrims* (2020) which accompanies a band of thirteenth-century travellers from England to Rome, Matthew Kneale acknowledges that 'Language in historical fiction is a dilemma. Ancient mouths uttering twenty-first-century slang can be jarring, if not downright ridiculous. An attempt to write a whole novel in thirteenth-century English will be well beyond most authors' capabilities, and is likely to appeal to a very small readership indeed.' His solution is to compromise, avoiding post-medieval words as much as possible but employing modern spelling and occasionally inserting archaic vocabulary 'to give a sense that this was a very different era, or to give a word an extra emotional resonance'.

Others have gone further down this route – most notably Paul Kingsnorth, whose debut novel, *The Wake* (2014), about an eleventh-century Lincolnshire farmer waging a resistance struggle against the victorious Norman invaders from a guerrilla base in the Fens, is written in what its author calls 'a shadow tongue – a pseudo-language intended to convey the feeling of the old language by combining some of its vocabulary and syntax with the English we speak today'. Like Kneale, Kingsnorth avoids modern speech ('To put 21st-century-sounding sentences into the mouths of eleventh-century characters would be the equivalent of giving them iPads and cappuccinos'). Like Kneale, but more drastically, he attempts a kind of linguistic quasi-authenticity:

> The first and most important rule was that I wanted to use only words which originated in Old English. The vast majority of the vocabulary of this novel consists of words that, in one form or another, existed in English 1000 years ago ... To achieve the sound and look I wanted on the page I have combined Old English words with modern vocabulary, mutated and hammered the shape of OE words and word endings to suit my purpose, and been wanton in combining the Wessex dialect with that of Mercia, Anglia and Northumberland – and dropping in a smattering of Old Norse when it seemed to work.

But, even when watered down and clarified, Kingsnorth's blend of Anglo-Saxon-lite ('in the brunnesweald nebbs all blaec hydan in the grene holt') runs a high risk of reader intolerance.

As in Kneale's *Pilgrims*, medieval folk on the move are portrayed in James Meek's novel, *To Calais, in Ordinary Time* (2019). The date is half a century or so later – 1348 – and Meek's travellers aren't journeying to Rome but making their way to Calais, captured for England by the nation's archers at the Battle of Crécy a couple of years before. They are also heading into the corpse-strewn path of the Black Death (England's first fatality from which was recorded in 1348). Like Kneale and Kingsnorth, Meek has said that he took pains to imbue his prose with period colour: 'I wanted a sense of strangeness but to avoid veering into the ways other people have used in the past of representing that era. So there is no "thee and thou" in the book even though it would be accurate. I also didn't want it to sound like Lord of the Rings – it is a narrow path you have to walk.'

Linguistic difference in Meek's book isn't just between the past and the present. It also signals social status, with contrasting registers used for his three main characters. Representing the Francophile nobility, Lady Bernadine, a knight's daughter in flight from a forced marriage (who refers to herself as a 'demoiselle' and is enamoured of the chivalric poem *La Roman de la Rose* with its code of courtly love), favours vocabulary with French roots. At the other extreme is a young ploughman, a bound labourer eager to win freedom through his prowess as a bowman, whose idiom is archaic and earthy. Contrasting, often comically, with it is the Latinate English of a scholarly lawyer whose 'scribal implements' fill the pages of his journal with locutions such as 'sylvan osculation', 'nigrous' and 'insomniate'

'To a degree,' David Mitchell remarked, 'the historical novelist must create a sort of dialect – I call it "Bygonese" – which is inaccurate but plausible.' For Mantel, the historical novelist 'must try to work authentically, hearing the words of the past, but communicating in a language the present understands'. This is, by far, the approach most commonly adopted. One of modern fiction's most versatile exponents of the genre, Barry Unsworth, used it with skilful assurance – especially in his novel, *Morality Play* (1995), where a troupe of fourteenth-century vagabond performers stumble on sinister secrets as they traverse north-east England. Like Kneale's

177

pilgrims and Meek's travellers, Unsworth's roving players show how useful geographical mobility proves to authors who travel back in time. Historically unfamiliar scenes take on added vividness when seen through the eyes of characters encountering scenes geographically unfamiliar to them.

In Unsworth's stark tale, eyes are opened in many ways. Its setting is a fourteenth century of plague and famine, destitution and lawlessness, where fields lie untilled and starving soldiers who have straggled back from the wars in France savagely resort to brigandry. Observing this harsh world, where many believe that the Last Days are imminent, is Nicholas Barber, a young cleric who has run away from Lincoln Cathedral where he was a subdeacon. The first thing he sees as the book gets under way is six shabbily but gaudily attired figures clustered in the dying light of a bitter December day around an expiring man. This tableau, which reminds Nicolas of 'the scene in the Morality Play when the besieged soul flies free at last', is one of many moments in the novel that suggest it could as well have been called *Mortality Play*. Death and deathliness pervade it. Plague mounds of those who died during the fetid summer bulge in graveyards. Two corpses are the motivating agents of the novel's plot. On St Lazarus's day, a feast commemorating the raising of someone from the tomb, a ghastly secret begins to be unearthed.

The mourners Nicholas sights are a band of players journeying to Durham. The death of one of their number puts them in a quandary as to how to find money to pay for his Christian burial. They will earn it, they decide, by performing some of their morality plays, with Nicholas standing in for the dead actor, at a small town their route takes them through. As they travel towards it, the reek of mortality from the cadaver in their cart becomes more and more unignorable. On arrival, they are plunged into an even more morbidly tainted atmosphere. In a climactic scene. Nicholas stumbles past a doorway from which wafts 'a stench of decay . . . not the smell of death but of disease, of poisoned tissue and corrupted blood, the rot of the living body'. This nauseating stink is merely the most open manifestation of noxiousness shrouding the town.

Soon after entering the little community huddled round the castle of a northern nobleman, the players learn that a local woman awaits execution for killing a twelve-year-old boy. When the townsfolk prove indifferent to such well-worn fare as the Play of Adam – preferring to watch a rival troupe of rope-walkers and fire-eaters – the actors boldly plan to attract an audience by dramatising the murder. The audacity of this is emphasised by Unsworth's reconstruction of the theatre-world these people have been accustomed to. For them, drama serves to exhibit God's designs, not man's depravities. The stagecraft by which the performers act out the customary biblical parables is enthrallingly re-created. Out of the property basket come such essential items as Eve's flaxen wig and glass beads, the red-painted paper apple to be plucked from the pasteboard tree, the Devil's fork, the wings worn by Lucifer before his fall, God's six-inch stilts and long robe. A mime repertoire of hand-movements – from the palm-out silencing gesture to the sinuous indication of tempting female allure – is demonstrated. Also rendering credible the players' need to attempt something new, Unsworth has them glumly aware of the ruinous competition now mounted by the wealthy guilds, which stage lavish cycles of mystery plays boasting costly special effects: realistic-looking beheadings of the Baptist, spectacular resurrections with the help of elaborate machinery.

The players' bid to retrieve their fortunes takes them towards ruin. As they re-enact their scenario of the strangled boy, his supposed murderer and a monk who claims to have witnessed the crime, improbabilities and inconsistencies increasingly deflect their improvisations in a new and ever more dangerous direction. The torch-lit makeshift stage in the inn yard isn't the only arena in which role-playing, masks and feigning hold sway. Nor does the chill this book strikes emanate merely from the glacial wintriness of its scenes: claddings of frost on cobblestones, snow drifted into eerie shapes, a swirling blizzard through which knights on horseback frighteningly break into view. Silhouetted against a background of mass graves, the death throes of feudalism and the demise of liturgical drama, *Morality Play* – focused like much of Unsworth's fiction on corrupt power, exploitation and deceit – works a bleak and masterly historical variation on the pervading modern concern with child abuse.

Francis Spufford

Fresh, observant eyes are provided by another rover in an outstanding novel about a later period, Francis Spufford's *Golden Hill* (2016). Throughout the ever-expanding vogue for historical fiction, the eighteenth century has been somewhat side-lined. Authors have tumbled over themselves to produce mock-Tudor tales. Pastiche Victorian and Edwardian novels have been published by the bushel. But the era in which the novel form rose to prominence with Fielding and Richardson, Smollett and Sterne has been oddly neglected. *Golden Hill* – which unrolls over the last few weeks of 1746 – winningly rectifies this.

When it starts, its hero, Richard Smith, is quivering with impatience on the deck of a ship slowly approaching New York harbour after a long Atlantic crossing:

> The brig *Henrietta* having made Sandy Hook a little before the dinner hour – and having passed the Narrows about three o'clock – and then crawling to and fro, in a series of tacks infinitesimal enough to rival the calculus, across the grey sheet of the harbour of New-York – until it seemed to Mr Smith, dancing from foot to foot upon deck, that the small mound of the city waiting there would hover ahead in the November gloom in perpetuity, never growing closer, to the smirk of Greek Zeno – and the day being advanced to dusk by the time *Henrietta* at last lay anchored off Tietjes Slip, with the veritable gables of the city's veritable houses

divided from him only by one hundred foot of water – and the dusk moreover being as cold and damp and dim as November can afford, as if all the world were a quarto of grey paper dampened by drizzle until in danger of crumbling imminently to pap – all this being true, the master of the brig pressed upon him the virtue of sleeping this one further night aboard, and pursuing his shore business in the morning.

Teasingly replicating prose of the period at its most long-winded, convoluted and pedantically facetious, this meandering, interminable-seeming opening sentence (which tests the reader's patience as much as the delay it dawdlingly describes tests Smith's) was a tactic, Spufford has said, to show how hard-to-take a novel offering unmitigated eighteenth-century pastiche would be. Swiftly shaking off this stylistic constraint, he goes on to write in more streamlined prose suffused with period colour. Pent-up energy – Spufford's as well as Smith's – is let loose as, once ashore, the new arrival races pell-mell, 'skidding over fish-guts and turnip leaves and cats' entrails, and other effluvium of the port', to a counting-house whose astounded owner, Lovell, he presents with a money-order for a thousand pounds. The bill seems vouched-for by an impeccably reputable City firm in London, but the sum is stupendous. During the highly eventful sixty days within which it must be paid, suspicion thickens around Smith, who appears to revel in the puzzlement he provokes. Is this jaunty young stranger a confidence-trickster? What were his circumstances in England? What business has brought him to the colony?

These and other mysteries keep the reader eagerly turning the pages of a cunningly crafted narrative that, right up to its *tour-de-force* ending, is alive with tantalising twists and turns. Like Fielding's Tom Jones, Smith is propelled through a hectic assortment of adventures and a colourful miscellany of social scenes: a King's Birthday dinner with the colony's grandees, a drunken fracas on 5 November ('Pope Day' in New York, when Papist effigies blaze on a bonfire), a prison cell under the cobbles of Wall Street. The plot teems with incident: a life-or-death scamper across the rooftops of Manhattan, *in flagrante* sexual embarrassments, a duel, and the prospect of dancing 'the Hemp Jig' from the gallows. Reproducing the racy vigour eighteenth-century fiction is also capable of, Spufford captures its pungency too: a drink-sodden jailbird, Smith reports in a letter, 'has a Nose swollen to the Likeness of a Piece of Crimson Fruit, ornament'd by as many black Pores as there are Seeds upon a Strawberry'.

High-fidelity literary mimicry combines with vivid evocation of pre-Revolutionary New York, an embryonic city whose Broad Way is a not-very-wide pebbled avenue leading to a common where cows graze, and whose skyscape is a jumble of stepped Dutch gables and church steeples against the background of a 'slow swaying fretwork of masts'. To Smith's eyes, Manhattan at first looks astonishingly wholesome. Its streets contrast pleasingly with the reek and filth of London. Its sturdy-seeming inhabitants are surprisingly unmarked by smallpox. There are no beggars, and, in this fledgling democracy, aristocratic arrogance has no inherited place. Only the presence of Black slaves – shuffling in irons, labouring in the fields, tricked out in powdered wigs to play minuets at soirées – strikes a sombre note.

Gradually, other uglinesses emerge. Nailed up in the fort, 'rustling congealments' that initially bewilder Smith turn out to be French scalps, an annual gift from Mohawks keen to display their friendliness to the Dutch and British settlers. Hidden machinations increasingly menace Spufford's spirited hero. Mired in vileness at the nadir of his fortunes, he learns of an appalling atrocity.

Resilient resourcefulness carries Smith over these crises, just as descriptive verve pulses through Spufford's novel. Little brilliancies of metaphor and phrasing gleam everywhere. The governor's banquet is 'all wigs and wide mouths and glittering eyes in the candle-light'. 'Fan-flutters and glance-exchanges' ripple through a fashionable church congregation. At a Christmas feast in a Dutch merchant's house, 'a red-faced patriarch with a square visage swagged north and south with white hair like a king on a playing card' utters sentences that 'growled along like barrels on a hard floor'. Acutely alert to sounds – 'blade skreeking against blade' in a sword-fight, Dutch-accented English ('eckshplayned') – Spufford has a superbly inventive visual responsiveness too.

As might be expected from an author whose first book, *I May Be Some Time* (1997), was a sizzling account of 'Ice and the English Imagination', Spufford is in his element with the coming of the New York winter. A 'bitter green pallor, the unmistakeable colour of impending cold' heralds the arrival of 'tiny flakes like feathered dust' that are soon 'furring the cobbles with a thin grey nap like velvet', then falling in 'fat, tumbling clots, as if the stuffing of furniture were being tossed over the balconies of heaven'. In sunshine, 'loose handfuls of crystal hissed off the rooftops in prismatic eddies'. As the white-shrouded little city hibernates, Smith takes part in a production of Addison's stilted tragedy, *Cato*. The result is often exuberant comedy, not least because the star performer is Euterpe Tomlinson, once a celebrated actress on the London stage, now much appreciated in the colony for her 'tremendous cleavage'. More central to the novel is Tabitha Lovell, a caustic, clever, tormented and tormenting young woman to whom Smith is drawn. Tingling with wit and wariness, their relationship adds an emotionally and psychologically deeper counterpoint to the themes of trust and doubt running through the novel's mysterious money-order plot.

Carys Davies and George Saunders

Golden Hill resurrected the America of three decades or so before the War of Independence. Another immensely engaging debut novel resurrected the America of three decades or so after it: Carys Davies' *West* (2018). Another restless traveller to America is its hero. In 1815, Cy Bellman, a thirty-five-year-old immigrant from England, now a widower, leaves behind his Pennsylvania farm and his young daughter, and heads for Kentucky. As often in modern fiction, bones spur the narrative into action. Excited by newspaper reports of 'monstrous bones ... prodigious tusks, uncovered where they lay, sunk in the salty Kentucky mud: teeth the size of pumpkins, shoulder blades a yard wide, jawbones that suggested a head as tall as a man', Cy sets out to explore what lies behind these 'giant remains'. A precursor of the nineteenth-century palaeontologists who more often feature in modern fiction, he 'has the pricking feeling ... that the giant animals were important somehow'. As he heads west into the wilderness beyond the Mississippi to investigate, surprising twists and turns unwind. Unexpected alliances – especially between Bellman and a Shawnee Indian boy – form. Scenes sparkle with wry comedy. Menace looms and ordeals are braved amidst breath-taking landscapes.

A writer of elegant and resonant concision, Davies produces a miniature masterpiece from a story set in motion by the finding of mammoth bones. In fewer than 150 pages, she works a beguilingly original variation on the Wild West genre (just as she would later do with the Raj fiction genre in her 2020 novel, *The Mission House*). Bellman's quest, flawed but bravely admirable, has all the ardent aspiration of the American Dream. Around him, evidence of racial oppression, territorial displacement, predatory atrocity and treachery show the pernicious colonial realities that debase it.

Within *West*'s slender span, wide horizons open and large concerns are broached. Its streamlined accomplishment puts historical novels dropsical with researched data to shame. Also published in 2018, a very different but also acutely creative refashioning of the genre focused on a few hours in the midst of America's Civil War: George Saunders's *Lincoln in the Bardo*. It would be an understatement to call it an extraordinary *tour de force*. Extravagantly strange in style and setting, it shows an author making a spectacular imaginative leap.

Over the preceding two decades, Saunders had won acclaim for his striking short stories. His speciality, as four volumes of stories and a novella exhibited, had been to focus with black zaniness on corporate hells: organisations whose activities are shrouded in sinister euphemisms, research labs where experiments are imperturbably ramped up into horror, theme parks where bureaucratic protocols mask cynical chicanery and worse. Darkly funny and oddly poignant, the stories began, though, to look somewhat formulaic. Repeatedly, ruthless bosses and sleazy institutional functionaries were shown harrying the weak and disadvantaged; bland business-speak and uplift motivational jargon grotesquely counterpointed damage and desperation. Diminishing returns became increasingly apparent as Saunders seemed stuck in a fictional mode reminiscent of Nathanael West, Kurt Vonnegut and William Gaddis.

Lincoln in the Bardo, his first novel, struck out in a new direction. Where the stories are set in the present or near-future, it turns back in time. Events are confined to a single night – 22 February 1862 – in a cemetery in Washington's Georgetown. Two days earlier, Abraham Lincoln, president of a nation bloodily tearing itself apart in civil war, has lost his favourite child, eleven-year-old Willie, to typhoid. Now, he pays a grief-stricken nocturnal visit to the crypt where the boy's body lies. It could be a scene from a Victorian novel – except that, around the silent tomb where the president cradles his son's corpse, the cemetery swarms with voluble spectral presences.

Garrulous graveyards and talkative tombs aren't new in literature. Edgar Lee Masters' *Spoon River Anthology* (1915) exhumed existence in a small Midwestern town though a sequence of verse monologues spoken by defunct citizens in its burial ground. Thomas Hardy's poem, 'Voices from Things Growing in a Churchyard' (1921), did something similar with a Dorset village.

Saunders' approach goes further. The 'bardo' in which the Lincoln of his novel's title (not Abraham but Willie) finds himself is the limbo-like realm that Tibetan Buddhism sees as a transition stage between death and rebirth. Populated with figures the reader gets to know solely through snatches of their speech (which comprise most of the novel), it's a place in which deceased beings still tethered to their previous existence by fixated traumas, gripping memories and unfulfilled longings are stranded.

It's territory that Saunders had touched on before. The title story in his first collection, *CivilWarLand in Bad Decline* (1996), hilariously portrayed a dilapidated Civil War heritage theme park plagued by ghosts hanging on from the era it tackily replicated. Located in the midst of the Civil War and thronged with ghosts, *Lincoln in the Bardo* – while not short on offbeat comedy – is far wider in scope and deeper in feeling. Melancholy, compassion and tenderness infuse its phantasmagoric scenes. One of its most eloquent spectres, a young man who slashed his wrists in misery at losing his male lover, recognised as he bled to death the terrible mistake he had made in ripping himself from life. Now craving for it, he persists in believing he will be 'revived'. So do the bardo's other inhabitants, who regard their coffins as 'sick-boxes' from which they will healthily re-emerge.

Through the yearnings of his ghosts, Saunders hauntingly celebrates the pleasures and the privilege of life. Its pains aren't forgotten either. From the section of the graveyard segregated for slaves, graphic accounts of abuse and degradation remind you of the hinterland of Black suffering surrounding Lincoln and which he is battling to alleviate.

The pathos of wasted lives and lost existences keeps piercing through the novel's surreal scenes. With uncanny mastery, Saunders encompasses both aching emotion and macabre fantasy. Like a latter-day Dante or Hieronymus Bosch, he conjures up post-mortem beings distorted in ways bizarrely emblematic of their plights. The young suicide hungry for the sensory delights he cut himself off from has mutated into a barnacled accretion of avidly bulging sets of eyes, ears, noses and hands. A man obsessed with property unstoppably swivels like a compass needle towards whichever of his lost houses he is currently brooding about. The bardo's longest-stay residents – bed-blockers of reincarnation, as it were – have eroded to near-limbless lumps like something out of Samuel Beckett.

Forking across this weird territory Saunders sends a suspense plot. It is crucial, you learn, that Willie – like other dead youngsters – should move on from the bardo before deformation engulfs him. Alternating with all this are chapters stocked with historical data: collages of engrossing extracts plucked from biographies of Lincoln, diaries and letters by his contemporaries, newspaper reports. They (and some invented snippets) assemble a complex and moving portrait of him, and open up fascinating, detail-packed vistas into his world. The father sorrowing over his son's coffin at the dead of night (as accounts testify was the case) is placed against a background of national mourning over the mounting carnage of the Civil War. Uncertain how to proceed with the conflict, Lincoln is presented as being in a transition zone himself.

Prodigiously inventive, *Lincoln in the Bardo* is a novel that takes enormous risks. What saves it from toppling into pitfalls of absurdity and freakishness is the subtlety and exactness of Saunders' writing (not least his flair for period pastiche), his power to convey strong emotion, and his phenomenal narrative panache. Set beyond the grave, it urges empathy among the living. Steeped in mortality, it is a triumph of vitality.

Pre-historical Fiction: William Golding, Jean M. Auel, Thomas Keneally and Raymond Williams

Golden Hill, West and *Lincoln in the Bardo* resurrect eras infrequently visited by historical novelists. Even thinner on the ground are books by what might be called pre-historical novelists, authors who have undertaken very long-haul flights of imagination into the past. Impelled by the pervading urge to scrutinise starting-points, some have peered as far back as the emergence of our species. Immeasurably the greatest writer to do this, William Golding, set an unsurpassed standard for such fiction with his 1955 novel *The Inheritors*, which displays how a tribe of peaceable, slow-thinking Neanderthals are exterminated by a band of aggressive, quick-minded *Homo sapiens*. Golding's scenario – encounter between Neanderthals and *Homo sapiens* seen as a grim warning of lethal things to come – was inverted and stretched out across six mammoth novels by the American author, Jean M. Auel, in her hugely bestselling series, *Earth's Children*. Beginning with *The Clan of the Cave Bear* (1980) and concluding with *The Land of Painted Caves* (2011), Auel offers *The Inheritors* turned upside down. Where Golding's novel ended with a sole surviving Neanderthal baby boy being adopted by a tribe of *Homo sapiens*, *The Clan of the Cave Bear* begins with a sole surviving Cro-Magnon little girl (orphaned after an earthquake engulfs her family) being adopted by tribe of Neanderthals. The authors' attitudes to 'the Others' (the term both Golding and Auel use for their *Homo sapiens*) are diametrically opposed. Where Golding sees them as baleful, Auel regards them as beneficent. Her Cro-Magnon heroine, Ayla, matures into an almost Californian-seeming, blue-eyed, long-legged lovely with rippling blonde hair, a lissom figure and voluptuous breasts. At first squinted at askance by the swart, squat, barrel-bodied Neanderthals as a creature sadly lacking the pelted allure of their own bandy-legged belles, she increasingly astounds them with her feisty refusal to be cowed into subservience as a female and by her feats of physical and mental agility. Prognathous jaws drop in amazement as she lopes around the tundra, applying tourniquets, braining hyenas, doing advanced maths and – to assist her unrivalled hunting prowess with a sling-shot – inventing the bra. Carnivores and curses, ostracism and earthquakes are all taken in her effortless Cro-Magnon stride: 'I would have been back earlier,' she murmurs modestly, 'but I got caught in an avalanche coming down the mountain.' Not one to trouble about linguistic incongruity, Auel has a Neanderthal reflect that the Others 'verbalised more fluently'. But, in her pages, Neanderthals themselves seem no slouches when it comes to verbalising (" "Iza, she is just perfect," Ebra raved. "I must admit I was a little worried when I learned you were pregnant after all this time" "). Though her publishers maintain that Auel's 'extensive research' into the Ice Age has 'earned her the respect of many renowned scientists, archaeologists and anthropologists around the globe', in her fiction the result is more plasticine than Pleistocene.

Another remote-harker-back, Thomas Keneally, worked a variant on the widely favoured format of two storylines that counterpoint two eras in *The Book of Science and Antiquities* (2019). Forty-two thousand years separate its protagonists but conspicuous links unite them. In twenty-first-century New South Wales, Shelby Apple, an octogenarian documentary film maker, is enthralled by the discovery of a Palaeolithic man's remains in the dried-up basin of an ancient lake. As the novel narrates Shelby's life story, that of Shade, the far-distant forebear whose excavated bones have excited his imagination, unrolls simultaneously. Affinities are stressed. Some are solid and specific: Shelby dies from a cancerous 'knot in my oesophagus', Shade from the lodging in his throat of a stone he has swallowed for ritual reasons. Others are hazier. The scientist who unearthed Shade's bones discloses that the Aboriginal's spirit manifests itself to him in dreams and 'definitely says to me that being human is a test that kills us'. 'He prodded at the universe the way we prod at it ... He chased love with the same sacred and profane mix of motives we do', he informs the marvelling Shelby. 'At the end of it, he was you, Shelby.' Misty intimations of mystic affiliations between Keneally's twinned heroes are floated throughout the novel. Less loftily, they share a penchant for odd-sounding erotic reminiscence. 'Images of black lingerie and unloosed breasts ... do not leave the supposed sexual Sahara of my groin unaffected', Shelby confides. Shade recalls the springings-up of his 'throbbing ... man-plant' and his wife Girly's enthusiasm for his 'man-root'.

Designed to confute racism in Australia by its forceful reverence for Aboriginal culture and vehement emphasis on there being a joint ancestor for Black and white peoples, Keneally's novel is very much historical fiction with a political agenda. A not dissimilar agenda manifests itself in *People of the Black Mountains* by the Welsh Marxist writer, Raymond Williams. Likewise stretching as far back as Palaeolithic lakeside life (here, in the Northern Hemisphere), the work was planned as a forty-millennia hindsight saga. Williams's death in 1988 before completing his intended chain of stories showing how folk in the Brecon Beacons region suffered affliction – meteorological, colonial, religious and economic – from the last ice age to the Second World War meant that its catalogue of Cymric woes only got as far as the plight of a Lollard refugee hunted for heresy in 1415.

What makes Williams's gargantuan enterprise noteworthy isn't just its projected length but its daunting density. It stands as a warning reminder of a major hazard facing writers of historical fiction: inordinate documentation. Heaping masses of data into its chapters, *People of the Black Mountains* (published in two volumes in 1989 and 1990 along with a list of the ninety-one books and periodicals 'which proved of most use in researching the background to the novel') does so not only historically but geographically. Its opening pages offer what is surely fiction's most disorientating exercise in scene-setting:

> See this layered sandstone in the short mountain grass. Place your right hand on it, palm downward. See where the summer sun rises and where it stands at noon. Direct your index finger midway between them. Spread your fingers, not widely. You hold this place in your hand.
>
> The six rivers rise in the plateau towards your wrist. The first river, now called Mynwy, flows at the outside edge of your thumb. The second river, now called Olchon, flows between your thumb and the first finger, to join the Mynwy at the top of your thumb. The third river, now called Honddu, flows between

your first and second fingers and then curves to join the Mynwy. The fourth river, now called Grwyne Fawr, flows between your second and third fingers and then curves the other way, south, to join the fifth river, now called Grwyne Fechan, that has been flowing between your third and your outside finger. The sixth river, now called Rhiangoll, flows at the edge of your outside finger.

This is the hand of the Black Mountains, the shape first learned. Your thumb is Crib y Gath. Your first finger is Curum and Hateral. Your second finger is Ffawyddog, with Tal y Cefn and Bal Mawr at its knuckles. Your third finger is Cadair Fawr. Your outside finger is Allt Mwr, from Llysiau to Cerrig Calch, and its nail is Crug Hywel. On the high plateau of the back of your hand are Twyn y Llech and Twympa, Rhos Dirion, Waun Fach and Y Das. You hold their shapes and their names.

Whether you would also hold them in your mind after this would-be handy guide to the book's topography is another matter. Historical content streams out on a similarly uncompromising scale. Myriads of meagrely individualised figures illustrating oppression, exploitation and injustice briefly mill in and out of the pages. Resolutely authentic language ('When the teyrn feels the frost, he remembers the taeog') adds further impediment to involvement.

Hilary Mantel

Problems in shaping a superabundance of researched material into compelling fiction have also dogged a writer of far greater skill, Hilary Mantel. From the start, fascination with history was entangled with her resolve to become a novelist. 'I began writing fiction in the 1970s at the point – paradoxically – where I discovered I wanted to be a historian', she has said. 'I only became a novelist because I thought I had missed my chance to become a historian.' Embarking on her literary career with what she recognised would be prolonged research for a novel about the French Revolution, she explained: 'I wasn't after quick results. I was prepared to look at all the material I could find, even though I knew it would take years'. True to this, the book, which eventually appeared as *A Place of Greater Safety* almost two decades after she began work on it in 1974, was her fifth to be published. Before it, she produced in quick succession four non-historical novels – *Every Day Is Mother's Day* (1985), *Vacant Possession* (1986), *Eight Months on Ghazzah Street* (1988) and *Fludd* (1989). Written 'as a way of getting a foot in the door', they enabled the belated publication of *A Place of Greater Safety* in 1992. 'A vast novel involving mountains of research', it was, at 873 pages long, a very different work from its small-scale predecessors.

In it, Mantel mentions that, after the guillotining of Louis XVI, the Sèvres porcelain manufacturers came up with a new design of coffee cup, decorated with a cameo of his severed head held in the executioner's golden hand and dripping golden drops of blood. This gruesome demitasse is typical of the bizarre detail that glints from the best scenes in her panorama of the French Revolution. It also epitomises what is often her own approach to it: the processing of revolution into rococo. Vignettes brushed in with deft little strokes ornament the brittle surface of her novel: Versailles court ladies resembling china on shelves as they perch in their rigid finery on benches at the fateful assembly of the Estates-General; Voltaire's cadaver, denied Christian burial, carried out of Paris in a coach under a full moon, propped upright and looking alive; Mme Roland in white muslin on her tumbril, seeing the hard edges of the guillotine silhouetted against a darkening sky.

The weird elegance of such miniatures isn't, as you might expect, a brief respite from an ugly welter of savagery and frenzy raging elsewhere. Throughout Mantel's chronicle of the Revolution, an unexpectedly high level of dandified urbanity prevails. Quizzical women are to the fore in the book's domestic and political scenes. Even in the most fetid depths of the Terror, characters keep up a steady line in imperturbable badinage. Mantel's revolutionaries tend to be as drawlingly ironic as any *ancien régime* lord. Her Mirabeau sounds like a predecessor of Oscar Wilde.

Although the novel's expansive canvas, stretching from 1763 to 1794, is crammed to dizzying point with people, three central figures stand out: Desmoulins, Danton and Robespierre. Of this trio, Mantel is most taken with Desmoulins, fondly referred to as Camille throughout the narrative while Danton and Robespierre never get beyond surname terms with their author. Even at the age of three, he is rather dotingly presented as a droll wit, disconcerting his papa with his sardonic gaze and quipping – when told not to be childish – 'Why not? I'm a child, aren't I?' Subsequent chapters establish him as a master of stylish mockery, partnered with a wife whose feline astuteness matches his own.

Flickers of quick sly wit playing over odd little scenes often galvanise Mantel's novels into sparky – indeed, Muriel-Spark-like – life. Here, though, her book stays stubbornly inert despite them. 'Writing is like running downhill; can't stop if you want to', it's remarked at one point; but while this near-900-page tome does increasingly seem interminable, irresistible momentum isn't one of its achievements. Since what will happen is well known – Robespierre's prim inexorableness sealing the doom of Danton and Desmoulins – there's no suspense to tighten the storyline. Tension from other quarters is absent, too. Fidgety zig-zagging between numerous characters, along with repetitious interludes of bantering repartee, mean that none of the nightmarish impetus of the revolution is captured. Further impeding the narrative's course are recurrent mounds of historical data tipped into the novel as if quarried straight from source books: 'By the end of the first week of February, France is at war with England, Holland and Spain. The National Convention has promised armed support to any people who wish to rise against armed oppression. At home there is a food shortage, soaring inflation. In Paris the Commune battles with the Girondist ministers . . .'

The result of long immersion in research, *A Place of Greater Safety* is, like many long-immersed things, bloated. As if conscious of this, Mantel kept her next historical novel, *The Giant, O'Brien*, an atmospheric excursion into late eighteenth-century Dublin and London, taut and shorter. But, with *Wolf Hall* (2009), the first book in the Tudor trilogy she continued with *Bring Up the Bodies* (2012) and *The Mirror and the Light* (2020), the pattern she had followed in *A Place of Greater Safety* reasserted itself in two ways: over-copious historical documentation and an almost fixated-seeming attitude to her central character.

Mantel's decision to set fiction in the Tudor era was something she described in militant terms: 'I decided to march on to the middle ground of English history and plant a flag.' To plant that flag, she had to push her way across territory already swarming with historical novelists. Colourful, savage and momentous, Henry VIII's reign has long exerted a magnetic pull on writers and readers. This is, Mantel has said, because it offers 'a distillation of all the stories that fascinate us about sex and violence and power and high politics, but being played out for us by royal people'. Certainly, fascination with crowned heads – especially ones dramatically lopped off – has ensured that the Tudor period has never lacked fictional chroniclers. Notably prolific among them was Eleanor Hibbert, the author of more than 200 novels who, besides turning out bodice-rippers, Mills & Boon romances, thrillers, murder mysteries, Gothic suspense (under the pen-name Victoria Holt) and family sagas (under the pen-name Philippa Carr), wrote (as Jean Plaidy) a dozen or so Tudor novels. Extending from *Murder Most Royal* (1949) about Anne Boleyn and Catherine Howard, to *Rose without a Thorn* (1993) in which Catherine Howard narrates her prematurely pruned life story, they include a novel about Catherine Parr and three about Catherine of Aragon. Elsewhere, Henry VIII's truncated matrimonies have come under fictional scrutiny from characters ranging from his court jester to his spouses' ladies-in-waiting. A stream of novels offering close female viewpoints on to the king – those of his wives, mistresses, sisters and sister-in-law – has issued from novelists such as Philippa Gregory and Alison Weir.

Mantel's observer of (and prime participator in) Tudor turmoil is Thomas Cromwell, the king's chief minister. Believing him unfairly overlooked or misunderstood by fictional chroniclers of the period, she thought and read about him for thirty years, she has said, before she started work on her trilogy devoted to his rise and fall. *Wolf Hall*, which took him from a brutalised childhood as the son of a thuggish Putney blacksmith to power and prestige as the *protégé* and close adviser of Cardinal Wolsey, was a feat of massive advocacy on Cromwell's behalf. Written 'from behind his eyes' (a technique that entailed frequent repetition of the awkward stylistic tic, 'he Cromwell'), the novel is an enormous receptacle for Mantel's plentiful information and admiring speculation about him. *Bring Up the Bodies*, in which Cromwell takes revenge on those who brought down his beloved patron, Wolsey, was more streamlined and more gripping. Tautness tightened its hold and, unlike its predecessor, it accelerated to a dramatic conclusion. In the eight years before the final volume in the trilogy, *The Mirror and the Light*, appeared, Mantel accumulated, she exulted, 'masses and masses of material for the third Cromwell novel'. Disgorged into a book over 900 pages long, this material swamped the gain in pace and focus she had achieved with *Bring Up the Bodies* (not much more than half its length). In *The Mirror and the Light*, Mantel's drawbacks as a historical novelist collide on a large scale with her skills.

Plunging you into the moments after the beheading of Anne Boleyn, with which *Bring Up the Bodies* ended, its opening pages are a masterpiece of gruesome finesse. Fallen belly down on the scaffold, the small body 'swims in a pool of crimson'. Sliding in the gore and sidestepping round the now blood-sodden cushion on which the queen had knelt, her veiled ladies 'lift what is left of her, holding her by her clothes . . . afraid the cloth will rip and their fingers touch her

195

cooling flesh'. A shuddering attendant, handed the linen-swathed head, 'genuflects with her soaking parcel'. Drenched in stomach-turning sensuousness, sharply focused, vivid, fast, it's a magnificently rendered scene – but, sadly, untypical of what follows in this bulging chronicle of Cromwell's last four years.

Mantel's Reith Lectures maintained that historical fiction should 'put the reader in the moment, even if the moment is 500 years ago'; it should be fiction that 'frees people from the archive'. Present-tense narration endows her trilogy (whose first words are 'So now') with in-the-moment immediacy. But freeing people from the archive proves more problematic, as reams of archival material are constantly dragged out with them.

Clogged with researched material, *The Mirror and the Light* can be a painfully slow read, sometimes like wading through a Sargasso Sea of Tudor haberdashery, sixteenth-century foodstuffs, aristocratic genealogies and dynastic matrimonial entanglements. Inventories are reeled out for everything from the music of the period ('The duets of Francesco Spinacino, the saltarellos of Dalza the Milanese, the *pavane alla veneziana, pavane alla ferrarese*: a new toccata from Capirola ...') to drapery ('Fourteen yards of black satin at six pounds and six shillings. Thirteen yards of black velvet for a nightgown and taffeta lining ... kirtles, partlets, bodices, sleeves, sundries'). There are lists of defunct Knights of the Garter, legendary outlaws ('Clym of the Clough, Adam Bell, Will Scarlet, Reynold Greenleaf ...') and debunked saints ('Guthlac and Gertrude, Hilda and Hubertus ... Odilia, Aiden and Alphege, Wenta, Walburga ...'). Emblems of noble families receive abundant attention: 'the Tudor rose', 'the Seymours' phoenix', 'the Howards' silver crosslets', 'the blue-tongued lion of the Fitzalans', 'the Rochford's sable lion', 'the Pole emblem, the pansy or viola', Catherine of Aragon's pomegranate, Anne Boleyn's white falcon, Anne of Cleves' swan.

Ominously prefaced by a five-and-a-half-page list of characters and two five-generation royal family trees, the novel is as over-populated as it is overloaded. Some artistic pattern is imposed by structural symmetries: *Wolf Hall* started with the fifteen-year-old Cromwell lying in his own blood on the cobbles of Putney after a brutal beating from his father, *The Mirror and the Light* closes with the fifty-five-year-old Cromwell lying in his own blood as he dies by the executioner's axe on Tower Hill. His beheading and that of Anne Boleyn strikingly bookend the novel.

Severed heads aren't uncommon in Mantel's fiction – not only in her Tudor trilogy (Thomas More's in *Wolf Hall*, those of Boleyn's alleged lovers in *Bring Up the Bodies*, Boleyn's and Cromwell's in *The Mirror and the Light*). Her novel set in Saudi Arabia, *Eight Months on Ghazzah Street* (1988), depicts a nation infamous for its decapitations. In *A Place of Greater Safety* (1992), the guillotine is kept busy. Alison Harte, the medium haunted by an abusive childhood at the centre of *Beyond Black* (2005), is bedevilled by flashbacks of seeing a woman's hacked-off head in a bath in the squalid squat where she was brought up. Beheadings in *The Mirror and the Light* are portrayed with an intensity often lacking from the rest of the novel. Since its main events are well known – Henry VIII's short-lived marriage to Jane Seymour, his distaste for her brief successor, Anne of Cleves, and the ruin this brings to her supporter Cromwell – there's scant suspense to add grip to its storyline.

Things are slackened further not just by multiple digressions into side-issues but by a high proportion of recapitulation. Episodes from the preceding novels are repeatedly harked back to: Cromwell's abused childhood at the fists and boots of his violent father, his years as a soldier and merchant on the continent, his time in the congenial service of Cardinal Wolsey until the prelate's fall from favour. Themes prominent in the previous books – caste-resentment of the commoner Cromwell by the grandees of ancient families, Henry's unnerving personal and religious vacillations – recur. So do rather one-note characters: the splutteringly belligerent Duke of Norfolk, the spitefully scheming Lady Rochford, the always snarling Bishop Gardiner.

For all its bulk, the book adds little to Mantel's already profuse portrayal of Cromwell.

Paradoxically, the novel seems at once voluminous and limited. Its concentration on the silky reptile pit of the court and the doublet-and-hose tribalism of the great families means that there's only a very distanced sense of the shattering cataclysms wreaked by Cromwell's religious policies. Though Mantel doesn't flinch from conveying pain – there's a searingly horrible scene of an agonised death by public burning – she is less effective at transmitting dread, the clammy terror hanging over the period. Fighting for his life under interrogation as a prisoner in the Tower, Cromwell verbally spars with his enemies with what can sound like Senior Common Room smartness and sarcasm. As in *A Place of Greater Safety*, repartee is surprisingly bantered on the edge of carnage.

In the novel's acknowledgements, Mantel expresses gratitude to the 'unseen army' of curators, librarians and academics who preserve 'what is left of the world of Thomas Cromwell'. Formidably knowledgeable about that world, she is paramount as a preserver of it herself. Her trilogy is a phenomenal achievement but, in *The Mirror and the Light*, it's more a phenomenon of amassed information and tireless enthusiasm than triumphant creativity.

C.J. Sansom

Mantel wasn't the only novelist to keep the Tudor flag flying in the bestseller lists. Some years before she began her trilogy, C.J. Sansom, an outstanding instance of a crime writer who found it fruitful to go back in time, had begun a Tudor fiction sequence that brought him, too, an enthusiastic readership. Like Mantel's trilogy, his first two novels – *Dissolution* (2003) and *Dark Fire* (2004) – are set during Cromwell's time as Henry VIII's chief minister. But, in contrast to her mannered approach and entranced concentration on Cromwell, his fiction has far swifter pace and fans out across a much broader field. In it a probing, scholarly intelligence combines with the suspense and surprises of the detective genre. A historian who had a career in law before he began writing his novels, Sansom found a well-chosen sleuth in his hunchbacked lawyer, Matthew Shardlake. He also found in the Tudor period a milieu that allowed him to engage with concerns that had long haunted him.

Atmospheres of oppression and scared wariness, in which careless words or an ill-advised allegiance can prove fatal, magnetise Sansom. Besides his Shardlake series, he has published two non-Tudor novels: *Winter in Madrid* (2006), a foray into spy fiction, mainly located in the devastated Spanish capital after the civil war, and *Dominion* (2012), an exercise in 'alternate history' that takes you into a 1952 Britain which, after surrendering to Germany in 1940, has become a dingy broken satellite state of the Third Reich. Franco and Hitler loom over terrorised societies in those books, as Henry VIII does in the Tudor novels.

In a 2018 interview, Sansom revealed what lies behind his compulsive (and viscerally potent) re-creation of nightmarishly authoritarian societies: traumatic memories of his ten 'terrible years as a pupil at George Watson's College, an Edinburgh private day school, which scarred me for life and nearly resulted in my death by suicide at 15'. In Tudor England, Franco's Spain and a Europe over which Hitler holds sway, he finds surrogate territories for the world of unremitting bullying, vicious scapegoating and emotional and psychological abuse that, he disclosed with angry, painful candour, almost destroyed him as a child. As with authors we have seen previously, scarring by early damage and the silences surrounding it spurred creativity.

In Sansom's fiction, this creativity has taken varying forms. *Winter in Madrid* is an espionage suspense tale; *Dominion*, a 'what-if' history novel exploring ambiguities of collaboration and resistance in an increasingly totalitarian Britain. The Shardlake novels were conceived as Tudor versions of differing types of crime novel: from a classic closed-community whodunit in a snowbound monastery (*Dissolution*) to a quest for a deadly weapon of war (*Dark Fire*), a political thriller (*Sovereign*, 2006), a sixteenth-century serial killer story (*Revelation*, 2008) and a legal thriller (*Heartstone*, 2010). The feature they share is portrayal of the havoc wreaked by Henry VIII's brutal political and ideological vacillations: a nation bloodily ripped apart by sectarian fanaticism, glories of ecclesiastical architecture reduced to rubble. Presiding over a country in turmoil and racked with fear, the monarch with the 'hard and savage' eyes caught in Holbein's portrait of him confronts Shardlake at a climactic moment in *Sovereign*. In *Lamentation* (2014), he reappears in a scene electric with peril, now so monstrously obese that he has to be winched and wheeled around his Whitehall Palace. *Tombland* (2018) unrolls his catastrophic legacy. Bankrupted by his foreign wars, the nation is in a ruinous state: the currency debased, poverty and destitution rife. Enclosures of common land by gentry greedy for the rich profits of sheep farming provoke large-scale uprisings, one of which, a peasant rebellion in Norfolk, was – Sansom argues in an essay appended to the novel – 'a colossal event that has been much-underplayed'.

Dread pervades Sansom's Tudor novels. Two kinds of violent death send tremors through them: criminal killings and official executions. The former – a monk crushed by a toppled statue, a poisoned novice, impalement by a shard of stained glass – give the books colourfully macabre whodunnit excitements. The latter – beheaded queens, hanged, drawn and quartered Catholics, out-of-favour nobles coming to a grisly end on Tower Hill – add a historical backdrop of jeopardy and slaughter.

As the Shardlake novels have progressed, the king's wives have increasingly come to the fore. *Dissolution* was set just after the death of Jane Seymour and in a world still shaken by the aftershocks of Anne Boleyn's beheading. *Dark Fire* takes place during the fiasco of the royal wedding to Anne of Cleves. *Sovereign* features the ageing Henry's ill-fated eighteen-year-old bride, Catherine Howard, accompanying him on a triumphal visit to York. In *Revelation*, a hesitant Catherine Parr ascends to the throne.

Saved by Shardlake, in that novel, from a maniac who murdered people in ways that luridly replicate torments in the Book of Revelation, she's a figure Sansom clearly finds especially sympathetic: sophisticated, intellectually curious, humane, morally serious but with an appealing sense of humour. Intrigued by her, he slows the momentum of his earlier Tudor novels so that he can linger round her predicaments and perils during Henry's last four years. *Heartstone* sees her at Portsmouth as England faces invasion provoked by Henry's calamitous war against France. *Lamentation* shows her menaced by his lurch away from Protestant reform in his final months.

Moving on a year or so from Catherine's death in 1548 and journeying from the cowed capital to the desperate provinces, *Tombland* – whose title takes the curious name of Tudor Norwich's most affluent locality and makes it grimly applicable to a whole nation – chronicles a doomed crusade for social decency and justice. From its wide cast of characters woven into a tapestry of little-known historical happenings, victims of cruelty – personal and political – affectingly stand out. Shardlake's vulnerability to abuse and attack – thuggish jeerings at his hunched back, superstitious recoilings from it, murderous hatred from power-figures he has crossed – is foregrounded in an environment of nerve-rending risk. Again, the scarifying microcosm of Sansom's wretched schooldays gives him a creative blueprint for a terrorised nation.

It isn't only because of this that the Tudor age fits his fictional purposes. Another factor is that he considers it 'the moment at which the medieval certainties that had endured for centuries were turned upside down ... in the space of a few years, the state took on a completely different meaning ... the more I read about it, the more I realised how like the twentieth century it was in its anxiety and uncertainty, even though people thought so differently then'. Countering suggestions that Shardlake's progressive views could seem anachronistic, he contends, 'It's difficult, perhaps impossible, to write a character well in the past who is not a projection back of modern sensibilities. My defence would be that the 16th century was the time when rational, sceptical enquiry was beginning. This is the age of the humanists; we're leaving medieval thought patterns behind. I'm not saying that a man like Shardlake did exist then, but he could have, where even 20 years earlier he couldn't. That's enough for me.'

Barry Unsworth

Sansom and historical novelists like him sought to show that – contrary to L.P. Hartley's much-repeated aphorism – the past isn't a foreign country and they often didn't do things differently there. In Barry Unsworth's case, it was a crisis of confidence that impelled him to emphasise this: writer's block brought on by the dereliction he witnessed when a writer in residence at Liverpool University in the 1980s. 'Going to Liverpool was a revelation,' he said. 'It was so awful. It was so devastated at the time. It was urban decay in a way I'd never seen it.'

What compounded the shock was that this encounter with depressed industrialism aroused memories not only of the city's past but Unsworth's own: 'It chimed in with the feeling that I'd always had that I should be writing about my own past – that is mining and the northeast. I should have been doing that rather than writing about exotic places and faraway things.' Self-reproach about not using his fiction to confront social and economic inequities such as he had witnessed among the deprived colliery villages of his youth, was accentuated not just by the place but also by the period. During a decade when Margaret Thatcher's monetary policies dominated Britain, Unsworth (who 'found the triumphalism and full-blown entrepreneurial spirit of the 1980s crass and distasteful') was appalled at the spreading divide between the privileged and underprivileged.

It sent his mind back to the world riven by gulfs of wealth and opportunity into which he had been born and from which his writing had distanced him. Gradually, qualms about having retreated into literary escapism turned into something more purposeful. He perceived how he could reconcile writing historical fiction with doing justice to his own past. 'For many years', he disclosed in a 1999 interview, 'I felt a certain kind of guilt that I wasn't dealing with my roots, that I was turning away from reality. I don't feel that any longer. I feel there is . . . an essential reality in the things I write about. And I don't feel they are dated or belong to the past. I think they are as true in terms of human behaviour and human nature as they ever were. The scenes have shifted, but the voices and the feelings are very much the same.'

In Unsworth's historical fiction, almost subliminal-seeming analogies with the colliery world of his formative years can sometimes be discerned. The sculptor in *Stone Virgin* who earns his livelihood by chipping away at rock isn't entirely dissimilar to the coal miners in Unsworth's family. The Black slaves clanking with ironmongery in the dark depths of the ship in *Sacred Hunger* are like monstrously more victimised versions of the miners with coal dust-blackened faces. Located in Unsworth's home territory of Northumbria, though back in the fourteenth century, *Morality Play* highlights the exploitation of the weak by the strong. So does *Sacred Hunger*, which sends parallels about economics-based callousness forking out from the eighteenth-century to the 1980s.

Its predecessor, *Sugar and Rum*, displays the psychological and literary manoeuvrings by which Unsworth overcame his historical novelist's block. Benson, his surrogate in the book, is an author unsuccessfully struggling to complete a novel about Liverpool's involvement in the eighteenth-century African slave trade. At one point, he is seen in a library familiarising himself with details of a celebrated 1782 court case concerning a slave ship, *Zong*, which, after leaving Liverpool, ran into difficulties that left it with insufficient fresh water to keep all its human cargo alive. Its captain's solution was hideously mercantile:

> If the remaining slaves died of thirst or illness the loss would fall upon the owners of the vessel, but if they were thrown into the sea they could be regarded as legal jettison, covered by insurance. Following this ... 132 slaves were thrown overboard in three batches. Back in England the owners claimed £30 insurance money for each of the jettisoned slaves. The underwriters refused to pay. The owners duly appealed. The appeal was heard at the Court of Exchequer, presided over by Lord Mansfield. After admitting that the law was with the owners, Lord Mansfield said, 'A higher law applies to this very shocking case,' and he found for the underwriters – the first case in which an English court ruled that a cargo of slaves could not be treated simply as merchandise.

Standing as an extreme instance of the almost literally dehumanising results of the lust for profit, an episode resembling the atrocity on the *Zong* provides the climactic turning point in the novel Unsworth, unlike Benson, went on to write: *Sacred Hunger*, which charts the journey of a merchant ship from Liverpool to the fever-coast of West Africa, then on to the wilds of Florida via the West Indies. In many ways a solidly traditional historical novel, comprehensively researched, endowed with such intense physical actuality that you almost smell the canvas and tar, the reek of branded flesh and the stench from the terrified captives crammed into the hold of its slave vessel, it is also stocked with analogies between its owner's rapacious appetite for gain and the commercial ethos prevailing in 1980s Britain. The past is resurrected not just as historical drama but to moral purpose and for its relevance to the present, as would continue to be the case throughout the rest of Unsworth's career right up to his next-to-final novel, *Land of Marvels*, set in 1914 Mesopotamia but quivering with premonitions of the fate of twenty-first-century Iraq.

Jim Crace

Some writers of historical fiction used the genre not merely to suggest parallels between past and present but to exhibit archetypes and paradigms. Jim Crace, a novelist of considerable restlessness whose books have ranged in time from the advent of the Bronze Age to Judaea two thousand years ago, early nineteenth-century England and a post-apocalyptic future America, finely achieved this with his novel, *Harvest* (2013).

When its story opens, a 'reapers' moon' hangs over an unnamed village in the depths of rural England. After an anxious summer, the harvest is in. But, as is recognised by Walter Thirsk, a middle-aged widower who relates what occurs over the next fateful week, it is the last harvest the village will see. Like omens of disaster, two plumes of smoke rise. One, at the border of the village, signals the arrival of newcomers establishing their traditional right to settle by having built a hut and hearth. The other comes from the flaming out of control of an attempt to scare away the local landowner's doves (resented for eating the villagers' grain).

These two conflagrations mark the end of a centuries-old way of life and labour. Hostility towards the outsiders blurs with panic about the fire at the manor to trigger a chain reaction of cruelty and injustice that culminates in a hideous death. As this ugly episode reaches its climax, the mercantile new heir to the land rides in and, with his 'chart-maker', prepares to fence off wheat and barley fields that will be 'surrendered to the yellow teeth of three thousand sheep'.

Crace's tale of the village's final week is at once a superb conjuring up of a doomed little world, a gripping horror story of appalling consequences and a resonant fable. His evocation of the rural setting exudes sensuous immediacy. A barley meadow 'bristling and shivering on the breeze' shows 'its ochres and its cadmiums, its ambers and its chromes' – signs, like the 'nutlike and sugary' smells wafting from it, that it is ready for scything. An ancient oak crouches within 'its swishing sleeves of ivy'.

For all its natural beauties, though, the village is no idyll. Grinding labour accompanies its seasonal rhythms. Events that hasten its disintegration – especially the maltreatment of two women and the little girl who is that year's newly crowned Gleaning Queen – are engineered by the new landowner. But the villagers themselves are far from blameless.

Enclosure of several kinds frames the novel: not just the fencing in of common land but the self-enclosure of an isolated community capable of barbarism in defence of its boundaries. Walter, who married into the village years earlier, finds himself mistrusted and assaulted when fears mount. Limitations – mental, physical, moral and emotional – manifest themselves as the planned wool-trade enclosures entrench on farmland. Atmospherically resurrecting a pivotal historical moment, Crace's simultaneously elegiac and unillusioned novel infuses it with almost mythic significance.

Robert Harris

To give the little world of *Harvest* wide symbolic resonance, Crace kept its village nameless, its region vague and its date hazy. More usually, novelists have found paradigms – especially political ones – in specific places and periods. Ancient Rome, from its republic to its imperial rise and fall, has been the most widespread source, and no writer has made keener use of it than Robert Harris.

Halfway through *Imperium* (2006), the first novel in his trilogy about the Roman orator Cicero, its hero indignantly exclaims, 'Politics? Boring? Politics is history on the wing! What other sphere of activity calls forth all that is most noble in men's souls, and all that is most base? Or has such excitement? Or more vividly exposes our strengths and weaknesses?' It's a paean of praise that is also a personal manifesto from an author steeped in and intensely informed about politics. Harris, who began his career as a BBC current affairs reporter before becoming political editor of the *Observer* and then a political columnist for the *Sunday Times*, initially wrote non-fiction books about the 1980s political scene and associated matters, such as the supposed finding of Hitler's diaries. When, in 1992, he switched to fiction, starting with a hugely successful debut novel, *Fatherland*, set in an alternative Europe where Hitler had been victorious in the Second World War, a passion for politics continued to animate his pages. Extensive knowledge about the Third Reich and the Second World War was mobilised in *Enigma* (1995), which fictionalised the urgencies and intricacies of code-breaking by intelligence personnel at Bletchley Park in 1943, and *Archangel* (1998) in which the discovery of a cache of Stalin's private papers threatened to unleash disruptive spectres of the past into Boris Yeltsin's Russia. Later novels – *Munich* (2017) recounting Chamberlain's last-ditch 1938 negotiations with Hitler, and *V2* (2020), a kind of companion piece to *Enigma*, in which a team of young women battle to sabotage German rocket attacks on England from Occupied Holland – continued his engagement with the Third Reich. But before them, Harris's fiction took a long swerve back into the distant past. With *Pompeii* (2003) he produced a novel about the 79 AD eruption of Vesuvius, which at first seemed cast in the spectacular-historical-catastrophe mode of precursors such as Edward Bulwer-Lytton's Victorian blockbuster, *The Last Days of Pompeii* (1834), to which it makes oblique allusion. As the book proceeds, however, it becomes apparent that concerns salient in Harris's earlier fiction have been transferred to this new territory.

Ingeniously adopting an unusual vantage point on to Vesuvius' fiery devastation, Harris takes as his central character a man whose element is water. Attilius, a young Roman from a dynasty of aqueduct builders, is sent south to take command of the Aqua Augusta, the great stone watercourse (the longest in the world) that irrigates the coastal plains and cities of Campania. Scarcely has he arrived before the system mysteriously chokes, jeopardising the teeming conurbations sweltering in the fierce August heat around the bay of Neapolis:

pleasure resorts like Stabiae or Baiae, Misenum where the imperial
fleet rides at anchor and – higher towards the forested green pyramid
of Mount Vesuvius – the prosperous trading town of Pompeii.

As Attilius deploys technical know-how, deduction and intuition
to locate and clear the blockage clogging the aqueduct, Harris provides
an engrossing tour of one of the great engineering achievements on
which the Roman Empire was based. By the time his hero – raising
sluices, plumbing reservoirs, probing filtration tanks and crawling
along finely graduated underground channels – has found and repaired
a tunnel floor that has unaccountably buckled in the vicinity of
Vesuvius, there's no doubt about the monumental accomplishment of
Roman hydraulic architecture. But even as Attilius is resourcefully
resolving the water problem, intimations of more terrible danger
make themselves felt as tremors shake the parched earth.

Harris evokes the world about to be engulfed by the volcano with
striking expertise, from its public baths and patrician villas to its
taverns and slave galleys. His depiction of a wealthy vulgarian's
banquet (the menu includes mice rolled in honey, parrot's tongue,
nightingale-liver stew and sow's udder stuffed with kidneys, with its
vulva served as a side dish) catches its grossness with such sickening
pungency as to make you feel like heading for the vomitorium. The
novel's portrayal of the Roman mentality is equally well-realised. But
its historical tableaux are never allowed to look remote. Analogies
with modern times are kept apparent. The book's epigraphs signal
affinities between Rome's world superiority and that of twenty-first-
century America (occasional use of terms like 'superpower' reinforces
this impression). Interviewed at the time of his novel's publication in
2003, Harris observed that 'the emergence of America as the world's
only superpower has suddenly made the Romans seem much more
relevant to us. This wasn't the case 20 years ago, when cold war rivalry
disguised the extent of America's military dominance. But now . . .
America truly stands supreme . . . Forget the Spanish empire in the
17th century, or the British in the 19th: nothing like this has been

seen since Rome.' Discounting one historian's likening of the Roman Empire to the Third Reich, he maintains 'The comparison ... is closer to America. Rome was not a single homogenised state: it was an ideal, to which people from all over its conquered territories could aspire ... And Rome's technological dominance, like America's, was not confined to the military.'

Pompeii is a bravura feat. Imaginatively excavating a doomed society busily pursuing its ambitions and schemes in the shadow of a mountain no one knew was a volcano, Harris gives full vent to his flair for thrilling narrative as Vesuvius erupts. Fast-paced twists and turns alternate with nightmarish slow-motion as desperate figures struggle to wade thigh-deep through slurries of pumice to what they mistakenly hope will be safety. Waves of flaming gas glaringly suffuse scenes of suffocating terror. Amid searing panoramas of Vesuvius' destructiveness, there's emphasis on Pompeii as a monitory image. It was, Harris has said, 'both a revelation of how advanced Roman civilisation had become, and a warning that nothing lasts for ever. What had happened to one town was emblematic of what eventually had overwhelmed an entire empire.'

Other emblematic aspects of the Roman world were spotlit in his next three novels. *Imperium* (2006), *Lustrum* (2009) and *Dictator* (2015) aimed 'to demonstrate that there are certain universal rules and themes in politics that remain constant whatever the era or culture'. Insights Harris had acquired through his immersion in politics combine with high-tension techniques honed in his earlier fiction. Painstaking reconstruction of Roman politics goes along with wider pertinence. Explaining why he went back in time to fulfil a long-held ambition to write a political novel, Harris said of his chosen era, 'the characters at that time were so extraordinary, and the issues they faced so modern, it was better to write about that time than do it in the present and risk a roman à clef'.

Cicero, the trilogy's hero, is for Harris 'the quintessential politician', 'the first to approach the business of politics in a professional manner, training himself in how to speak, working out who were the important people to get to vote for you, developing his image and cultivating voters'. The novels watch him doing this. *Imperium* portrays his acquiring of power, official and political. *Lustrum* depicts his supremacy as Rome's most acclaimed and feared orator. *Dictator* charts the aftermath.

Their narrator is Tiro, a former slave. Looking back in old age over his thirty-six years as Cicero's confidential secretary, he records in the first book of the trilogy his master's remarkable ascent, between 79 and 64 BC, to fame and the ultimate power pinnacle of the consulship. As a close-quarters observer of political struggles and the inventor of a brilliantly efficient system of shorthand (much needed to keep up with Cicero's courtroom torrents of eloquence and invective), he is well placed to write these memoirs. His ability to jot down speech at speed also proves of saving value in two crucially decisive episodes.

Lacking the traditional means of access to political power in Rome (membership of the patrician caste, leadership of an army, enormous wealth), Cicero – initially an unprepossessing young advocate from the provinces beset by nerves, insomnia and a stutter – attains it by strength of will and suppleness of intellect. Visits to celebrated orators in Athens and Rhodes school him in rhetorical techniques: the telling effect of a sudden drop into quietness or a prolonged pause, the importance of clearly defined body language, the deadly impact of a perfectly targeted thrust of mockery that will linger in listeners' minds after everything else in a speech fades away. These skills are dauntingly tested in the first great case of his career: his prosecution of Gaius Verres who, protected by powerful allies, had used his governorship of Sicily as an opportunity for wholesale looting (everything from archaic Greek bronzes to wrenched-off ancient sanctuary doors), extortion, enslavement, torture, floggings to death and the hanging or crucifixion of anyone who defied him.

Race-against-time scenarios generated page-turner tension in Harris's earlier novels: a desperate bid to unearth the truth about the

Nazi death camps in *Fatherland*, the urgent drive to break the Nazi code in *Enigma*, a dash to reach an Arctic hideout before winter locks it away behind snow and ice in *Archangel*, the frenzied stampede from Vesuvius in *Pompeii*. In *Imperium* suspense is escalated by the need to gather evidence against Verres in a challengingly short space of time, and to compress the indictment so that it can be trenchantly delivered within the brief period of a trial cynically curtailed by Verres' supporters .

Cicero's against-the-odds defeat of Verres entitles him to assume the rank of the man he has routed – the first step in a climb to dominance portrayed in the next novel and watched fatally declining in the final book. Throughout this trajectory, Republican Rome in its last days is re-created with a wealth of arresting detail. Resurrecting a society two millennia away from ours, Harris contrives to make it appear at once distant and familiar. 'The whole point of my book', he said, 'is that politics never changes. In 2000 years, absolutely nothing has changed.' Electoral predictions in Rome may be based on auguries and entrails rather than focus groups and opinion polls but, behind colourful surface differences, the prototypes of our own politics are visible. Tiro seems a precursor of the legal reporter and the lobby correspondent. As even Cicero becomes tainted by compromise and concession, Harris dramatises enduring political issues. His Roman scenarios of democracy under pressure from autocracy, of populist anger self-interestedly whipped up by corrupt billionaires, of concentrations of power clenched in dangerously few hands and a constitution buckling under strain crackle with immediate pertinence.

Harry Sidebottom

During the Victorian and Edwardian imperial heyday, Rome – the classic prototype and paradigm of empire – was often seen (not least on colossal canvases by artists such as Thomas Cole whose five-painting sequence, *The Course of Empire*, panoramically displayed its span from healthy primal state to 'Consummation', 'Destruction' and 'Desolation') as a warning of inexorable downfall. Although it was the British Empire and its aftermath to which the multitude of novels about imperialism published over the last half century harked back most widely, the disintegration of the Roman Empire received considerable attention too. No novelist focused on it with fiercer knowledgeability than Harry Sidebottom. A classics don at Oxford specialising in Roman history and ancient warfare (about which he wrote an admired study), he merged the two in novels which it would be an understatement to describe as full-blooded. Rarely has erudition been more steeped in gore.

Sidebottom's academic credentials stand out as impressive even in a period when authors of historical fiction have often put in prodigious amounts of preliminary research (Robert Harris's filling the boot of his car with the twenty-nine volumes of the Loeb Classical Library edition of Cicero's works purchased at Blackwell's prior to writing his trilogy, Hilary Mantel's decades-long delvings into Tudor archives, C.J. Sansom's equally prolonged immersion in the period, Barry Unsworth's amassing of a plethora of data before using, he reckoned, 'about 20%' of it in his fiction). Appendices to the novels in Sidebottom's six-book *Warrior of Rome* series and his subsequent *Throne of the Caesars* trilogy bristle with cross-reference to articles in learned journals such as 'Herodian's Historical Methods and Understanding of History' (*Aufstieg und Niedergang der Römischen Welt* II.34.4 [1998]) or *Oration XI, In Praise of Antioch*, by the fourth-century AD orator Libanius (translated by G. Downey in *Proceedings of the American Philosophical Society* 103.5 [1959], 652–686). Copiously recommended background reading ranges from Eusebius' *History of the Church* and *Tertullian: A Historical and Literary Study* to *The Age of the Galley: Mediterranean Oared Vessels since Pre-Classical Times* and *Looking at Lovemaking: Constructions of Sexuality in Roman Art 100BC–AD250*. Glossaries, sometimes running to 25 pages or more, elucidate recondite words and phrases. There are appended disquisitions on topics such as Senatorial

Careers, Provincial Governors, Die-Cutting and Coin-Striking and The Measure of Time.

What gives Sidebottom's fiction its peculiar distinctiveness is that this scholarly apparatus coexists with mounds of butchery. Imperial disintegration and physical dismemberment receive equal attention. Chronicling the Roman empire's third-century AD disasters on its distant frontiers – in the North, in Africa and especially in the East, where the Sassanid Empire is making devastating inroads – the novels contain a spectacularly high body count. Scarcely have they begun before stabbed and gruesomely hacked fatalities start to pile up. *Fire in the East* (2008), the novel which launched Sidebottom's *Warrior of Rome* sequence, opens with the assassination of a Roman emperor and his son. *Iron and Rust* (2014), which launched his later series, *Throne of the Caesars*, opens with the assassination of a Roman emperor and his mother. Violent death is the favoured opening gambit throughout Sidebottom's fiction. *Fire in the East*'s successor, *King of Kings* (2009), begins with a man impaling himself on his sword ('coils of intestines slithered out with the blade. Shiny, and revoltingly white, they looked and smelled like unprepared tripe'). *Blood and Steel* (2015), the aptly titled successor to *Iron and Rust*, gets under way with the assassination of the commander of the emperor Maximinus' Praetorian Guard.

Sidebottom's hero, Marcus Clodius Ballista (an Anglo-Saxon nobleman brought to Rome when young as a hostage and carried to prominence by his military prowess) receives so many wounds during the two fictional series in which he plays a commanding role that you feel he can't be much more than ambulant scar-tissue by the time they conclude. Nevertheless, Sidebottom plunged him into a particularly strenuous scenario in the first of the stand-alone novels that came next. *The Last Hour* (2018) – a twenty-four-hour-timeline thriller in which Ballista is hunted by a band of killers as he strives to save the emperor Gallienus from assassination at the Colosseum – opens with him slaughtering three of them before clambering onto the dizzyingly towering roof of the Mausoleum of Hadrian (which, as Castel Sant'Angelo, would later be the site of Tosca's suicide-leap in Puccini's opera) from which he dives into the Tiber, surfacing battered but, improbably, alive.

With its formulaic ferocities and sword-and-sandal savageries, Sidebottom's fiction could look as though it merely offers strenuously violent excitements – an impression not weakened by his comments about the solo books that followed his linked novels. *The Last Hour*, he explained, was devised as an ancient Roman version of the American TV action drama, *24*, with its twenty-four-hour time scheme and counter-terrorist-agent hero. *The Lost Ten* (2019), about a perilous rescue bid by a crack Roman squad behind enemy lines in Persia, was conceived as '*Bravo Two Zero* meets *Gladiator*'. *The Return* (2020), his first murder mystery, aims 'to bring the dark brooding menace of the best Scandi and Italian Noir to the past, while not stinting on the military action of the historical novel.'

Coexisting with the slashing and the slaying, though, is cutting-edge scholarship. In keeping with Sidebottom's belief that 'Historical novelists are the gatekeepers of history. We have a duty to get things right', massacre occurs in meticulously researched milieux, authenticated down to the last particular. Dramatic set pieces like the siege of a Roman outpost in Mesopotamia ringed by the ferocious Sassanid army brim with information about warfare of the period.

Politically, too, the novels display authoritative knowledge. The entangled power struggles that reduced the vastly extended Roman Empire to a low ebb in the third century AD are compellingly exhibited and explained in the *Warrior of Rome* and *Throne of the Caesars* series. *The Return*, set in the Calabria of 145 BC, gives a fascinating picture of Roman expansionism in its early years, as a legionary arrives back at his family's farm in territory that is still an unruly, resentful colony of the Republic.

Beneath their entrail-splattered, blood-drenched surface, Sidebottom's novels share the modern engrossment with empire – from its rough beginnings to its decline into decadence and breakdown. Other prevailing themes are evident too. 'Combat stress', frequently focused on in novels about twentieth-century wars and their aftermath, is seen in an ancient Roman context. Killings during the sack of Corinth leave the legionary in *The Return* hag-ridden by trauma, which surfaces in his nightmares as apparitions of the avenging Furies. Ballista, Sidebottom's series hero, isn't only a formidable exemplar of physical scarring but also suffers from post-traumatic stress disorder, which shows itself in terrifying hallucinatory visions of an emperor he has murdered.

Like many historical novelists as well, Sidebottom emphasises that the period in which he has immersed himself has continuing relevance: 'I like to explore important themes of Roman history in my fiction. These themes were important then, and they remain so today. The Romans are always "good to think with" about both the past and the present.'

He shares another widespread trait: that of linking novels into series. A marked feature of historical fiction in recent decades has been the number of works published as parts of an ongoing sequence. Legions of ancient Rome novels have appeared in this form: from Steven Saylor's sixteen-book *Roma Sub Rosa* detective series and Simon Scarrow's twenty-one-book *Eagles of the Empire* series to Lindsey Davis's twenty-novel crime series narrated by an imperial 'informer', Marcus Didius Falco, and her subsequent ten-book series narrated by his adopted daughter, Flavia Albia. Another veteran of the genre, Edith Pargeter, wrote, as 'Ellis Peters', twenty murder mystery novels following the whodunit exploits of a twelfth-century Benedictine monk, Brother Cadfael. Besides publishing a quartet of novels about the American Civil War, a trilogy about King Arthur, another about fourteenth-century Europe, and a thirteen-novel series about Alfred the Great and his descendants, Bernard Cornwell, a particularly prolific unroller of historical fiction, chronicled the Napoleonic Wars era in more than twenty books starring his scarred and wayward British soldier, Richard Sharpe.

Patrick O'Brian

Naval life during the Napoleonic era was expansively chronicled in Patrick O'Brian's twenty-volume Aubrey–Maturin sequence, launched in 1969 with *Master and Commander* and continued to *Blue at the Mizzen* in 1999, published just months before he died, leaving behind an unfinished further addition to it. A character in its fourteenth book, *The Nutmeg of Consolation* (1991), defines a novel as 'a work in which life flows in abundance, swirling without pause: or, you might say, without an end, an organized end'. It's a definition that, not least in its watery imagery, certainly fits O'Brian's marine saga.

The two friends at its centre are neatly antithetical. Jack Aubrey, the crests and plunges of whose naval career from lieutenant to rear-admiral are charted across the novels, is a sunny-natured extrovert, open in behaviour and never happier than when flinging himself into strenuous action. Stephen Maturin, his saturnine ship's surgeon who also works as an undercover agent against the French, is guarded in manner and intellectually keen, using voyages around the world to pursue his researches into natural history. As skilled amateur musicians playing Mozart or Corelli – Aubrey on the violin, Maturin on the cello – they achieve harmony through counterpoint. The novels show their contrasting personalities having the same effect.

There is one other continuing contrast: Aubrey, nerve and muscle, eye and mind in formidable control when facing peril on the ocean, is repeatedly shown as all at sea when ashore, floundering amid the murky undercurrents of civilian life. Apart from this, O'Brian's epic doesn't present much pattern. Narrative often moves forward with almost arbitrary-seeming jerkiness. Episodes in one novel sprawl on into the next. As if by afterthought, retrospective light is cast from a later book on to events in a predecessor. Meanderings and circlings back are common. The sequence has often been called a *roman fleuve* but a better term would be *roman océanique*. Encompassing an enormous range of late Georgian naval life, it surges across many seas

– from the Mediterranean to the Baltic, the Pacific, the Atlantic, the Indian Ocean and the South China Sea. Characters are seen singing the Old Hundredth during a shipboard service near Tristan da Cunha under the low grey skies, sleet and spindrift of a southern winter echoing with penguin calls or playing makeshift cricket in tropic heat and an atmosphere 'wet as a living sponge' after running aground on an uncharted reef. From the spice islands of the East Indies to the prison colonies of New South Wales, from the rigours of the Antarctic to the treacherous languors of the Malay archipelago, the geographical span is vast.

What O'Brian packs into it is a historical era resurrected in extraordinary detail. In one of his rare interviews, he insisted that 'A novelist must know everything about his time.' By 'his time' he meant not the twentieth century he lived in but the eighteenth and early nineteenth century he mentally and imaginatively inhabited. 'There is something the English would say is at times a bit precious about Patrick, something even a bit incomprehensible. His language, his address. He doesn't really belong in this century', his British editor observed. His American editor remarked that 'O'Brian wasn't writing about the early nineteenth century; he seemed to be writing from within it.'

O'Brian went to considerable lengths to achieve this effect. Like other historical novelists we have seen, he was a voracious researcher. Long before he began to write his Aubrey–Maturin novels, he said, he 'had been reading naval history for years and years'. An avid frequenter of the National Maritime Museum at Greenwich and the British Public Records Office, he soaked up information about Nelson's navy from captains' logs, plans of ships, the memoirs and letters of admirals and commanders. *The Naval Chronicle*, a monthly journal brimming with first-hand accounts of sea battles as well as day-to-day life in the Royal Navy, was a source he acknowledged as especially indispensable ('when I describe a fight I have log-books, official letters, contemporary accounts or the participants' own memoirs to vouch for every exchange'). Declaring that 'authenticity is a jewel', he went even further in pursuit of it, assembling around himself an eighteenth- and early nineteenth-century milieu. His favourite authors were Jane Austen and Samuel Richardson, with Henry Fielding and Tobias Smollett not far behind (it's no accident that two valued members of Aubrey's crew are named Richardson and Fielding). Nikolai Tolstoy, his stepson and biographer, reported that 'he frequently emphasised to me the pleasure of reading classic novels, if not necessarily in first editions, at least in those published during the authors' lifetime. Elegant binding, distinctive print, the thought that the work had been read by the authors' contemporaries, and the idiosyncratic smell of early editions add materially to the pleasure of reading'. 'You see the print they saw', O'Brian explained. 'You have the smell of the binding in your nostrils. It makes the era palpable and helps its apprehension. Take a newspaper account of Waterloo or Trafalgar, with all the small advertisements: it seems much more real than reading about it in a history book.' A keen period bibliophile, he swapped his manuscript of *Master and Commander* for a first edition of *Emma*. A fine set of the 1810 edition of the *Encyclopaedia Britannica* was particularly prized as an infallible guide to the state of knowledge at the period of his fiction and a guard against anachronism.

O'Brian's appetite for authenticity was unsparing. Guests who paid handsomely to attend a banquet held in his honour in 1996 in the ornate Painted Hall of Greenwich's Royal Naval College may have been surprised to be served, at his insistence, turnips and corned beef, preceded by pea soup and followed by 'figgy-dowdy', a shipboard stand-by of suet and raisins. Indigestibility of another kind – hard-to-take-in nautical vocabulary – can be a drawback in his fiction. Readers unfamiliar with the whereabouts and function of futtocks, gingalls, gaffs and orlops, or what exactly is entailed by being 'furled in the loose bunt, swagging horribly, with gaskets all ahoo' won't find much enlightenment in the books in which they feature (aware of this, O'Brian's first biographer, Dean King, additionally published a 400-page lexicon to the novels). A further discouragement is sometimes stodgy humour, as in recurring jocosity about Aubrey's muddling of proverbs ('They have chosen their cake and must lie on it', 'There's a good deal to be said for making hay while the iron is hot'). Women in the books – Aubrey's two-dimensional wife Sophie, his shrewish mother-in-law Mrs Williams, the supposedly irresistible *femme fatale* Diana Villiers, the seductive American spy Louise Wogan, a throat-slitting Borneo pirate queen – aren't much more than pasteboard.

But the epoch within which O'Brian places these figures is rendered with astonishing copiousness, breadth and immediacy. It isn't only geographically that the range is confidently wide. His imagination seems as at home in the flame-lit courtyard of a Malay palace where a Sultan's faithless catamite is meeting a hideous fate as in the polite backgammon room of a London gentleman's club. Detail is assiduously exact – right down to items such as the twists of differently coloured thread with which Chinese firework-makers in Malaysia label their small cotton bags of chemicals. Verbally there's the same precision: when a fellow-botanist offers Maturin a 'nondescript' plant, he doesn't mean it's featureless but (true to the period meaning) not yet scientifically identified and categorised. As might be expected, water is constantly scrutinised: as a ship leaves Bombay, it's noted how 'the fetid ooze of the Hooghly gave way to the clearer sea of the Bay of Bengal, to the right dark blue of the Indian Ocean'. Weather signs are also acutely registered as when 'deep purple' massing beneath 'a dark coppery glare' gives forewarning of a typhoon.

There are teeming panoramas of the gaudy polyglot diversity of early nineteenth-century ports: Lisbon, Malta, Bombay. Gibraltar, seen from a ship in its bay, is dazzlingly conjured up:

the brilliance of the sun makes colours glow and sing: a military band was playing on the Alameda, its brasses blazing like gold beneath the shade, while through the gardens and up and down the Grand Parade flowed an easy crowd of red coats, blue jackets, and a wonderful variety of civilian clothes from Europe, Morocco, the Turkish provinces of Africa, Greece and the Levant, and even from much further east. White turbans and the pale, dust-blue robes of Tangier Copts, the dark red and broad straw hats of Berbers and the black of Barbary Jews moved in and out among the pepper-trees, mingling with tall Moors and Negroes, kilted Greek seamen from the islands, red-capped Catalans, and small Malays in green.

The look and sound of the early nineteenth century around the globe is caught with extraordinary skill. So is its political and intellectual climate. Two background figures loom as particularly influential on O'Brian's protagonists: Nelson, the naval hero who is Aubrey's idol, and Joseph Banks, the naturalist and explorer who is Maturin's mentor (and whose biography O'Brian wrote). What the series most compellingly transmits – matching even Mantel's enthral-ment with the Tudor age – is its author's intensely knowledgeable involvement with his chosen period. 'The tale or narrative set in the past may have its particular time-free value', O'Brian once asserted. It's a belief that, as we have seen, many historical novelists have subscribed to, highlighting aspects of the era they focus on as having modern parallels. But, with O'Brian, this hardly seems to be the case. Complete immersion in a now-distant epoch is an end in itself.

William Golding's *To the Ends of the Earth* Trilogy

Another novelist drawn to shipboard life in the Napoleonic era was William Golding. The sea had always been a significant element in his life. Sailing was one of his keenest passions. Service in the Royal Navy during the Second World War gave him experience of cruisers, destroyers and minesweepers; he was one of the sailors who took part in the sinking of the *Bismarck*; during the D-Day operation, he commanded a rocket-launching craft. After the war, as a teacher at Bishop Wordsworth's School, he introduced naval uniform and the study of knots, semaphore and seamanship to the Combined Cadet Corps under his charge. In his boat, the *Wild Rose* (a converted Whitstable oyster smack), he sailed the Dutch waterways and around the North Sea and the Baltic. A further plan to explore the canals of Europe was scuppered when his later boat, the *Tenace*, was run down and sunk in a collision with a tanker off the Isle of Wight in the English Channel. In his fiction, watery menace made its presence powerfully felt: the sea surrounding the island on which schoolboys are marooned in *Lord of the Flies*, the rivers the Neanderthals are terrified of crossing in *The Inheritors*, the freezing Atlantic pounding at the swept-overboard protagonist of *Pincher Martin* on his rock.

With *Rites of Passage* (1980), Golding launched one of English literature's great fictional voyages. At its start, passengers embark on an antiquated ship of the line that has been converted to carry them across the dangerous seas of the Napoleonic era to Australia. By the time the next book, *Close Quarters* (1987), begins, the decrepit old vessel is just south of the Equator, labouring in the doldrums where its hull has become choked with weed. *Fire Down Below* (1989), the finale to the trilogy (which Golding revised into a one-volume edition, *To the Ends of the Earth*, in 1991), carries the crippled ship and its storm-tossed freight of humanity to landfall in Sydney Cove.

As always in Golding's fiction, the physical setting is pungently and ruggedly actual. Life on the Australia-bound sailing ship reeks and resounds with authenticity. Its sand and gravel ballast stinks. The sweetish odour of laudanum hangs over its fetid sick-beds. Wind whistles in its rigging and thunders in its sails. Its planking resounds to 'the leathery slap of the seamen's naked feet'.

But, again as usual, Golding is as keen to re-create his characters' inner worlds as he is to reconstruct their external milieu. For most of

Rites of Passage, the reader is confined within the narrow, snobbish mind of Edmund Talbot, a supercilious young man keeping a journal of the voyage to entertain and gratify a politically powerful aristocrat back in England who is his godfather and patron. Bound for a government post in the upper colonial echelons of Australia, Talbot reports on the turbulent journey in sedulously *blasé* tones. Exuding condescension, reeling out classical allusions as shibboleths of class distinction, alternating between seigneurial disdain and sycophantic regard for rank, his journal lets you hear the last, jaded accents of Augustan civilisation.

Golding's purpose, it becomes evident, isn't just to chronicle the hazards of an early nineteenth-century voyage across the globe but to chart the eddies in a crucial watershed in British cultural history. In *Rites of Passage*, ebbing Neo-Classicism and the first waves of Romanticism meet. For, also on board ship, is a gawky, evangelical clergyman, Robert Colley. Viewed through Talbot's derisive gaze, he seems a clownish bumpkin, outlandish in manner and unmodish in dress. Then, after a murky incident below decks leads to Colley's collapse into catatonia and death, a journal he also has written comes into Talbot's possession. And, as it is unfolded to the reader, the narrative enters a new world.

The last and best of the figures of ungainly decency Golding often introduces into his fiction, Colley turns out to have been alive with Romantic susceptibility. His response to the journey glows with entranced appreciation of natural splendour. In contrast to the cynicism and smart knowingness that are Talbot's forte, his vision of their voyage is rapt and receptive. Turner-esque seascapes of mist and lightning, gleam and vapour, majestically awe him.

But Colley's uncircumspect responsiveness finally destroys him. Gradually, the novel discloses how, after he has been plied with drink, his suppressed homosexuality has been jeeringly made play with by one of the young crewmen whose bronzed bodies he has innocently rhapsodised about in his journal. As Colley subsequently wills himself to death out of shame, Golding invests with fierce desolation a theme that always haunts his pages: the damage done by human cruelty.

Not that *Rites of Passage* is a cheerless book. In it, Golding's gifts of irony and humour are often deployed to hilarious effect. Talbot's callow satirisings, crowing over the absurdities of his fellow-passengers, are themselves satirised with mature finesse, tinged with a tolerance for his youth. Around him, there are scenes of exuberant comedy. Mr Prettiman, an irascible rationalist, stalks the after-deck with a blunderbuss, hoping to bring down an albatross and thus explode the superstition Coleridge's *Rime of the Ancient Mariner* has, he believes, deplorably promoted (the poem's relevance to the victimisation of Colley taking place on the ship goes unnoticed by him and everyone else). Talbot is entangled in a grotesque *amour* with a rouged *belle*, Zenobia Brocklehurst, and unnerved by a snappishly intelligent governess, Miss Granham, who seems disconcertingly indifferent to his assumptions of social superiority.

As characters literally tread the boards and the ship becomes increasingly bedecked with theatrical metaphor, all this seems like a brittle comedy of manners played out above an underlying physicality and brutality, and surrounded by vast dimensions of ocean and cosmos.

The collision between eighteenth-century rationality and nineteenth-century romanticism in *Rites of Passage* sometimes calls to mind the novels of Jane Austen. With *Close Quarters*, Golding steers his fiction even further into the atmosphere of her world. When the emigrants' ship is becalmed alongside another – so that, it is observed, the two vessels resemble adjoining streets in a country village – the voyagers enjoy a social life very like that in an Austen novel. As if responding to the complaint that her fiction parochially ignores the Napoleonic Wars, Golding suggests what it might have been like if it hadn't. Jubilant when they receive news of Boney's defeat, dashing young officers, a puffed-up aristocrat, his sentimental wife and their spirited ward, who has captivated Talbot, exchange visits and notes, meet for a dinner party and attend a ball. In the background, new and old attitudes clash as Benét, a lieutenant of Byronic disposition, devises a bold scheme – stubbornly opposed by the ship's cautious second-in-command, Summers – for scraping the weed from the hull.

In *Fire Down Below*, the antagonism between Benét and Summers is brought to the fore. The ship's progress to Sydney Cove, already so dangerously prolonged as to threaten provisions is now jeopardised by a new menace. Having worked loose, the foremast is splitting the huge block of timber, 'the shoe', at its base. With characteristic panache, Benét proposes sealing the cracked shoe by inserting red-hot irons which, bolted to metal plates, will pull the wood together as they cool and contract. Summers horrifiedly contends that this will ignite the core of the timber. Overruled, he watches with chagrin as Benét's risky ploy apparently succeeds. Then, in one of the most blazingly exciting sequences Golding ever wrote, he is proved fatally right.

Fire down below isn't just a real hazard in this novel. It is also the main image running through it. Potentially calamitous heatedness smouldering in the depths of the personality is the book's subject. On the fraught ship, opposing factions gloweringly coalesce. Anger and banked-down sexuality flame out. Jealousy flares. Not only do sparks fly between the flamboyant Benét and staid Summers but, beneath the latter's dispassionate exterior, dangerous elements kindle: resentment, ambition and suppressed homosexuality. Subtly, Golding makes it evident to the reader, though never to Talbot, that Summers is in love with him, tactfully contriving ways to help and protect, without embarrassing, him. There are interludes of delicate tension where the two men, sharing the watch in the middle of the night, exchange quiet confidences, Summers's just perceptibly tinged with bitterness welling from his thwarted tenderness.

The atmospheric nature of these and other scenes is heightened by the transformation effected in Talbot's narrative style after his reading of Colley's awed account of the voyage. Talbot's own Augustan prose – epigrammatic, neat and witty – now often also comes alight with visual responsiveness: in full moonlight, dazzlingly blanched sails hang above a ghost ship of silver and ivory; its wake bursts into 'a splendour of diamonds'; crenellated clouds tower up like ominous 'castles of storm'.

Brilliantly navigating a range of period styles, the novel has grotesque set pieces, such as a hideously incongruous wedding ceremony at sea, that recall Smollett, one of the eighteenth-century authors Talbot plumes himself on emulating. But, most of all, as Talbot's pride and prejudice give way to sense and sensibility, similarities to Jane Austen flood into the book. Behind a glitter of witty, politely edged verbal skirmishing, faults of inexperience are rectified; education is achieved through admission of error; moral growth entails recognition of limitations.

The journey to the other side of the globe salutarily overturns Talbot's preconceptions and widens his horizons. Where his view of other people was once shallowly mocking, he now registers deeper dimensions – helped by the way characters he thought farcical caricatures undergo a sea change. Mr Prettiman, for instance, initially 'our comic philosopher', swells, after incurring grave physical injury, into a painfully suffering fellow creature.

Talbot's maturing includes a developing respect for Prettiman's utopian scheme of founding a model community, purged of privilege and superstition, in the pristine heart of Australia. This project adds a second connotation to the image of fire down below. Under the gleaming constellations of the Southern Hemisphere, Prettiman, a romantic rationalist, speaks of his Promethean ideal of people as visionaries: 'we, a fire down below here – sparks of the Absolute – matching the fire up there'. This is a height, Talbot ruefully recognises, that he himself can never attain. His career will be more worldly. Indeed, for a time, it looks likely to be merely mundane. Up-ending his plans on his arrival in the Antipodes is the news that his influential godfather has expired of apoplexy brought on by overenthusiastic celebration of Britain's victory over 'the Corsican Tyrant'.

A sequence of brisk ups and downs, cunningly held in reserve to keep anti-climax at bay after the narrative has docked at Sydney Cove, finally takes Talbot to a happy, Jane Austen-ish ending with an ironically commonsensical young woman. But round the edges of this prospect – in a book whose atmosphere is as ever-shifting as its seascapes – melancholy drifts in. The elderly Talbot penning the pages looks back with wondering wistfulness at the ability he once had to experience intense emotion. Regret at not being able to rise to the challenge of Prettiman's idealism still sometimes surfaces in his dreams.

Starting as an arrogant social figurehead, Talbot ends as a decently self-questioning human being. This interior journey is charted with psychological and emotional nuance, while the marathon sea voyage during which it occurs gives full leeway to Golding's skills at vigorous action-writing. Throughout the book, idioms now dryly stranded in the English language – 'taken aback', 'pipe down', 'sailing close to the wind' – are drenched in the immediacy of their maritime origins. In *Fire Down Below*, pouring oil on troubled waters isn't just something characters metaphorically attempt during stormy disputes but a literal manoeuvre desperately undertaken as cliff-high waves crash around the ship and miles of ocean seethe up under its precarious timbers.

Maritime Microcosms: Julian Barnes's
A History of the World in 10½ Chapters

Golding's battered, barnacled old sailing ship creaking its leaky way over the Equator to the Antipodes is an especially memorable fictional vessel, but it was far from the only symbolic craft set afloat in modern novels. Maritime life as microcosm held sway on boats from many points of the literary compass. The *Sincerity*, Matthew Kneale's Victorian ship en route to the Antipodes in *English Passengers* took on board, along with its crew of smugglers and cheats, two ripe specimens of colonial and religious bigotry: a physician with unlovely views about 'racial types', and a fanatical Creationist clergyman. Amitav Ghosh's trilogy about early nineteenth-century colonialism in the East – *Sea of Poppies* (2008), *River of Smoke* (2011), *Flood of Fire* (2015) – stocked a former slaving schooner with characters embodying other kinds of enslavement: domestic bondage, caste servitude, indentured labour on sugar plantations, the entrapments of the opium trade. In Joseph O'Connor's *Star of the Sea* (2004) a 'famine ship' transported a range of representative voyagers – dirt-poor emigrants, refugees, servants, writers, revolutionaries and aristocrats – from the starving Ireland of 1847 to New York.

The most frequently sighted vessel reconditioned for emblematic purposes was Noah's Ark. The cosiest make-over it received was Barbara Trapido's *Noah's Ark* (1984), the tale of a variegated family that a man named Noah protectively sheltered under his roof. More often, it was commandeered by feminist writers eager to deconstruct and remodel a patriarchal archetype which had previously accommodated only conventionally connubial and hetero-normative pairings. The results – Jeanette Winterson's *Boating for Beginners* (1985), *Arky Types* (1987) by Sara Maitland and Michelene Wandor – could be freighted with whimsical preachiness. But the best of the novels in this line, Michèle Roberts's *The Book of Mrs Noah* (1987), which converted the ark into a floating conference centre where women from different backgrounds congregated, debated and wrote, adroitly combined the buoyant and the substantial. Steering her ark to Venice – a city whose associations with androgyny, carnival and moist intricacy made it a favoured feminist port of call – Roberts further emphasised its removal from its patriarchal origins.

The most virtuoso literary response to Noah's Ark, Julian Barnes's *A History of the World in 10½ Chapters* (1989), contained a few elements that had featured in the little flotilla of works that preceded it. One of the participants in *Arky Types* was a chatty worm: Barnes's opening chapter gives a woodworm's view of life on the ark. Another chapter elaborates on something Winterson's novel alluded to: an American expedition to Mount Ararat in search of relics of the ark. But Barnes's novel is a work of far greater span than any of its predecessors. The *Titanic*, the raft of the *Medusa*, Columbus's galleon, a boat crammed with Jewish refugees, an Australian dinghy trying to escape nuclear fallout, a nineteenth-century Turkish steamer chugging towards Trebizond: ships of all kinds – even a spaceship – are brought into view in it. But the vessel most frequently cited is Noah's Ark. Turning up as a child's toy or an ark-shaped fundamentalist church in North Carolina, figuring in a sarcastic joke or as an object of pious pilgrimage that respectively draws a Victorian spinster and an American ex-astronaut out to search for its rumoured resting place on Mount Ararat, it is never allowed to sink below the book's imaginative horizon.

The first chapter sneaks you on to it during the Flood. Narrated by a woodworm that has surreptitiously wriggled aboard, this opening account of life on the ark sardonically undermines one of mankind's venerated myths. As the inside story of Noah gets told, the official version is revealed to be full of holes. The ark, the subversive stowaway discloses, was run like a prison ship. Numerous species – unicorns, salamanders, hippogriffs – were lost through human stupidity, greed and fear. With creatures segregated into 'clean' and 'unclean', vicious divisiveness ruled. Equating difference with inferiority, humans shamefully maligned and mistreated their fellow animals.

At the end of this exuberantly mordant little tale, the ark scrapes to earth and its illicit passenger wriggles off to go forth and multiply. But the cargo of concerns weighing down life on the boat – bigotry, aggression, tyranny, ignorance, misguided motives – also spills out across the world. Ensuing narratives illustrate different ways in which these issues have lumbered mankind's subsequent progress.

'The history of the world?' one passage rhetorically enquires. 'Just voices echoing in the dark, images that burn for a few centuries then fade; stories, old stories that sometimes seem to overlap; strange links, impertinent connections.' It resembles, Barnes suggests, 'a multi-media collage'. To match this, his novel is extravagantly heterogeneous: a bravura miscellany of facts and fictions, pastiche, autobiography, essays and reportage, meshed together by recurring images and motifs.

Fanning out to fulfil the flippant promise of its title, Barnes's anthology ranges from the Aegean to Australasia, from a law court in medieval France to a modern film unit in the Amazonian jungle. Parody gives way to documentary. Jokes jostle horrors. Satiric mimicry is counterpointed with intimately personal talk. 'Everything is connected', one character asserts. She is referring to the planet's webs of ecology that are being ripped apart by chain reactions from disasters such as Chernobyl. But her concern with large-scale integration is itself linked to Barnes's purposes. Interfusing his diverse-looking conglomeration is underlying unity. Sometimes this is signalled by superficial concurrences and contrivances: one chapter describes the genesis of a painting by Géricault; in the next, a young lady views it on its 1821 exhibition in Dublin's Rotunda; soon afterwards, she sets out for Mount Ararat where she perishes; her remains, mistaken for those of Noah, turn up in a subsequent story.

More substantial connections are established by persisting preoccupations. One theme particularly prominent in this acutely intelligent medley of writings is the propensity of humans to misuse, or fail to use, their intelligence. A calmly appalling catalogue of the gross misjudgements, panicky disorder and insane violence that cause the wreck of the *Medusa* and the survivors' thirteen-day ordeal on their raft, gets one chapter under way. Another section, supposedly a sixteenth-century manuscript recording arguments in an ecclesiastical court, where woodworms are being tried for sacrilegiously damaging the bishop's throne, burlesques the ability of *Homo sapiens* to combine mental ingenuity with crazy premises. Reference in another tale to the nuclear bomb gives a sombre contemporary twist to the notion of the human mind being simultaneously too clever and too obtuse for its own good. Another aspect of the brain's ability to mislead itself, on which the book seizes, is the tendency to confuse knowingness with intelligence. Inane smartness is impaled with nicely spiked wit in two stories about media men: a suave TV personality and a modish film-actor. Both of these strenuously *au fait* characters display a vacuous sexual vanity – in contrast to which Barnes upholds love. A twenty-two-page, very personal-sounding meditation presents it as the redeeming factor in mankind's history; not because it necessarily brings happiness but because it can 'teach us to stand up to history, to ignore its chin-out strut'.

At the opposite extreme to love's strong tender responsiveness to individuality, Barnes locates regimentation and prejudice: the roping-off of people into despised or victimised groups. Segregation along racial, national, social, sexual or ideological lines slices through his book's rich jumble of human diversity. Its second chapter, a chilling modern variant on the archetypal myth comically debunked in the opening piece, has assorted couples ascending the gangway of a lecture cruise ship under the mocking eye of a widely travelled sophisticate. Spotting giveaway signs of which nation they hail from is, for him, a superior game. But when the boat is hijacked by terrorists and a systematic culling of the passengers begins, distinguishing national marks become a matter of life or death.

Political fanaticism lies behind this hideously methodical massacre. Elsewhere, religion's ability to constrict sympathies and blinker vision is satirically demonstrated. But, careful not to pigeon-hole himself as a reductive rationalist, Barnes also acknowledges its power to foster aspiration. Not that he holds any brief for eternity. His closing chapter – a dream of heaven – presents an endless after-life of instantly gratified wishes as hellishly boring.

Where Barnes's brainy talent displays itself most effectively is in sequences such as his dazzling deconstruction of Géricault's painting, *The Raft of the Medusa*. With this essay on art's false starts and ambiguous ends – as good as anything in his previous masterpiece in this line, *Flaubert's Parrot* – the book is a long way from fiction but close to what Barnes calls 'fabulation': making patterns with facts and fantasies in order to comprehend life.

Seeing crude categorisation as a major destructive factor throughout human history, Barnes's hybrid book inventively defies classification. Different ways of viewing the world – artistic, scientific, religious, 'sophisticated', 'primitive', cynical, hysterical – are inspected from different perspectives and, with postmodern *élan*, in different literary genres. But throughout this diversity, the Noah's Ark motif emphasises that, essentially, the planet's infinitely diverse population are all in the same boat.

Noah's Ark novelists weren't the only ones to pillage the Bible for material. From Howard Jacobson's fictionalising of Adam and Eve's life after their expulsion from Eden, *The Very Model of a Man* (1992), to Joseph Heller's *God Knows* (1984) in which the aged dying David gives a revisionist account of his career as recorded in scripture, Allan Massie's not dissimilar retrospect, *King David* (1995) and Dan Jacobson's *The Rape of Tamar* (1970) about the assault of King David's daughter by her half-brother Amnon, Old Testament tales have been retold and remoulded by many modern novelists. The Book of Books was far from unique in this. For, as we shall see, in late twentieth- and early twenty-first-century fiction reinterpreting and repurposing the literature of the past escalated into a widespread, multi-faceted phenomenon.

Part IV

Post-scripts:
The Literary Past and
Its Afterlife

Consciousness of the Literary Heritage

Resurrection writing went well beyond novels written about the past. Novels written in the past were retrieved and refurbished too. Nineteenth-century novels, in particular, were given modern makeovers – sometimes with impressive ingenuity and panache. Relocating *David Copperfield* to twenty-first-century drug-ridden Appalachia, Barbara Kingsolver's *Demon Copperhead* (2022) in which David's bullying step-father, Murdstone, becomes Stoner, a tattooed thug who battens on the hero's OxyContin-addicted mother, re-fashioned Dickens's tale to encompass America's current opioid crisis (giving her narrator an idiom indebted both to Huck Finn and Holden Caulfield, she added another layer of vitalising literary indebtedness as well).

With many novelists having academic backgrounds as professors of creative writing or teachers of and researchers into past literature, drawing upon the literary heritage became common in modern literature. Sequels, prequels and other offshoots sprouted around classic texts. Admiration and affection could be motives for this as when P.D. James, a lifelong devotee of Jane Austen, added a corpse to the corpus with her final murder mystery novel, *Death Comes to Pemberley* (2011).

At the opposite extreme, a condescending, indeed confrontational, attitude towards past masterworks could be found as authors sought to reprove and improve them. Resurrection for recrimination wasn't uncommon. But, whatever the motivation, using past literature as material for modern literature flourished to an extraordinary extent.

Resuscitations

A record-breaking bestseller later turned into a spectacularly successful film, Michael Crichton's science fiction thriller *Jurassic Park* (1990), was a significant modern novel. Its significance was two-fold. As a story of retrieval and re-creation by cloning, it offered a metaphor for what has been a remarkable literary phenomenon. As a re-working of Arthur Conan Doyle's *The Lost World* (1912) and H.G. Wells's *The Island of Doctor Moreau* (1896), it was itself a striking instance of it. In Wells's novel, a megalomaniac scientist seeks to reshape animals into humans through excruciating surgery (a spine-chilling moment when the howls of a puma undergoing vivisection mutate into human screams signals his horrible triumph). In Crichton's novel, DNA extracted from dinosaur fossils enables a megalomaniac tycoon to reproduce primeval monsters (such as those Conan Doyle showed surviving on a remote plateau in the Amazon) which break loose and start making lethally mauled humans scream.

Reviving the past is an imaginative impulse that has spread through modern fiction on an unprecedented scale. Nowhere did it manifest itself more extensively and with such fertility as in the resuscitation, reinterpretation and reshaping of earlier literature – and literati. There have been frequent fictional resurrectings of Shakespeare, Dickens, the Brontës, Thomas Hardy and Oscar Wilde. Marlowe, Milton, Congreve, Chatterton, Blake, John Clare, Jane Austen, Byron, Keats, Tennyson, Ruskin, Browning, Lewis Carroll, Tolstoy, Dostoevsky, Chekhov, Bram Stoker, H.G. Wells,

Robert Louis Stevenson (revisited in his last years in Samoa by two novels), Kipling, Thomas Mann, Wilfred Owen, Siegfried Sassoon, Robert Graves, D.H. Lawrence, Virginia Woolf and Somerset Maugham have all received a fictional kiss of life.

A surprising number of dead authors found posthumous re-employment as private detectives. Robert Browning investigated murders that mimicked macabre punishments in Dante's *Inferno* in Michael Dibdin's *A Rich Full Death* (1986), set among the Anglo-American colony of nineteenth-century Florence. Elsewhere, Aristotle, Chaucer, Shakespeare, Dr Johnson, Mark Twain, the Brontë sisters, Henry Adams, Conan Doyle, Agatha Christie and her fellow crime writer Josephine Tey have reappeared as sleuths.

In a thirteen-book series by the American author Stephanie Barron, starting with *Jane and the Unpleasantness at Scargrave Manor* (1996) and continuing to *Jane and the Waterloo Map* (2016), Jane Austen featured as a kind of Regency Miss Marple. During this sequence of what could be called pelisse procedurals, she encounters a strangled French *femme fatale* at the races in Kent, two corpses on the ancient Pilgrims' Way to Canterbury, a stabbing at a masquerade in Bath, a man dangling from a makeshift gibbet in Lyme Regis, the body of a mutilated cross-dresser in Derbyshire and a lieutenant with a broken neck in the snow near Steventon Rectory. She also stumbles on a corpse in the cellar of Chawton Cottage and another in the Prince Regent's Library at Carlton House. In one book, she proves of assistance to Lord Byron after he awakes in Brighton to find the lifeless body of a society beauty lying in bed next to him and, in another, to Lord Castlereagh after a Russian princess with a slit throat is discovered on his doorstep. Small wonder that, at one point, she fears she 'has lost her youthful bloom'.

It wasn't only authors who had new life breathed into them. Their relatives and associates were recuperated too. Figures – especially female – once shadowy in the background were brought into fictional limelight: Shakespeare's Dark Lady, Pepys's wife, Newton's niece,

Jane Austen's sister, Elizabeth Barrett Browning's maid, Einstein's daughter, Proust's mother, John Synge's mistress.

Throngs of literary characters took on new leases of life. Mrs Gulliver was launched on voyages of her own. Mr Rochester's first wife told her story. Anna Karenina's son was re-encountered as an elderly *émigré* in 1947 London (in a novel with an epigraph from a letter by Tolstoy: 'My God, if only someone would finish *Anna Karenina* for me!'). Dr Watson's wife Mary and Sherlock Holmes's housekeeper Mrs Hudson set up as sleuths in their own right. Sherlock Holmes himself has been plucked back from the dead many times (and in one novel unmasked as Jack the Ripper) since Conan Doyle had second thoughts about finishing him off at the hands of his arch-foe Moriarty at the Reichenbach Falls. A near-industry fabricating further adventures for him has tirelessly expanded.

Another has burgeoned around Jane Austen's work. The Austen Project, launched by the publisher HarperCollins, commissioned well-regarded contemporary authors to give her books modern makeovers. Joanna Trollope took on *Sense and Sensibility*, Val McDermid *Northanger Abbey*, Alexander McCall Smith *Emma*, and Curtis Sittenfeld *Pride and Prejudice* (relocating it to Cincinnati, with characters such as a Jane Bennet who is a yoga instructor, a 'Chip' Bingley who has starred on a reality TV dating show and a haughty neurosurgeon Darcy).

When Austen wrote in *Mansfield Park*, 'Let other pens dwell on guilt and misery', she had no idea what she was letting her novels in for. Other pens have proved only too ready to fill what have been seen as prim gaps in her fiction. Extensions of her storylines have shown Alzheimer's reducing Miss Bates to embarrassing foul-mouthed lapses, John Knightley degenerated into a buffoon, Frank Churchill propositioning Mr Knightley while suggestively fondling a billiard cue, Charlotte Lucas flagellating Mr Collins or being orally pleasured by a harpsichord-tuner behind one of Pemberley's box hedges, Henry Tilney alarming Catherine Morland by hauling fearsome-looking sex toys out of a cupboard in Northanger Abbey, Jane Bennet entangled in a threesome with the Bingley sisters, Jane Fairfax as a bride jilted at the church door, Mrs Bennet having problems with the menopause, Colonel Brandon mowed down in Spain during the Peninsular War, Marianne Dashwood hobbling around on a severely ulcerated leg, Mrs Jennings felled by dropsy and senile dementia claiming Mrs Dashwood.

The married lives of Austen's heroines have been a continuing source of fictional conjecture. Bulletins on their marital fates have seen Elinor Ferrars almost starving in an impoverished parsonage where she subsists on pease pudding and whey, Emma Knightley tempted into a lesbian fling with a dubious French baroness, and Elizabeth Darcy faced with murder in the grounds of Pemberley. Even more lurid scenarios were unrolled with the advent of 'mash-up' fiction, a genre which scrambled Gothic and sci-fi sensationalism into classic novels. Opening with the line 'It is a truth universally acknowledged that a zombie in possession of brains must be in want of more brains', Seth Grahame-Smith's *Pride and Prejudice and Zombies* (published on 1 April 2009) had Elizabeth and Darcy battling hordes of the undead (and in Elizabeth's case fighting – and winning – a duel with Lady Catherine de Bourgh). In its successor, *Sense and Sensibility and Sea Monsters* (2011), giant lobsters, carnivorous jellyfish and a sea serpent known as the Devonshire Fang Beast present new hazards to the Dashwood family. Reluctant in Austen's novel to marry Colonel Brandon because he wears a flannel waistcoat, Marianne in Grahame-Smith's book needs to overcome an initial disinclination because (part man, part mutant squid) he sports tentacles instead of sideburns.

Zombies, apt presences at a time when few authors have been left to rest undisturbed in their grave, surfaced in re-jiggings of other novelists' books too. Opening with the line, 'Marley was dead, to begin with', Dickens's *A Christmas Carol* all but urged them to pop up. Adam Roberts, a professor of nineteenth-century literature and writer of science fiction, seized on this with gruesome relish. His novel *I Am Scrooge* (2009) opens with the lines, 'Marley was dead, to begin with. Dead for about three minutes, that is: then he got up again.' Butchering a clergyman, a clerk and an undertaker, his reanimated corpse embarks on a brain-slurping rampage. As the story ends, Tiny Tim's festive toast, 'God bless us, every one!', is replaced by a rallying cry from Scrooge, urging fightback against the marauding zombies: 'GO BASH 'EM, EVERY ZOM!'

Tiny Tim was given an unexpected afterlife elsewhere as well. Discarding his crutches and acquiring a more cynical disposition in Louis Bayard's *Mr Timothy* (2003), he grows up to take a job in a brothel and uncover a paedophile ring. As we shall be seeing, shovelling retrospective squalor into Victorian fiction has been a heftily expanding activity in modern novels. Plunging Victorian authors into it has been an accompanying side-line: ripely exemplified by Frederick Busch's *The Mutual Friend* (1979) where Dolby, an alcoholic and tubercular ex-secretary of Dickens, decaying amid a 'chorus of gagging' in a charity ward, gives an account 'punctuated by spitting and coughs' of his former employer's career. Pungent recall of 'the foul brown spit' of tobacco-chewing Americans goes along with reminiscences of phlegm-slimed gin-shops. Regurgitating figures from Dickens's past, Dolby declares 'I spit them out upon the page.' *Great Expectorations*, it strikes you, would have been a more appropriate faux-Dickensian title than *The Mutual Friend*.

Continuations

Where historical novelists – Mantel, Sansom, Sidebottom, Saylor, Davies, Cornwell, O'Brian, Golding – wrote continuation narratives for their own characters, an increasing number of novelists wrote them for other authors' characters. Among factors motivating historical novelists – reluctance to relinquish a character they had become attached to, who inhabited an era that engrossed them or who had proved a draw in attracting readers – it was the last that was most evident among novelists who took over other novelists' creations. Topping the pile when it came to literary recyclings were sales-boosting fictional figures.

James Bond was re-licensed to kill in multiple spin-offs, the first of which – *Colonel Sun* (1968), a Bond continuation novel written by Kingsley Amis under the pseudonym Robert Markham – saw publication just four years after Ian Fleming's death. Beginning with *Licence Renewed* (1981), the spy and thriller writer John Gardner piled up fourteen 007 continuations; the fifth, rather ironically, given Gardner's persistence in keeping Bond alive, called *Nobody Lives for Ever* (1986). Another thriller writer, Raymond Benson, produced five Bond novels, among them *Never Dream of Dying* (2001). More sparingly and with greater literary accomplishment, Sebastian Faulks wrote one – the stylish *Devil May Care* (2008) – as, less surely, did Jeffrey Deaver and William Boyd. Anthony Horowitz channelled thriller skills first exercised in young adult books about the teenage spy Alex Rider and murder mystery screenplays for television into two Bond continuity novels. His snappily titled *Trigger Mortis* (2015) didn't only resurrect Bond but brought back Pussy Galore (last seen in Fleming's pages bobbing on a life raft off the coast of Canada with 007 after he had ejected a sadistic Korean psychopath from a plummeting BOAC jet and strangled the malign tycoon Goldfinger). Horowitz's *Forever and a Day* (2018) wasn't strictly a continuation novel but a prequel – to the first Bond novel, *Casino Royale* (1953): in key with the prevailing impulse to go back to starting-points, it portrayed 007 on his first mission.

Parodying *Casino Royale*'s opening line ('The scent and smoke and sweat of a casino are nauseating at three in the morning') with 'The smell and noise and confusion of a hallway full of schoolboys can be quite awful at twenty past seven in the morning', Charlie Higson's series of young adult spy novels begun with *SilverFin* in

2005 went back even further to Bond as a thirteen-year-old at Eton in the 1930s. Following another trend, Kate Westbrook's trilogy *The Moneypenny Diaries* – *Guardian Angel* (2005), *Secret Servant* (2006) and *Final Fling* (2008) – cast a quizzical female gaze on to Fleming's ultra-male world.

Bond wasn't the only iconic crime-fighter to be revived. The Chandler estate passed the fedora and silver-tipped swordstick of Raymond Chandler's gumshoe, Philip Marlowe, to continuation writers they had chosen. One was Robert B. Parker, whose own hard-boiled private investigator, Spenser, owed much to Marlowe. Parker's first excursion into Chandler's fictional world, *Poodle Springs* (1989), was a variant on the continuation novel: the completion novel, in which books left unfinished at their author's death are rounded off by other hands (Jane Austen's *Sanditon* and Edith Wharton's *The Buccaneers* fell victim to particularly ham-fisted instances of this). Parker's completion of Chandler's four-chapter work in progress when he died, provisionally called *The Poodle Springs Story*, was well received; *Perchance to Dream*, his 1991 sequel to *The Big Sleep*, less so. After his own decease in 2010, he became the subject of continuation writing himself: a string of sequels by Ace Atkins provided Spenser with further sleuthing challenges.

Over past decades estate-approved and often estate-commissioned extensions of a popular dead novelist's *oeuvre* have been prolific and proved highly profitable. Doubtless impressed by the sales figures (more than 40,000 copies sold within four days of publication) for Faulks's Bond pastiche, *Devil May Care*, commissioned by the Fleming estate to celebrate the centenary of the author's birth, the Chandler estate approached novelists of comparable calibre to write follow-up Marlowe novels. At their invitation, John Banville, under the pseudonym he used for penning his own crime fiction, Benjamin Black, reanimated the Marlowe of the 1950s in *The Black-Eyed Blonde* (2014). *Only to Sleep* (2018) by Lawrence Osborne, who was next commissioned, had an ageing Marlowe persuaded out of retirement in 1988. The Agatha Christie estate followed suit by commissioning (with their first granting of permission for a continuity novel) a Poirot whodunnit, *The Monogram Murders* (2014), from the crime writer Sophie Hannah, who went on to confect further murder mysteries to test the Belgian sleuth's little grey cells with *Closed Casket* (2016), *The Mystery of Three Quarters* (2018) and *The Killings at Kingfisher Hill* (2020).

Financial incentives were clearly paramount with publishers, who saw dead novelists' popular fictional characters as opportune commodities, ripe for re-marketing as new lines of a once-lucrative brand (and, as an added bonus, boosters of the back-list they were lifted from). Writers of continuity novels tended to cite 'homage' as their motivating factor. Some took pains to bestow it as fittingly as possible. 'Intrigued' by his invitation from the Fleming estate, Faulks re-read the Bond series, then decided to extend it with a novel set in 1967, giving 007 sufficient time to recover from the hospitalised condition he was left in at the end of Fleming's final thriller about him, *The Man with the Golden Gun* (1965). Drug-dealing came to mind as a subject appropriate to the Summer of Love (and usefully one that Fleming himself had not much touched on).

Besides searching for a subject Fleming hadn't tackled, Faulks sought a setting he hadn't made use of, and alighted upon the Middle East (pushed aside by Fleming as just 'full of thieves and crooks'). Memoirs of the region in the 1960s, consultations with experts on it, and internet research into matters such as Indo-Chinese torture techniques, reinforced Faulks's hunch that it would suit his purposes. Inspiration for that recurrent feature of Bond fiction – a villain's grotesque physical deformity – came from Faulks's memories of his father talking about a misshapen hand that had afflicted a fellow undergraduate.

Before elaborating his storyline, Faulks drew up an inventory of the regulation fitments of Fleming's Bond books: the Bentley and the Morland cigarettes, the sea-island cotton shirts, the loafers, the shoulder-holster guns, the martinis, the meals, the torture, the gadgets, the girls. Critical acumen came in too. The novels, he noticed, tend to start with an incident from which Bond is absent – a device replicated in *Devil May Care*, which teasingly begins in a rainy provincial France of glistening slate roofs, more likely to be seen as typical Faulks, not Fleming, territory. Tracing other patterns in Fleming's thriller scenarios, Faulks simulated them so convincingly that, to his gratification, 'the head of the Bond film company, Eon, declared: "If you told me you'd found this in Ian's desk drawer, I would have believed you."'

Fleming's prose style Faulks identified as 'a pretty straightforward sort of newspaperman's style . . . a good way of getting information across, fast and accurate. I don't see any overwriting, any clichés – except little bits of purple here and there, which largely are to do with machinery, actually. He's really more turned on by machinery than by sex.' It was a style he found fairly easy to imitate as it is 'standard journalistic: no semi-colons, few adverbs, few adjectives, short sentences, a lot of verbs, a lot of concrete nouns.' More distinctive, he felt, was the tone, 'a sort of slight hauteur that was a little bit harder to catch – a little bit cold and a little bit superior in places'. To capture its cadences of 'I'm more worldly than you', he sometimes 'imagined myself sucking on my teeth, with perhaps a cigarette-holder' as he wrote.

With less-focused continuity novelists, tribute to their predecessor's talent could be unintentionally conveyed by deficiencies in their own. Slackness and meanderings in Sophie Hannah's over-prolonged Poirot books remind you of the brisk craftiness with which Christie's whodunnits exert their inimitable grip. Protracted facetiousness and ploddingly drawn-out escapades in Ben Schott's *Jeeves and the King of Clubs* (2018) and *Jeeves and the Leap of Faith* (2020) make you very conscious of the fast-paced comic choreography (tuned to a fine art by early years of working on Broadway and West End musicals) that dances through P.G. Wodehouse's own novels. Further heightening the contrast, Schott's Bertie Wooster is far from pitch-perfect, recounting events with a barrage of wisecracks, neat ripostes, knowing allusions and puns (sometimes bilingual) that would have left Wodehouse's chinless wonder gaping.

Literary ventriloquism was sustained with far more accurate *élan* by Peter Ackroyd whose *The Last Testament of Oscar Wilde* (1983) was expertly attuned to both the epigrammatic idiom and the excruciated sensibility of the man who, after years of coruscating on thin ice, had plummeted to chilling depths. Henry James found an impressive emulator too. Though his eerie tale, *The Turn of the Screw*, attracted the attention of several later hands, his works seemed largely resistant to continuation (ending with its spinster heroine picking up her knitting 'for life, as it were', his novella *Washington Square* looks definitively sequel-proof). Amid the flurry of continuation writing in recent decades, no one seemed inspired – or bold enough – to add further touches to *The Portrait of a Lady*, his famously open-ended masterpiece about the young American heiress, Isabel Archer, until John Banville took up the challenge with *Mrs Osmond* in 2017.

It wasn't an altogether surprising move. With his Raymond Chandler pastiche, *The Black-Eyed Blonde*, Banville had previously brought considerable expertise to replicating another author's fictional world. An outstanding feat of literary ventriloquism, *Mrs Osmond* showed even more engagingly that his fiction could have livelier appeal when written in imitation of another author than in his own style. 'I'm not saying I'm possessed by the soul of Henry James, but some part of my brain is able to cease to be me while I'm working on it', Banville said of *Mrs Osmond*. Since that more personal part of his brain could exude prose of some preciosity (characters emitting a 'plumbeous' smell, taking a 'balneation' not a bath, and marvelling at 'the act of pandiculation'), its absence proved fortunate. Pastiche liberated him from the affectation that had stilted even his 2005 Man Booker-winning novel, *The Sea*.

Banville's novel begins where James's novel ended: with Isabel's decision to return to Rome, which she had left after discovering that her idealistic marriage to the aesthete Gilbert Osmond was contrived by him, in league with his former mistress, Madame Merle, for crudely mercenary motives. It's a decision much debated by readers over the years, and which James was sometimes urged to write a sequel to explain. Providing such a sequel, Banville unfolds the reasons for Isabel's resolve as he accompanies her back to her pernicious husband via stays in London, Paris and Florence.

The scenario he devises is engrossing, but his book's real triumph is as a discerning tribute to James's genius. The stylistic emulation is masterly. Banville captures James's prose mannerisms ('They conversed, the two friends, late into the night'), his mergings of nuance and vivid metaphor, his ironic elegancies, his precision and complexity. Atmospheric scenes remind you of his unsurpassed skill at evoking place. One episode, indebted to *The Bostonians*, recalls his gift for buoyant satire as Isabel dines on boiled greens with a severely vegetarian Suffragist, 'a person of pamphlets and polemics, of parades and protests'. Others, inspired by *The Awkward Age* and *The Golden Bowl*, impressively replicate James's portrayals of feral impulses just perceptible beneath silky social interactions. Deepening the malignity of Osmond and Madame Merle, Banville makes Isabel's encounters with them electric with animosity. James's central concerns – the hazards and rewards of freedom, treachery, renunciation, interplay between American and European values – are skilfully mirrored. It's an admirable display of creative empathy generating a sequel of high finish.

Sherlock Holmes

The character most widely supplied with an afterlife was Sherlock Holmes. Often reintroduced in plots that Conan Doyle's creation would have found woefully inferior, he was also reincarnated in works of high-level appreciation. One was Anthony Horowitz's *The House of Silk* (2011), set in 1915, a year on from Holmes's peaceful death in the farmhouse on the Sussex Downs where he had retired to keep bees. Lonely, weary and still plagued by the bullet wound in his shoulder from the Second Afghan War, Dr John Watson, MD, OM – who had modestly declined an invitation to speak at his distinguished friend's memorial service in Westminster Abbey – sits down to pen a final tribute to him. To complete the canon of the great detective's adventures, he has resolved to add to the fifty-six tales and four novellas he had previously made available the story of the House of Silk: a case so scandalously horrible that there was no question of its being made public at the time and which he still wishes to be held back for a century or so before publication. From the nursing home where he is confined, he sends his memory back to the Baker Street of 1890. A dank November fog blurs the gas lamps. As he climbs the seventeen stairs to the door of 221B, Sherlock Holmes, pipe in hand, turns to greet him.

From parody – most boisterously let rip in spoofs such as *The Bound of the Haskervilles* and *The Freckled Hand* by Charles Hamilton (the begetter of Billy Bunter) – to respectful pastiche and ingenious re-workings, so many authors have tried out ways of producing their own Holmes stories that finding a fresh angle constitutes a three-pipe problem in itself. Horowitz's approach (which won him the first seal of approval from the Conan Doyle estate) is to replicate the style, suspense and atmosphere of the original stories while incorporating new dimensions. Familiar characters are given aspects beyond their customary roles. Prints of Inspector Lestrade's square-toed boots in the mud of a crime scene are, Holmes scornfully notes, 'heading in quite the wrong direction, missing everything of importance'. But, as the plot proceeds and deadly jeopardy endangers the super-sleuth, Lestrade proves a shrewd ally. Even Moriarty, disgusted at the iniquity Holmes is combating, unexpectedly offers help too. So urgent is the threat that Mycroft uncharacteristically scurries from the Diogenes Club to advise his brother.

A veteran of crime mystery writing, Horowitz has no difficulty assembling a twisty narrative littered with bewildering corpses. A Holmes aficionado steeped in the canonical stories, he is in his element plausibly inserting this new adventure among them. When the tale starts, Watson, whose wife Mary is away, is temporarily returning to 221B Baker Street: partly to supervise Holmes's recovery from the effects of having starved himself in order to unmask a murderer, as recounted in 'The Dying Detective'; partly in the hope of reviving the mystery-solving excitements they once shared.

Immediately, things fall into their former pattern. Scarcely has Holmes confounded Watson by a virtuoso display of deduction than an agitated client is ushered in by Mrs Hudson. Reminders of other favoured Conan Doyle themes and techniques follow. As in *A Study in Scarlet*, gory happenings in America breed grisly revenge in London. Confronted with what seem mystifyingly murky events, Holmes observes 'The picture becomes clearer by the minute.' But before the case can be resolved he and Watson are violently side-tracked into what at first looks like a separate investigation.

Although Horowitz is deft at capturing the ironic humour – caustic from Holmes, genially bantering from Watson – that glints through the stories, he frequently makes the mood more sombre. The half-a-dozen street Arabs who Holmes employs as look-outs and jokily calls his Baker Street Irregulars aren't the usual chirpy ragamuffins but realistically destitute youngsters. When the hideously battered body of one of them is discovered with a white silk ribbon tied to his wrist, Holmes is galvanised into tracking down the perpetrators, an increasingly perilous quest that takes him to venues ranging from an Elizabethan manor in Gloucestershire to an opium den in Limehouse and the cells of Holloway prison.

Narrative gusto is counterpointed by the elderly Watson's sober reflections on evils his earlier stories failed to explore: most especially 'the greatest curse of our age, the carelessness that had put tens of thousands of children out on to the street'. Horowitz's decent feelings about them result in one denouement that (in the context of modern alertness to child abuse) isn't unpredictable. But he follows it with a second narrative twist which is a master class in Holmesian ingenuity. Tiny slips that wouldn't have eluded Holmes's magnifying glass ('momentarily' intended to mean 'in a moment', 'Baliol' College) occasionally speckle the period prose. But, brimming with informed enthusiasm, Horowitz's adeptly crafted homage is so perfectly pitched that, as it concludes to the strains of Holmes playing his Stradivarius, fans of the great detective should applaud.

Not only Holmes but his creator could sometimes be exhumed, as in Julian Barnes's *Arthur & George* (2005). In Great Wyrley, a village in the depths of Edwardian Staffordshire, a dead rabbit is found skewered to the vicarage lawn. Broken eggs are laid out on the doorstep, dead blackbirds discovered in a soup tureen. Anonymous letters – obscene, misspelt, rabid with religious mania – slither through the letter box. Gallons of black paint and slurries of coal are disconcertingly delivered. In the local paper, advertisements announce that the vicar is running a matrimonial agency, is selling horse manure and will dispatch specimens of ladies' corsetry on demand. When cattle in the vicinity are viciously slashed, things take an even more macabre turn. Soon the press is clamouring about 'the Great Wyrley Outrages'. It sounds like a case for Sherlock Holmes. And, indeed, the sleuth who sets out to disentangle the affair is Holmes's creator, Conan Doyle. Unlike Holmes's cases, though, the situation at the centre of Barnes's novel isn't fantasy but fact. Taking a real-life whodunnit, *Arthur & George* transforms it into an enthralling exercise in detective fiction of more kinds than one.

Barnes has always had a penchant for writing fiction much indebted to actuality – especially the lives of creative prodigies. Delius inspired a story in his collection *Cross Channel* (1996), as did Sibelius and Turgenev in *The Lemon Table* (2004). *Flaubert's Parrot* (1984) paid elaborate homage to Barnes's favourite novelist. *Arthur & George* turns his admiring attention to two authors: Conan Doyle,

who stamped his image of the great detective on the world's imagination, and George Edalji, who made a more modest impact with his
1901 publication, *Railway Law for the 'Man in the Train'*, a manual
on the rights of the travelling public.

In most respects the men seem opposites, as deft intercutting
conveys. Arthur, born into shabby gentility in Edinburgh, comes
from a Catholic family conscious of its aristocratic lineage; George is
the half-Indian son of a Parsee immigrant now a Church of England
vicar in Staffordshire. Where Arthur is highly imaginative, thrilled
as a child by his mother's stories and later pouring out his own,
George is earnestly factual and becomes a solicitor. Vigorously
participating in boxing, football, golf and cricket (once bowling out
W.G. Grace), Arthur bounds with energy; staid and myopic, George
is sedentary. Exuberant Arthur, pukka in appearance with his tweeds
and walrus moustache, is a family man; shy, nervy, odd-looking
George remains a bachelor.

Having established the gulfs between his protagonists, Barnes
chronicles the happenings that draw them together. Powerful pages
document the ordeal George undergoes after the Edaljis report the
harassment of their vicarage to the police. Startlingly, he finds that
he himself is under suspicion. Although he lacks motive and opportunity and the evidence against him is derisory, this solicitor of
impeccable probity is charged with mutilating local livestock. Further
travesties of justice result in his being sentenced to seven years' hard
labour. Public outcry gets him released after three years. But, with
the guilty verdict still standing, he exchanges prison for legal limbo.

A matching account of how Arthur has been faring reveals that,
in another way, he too has been imprisoned. As nurse-attendant to
his consumptive wife Touie, he spends thirteen chaste, dutiful years
keeping her and their debilitated marriage alive. Sixteen stone of
wholesome, pure-hearted manliness, Arthur was Sir Galahad
surviving into the twentieth century. Chivalry – especially towards
women – was his watchword. Faithfully, he stayed at Touie's side

despite falling in love with another woman, Jean, with whom he shared ten years of semi-secret platonic devotion. After Touie's death, guilt at what he sees as his dishonourableness holds him back from marrying Jean and plunges him into depressive lethargy.

What spurs him out of it is a new appeal to his chivalry and sense of fair play: a letter from George, seeking help in clearing his name. In no time, the game's afoot. Pausing only long enough to be dissuaded from equipping himself with a false beard, Arthur hurtles down to Great Wyrley and probes, as Holmes might have done, the murky circumstances of the Edalji affair. What emerges is a racist welter of yokel malice, police ill intention and gross prejudice in high places. George's innocence is proved (as a consequence of his case, the Court of Criminal Appeal was put in place) but a blandly equivocating Public Inquiry refuses to over-rule the verdict and insists that everyone implicated in the miscarriage of justice was blameless.

Arthur's investigation is only one of many in this novel, which explores the lasting effects of upbringing, the importance of scrutiny and evidence, and the role played in lives by narratives and beliefs. Around these issues, Barnes captures an era with atmospheric sureness. Handsomely retro-styled to resemble a volume from an Edwardian bookcase, its dark-mustard-yellow cloth binding embossed with what looks like an illustration from *Punch*, *Arthur & George* has strong affinities with Edwardian fiction. Its central figures – contrasting types of stoical decency – are portrayed with a leisurely fullness redolent of the period. Like many Edwardian novels, it is about close-to-home savagery behind the imperial façade, and unruly impulses beneath a veneer of decorum (in one scene, as Arthur confronts Staffordshire's Deputy Lieutenant in his lamp-lit study, ugly assumptions horribly surface through formidable urbanity). Barnes's elegant prose – crisp with precision and irony – is put to skilled use in a true-life tale as terrifically told as any by its hero Conan Doyle himself.

Charles Dickens

Where writers of what could be called post-script fiction usually resurrected either a fictional character or a dead author, one novel reincarnated both and made them collide. Swarming with a motley throng of exuberantly colourful characters in a nineteenth-century London of pea-souper fogs and flaring gaslights, escutcheoned carriages in the West End and child-felons in the slums of Seven Dials, Peter Carey's *Jack Maggs* (1997) is the most Dickensian novel Dickens never wrote. Freakish figures with quirky mannerisms and odd names – Mrs Halfstairs, Captain Constable – lurk in skew-whiff little rooms or down narrow corridors lined with ancient, mildewed ballgowns. Out on the mudflats of the Thames, scavengers find curious jetsam such as an infant dropped from London Bridge. Strange legacies and outlandish lawyers twist lives in fateful new directions. In the foreground are cosy snuggeries and convivial dinner tables replete with steaming tureens of eel soup. In the background, overshadowing the metropolis's warrens of gin-sodden destitution and lawlessness, is the gallows.

The person most at risk of dancing 'the Newgate jig' from its dangling noose, Jack Maggs, is a character who has side-stepped into Carey's imagination from Dickens's *Great Expectations*. A version of Magwitch, the convict transported to Botany Bay in that book, he is made central to a novel that takes an acute aslant look at the imaginative psychology of the writer who has so enrichingly influenced Carey. Like Dickens, Carey smuggles his convict back into England to meet the *protégé* whose rise in society he has funded with wealth acquired in Australia, because of a long-ago kindness. Unlike Dickens, Carey also brings his convict into contact with a flashily dressed young Cockney author just beginning to captivate the nation with his novels.

Titus Oates – 'the Prodigy' – is immediately recognisable as a nattily dressed version of Dickens ('the Inimitable'). Living with his ill-suited wife and her younger sister whom he idolises, he has had a comfortless childhood for which he now compensates by near-manic celebration of the pleasures of family and friends. Alongside these domestic instincts, anarchic impulses quiver. Energy almost visibly vibrates from him (he believes in 'animal magnetism' and has powers as a mesmerist). Romping through formidable amounts of work, he travels hectically, roams around London from its plush townhouses to its fetid rookeries and is fascinated by the gruesome (he has toured the Paris morgue, and among specimens of human disorderliness stored in his neat pigeon-holes is a thief's hand purchased from a shop in Whitechapel). The 'criminal mind' fascinates him.

Given this, a chance encounter with Maggs, a clandestine 'bolter from New South Wales', seems a godsend. Soon, Oates is ransacking him of his secrets and emotional privacies. And, as the ruthless larceny of the novelist is counterpointed with Maggs's humiliated memories of the robberies he was forced into as a boy, the book brims with sympathy for the exploited. True to his sensitive but utterly unsentimental involvement with the damaged and cast-out, Carey keeps you aware of the lashed back under Maggs's swagger clothes and bruiser demeanour, and of the maltreated decency and dignity deeper still.

Other luckless social casualties – girl-prostitutes, a suicidal homosexual, a woman crazed by penury – are caught sight of as Carey sends his narrative through an often dark world. Small victims of an orphanage fire exhibit the ravages of official neglect: a tot lying 'in her little box with all the solemnity of a matron at the Communion rail', a boy's corpse 'wet, bubbled, like meat, the blue-white bones broken through the charred and blistered skin'. Emblematically named Ma Britten, a corrupt Britannia who purveys miscarriage pills, aborts potential in many ways. Less allegorical malignity is also observed as a subplot charts the deterioration of a dapper, benign bookworm into a shameful, jealous antagonist of Maggs.

What saves Maggs is the pluck and good sense of a servant girl who induces him to jettison his fantasies about his surrogate English 'son' and go back to his genuine offspring in Australia. Adeptly, Carey melds the colonial concerns widespread in modern fiction with the equally prevalent turning back to classic texts. His style adds lustre and depth. Carey uses words as an artist uses line and pigment – to vibrant visual effect: a nocturnal burglar's 'heavy limbs bled into the darkness'; sliding from a roof, a woman 'skittered towards the guttering, her skirt ballooning out like a spill of ink, her pale hands flapping fish-like against the tiles'. Vivid, exact, unexpected images and language match the quick, witty intelligence flickering through this ingenious post-script novel, and make it a triumph of ebullient indictment, humane insight and creative generosity.

Continuance of Being

Extending even as far back as Grendel's mother – the marsh-monster in the Old English epic poem *Beowulf* who was rehabilitated in Maria Dahvana Headley's novel *The Mere Wife* (2018) as a veteran female marine in twenty-first-century American suburbia suffering from post-traumatic stress disorder – the exhuming of past literary figures has been wide-reaching. One novel, Christine Brooke-Rose's *Textermination* (1997), played postmodern games with the after-lives of scores of eighteenth-, nineteenth- and early twentieth-century fictional characters who have travelled – by 'aerobrain' – to the San Francisco Hilton for their annual convention. During this 'international ritual for the revival of the fittest', which Brooke-Rose conjures up with intertextual brio, Austen's Emma Woodhouse (sometimes, to her vexation, mistaken for Flaubert's Emma Bovary) tells *Middlemarch*'s Mr Casaubon, 'We are all gathered here to pray together for our continuance of being, but also for all our brethren, far more numerous than even we who are here, who remain dead in never-opened books, coffins upon coffins stacked away in the great libraries of the world'. Liberating characters from this fate and mobilising them in often unexpected new directions has been a large-scale enterprise among modern novelists.

Stevenson's Dr Jekyll and Mr Hyde was reanimated as a 1980s female depressive whose medication was going awry. The fraught governess from James's *The Turn of the Screw* faced surprising new twists during the First World War. Ezra Pound's Hugh Selwyn Mauberley re-emerged in the 1930s to demonstrate modernism's collusions with fascism. Lady Chatterley became a Tinder bot. Mrs Dalloway reappeared in 1990s Greenwich Village (as did Virginia Woolf in twenty-first-century Manhattan). Mrs Danvers cast her baleful shadow over a pallid sequel to *Rebecca*. No character seemed too lowly for fictional revival. Flashman, the bully from *Tom Brown's Schooldays*, cut a caddish dash through George MacDonald Fraser's ebulliently wide-roaming series of historical novels. Even Billy Bunter's adult career was chronicled (re-encountered as a globular octogenarian, the Fat Owl of the Remove was revealed as responsible for sinking the *Titanic*, prolonging the First World War and causing the General Strike). Classic texts – *Wuthering Heights, Jane Eyre, A Christmas Carol, Peter Pan* – have had surprising variations worked on them. So have most of Shakespeare's plays (in the case of *Henry IV, Part I,* with dogs as protagonists: Prince, who narrates, is a black Labrador; Falstaff is an irresponsible Springer Spaniel).

Commandeering someone else's fictional characters isn't a new phenomenon, of course. But, formerly, it happened far more rarely and most usually with satiric intent, as in Henry Fielding's 1741 novella *Shamela* (which opens with a letter from a man called Ticklctext). A swingeing debunking of Samuel Richardson's moralising novel *Pamela* (1740), Fielding's lampoon exposes Richardson's pious heroine – a maidservant who rigidly retains her virtue under sustained lecherous encroachment from her master, Mr B – as a sly hypocrite, well aware that holding off the advances of her 'Mr Booby' (while never placing herself at too great a distance from them) will inflame and frustrate him into wealthily wedding her. The subtitle of Richardson's book is 'Virtue Rewarded'. Fielding's squib could have been subtitled 'How to Marry Your Molester'.

Derision similarly fuelled quite a number of late twentieth- and early twenty-first-century re-figurings of classic texts. So did condescension. Nineteenth-century fiction, in particular, was often posthumously patronised, most usually on the grounds that it was lamentably lacking in sexual explicitness. As we have seen, Jane Austen's novels underwent much present-day dishevelment to supply this – not least in Arielle Eckstut's would-be rollicking *Pride and Promiscuity: The Lost Sex Scenes of Jane Austen* (2001).

Charlotte Brontë attracted gamey revisionism too. In 1999, a novel purportedly based on factual research, James Tulley's *The Crimes of Charlotte Brontë*, accused her of being a murderess who colluded with her husband-to-be (her father's curate, the Rev. Nicholls) in poisoning Branwell, Ann and Emily (whom Nicholls had made pregnant). With *Charlotte* (2000), D.M. Thomas, a novelist never loath to give a lewd turn to things, put *Jane Eyre* in the dock for prudery.

English literature's most famous opening to a final chapter, 'Reader, I married him', gave Thomas his starting point for a very different slant on Jane's marital life. Brontë's Jane, the proud mother of a healthy son, rejoiced that: 'No woman was ever nearer to her mate than I am: ever more absolutely bone of his bone and flesh of his flesh.' Thomas's Jane, it soon emerges, has never been flesh of Mr Rochester's flesh at all. Perplexed at having failed to conceive a child after years of marriage, she consults her friend Maria (more familiar to readers of *Jane Eyre* as the devout schoolmistress, Miss Temple). From this unlikely source she receives a brisk account of the physiology of the penis and is aghast to realise that her marriage is unconsummated. Upheaval ensues. Shamed at Jane's discovery, Rochester abandons her, then breaks his neck in a fall from his horse. Jane is shaken by disclosures of sadomasochistic relations between Rochester and his deranged first wife and strange reports of misplaced offspring. Resolved to get to the root of it, she journeys to the West Indies where she finally attains sexual fulfilment and pregnancy with a young Black lover.

This allegedly 'realistic' version of Brontë's 'romantic' narrative is the work, it emerges, of a literature lecturer, Miranda Stevenson, attending a feminist symposium in Martinique. Her purpose in penning it is 'to bring out some of the repressed issues' in Brontë's novel. Releasing repressions is, it soon becomes clear, a speciality of Miranda's. Most of her time in Martinique is spent in hectic and graphically rendered copulations with assorted locals, from a hefty cane-cutter to a mixed-up drag queen. Back in Britain, she regales her elderly father with tape recordings of these steamy sessions. Capering in the lingerie and suspender-belt of her dead mother (a wildly promiscuous manic-depressive), she also performs kinky charades for the old man, who resembles Mr Rochester in being almost blind. As other nudging analogies further intimate, these antics supposedly give a healthily open modern-day upturn to *Jane Eyre*.

Thomas's own authorial imprint is most discernible in his book's bid to persuade you that the seamy sexuality on display constitutes bold free-spirited defiance of timid bourgeois inhibition. Miranda's husband is denounced as 'a sour little puritan' for objecting to her father's habit of sexually playing with their infant daughter in the bath. The old goat's leering, voyeuristic relationship with Miranda is presented as evidence of their joyfully unfettered artistic natures.

Sexual and textual waywardness have often featured in Thomas's fiction. Before tampering with *Jane Eyre*, he played games with authors as diverse as Pushkin and Rider Haggard. In *Charlotte*, as earlier, what results looks little more than grubby doodling on a classic text. For all his excitability about coupling sex and creativity, Thomas never comes up with anything of substance. Despite the erotic entanglements she is pushed into, Miranda remains a nullity. Said to be an intellectual, she is most characterised by mindlessness. Vacuous opinions issue from her unremittingly. Economic dependence as apparent in modern Martinique is, she considers, far worse than slavery imposed by shackles and the lash ('The plantation slaves of the last century could rebel . . . But there was no escaping from the soft life'). Besides travestying *Jane Eyre*, Thomas's novel reduces to absurdity the opening up of feminist and colonial perspectives around Brontë's book that Jean Rhys's *Wide Sargasso Sea* (1966) had influentially pioneered.

Exhibiting what had been backgrounded in or omitted from classic novels became of increasing concern in modern fiction. Retrospective rebuke was administered in works that weren't so much extensions as expostulations. *Treasure Island*, Robert Louis Stevenson's adventure yarn for boys, was a case in point. A fertile spawner of spin-offs, it didn't only generate a spate of swashbuckling 'shiver me timbers' sequels and prequels – *Jim Hawkins and the Curse of Treasure Island* (2001), *Flint and Silver* (2008), *Pieces of Eight* (2009) and the like – but, in Andrew Motion, found a novelist keen to steer it into areas beyond Stevenson's 'buccaneers and buried gold'. His first sequel to it, *Silver* (2012), righted gender imbalance by pairing Jim Hawkins's son with Long John Silver's daughter and highlighted racist atrocity by sending both back to a Treasure Island where they undertook the rescue of Black slaves. *The New World* (2014), Motion's sequel to that sequel, carried them on to Louisiana and Texas where the brutal displacement of Native Americans confronted them.

In an entertaining and acute review of a 1996 novel, *Emma in Love: Jane Austen's Emma Continued*, the critic David Grylls drew attention to the jacket's description of its author Emma Tennant as the creator of 'a new literary genre ... the classic progression'. It was, he sardonically noted, 'A nice phrase – for "classic" assimilates to the sequel the unquestioned status of the original, while "progression" suggests positive improvement.' His review's conclusion about the novel was that 'Like previous "classic progressions" by Tennant, it confirms that nowadays the real danger to dead authors isn't the malicious biography but the avaricious sequel.' Sequels were certainly Tennant's abundant stock-in-trade. A kind of literary parasite, she attached herself to a long line-up of host works besides *Emma*: *Sense and Sensibility*, *Pride and Prejudice* (in two novels), *Jane Eyre* (also in two novels), *Wuthering Heights, Tess of the d'Urbervilles, The Aspern Papers, The Turn of the Screw, Dr Jekyll and Mr Hyde, Kidnapped, Confessions of a Justified Sinner* and *Faust*.

Over recent decades, there has seemed no end to sequels – or to prequels or to what Philip Pullman called 'equels' (novels running parallel to events in a primary text). Hope of profiting financially from association with a widely popular work often clearly prompted them. So did ideological revisionism – the inserting of *bien pensant* afterthoughts into classic texts deemed neglectful or ignorant of issues that have become pressing modern preoccupations. Setting right supposed wrong-headedness or inadequacy (of coverage, frankness, indignation or condemnation) in literary works of preceding periods is a retrospective crusade that has swelled inordinately. At the same time, novelists have found ways to cast admiring, exciting and enticing new light on past masterpieces. The full gamut of all these responses, from censure to celebration, is particularly on view in modern fictional treatments of the works of the pre-eminent figure in our literary past: William Shakespeare.

Shakespeare

Not long after HarperCollins launched its Austen Project with Joanna Trollope's remake of *Sense and Sensibility* (2013), the Hogarth Press initiated a similar venture, the Hogarth Shakespeare series, for which 'some of today's most celebrated and bestselling authors' were invited to 'reimagine Shakespeare's plays for the 21st century'. The first to appear was *The Gap of Time* (2015), described by its author, Jeanette Winterson, as a 'cover version' of *The Winter's Tale*.

Shakespeare's play, Winterson revealed, held 'talismanic' significance for her: 'It's about a foundling. And I am.' Since her earlier books about being a 'foundling' (or, more accurately, adopted) – her first novel *Oranges Are Not the Only Fruit* (1985) and her memoir *Why Be Happy When You Could Be Normal?* (2011) – pulsed with vitality, the enterprise sounded promising. Certainly, it was ambitious. *The Winter's Tale* is unusual both in tone and structure. Its first section, in which Leontes, king of Sicilia, falsely believes his wife Hermione to be pregnant by his childhood friend Polixenes, is a crescendo of virulently expressed sexual jealousy and pathological rage culminating in violence, death and the casting out of Hermione's newborn baby into the wilderness. Leaping forward sixteen years, the rest of the play, mainly set in Polixenes' kingdom of Bohemia where the abandoned baby, Perdita, was found and raised by a shepherd, is largely an idyll of reunion, reconciliation and requited love.

Winterson's take on this has Leo, a megalomaniac banker who runs a hedge fund called Sicilia, insanely jealous of his wife MiMi's closeness to his friend Xeno from New Bohemia, a city in America. Cranking things up further, Leo and Xeno weren't just boyhood friends but teenage lovers, romping in the shower and dorm. While Xeno grows up openly gay, Leo represses his homosexuality, with toxic results. In Winterson's equivalent to Leontes' feverish broodings about sexual betrayal, he throbs with arousal about Xeno while watching via a webcam what he mistakes for a sex scene between him and MiMi (an 'eight-inch purple silicone dildo' that excites his attention is actually a pencil case).

The crudity of Winterson's animus against Leo (made a rapist and the crony of an unsavoury oligarch, Vladimir Oshitavitch) is matched by the freakishness she projects on to other characters. Diminished to MiMi, Hermione becomes a 'small slight boyish' singer and actress (whose debut was 'in Deborah Warner's adaptation of *The PowerBook*, a novel by . . . Jeanette Winterson'). Raised in Paris, she is, we're told, 'bilingual in French and English': a claim that rings oddly, given her linguistic gaffes ('Les Fleurs du Mals'). Paulina, the noblewoman who – in one of Shakespeare's most electrifying scenes – fiercely defends Hermione against Leontes, suffers an even more bizarre transmutation: into a cartoonish twist on the Jewish momma stereotype who, when not 'pulling her *oy vey* face', wishing people 'Mazeltov' or telling them to 'have a little slufki', goes to Golders Green to get her hair done ('Schlepp it up, Elaine').

Found and adopted by Shep, owner of a piano bar in New Bohemia, Perdita becomes a singer with a girl-group, whose other three performers 'ggigggled with six gs'. Eccentric typography pervades the pages. Dozens of lines are in block capitals. At times, Winterson seems to be having difficulties with her Caps Lock ('terrorISed, TErrorised, terrORised') and her spacebar ('hecan'tgete noughofyouyouhavebeenthemakingofhim'). Even in layout, her 'cover version' of *The Winter's Tale* looks out of kilter.

As with the Austen Project which petered out after feeble updatings of just four novels, the Hogarth Shakespeare – which went on from Winterson's garish re-hash to a heavy-handed take on *The Merchant of Venice* from Howard Jacobson and a disappointingly lacklustre retelling of *The Taming of the Shrew* from Anne Tyler – began to look similarly unworthwhile. But, with *Hag–Seed* (2018), Margaret Atwood's version of *The Tempest*, it struck gold.

Shakespeare's play, in which enemies of the deposed duke Prospero fall into his power when shipwrecked on the island where he has found refuge, offered Atwood a trove of opportunities she adeptly seized. *Hag–Seed* is at once a winningly inventive (and often very funny) re-fashioning of *The Tempest*, a brilliant scrutiny of it, a celebration of the potency of theatre, and a lively revisiting of themes that have always stirred Atwood's imagination. Outstanding among them is revenge which, often smouldering through her fiction, even infiltrated her non-fiction study of debt and restitution, *Payback* (2008).

In *Hag–Seed*, the Prospero-like figure seeking payback is Felix Phillips, once a charismatic Canadian theatre festival director, famed for his sensational, risk-taking Shakespearian productions (*Pericles* with spaceships and extra-terrestrials, a shockingly graphic *Titus Andronicus*) until ousted by his scheming assistant, Tony. Brooding on vengeance while in embittered exile, Felix eventually becomes a teacher on a 'Literacy Through Literature' programme at a local prison. Here, under an assumed name, he directs inmates in an annual production of a Shakespeare play. After success with *Julius Caesar*, *Richard III* and *Macbeth* ('Power struggles, treacheries, crimes: these subjects were immediately grasped by his students'), he embarks on a production of *The Tempest*. News arrives that perfidious Tony, now a politician on the make, plans to attend with his cronies as a PR exercise . . .

Hag-Seed isn't the first Canadian novel to chart turbulence swirling around a staging of *The Tempest*: Robertson Davies' *Tempest-Tost* did so in 1951. But the likeliest inspiration for Atwood's scenario is the Shakespeare Festival Theatre in Stratford, Ontario, whose founding director, the great theatrical innovator, Tyrone Guthrie, seems the model for Felix's mix of maverick recklessness and genius.

There are satiric cameos of Felix in his high-handed heyday, brushing aside mundane irritants such as 'a dry-cleaning bill from a front-row theatregoer's unwilling interactive participation in a splatter scene: Macbeth's gore-drenched head flung too vigorously onto the stage, Gloucester's gouged-out eyeball slipping from the grasp of its extractor, with vile jelly staining the floral silk print, so hard to get out'. But his theatrical wizardry and directorial verve are never in doubt.

Atwood exultantly captures the aplomb with which he controls his jauntily nicknamed inmate actors (PPod, Bent Pencil, SnakeEye, 8Handz). Skills as con artists, fraudsters, identity thieves that have put them behind bars prove invaluable when re-directed into work on the play. At a party where their video version of *The Tempest* is screened, drama's ability to humanise and energise, tap emotions and open minds, is conveyed with fleeting poignancy: 'Watching the many faces watching their own faces as they pretended to be someone else – Felix found that strangely moving. For once in their lives, they loved themselves.'

A lonely moment in the snowy countryside when Felix hears 'a glassy whispering: it's the dead weed stalks that are sticking up through the drift, glazed with ice, stirred by the wind. Tinkling like bells' strikes a similarly haunting note (and reminds you that Atwood is a poet as well as a novelist). But the prevailing mood is exhilaration. Atwood throws her imagination into the preparations for the play with zestful ingenuity. Costumes are foraged for in fetish emporiums and ski-wear stores. A screengrab from the Tornado Channel gets the video-ed production off to a roaring start. 'Technical gnomes and gremlins' do the work of Prospero's spirit-helpers. The casting of Ariel – problematic at first since no one in prison wants to play 'a fairy' who sings about sucking where the bee sucks – becomes more appealing when Felix points out that, with his battery of electrifying spells, he's 'the special-effects guy'. Noting that lines in the play can resemble rap (''Ban 'Ban Ca-Caliban'), Felix gives his staging a hip hop opening: 'What you gonna see, is a storm at sea: / Winds are howlin', sailors yowlin' . . .'.

Felix's production takes place within Atwood's own replication of *The Tempest*. Structured in five acts with a prologue and epilogue, her novel mirrors its form and its themes: revenge and reconciliation, imprisonment and release, fatherly affection, cathartic conjurings-up of illusion. Though the title spotlights Caliban (given a vigorous stomp number, 'Hag-Seed': 'My mom's name was Sycorax, they call her a witch,/ A blue-eyed hag and real bad bitch . . .'), the book illuminates the breadth and depths of the whole play. The troupe's workshops on it sizzle with perception as Atwood transmits the pleasurable buzz of exploring a literary masterpiece. A glowing tribute to Shakespeare in his 400th anniversary year, *Hag-Seed* was a triumphant display of what could be achieved by sending fresh imaginative energy playing over a classic text.

Shakespeare's plays were frequently re-wrought into receptacles for insistent modern concerns. *Pericles* gave Mark Haddon a template for *The Porpoise*, one of numerous modern novels exposing sexual abuse by a father. Female turpitude in Shakespeare's tragedies was often traced back to male malignity. Relocating *King Lear* to a ranch in Iowa, Jane Smiley's *A Thousand Acres* (1999) added revelations that the villainous older sisters had been sexually abused by their patriar-chal parent. *Macbeth* was bloodily re-envisioned in a bleak industrial town in 1970s Scotland by Jo Nesbø, whose thriller of that name featured an Inspector Macbeth and his partner Lady (who had been traumatically abused by her father). An earful of poison, it was inti-mated in Rebecca Reisert's *Ophelia's Revenge* (2002), was the least King Hamlet deserved after his marital brutality to Gertrude and coercive control of her ('She does not say him nay, even when he beats her,' Yorick sadly testified).

Ophelia herself was seen as a regrettable role model for today's female teenagers and much in need of bracing up. Fatally compliant to male authority in Shakespeare's tragedy, she reappeared as a far feistier presence in several young adult novels. Spotting that 'in the play we never see her drown' and reasoning that 'even when Hamlet jumps in the grave and embraces her body, presumably she's wound in a sheet, so how do we know that was actually Ophelia's body?', Lisa M. Klein, in *Ophelia* (2006), showed her re-surfacing as a strong swimmer, surviving Elsinore's murderous mayhem by feigning madness, faking her death and getting herself to a nunnery where she gives birth to a child conceived by Hamlet, later taking Horatio as her partner. In Lisa Fiedler's *Dating Hamlet* (2002), far from confining herself to the distribution of metaphorically significant herbs and simples around the Danish court, Ophelia is a formidable herbalist who brews a poisonous potion to kill Claudius. Faking madness and drowning by her first-rate acting skills, she also vigor-ously thwarts attempted rape by the royal guard, Barnardo ('Using the heat of all my hatred, I fold a fist and land it hard upon his jaw ... with every ounce of strength I possess I direct my knee into the spot he described as south of his stomach'). A vehemence of utter-ance denied to Shakespeare's Ophelia rings out as she curses Claudius: 'Damn his soul to hell! ... Damn his eyes, and his vile heart, and his nose, and each one of his gnarled teeth, and damn every last follicle of hair on his body.'

Jeremy Strafford, the author of a prequel to *Hamlet* in which the prince secretly weds Polonius' daughter before departing to fight against the Poles, explained in an introductory note to his *Ophelia* (2001) that 'one of the purposes of my book is to fill in the blanks'. The prevalent urge to remedy perceived literary gaps inspired novelists in other ways too. Noting a lacuna in the sequence *Henry IV (Parts One and Two), Henry V, Henry VI (Parts One, Two and Three)* and *Henry VIII*, Robert Winder inserted a 100-page play to fill it into his novel *The Final Act of Mr. Shakespeare* (2010): a brave pastiche written with bravura panache, 'The Tragicall History of Henry VII' showed the dramatist defiantly venting his prudently long-suppressed feelings about the Tudors as his career neared its close. The following year saw another fictitious Shakespearean drama come to light. Arthur Phillips's novel *The Tragedy of Arthur* (2011) included a hitherto unknown text of *The Tragedy of Arthur, King of Britain, Newly Corrected and Augmented by William Shakespeare*.

It was around *Hamlet*, though, that most retrospective gap-filling took place. When the prince expired gasping 'the rest is silence', he couldn't have been more mistaken. A post-mortem clamour of additions and adjustments to the play has persisted across the centuries and become particularly insistent in recent decades. Maggie O'Farrell's *Hamnet*, which won the 2020 Women's Prize for Fiction, used it as a way into a recuperation narrative about Shakespeare's wife (who it calls Agnes, the name by which she was referred to in her father's will). Beginning with the death from bubonic plague of their eleven-year-old son Hamnet (a name interchangeable with Hamlet in the sixteenth century), it ends with Agnes watching *Hamlet*, three years later, at the Globe, first in outrage, then with the realisation that it is her husband's attempt to perpetuate their lost child. In between, as Shakespeare, never named in the novel and barely given a speaking role, largely remains in London, his wife takes centre stage, causing awe in Stratford by her paranormal powers of perception, uncanny skill with herbs and other 'unusual abilities'.

The most ingenious prequel to *Hamlet* came from Ian McEwan whose 2016 novella *Nutshell* was narrated by a nine-month-old foetus in the womb of Trudy, an unfaithful wife who is the mistress of her husband's property developer brother Claude. Always fascinated by differing mindsets, McEwan slipped with brainy relish into one of literature's most famous consciousnesses. Playing with the conceit of Hamlet as a foetus eavesdropping on a plot to murder his father, he simultaneously spoofed crime fiction and found a witty mouthpiece for a mordantly funny and incisively intelligent commentary on the modern world. The book ended with the newborn Hamlet declaring 'The rest is chaos.'

The most expansive and ravishingly textured prequel to *Hamlet* was written by John Updike, whose novel *Gertrude and Claudius* (2000) depicted three decades of events in Elsinore prior to those in Shakespeare's play. Alerting you to the existence of earlier versions of the Hamlet story, the names of Updike's characters change as his novel moves forward. Those in Part One (where, at the behest of her royal father, young Gerutha marries Horwendil while attracted to his brother Feng) derive from a twelfth-century narrative. Those in Part Two (where Geruthe betrays her husband Horvendile with Fengon) are from a sixteenth-century source. Part Three follows the newly married Claudius and Gertrude into the opening scenes of Shakespeare's drama.

Updike's version of the *Hamlet* scenario initially seems designed as ironic comedy. Suavely anachronistic, he juxtaposes modern attitudes with medieval situations. Feminist ripostes reverberate within the craggy walls of Elsinore. Gerutha pouts that her warrior husband-to-be (who might have passed muster 'in the dark old days, when the deeds of the sagas were being wrought') is 'unsubtle'.

Subtlety, of course, was Updike's forte as a novelist, and he never displayed it with more finesse than in this novel. Psychological and emotional nuance are delicately traced. Physical details are responded to with rapt precision. Gerutha's hair glints with 'the red of copper

266

diluted by the tin of sunlight'. Dismounting on the way to poison his brother, Fengon glimpses a reflection of himself, 'squat and miniature, a bearded troll, in the long-lashed orb of the horse's purple-irised eye'.

Sensuousness and sensuality evoked with luscious minuteness put Updike's artistic hallmark on this novel. But, infused with the literary critical acumen he usually reserved for his book reviews, it also constitutes a brilliant commentary on Shakespeare's tragedy. The uneasy coexistence of conflicting codes of conduct in medieval Denmark ('Viking blood-hunger crammed into the outward forms of Christianity') is spotlit: spliced into the royal throne are bits of the True Cross and of the primal Norse tree Yggdrasil. Heightening the sense of a society in transition, Gerutha scorns the glorified butchery of the sagas (lopped-off limbs, shattered shields, slaughtered foes) for the amorous raptures in the romances on vellum manuscripts which she reads. Constraints upon public role – kingship, regal wifehood – hamper personal aspirations. Chilly provincial Elsinore contrasts with the sultry glamour of the Italian and Byzantine realms from which cosmopolitan Fengon beguilingly returns with graceful manners, exotic tales and sophisticated views.

In keeping with their warm-blooded, connoisseur responsiveness to the allure of the civilised south, Updike makes the queen and her lover humane figures opposed to the cold rigidities of the north. Even Fengon's murder of his brother is presented with some mitigation as partly a bid to stop the king subjecting his court chamberlain to barbaric torture and execution.

By the time of the poisoning of the sleeping monarch in his orchard (an episode rendered with voluptuous mellowness: rotting apples and pears filling the air with the scent of fermentation, waning sunlight gold on the unscythed grass), Updike's novel has begun to segue into Shakespeare's play. Throughout the book, there have been anticipations of it (talk of a brocaded arras, complaints of things being 'out of joint'). The final pages, decked with theatrical imagery, wittily paraphrase Shakespeare's opening scenes: Hamlet 'wordily implied, with the whole court listening, that only he was truly grieving'.

Updike's novel everywhere shows his creative attention to Shakespeare's play. His Polonius is as fussily prolix as Shakespeare's ('The gentlemen from Poland, as I say, are prone to divagate, prevaricate, and expostulate', he elaborates even at a moment of crisis). His Ophelia quivers with ambivalence prompted by her Shakespearian namesake. Even touches that seem characteristically Updike's actually sprout from Shakespeare's text. Geruthe's erotic surrender to Fengon occurs over several meetings in a turret room from which are first seen 'buttons of pale-green leaf, budded but yesterday', then vegetation that has unfurled from 'button-like solidity to the particulate leafiness of tiny cabbages', and finally (as she yields) foliage 'loosening enough to fill the woods with a yellow-green fog'. The motif of gradual relaxation into lush openness is Updike's, but it stems from a comparison of spring buds to 'buttons' which Shakespeare gives to Ophelia's brother, Laertes.

Shakespeare's plays have had many offshoots. They have been amplified into operas and reprised as musicals. Later playwrights have dramatised the points of view of characters such as Shylock, King Lear's wife and daughters, Rosencrantz and Guildenstern. Novelists have transposed *Twelfth Night* to a seaside town in Wales and *A Midsummer Night's Dream* to 1930s Hollywood. *Gertrude and Claudius*, however, stands out – like Atwood's *Hag-Seed* – as a superlative homage from one imaginative veteran to another.

Victoriana

Shakespeare's plays gave rise to a wide range of fictional after-works. So did the novels of Jane Austen. But it was the Victorian age to which post-script writers were most drawn. The books of Dickens, the Brontës, Hardy, Conan Doyle, H.G. Wells and Robert Louis Stevenson generated numerous fictional spin-offs as the period exerted a magnetic pull on the imaginations – and often the indignations – of late twentieth- and early twenty-first-century novelists. It was a pull that sometimes manifested itself in appealing and original ways. Posy Simmonds, much enjoyed and admired for her neat satirisings of the foibles and fashions of the arty liberal bourgeoisie in cartoon strips for the *Guardian*, extended them into a trio of graphic novels which used nineteenth-century fictional prototypes to frame present-day pretensions and perfidies. *Gemma Bovery* (2000), a smart makeover of Flaubert's masterpiece, portrayed a flighty English expat living in a Normandy village with her dull furniture restorer husband. In *Tamara Drewe* (2007), Bathsheba Everdene, the headstrong heroine of Hardy's *Far from the Madding Crowd*, became a metropolitan journalist who files her column 'Away From It All' from a West Country village with an upmarket writers' retreat. *Cassandra Darke* (2018) updated Dickens's *A Christmas Carol* with a grouchy twenty-first-century female Scrooge – a flint-hearted Chelsea art dealer – who achieves redemption amid visually and verbally sharp vignettes of contemporary London.

Simmonds's entertaining take on *Far from the Madding Crowd* was a more appreciative response than Hardy's fiction tended to arouse. Revisitings of his novels and reinspections of their author were more often accompanied by disapproval, indeed disgust. Born a hundred years to the day after Hardy, the hero of Howard Jacobson's *Peeping Tom* (1984) is appalled by the suspicion, awakened under hypnosis, that he may be a reincarnation of the man he regards as a 'prurient little Victorian ratbag'. In Emma Tennant's *Tess* (1993), the ratbag acquires even more loathsome features: 'His is the male, controlling imagination that devours women in its lair. Monster eats the Muse.'

Transporting Hardy's scenario from a village in nineteenth-century Wessex to a late twentieth-century boarding school in Dorset, where self-centred Beth attracts three boyfriends – just as Bathsheba attracted three suitors – F.J. Campbell's *The Islanders* (2019), its press release promised, 'retold *Far from the Madding Crowd* for a new generation . . . with added sex and drugs'. Adding sex (and sometimes drugs, especially opium) was something later hands kept doing to Victorian fiction. Seen as erotically desiccated, its classic novels were retrospectively drenched in body fluids. Sexually fortified remixes of canonical fiction abounded, as did pastiche nineteenth-century novels that – unreceptive to the subtlety, obliquity and ingenuity with which Victorian writers had found ways of treating sexual material – let loose a kind of reproving blatancy.

Michel Faber's *The Crimson Petal and the White*, published amid much hype in 2002 and hailed by one reviewer as 'the novel Dickens might have written had he been allowed to speak freely', opened with a prostitute performing ablutions with a 'contraceptive bouillon', perched characters on chamber pots, and never missed an opportunity of itemising bodily emissions as it charted the descent into madness of a near-child-bride who believes that menstruation is a religious phenomenon like stigmata. Priding itself on adding dimensions excluded from Victorian fiction, it was in fact far more vacant than the typical Victorian novel. Stretched out to the length of a nineteenth-century triple-decker, it had none of the breadth and depth and abounding human diversity you would expect to find in one. Its tally of characters was sparse compared with the antecedents it patronised. Characterisation was clichéd, and Victorian hypocrisy exhibited repetitively and with platitudinous crudity. A respectable-seeming paterfamilias was unmasked as a sex-fiend. Religious characters routinely seethed with repression. Its two main female figures stereotypically represented the Pure Woman and the Fallen Woman: the latter, a prostitute named Sugar, was also an improbable proto-feminist prodigy of emancipation. A meagre plot, devoid of the narrative grip and virtuosity of genuine Victorian fiction, straggled across almost 900 pages before petering out inconclusively.

Promoted by its publishers as 'the first great nineteenth-century novel of the twenty-first century', *The Crimson Petal and the White* was far from alone in presenting itself as the kind of fiction the Victorians would have written if they had had the freedom from censorship (and the post-Freudian insights) available to later writers. Published a couple of years before it and running to more than 1,200 pages, Charles Palliser's *The Quincunx* (1989) had pioneered what would become a sub-genre of hefty, replica Victorian novels. Generating a stir in literary quarters as an exciting new phenomenon, it was extensively and overtly indebted to Dickens. John Huffam the name its harried hero eventually discovers to be his real one, is lifted from Dickens's three first names: Charles John Huffam. Numerous other characters have Dickensian-seeming surnames: Thackaberry, Fortisquince, Maliphant, Bellringer, Limpenny. A family of Digweeds sound like distant cousins of the Smallweeds in *Bleak House* (which provides an obvious blueprint for the entangled and ruinous legal proceedings of Palliser's plot). *Oliver Twist* (a gang of thieves), *Nicholas Nickleby* (a sadistic boarding school), *The Old Curiosity Shop* (Punch and Judy men), *David Copperfield* (the narrator's disastrously ineffectual mother), *Little Dorrit* (a debtors' prison), *Our Mutual Friend* (unsavoury scavengers on the edge of the Thames) and *Great Expectations* (a mysterious young girl first encountered in the courtyard of a dilapidated great house) contribute sizeably too. But *The Quincunx* isn't intended as a sequel, prequel or alternative version to Dickens's books. Essentially (with some postmodern attachments), it is a huge attempt not to rectify or rebuke but to reproduce nineteenth-century fiction: a neo-Victorian novel.

Others followed. *The Meaning of Night* (2006) by Michael Cox demonstrated, even before its publication, that pastiche Victorian fiction was a very bankable commodity. The publisher John Murray who acquired it (winning what was then the highest-bidding British auction for a debut novel) reportedly paid its author an advance of £500,000. Presented as 'one of the lost curiosities of Victorian fiction' discovered by a professor of 'Post-Authentic Victorian Fiction', Cox's book was an emulation of the 'sensation novel': the nerve-tingling secrets-shocks-and-suspense sub-genre launched by Wilkie Collins's masterpiece, *The Woman in White* in 1860, and luridly continued with works such as Ellen Wood's *East Lynne* (1861) and Mary Elizabeth Braddon's *Lady Audley's Secret* (1862). Narrated by the embittered heir to a great baronial estate denied his rightful heritage, Cox's book is crammed with the paraphernalia of the sensation novel: murder, madness, treachery, jeopardy, revenge, marital cruelty, concealed parentage, aristocratic heartlessness, a cigar-smoking villain, sexual obsession, opium, fog, legal skulduggery, a hidden affidavit, melodrama in a mausoleum, dastardly conspiracies and clandestine encounters, fatally misplaced trust and appalling revelations. But none of this activates excitements like those pulsing through the Victorian works Cox seeks to imitate. Often meandering into extensive digressions about antiquarian bibliography, narrative pace is slow and hobbled by a weighty apparatus of explanatory annotation. More than 300 textual notes – two before you've reached the end of the first sentence – constantly impede momentum. While it soon becomes evident that Cox (who said he had spent thirty years working on the novel) was minutely knowledgeable about the Victorian period, it also becomes apparent that he didn't notably absorb any of the qualities that made its fiction so compelling.

At the end of another profusely annotated ersatz Victorian novel, *Kept* (also published in 2006), its author D.J. Taylor declared: 'I acknowledge the direct influence of Charles Dickens, George Eliot, Elizabeth Gaskell, George Gissing, Jack London, Mary Mann, Henry Mayhew, George Moore, Alfred, Lord Tennyson, Anne Thackeray Ritchie, W.M. Thackeray and Anthony Trollope.' It's hard to see how he could not do. For his novel is a collage of literary snippings. Its characters are like papier-mâché figures made from pulped up pages of Victorian novels. Where they're taken from is written all over them. The main narrator sounds like Thackeray. There's a 'mad' woman incarcerated in an attic (so Charlotte Brontë surely deserved an acknowledgement too). A sleuth-like lawyer closely resembles Dickens's Tulkinghorn in *Bleak House*. A civil servant could well be on leave from one of the offices in Trollope's fiction; Hiram's Hospital from *The Warden* gets a mention and there are regular extracts from the diary of Josiah Crawley, the paranoid clergyman in *The Last Chronicle of Barset*. When the storyline moves into the slums of Clerkenwell, it's obvious that Gissing had been there first. When it accompanies a young servant girl as she trudges up the long drive to a country mansion, it's no surprise to find that, taken from George Moore's *Esther Waters*, her first name is Esther. A savage grey wolf that a sinister squire unwisely keeps in his grounds looks on loan from the same menagerie as Conan Doyle's 'The Brazilian Cat' and 'The Hound of the Baskervilles'. An expedition to the Yukon has clearly been mapped out in advance by Jack London.

In a lively, astute review of Taylor's novel in the *Times Literary Supplement*, Daniel Karlin, a professor of nineteenth-century literature, highlighted not just its copious borrowings but its often slack grip on Victorian idiom and society. Noting that the book's subtitle is 'A Victorian Mystery', Karlin observed that its 'real mystery' was 'as Trollope might have said – Why Did He Do It?' It's a question that hangs over a great deal of Victorian-lookalike literature. What motivated so many writers to devote so much time and energy to fabricating facsimiles of great works from fiction's golden age?

One possible answer that immediately comes to mind is: a kind of *déformation professionnelle*, the dyer's hand ('subdued to what it works in') syndrome. Taylor is a literary critic and biographer of Thackeray. Cox was a biographer of M.R. James, editor of an anthology of Victorian detective stories and co-editor of *The Oxford Book of Victorian Ghost Stories*. Palliser was a lecturer in English and has written introductions to works by Wilkie Collins and Conan Doyle. Often not so much writing as regurgitation, their pseudo-Victorian fiction could be seen as a spillover from their other occupations. More generally, a potent moulding force on modern fiction has been the fact that a high proportion of its writers have – as literary academics and/or teachers in creative writing departments – led very book-furnished lives. The immersion in past literature required by their professions seeps its after-effects into their own.

Behind novels simulating those of the great Victorian storytelling social chroniclers are other likely incentives too: consciousness of the wide appeal such fiction held (and still does) and, as with the writing of continuation narratives for popular characters from deceased authors' books, hope of comparably large sales that might ensue. Where nineteenth-century novels were retrospectively rebuked for prudery and hypocrisy by modern novels that racily rewrote and didactically travestied them, they were hopefully imitated by modern novels that plundered and pastiched them.

The pull towards neo-Victorian writing has had a long reach. The New Zealand writer Eleanor Catton, whose novel *The Luminaries* won the 2013 Man Booker Prize, relocated tropes and themes of nineteenth-century fiction to a mining settlement on her country's South Island during its 1860s goldrush. Constructing a novel almost as vast (at 864 pages) as *The Quincunx*, Catton further resembled Palliser in encasing Victorian voluminousness within an arcane framework. Where the five-point 'quincunx' symbol gave structure to his novel, hers was controlled by an elaborate network of astrological patterns and zodiacal symbolism.

Even novelists who had made a name for themselves as close-to-it-all chroniclers of modern life and its pressing issues could be drawn away from what they excelled at into Victorian impersonation. Edmund White was a case in point. After reportage-like fiction alive with autobiographical immediacy – especially in his trilogy that charted the trajectory of gay life from the repressions of the 1950s through the liberations of the 1960s and 1970s to the AIDS calamity of the 1980s: *A Boy's Own Story* (1982), *The Beautiful Room Is Empty* (1988) and *The Farewell Symphony* (1997) – he tried his hand at masquerading as a Victorian author with *Fanny* (2003).

Literary identity theft, the novel soon exhibited, was not his forte. Presented, as often with historical pastiche works, as 'an important literary discovery', it purports to be a book that Fanny Trollope, mother of the novelist Anthony, left unfinished when she died in 1863. In it, she attempts a biography of her one-time friend, Frances Wright, the Scottish heiress and radical who in 1827 induced her to cross the Atlantic to join a utopian community in the backwoods of Tennessee. Finding that this promised Arcadia consisted of three roofless, malaria-ridden shacks, Fanny Trollope hastily moved on to Cincinnati. Further disillusionments there propelled her back to England where she completed her first book, *Domestic Manners of the Americans* (1832). With its scathing commentary on transatlantic boorishness, it proved an instant hit in Britain and launched her, at the age of fifty-three, on the indefatigable literary career (41 books in 115 volumes over 24 years) with which she kept her family afloat.

Allegedly a forty-second book from her prolific pen, White's novel begins with acerbic *élan* as Fanny (sounding not unlike Muriel Spark) casts a withering eye over her former soulmate ('she decided she was an Epicurean ... I gather what she had in mind was an imperviousness to Opinion and an indifference to Reputation'). Soon, Wright emerges as a monster of egotistical double standards: a vehement feminist who chases elderly males with big reputations, a clamorous denouncer of slavery who treats her associates like serfs.

The spoof editorial commentary (another routine feature of pseudo-period fiction) with which the book is tricked out asserts that Mrs Trollope's last words were 'poor Fanny'. In actuality, they were 'poor Cecilia', a reference to the consumptive daughter whose prolonged and ultimately very painful death had much distressed her. White's replacement of this poignant utterance with a more slyly ambiguous one (is Fanny pitying Fanny Wright or herself?) signals his novel's double focus. As Mrs Trollope scribbles on, she discloses more about herself than her supposed subject.

Not content with recasting Fanny's last words, White recasts many of her preceding ones. His retelling of her American adventures is largely made up of paraphrase of, or extrapolation from, her transatlantic travelogue. In an afterword, he claims his 'usual method has been to take an occasion only briefly presented by Mrs Trollope and to reimagine it entirely'. As an instance, he cites her visit to a fire-and-brimstone revival meeting. But Trollope's account of this is several pages longer than his and, as an on-the-spot response, infinitely more interesting than his synthetic simulation.

When White adds invented material, it sticks out with garish artificiality. A particularly embarrassing episode imagines Mrs Trollope, the fifty-two-year-old mother of six children, embroiled in a torrid, sexually awakening affair with a brawny escaped slave from Kentucky who is working as the local blacksmith. 'I had turned into big black Cudjo's little yellow girl', she improbably exults, blissfully recalling 'that fruit-pink mouth and tongue obscenely battening off my very life's force'.

Blunders blotch White's feigned nineteenth-century pages. Fanny Wright trills that 'the pure source of human felicity' is '*sex*, of course . . . The pleasures of the body'. But Victorians didn't use the word 'sex' to denote intercourse, only gender. Since Fanny Trollope wasn't American (and was mocking of the nation's idioms), she is unlikely to have spoken of 'finishing up' a letter.

White undertook his increasingly pointless-seeming exercise because, he said, his leading characters are 'largely and unfairly forgotten'. But two acclaimed biographies of the far-from-forgotten Fanny Trollope had appeared not long before (and her well-known *Domestic Manners of the Americans* is easily accessible). They serve her reputation far better than White's off-key ventriloquism.

Metropolitan Prototypes: Tom Wolfe

In 1989 another American novelist, Tom Wolfe, published an essay, 'Stalking the billion-footed beast', in *Harper's Magazine*. It was a manifesto urging his fellow US novelists to channel their energies

276

into producing fictional panoramas of present-day metropolitan life similar to those pioneered by the great nineteenth-century European novelists. With his own recent first novel, *The Bonfire of the Vanities* (1987) which cast a satiric glare over contemporary New York, he had aimed, he said, to write 'a novel *of the city*, in the sense that Balzac and Zola had written novels of *Paris* and Dickens and Thackeray had written novels of *London*, with the city always in the foreground, exerting its relentless pressure on the souls of its inhabitants'.

It was an ambition Wolfe had harboured for two decades. When he began his career as a writer in the late 1960s, 'The New Journalism' and the 'non-fiction novel' were in vogue as the modes best-suited to the capturing of modern life. Behind their innovative-sounding labels, what they essentially amounted to was high-octane reportage. Expertise acquired during Wolfe's years as a leading practitioner of it – needle-sharp alertness to fads and fashions, finger-on-the-pulse receptivity to current issues, immediacy of evocation, prose of exceptional verve – served him thrillingly when he moved on to fiction with *The Bonfire of the Vanities*.

It was a novel that melded the up-to-the-minute with harkings back. An enthusiast for the vast span, narrative energy and surging human variety of the nineteenth-century novel, Wolfe had regarded with disfavour the types of fiction that had come to the fore in the 1970s: self-referential novels whose focus fell on their own fictionality, novels of magic realist fantasy, absurdist novels, and works of austere minimalism, fictional starvelings generated in accord with the anorexic aesthetic laid out by one of its leading postmodern proponents, John Hawkes: 'I began to write fiction on the assumption that the true enemies of the novel were plot, character, setting and theme, and having once abandoned these familiar ways of thinking about fiction, totality of vision or structure was really all that remained.'

For Wolfe, the 'headlong rush to get rid of not only realism but everything associated with it' could hardly have been less congenial. 'The introduction of realism into literature in the eighteenth century by Richardson, Fielding, and Smollett', he contended, 'was like the introduction of electricity into engineering.' Its galvanising power made possible the dynamic masterworks of nineteenth-century fiction: 'It was realism that created the "absorbing" or "gripping" quality that is peculiar to the novel, the quality that makes the reader feel like he has been pulled not only into the setting of the story but also into the minds and central nervous systems of the characters.'

'One of the specialities of the realistic novel, from Richardson on,' Wolfe noted approvingly, 'was the demonstration of the influence of society on even the most personal aspects of the life of the individual.' A factor that differentiated contemporary New York from the metropolitan societies on view in fiction a century or so earlier – the London of *Vanity Fair* and Dickens's novels, the Paris of Balzac and Zola, Tolstoy's St Petersburg and Moscow – was 'overt racial conflict'. Wolfe made it central to his trio of novels about huge American cities: New York in *The Bonfire of the Vanities*; Atlanta, presented as the premier city of the American South in *A Man in Full* (1998); and Miami, seen as a hotbed of multi-racial turmoil in *Back to Blood* (2012). But, around it, he assembled fictional tropes and techniques learned from the nineteenth-century classics that had engaged and animated his imagination. It was an imagination that, dismayingly, became more and more inflamed as time went by until – mountingly obsessed by power struggles, brutal jockeyings for status and rampant grossness – Wolfe didn't so much satirise excesses as hyperventilate over them. Yet with *The Bonfire of the Vanities* he flamboyantly demonstrated what could be achieved by reactivating the blueprint of the nineteenth-century social novel.

Initially appearing, like many of its Victorian antecedents, in serial form (fortnightly instalments of Wolfe's first version of it were published in *Rolling Stone* magazine), it is a tale of two city boroughs: Manhattan and the Bronx. The former toweringly brandishes the city's pinnacles of wealth and fashion: 'there it was, the Rome, the Paris, the London of the 20th century, the city of ambition, the dense magnetic rock, the irresistible destination of all those who insist on being *where things are happening*. Nearby, the 'Sargasso Sea of the Bronx' festers with its rotting depths of dereliction.

It is the kind of starkly polarised society that Wolfe's literary idols – Dickens, Balzac, Zola – were often impelled to display: exhibiting the gaping gulfs between penury and plutocracy, then chasteningly closing them by some factor (such as disease spreading from neglected slum to neglectful salon) that calamitously brings home to the affluent the consequences of their indifference towards the destitute. In Wolfe's novel, such retribution is brought about by a car.

Automobiles had always been significant objects in his writing. The work that carried him to prominence as a pioneer of America's New Journalism, *The Kandy-Kolored Tangerine-Flake Streamline Baby* (1965), was a zippy survey of custom car shows with their gaudy vehicles sporting 'diamond dust' paint jobs. A later article on demolition derbies – gladiatorial encounters between buckled, baroque stock cars – kept his interest on the same track.

The car at the centre of *The Bonfire of the Vanities*, an elegant black Mercedes two-seater, is less garishly ostentatious but still stands out spectacularly because it is being driven, in increasing panic and disorientation, round the scary wastelands of the South Bronx. In it are Sherman McCoy, an ace Wall Street bond salesman, and his mistress, Maria Ruskin, the young wife of an old millionaire with a palatial Fifth Avenue apartment. Straying into the wrong lane when driving Maria from the airport after one of her European shopping jaunts, Sherman finds himself funnelled into the Bronx in what turns out to be his first unlucky turning on a journey to disaster.

Sometimes opening up into full-throttle bursts of present-tense narrative, Wolf sends his couple skidding with accelerating alarm round blocks razed to the ground, down pot-holed streets, through nerve-wrenching blasts of noise from crumbled buildings and past glimpses of ugly fights. Lost in what seems a giant junkyard over which darkness is falling, they cower – she in her smartly shoulder-padded Avenue Foch couture, he in his Huntsman jacket and Jermyn Street shoes – as what seem to be faces from another species appear and leer through the electronically locked windows of the deluxe car halted at a red traffic light.

Finally, screeching under an expressway, they run into tyres strewn by ambushers and a terrifying skirmish with a couple of Black muggers follows. One of the assailants, himself eerily shaking with fear, is knocked over as Maria reverses the car into him before swerving off with Sherman to the sanctuary of Manhattan. There, as they make love – awash with sweat, adrenaline and euphoric relief – they congratulate themselves on having faced New York's worst nightmare and escaped unscathed. But already nemesis is slithering towards them.

Even before this, Sherman has seemed to be courting a comeuppance. Handsome, Yale-educated, impeccably tailored, possessing a fashionably thin wife and a daughter satisfyingly enrolled at an exclusive nursery school, he lives in an opulent Park Avenue cooperative which, with its marble floors, walnut curve of staircase and swank antiques, lavishly buttresses his smug sense of superiority. Also boosting this is his pre-eminence in the bond-trading room of Pierce and Pierce, an investment banking firm. Near the peak of his profession on the fiftieth floor of a glass tower on Wall Street, Sherman revels in the rousing daily din of 'well-educated young men baying for money' into their phones. Satellite-linked wheelings and dealings and an astronomical salary give him a heady sense of floating above mundane constraints.

What drags him down from this is a twisting plot that wraps itself round him inescapably. The mugger hit by the car, Sherman learns with horror, is in a dangerous coma. Worse, a campaign is being mounted on his behalf. An ambitious District Attorney seeking re-election in the Bronx wants justice wreaked on the white hit-and-run driver so he can get the ethnic vote. A Black activist, astute at capitalising on anti-capitalist crusades, also hopes to reap dividends out of his hunting down.

Further contributing to the bringing down of Sherman is the District Attorney's assistant, Larry Kramer. An *habitué* of the Bronx County Building – a massive slum-beleaguered courthouse ornamented (in what now seems monumental irony) with allegorical statues of the civic virtues – he provides the eyes and ears through which Wolfe trains attention on the overflowing horrors of the district: the 40,000 annual arrests; the daily debouching of vanloads of criminals, psychopaths and ordinary folk pushed beyond breaking point; the courtrooms resounding with obscenities, harassed official reprimands and endless tangled tales of woe and atrocity.

It's to the detention pens here – fetid with race hate, squalor and thuggery – that Sherman is eventually hauled, ratted on by Maria and seized on by political opportunists as that godsend in the Bronx, a white defendant. Diverse legal types (criminal lawyers, plea-bargainers, legal aid lawyers, a judge, a DA and assistant DAs, clerks, jurists, court reporters, warders, detectives) swarm through these pages of the story in a way reminiscent of *Bleak House*. There is a similar stress on the law's chicaneries and delays. And finally, as the novel's neatly inconclusive conclusion discloses, Sherman metamorphoses, like some latter-day Miss Flyte, into a permanent haunter of this world. Battling his way through writs and re-trials, he becomes a 'career defendant'.

A bursting compendium of resources used to signal caste and prestige, the novel is heaped high with snob commodities and showy trade names. Sartorial styles – from the thermal jackets and unlaced sneakers sported by militant young Black men to sprigged yellow ties signalling low executive rank and top-drawer togs such as two-button single-breasted Savile Row suits – are held up for inspection. Extremely good at taking you, with an informed sharpness worthy of Balzac, into the milieux of journalism, finance, law and city politics, Wolfe is at his best as a guide to the sphere of social display. Vanity Fair, in all its variety, is surveyed.

Making the book more comic than balefully monitory is the fact that Wolfe is fascinated by what his prose flagellates. Enormously knowledgeable about the trivia he mocks his characters for adulating, he wittily impales trends and fads, pretensions and swaggerings. There is not much amiable humanity in the book – with the ironic exception of the ill-fated Bronx mugger Henry Lamb, who, it transpires, was a well-meaning youth pressured into the assault on the Mercedes by a tough drug-peddling neighbour.

Around this shred of doomed decency, the novel is an inferno. As a journalist with a dislike of 'pale beige tones', Wolf had always deployed a high-coloured palette. Writing like a Day-Glo Dickens, he depicted freaks and villains with such chromatic intensity – 'all the new electrochemical pastels of the Florida littoral: tangerine, broiling magenta, livid pink, incarnadine, fuchsia demure, Congo ruby, methyl green, viridine, aquamarine, phenosafranine, incandescent orange, scarlet-fever purple' – that dark glasses almost seemed advisable for reading him.

The Bonfire of the Vanities hits the retina with similar force. 'Blazing' is a favourite word. Drawing rooms are irradiated with lamps swathed in shades of Chinese red or burnt apricot. Watching television, someone's face is bathed in 'tones of first-degree-burn pink'. Everywhere from red *moiré* braces to an empurpled sky – there are hot tints. Everywhere, too, the temperature is high, literally and metaphorically: studio lights scorch down in the opening scene; the identity of the female 'hot number' with Sherman in the car is feverishly sought by the media. From the Bronx's flashpoints, fuelled by desperation, to a Wall Street skyscraper in which a real fireplace is a glowing status symbol, the novel keeps incendiary images to the fore. In this heated world only warmth is missing: typically, characters who shun racial bigotry don't do so out of decency but because it indicates 'low rent origins'. Particularly kindled by Wolfe's admiration for Thackeray's *Vanity Fair*, blistering social satire made *The Bonfire of the Vanities* a blazing success.

Margaret Thatcher and the Two Nations

Tom Wolfe wasn't the only author inspired by Victorian fiction's accusatory highlighting of social inequalities. As we have seen, *The Radiant Way*, Margaret Drabble's novel about the divide between England's North and South, shuttled between both regions and showed a desire, reminiscent of Elizabeth Gaskell, to explore factors separating them.

In 1980s Britain, nineteenth-century 'condition-of-England' novels provided models for literary response to the political ideology of Margaret Thatcher. No British prime minister had more impact on fiction. Partly, this showed itself in the frequency with which she bustled into books. Her distinctive, rapid, somewhat hen-like gait repeatedly drew authors' notice. Philip Hensher's *Kitchen Venom* (1997) observed that 'When she walked she seemed to extinguish a cigarette beneath every pace.' Alan Hollinghurst's *The Line of Beauty* (2004) watched her 'gracious scuttle'. Mark Lawson's novella, *Bloody Margaret* (1991) followed her 'funny, crouching Groucho run' as, spiked and hinged scoop in hand, she scurried about, spearing up carefully arranged garbage in St James's Park for a 1988 PR photo opportunity. Hilary Mantel's story 'The Assassination of Margaret Thatcher' (2014) listened to the sound of her 'High heels on the mossy path. Tippy-tap. Toddle on', as she came into the sights of an IRA gunman. Mantel's homicidal fantasy was the product of what she called 'boiling detestation' of Thatcher (who had made an earlier appearance as a Secretary of State for Education with a voice like 'shards of glass' and hair that 'lay against her head in doughy curves, like unbaked sausage rolls' in Mantel's partly autobiographical 1995 novel, *An Experiment in Love*). J.G. Ballard, a fan of the prime minister, showed her surviving an assassination attempt at her home in Dulwich and undauntedly emerging with tea and biscuits for the rescue services.

Authors of a right-wing disposition tended to dwell admiringly on Thatcher's toughness. In Len Deighton's thriller *XPD* (1981), the director-general of MI6 squirms in his chair as she subjects him to piercing looks and refuses to let him smoke a cigarette. *First Among Equals* (1984) by Jeffery Archer (soon to be made deputy chairman of the Conservative Party) shows her in robust control of a Cabinet meeting about a Libyan terrorist crisis. Brusquely barking out commands to her defence secretary – 'Report any news you hear direct to me. I shan't be sleeping tonight' – Archer's Thatcher is so macho a leader that he becomes confused as to her gender. There is speculation, he writes, as to 'whether Mrs Thatcher would now make way for a younger man'.

There's no doubt about her femaleness in D.M. Thomas's *Lying Together* (1990), where a Russian dissident tells of a heavy petting session he has enjoyed with Mrs Thatcher in 10 Downing Street. While novelists most usually lamented her tight monetary policies, Thomas's character enthuses about her 'wonderful taut nipples' ('She loves having them sucked. It drives her wild.') 'Essentially', it's disclosed, 'the Iron Lady is a young girl still, the daughter of a grocer who had ruined her with discipline; a girl bursting with suppressed sexuality and fun.'

Suppressed sexuality and fun remain firmly so in Laurence Rees's thriller *Electric Beach* (1990) where Margaret Thatcher has eyes 'as sharp as frost', a coiffure like 'a Viking helmet' and teeth that look 'specially sharpened'. Her 'glittering helmet of hair' reappears in Mantel's story as something that provides an easy target for the IRA marksman. In *Operation 10* (1982) by Hardiman Scott, a former political editor of the BBC (an organisation towards which Thatcher was not benign), she is kidnapped by the IRA, imprisoned and forced into a flannelette shift after having her face scrubbed with carbolic soap and her hair cropped until she resembles 'the inmate of some turn-of-the-century charity ward'. Reduced to this plight, she murmurs with unexpected meekness 'I have no objection to emptying my own slops, if you will show me where.'

Attention was often paid to Margaret Thatcher's clothing. One of the observers whose monologues make up *Bloody Margaret* is her wardrobe adviser, an 'Image Man' hesitating between 'a two-piece in cruise-missile grey' or 'the usual Tory-blue suit' for her speech in Blackpool's Empress Ballroom during the 1987 Conservative Party Conference (where, it's suggested, the Special Branch's codename for her is Boadicea). But her most sartorially significant clothes are on view in David Caute's 1989 novel *Veronica: or, The Two Nations*, where she wears 'a terracotta outfit . . . with a busy pattern of what looked all too like snakes and ladders'. It's a pattern whose motif of escalated rise and unlucky descent is also woven into the novel's fabric. Though Thatcher's call for a return to 'Victorian values' failed to win any appreciable response from novelists, desire to document the social repercussions of her policies (the 'sado-monetarism' Malcolm Bradbury satirised in his 1987 novella, *Cuts*) did impel a number of them back to a Victorian literary template. One undoubted beneficiary of Thatcherism was a sub-genre of nineteenth-century fiction that it reanimated. As its title signalled, Caute's novel, whose narrative view-point is polarised between a Conservative Cabinet minister and a left-wing journalist from the East End slums, purposely evoked a notable Victorian novel. Behind Caute's depiction of a bifurcated Britain stands an earlier portrayal of the country as deplorably split between rich and poor: Benjamin Disraeli's *Sybil, or The Two Nations* (1845).

Nineteenth-century condition-of-England novels became regular background presences to fiction of the 1980s and 1990s, invoked by authors who felt that the divides such books had aimed to narrow were being prised wide apart again by Thatcherism. David Lodge's elegant, ironic *Nice Work* (1988) was a prime instance of this. As a post-structuralist feminist lecturer and an unreconstructed Midlands industrialist learn about each other's very different field of employment through a job-swap scheme, Lodge makes witty play with allusions to, and plot patterns from, books such as Disraeli's *Sybil*, Charlotte Brontë's *Shirley* (1849), Elizabeth Gaskell's *North and South* (1854) and Dickens's *Hard Times* (1854). Like them, his novel looks at a nation cleft by social, economic and regional gulfs.

Where there's a difference is in his central characters' awareness that real power and prestige in their time lies outside both their spheres: in the City of London.

After their vogue during the Thatcherite 1980s, updated Two Nations or condition-of-England novels went into abeyance for a while. But a resurgence was triggered several decades later by the 2008 financial meltdown and the 2016 Brexit referendum. John Lanchester's *Capital* (2012) was a response to the former. As its two-way title indicates, it is about both money and the metropolis. Centring on a gentrified street south of the Thames as the recession closes in, it unfolds into a panorama of modern life in the city – and City – of London.

Pepys Road, the nub of Lanchester's chronicle, is a stretch of late Victorian terraced housing originally designed for the upwardly striving lower classes. By 2007 when his story opens only Petunia Howe, an elderly widow born – and now dying – in the home her grandfather bought, is a reminder of these humble origins. Far more typical of the street's current demographic are Roger Yount, an investment banker, and his high-maintenance wife Arabella.

As well as their £3.5 million house in Pepys Road, its interior in a perpetual state of pricey makeover to accommodate Arabella's ever-changing whims about decor, the Younts possess a Georgian parsonage in Wiltshire which has proved slightly disappointing ('going there for your year's major summer holiday was a little bit dowdy, Arabella felt'). Ambitions to supplement it with a Mediterranean villa ('It was said you could get somewhere pretty habitable on Ibiza for a million quid'), along with routine running costs such as a timeshare on a yacht, private jet hire, three cars, a Spanish nanny and an Australian 'weekend nanny' (not to mention a Hungarian 'crisis nanny' to cope with child-care at Christmas), all make Roger jumpy about his impending annual bonus. With incredulous aghastness, he starts to fear that, far from the seven-figure sum he hopes for, it could be as low as his basic salary of £150,000. News that he will be receiving only a five-figure emolument causes him to vomit with shock.

Bankers' engorged expectations are put on satiric display in *Capital* with the same lethal knowledgeability Lanchester brought to his factual account of financial bunglings in his book about the economic meltdown, *Whoops!* (2010). Surveying the exorbitances of the super-rich – from Arabella's airhead expenditures to gross treats laid on during a shooting party on an oafish multi-millionaire's Norfolk estate – is a speciality. But the novel extends considerably beyond this. Taking you into the minds and circumstances of a wide variety of Londoners, assorted narratives (that, in big-city fashion, intersect but rarely interconnect) spotlight a female refugee from Zimbabwe illegally employed as a traffic warden, a terminally ill old lady, a teenage football prodigy from a two-room shack in Senegal, an industrious young Polish builder and his svelte Hungarian girlfriend, and the Kamals, a Muslim family who own Pepys Road's corner shop.

Providing a kaleidoscope of perspectives on to the metropolis, Lanchester's characters are never merely representative types. They surprise and engross by believably revealing unexpected aspects of their personality. Initially a carpingly aggrieved comic turn, Mrs Kamal grows into a formidable force for justice when her amiable son is mistakenly detained as a jihadi suspect. Intermittent realisation of how he is being humanly impoverished by immersion in the wealth industry gradually starts to save Roger.

To pull together his novel's diverseness, Lanchester threads a mystery story through it. Pepys Road's residents are perturbed when postcards declaring 'We Want What You Have' recurrently drop through their letterboxes: rather as a range of Londoners are disturbed by the phone message, 'Remember you must die', in Muriel Spark's *Memento Mori* (1959), about which Lanchester has written admiringly. But this plot scarcely seems necessary as a unifying device. Money already serves that purpose. References to it cascade through the pages. Pepys Road homeowners effortlessly accumulate wealth as house prices soar. Incomes and spendings are precisely itemised. A rogue trader ruins a bank. A parking ticket has disastrous consequences. Finding half a million pounds in hoarded banknotes presents a moral test. Insurance lawyers haggle over the value of an injured knee, and a Banksy-like artist makes a fortune out of installations purporting to scorn the 'commodification' of art.

Builders' skips and scaffolding clutter Pepys Road as lucrative renovation of its Victorian properties hectically proceeds. Lanchester's book itself rewardingly refurbishes the condition-of-England novel. Presenting London as a microcosm of early twentieth-century inequity and diversity, it takes you from the top of the London Eye to a cell in Paddington Green police station, from scruffy-chic art hangouts in Hoxton to a plutocratic banquet in the City, an asylum-seekers' refuge in Tooting, a Clerkenwell gambling club, a Premiership League soccer club's training ground, an African Anglican church in Balham and a host of other vividly rendered venues.

Social and regional divides heightened by economic inequalities slipped somewhat into the fictional background as Brexit bifurcated the nation. Soon, it was Leaver and Remainer divides that novels such as Jonathan Coe's *Middle England* (2018) sought to map with the help of a Victorian blueprint. Nodding towards George Eliot's *Middlemarch* with its title and focusing on the same region, it interwove socially and ideologically illustrative types such as a pro-European art historian and a writer of op-ed pieces for the *Guardian* with a Brexiteer driving-instructor, a Eurosceptic anti-immigrant bigot and the leader of a right-wing think tank called Imperium.

Edwardian Emulations

It wasn't only Victorian novels that were used to underpin fiction portraying modern life. Two contrasting instances showed how classic Edwardian novels could be utilised too: Zadie Smith's *On Beauty* (2005) and Sathnam Sanghera's *Marriage Material* (2013).

E.M. Forster, who famously urged 'Only connect' in the epigraph to his novel *Howards End*, would have been startled to see the way in which Smith followed his advice. Fastening on to *Howards End*, *On Beauty* takes over and makes over its characters, plot patterns, themes, situations and phrases. The setting of Smith's book is a university town in Massachusetts. From street-savvy youths in hoodies to academics bristling with postmodern theory, twenty-first-century types stream across its pages. 'This isn't 1910', someone is made to snap. But, constantly, *On Beauty* looks back to Forster's 1910 condition-of-England novel. *Howards End*'s studiedly casual opening line, 'One may as well begin with Helen's letters to her sister', is restyled as 'One may as well begin with Jerome's emails to his father.' An awkward mix-up over an umbrella is updated to an awkward mix-up over a Discman. Forster's South London clerk shabbily excluded from the cultural establishment becomes a Black American rapper.

Happenings in *Howards End* – a false-start engagement and its ensuing embarrassments, a Christmas-shopping expedition, a trip to the country that gets no further than the railway station, a sudden friendship, an unexpected funeral, a suppressed bequest – are replicated. Forster's fey description of Beethoven's Fifth Symphony performed in London's Queen's Hall is paralleled by a fey description of Mozart's Requiem performed on Boston Common (where Forster hears elephants and goblins in the music, Smith hears apes and mermaids). Through both books spreads a mesh of tensions and attachments between two families who embody – liberal versus conservative – opposing attitudes and ideologies.

All but daubed with highlighter pen, *On Beauty*'s re-workings of *Howards End* aren't difficult to spot for readers familiar with Forster (others will be understandably bemused by some of the book's far-fetched twists and turns). What is harder to see is their purpose. Smith's preface speaks of offering '*hommage*' to Forster. But cannibalising one of his novels, giving its components a gaudy re-spray and recycling them into what turns out to be a ramshackle vehicle for an ill-sorted heap of concerns seems a curious mode of going about this.

Despite its commandeering of the framework of *Howards End*, *On Beauty* isn't any more successful than its predecessors, *White Teeth* (2000), which borrowed plentifully from Salman Rushdie's *The Satanic Verses*, and *The Autograph Man* (2002), which was sizeably indebted to Martin Amis's *Money*, in curbing Smith's taste for meandering as her whimsy takes her. Initially focused on the households of two rival academics – Howard Belsey, a white English art historian of radical bent, and Monty Kipps, a Black art historian and reactionary campaigner against PC pieties – the narrative soon strays away from this set-up. Swerving about, Smith seems unable to decide what kind of novel she wants to write: a campus satire, an amused survey of North London and East Coast American lifestyles, a study of infidelity and its hurts (after twenty-eight years of happy marriage, Howard has been unfaithful to his wife Kiki), a jaunty celebration of youth culture, an exploration of the relationships between beauty and power, creativity and criticism, experience and analysis, or a conscience-pricking portrayal of the gulf between the pampered existences of affluent Black Americans and the exploited plight of Third World Black people, especially Haitian refugees who, as cleaners, drivers and street-peddlers, constitute – rather as in Tom Wolfe's fiction – a populous underclass in this book. Skimming inconsequentially around among this medley of material, *On Beauty* fails to get a satisfactory purchase on any of it.

Slackness lets inconsistencies slip past. Images go awry. At one point it is remarked how 'the democratic East Coast snow was still falling, making the garden chairs the same as the garden tables and plants and mail-boxes and fence-posts'. Momentarily attention-catching, the image rapidly melts into meaninglessness. Since the things it falls on keep their differing shapes, the 'democratic East Coast snow' can't make them the same – and, of course, snow in even the most undemocratic zones of the globe would have the same effect.

Inability to sustain tone is a more general difficulty. Characterised as 'soft and open, with a liberal susceptibility to the pain of others …

overwhelmed by the evil men do to each other', Howard and Kiki's younger son Levi reflects about Haiti: 'there's this little country, a country *real close to America that you never hear about*, where thousands of Black people have been enslaved, have struggled and died in the streets for their freedom, and had their eyes gouged out and their testicles burnt off, have been macheted and lynched, raped and tortured, oppressed and suppressed and every other kind of pressed'. The segue from the catalogue of horrific atrocities to the careless flippancy of 'every other kind of pressed' grates. Smith's fiction can seem too receptive to the cool and offbeat. Zany quirks are what readers will remember of many of her characters (such as a lecturer who repetitively burbles about the virtues of '*pah*-point presentation'). Even Kiki, who looms corporeally large – she weighs in at 250 lb and her obesity is a frequent topic – seems fairly substanceless when it comes to psychological and emotional believability. Significantly, the novel's most engaging feat of characterisation (shambling, mumbling, well-intentioned Levi) is the one where it pulls most free from its self-consciously bookish background. Elsewhere, the sense of arch appropriation and skittish cross-reference thickens the atmosphere of self-indulgent waywardness that has overwhelmed the book by the time Smith reaches her Howard's end.

More purposeful updating of a classic work was accomplished by Sathnam Sanghera in his novel, *Marriage Material*, for which, he explained, he 'shoplifted characters and elements of plot' from Arnold Bennett's Edwardian masterpiece, *The Old Wives' Tale* (1908). The choice of verb is appropriate. A shop is central to each book: in *The Old Wives' Tale*, a drapery store in Staffordshire; in *Marriage Material*, a newsagent's run by a Sikh family in Wolverhampton. Further similarities soon emerge. Each novel spans three generations, starting with a bedridden overbearing father and his tradition-bound wife, then shifting to their contrasting daughters (one conformist, one a rebellious runaway) before moving on to the stay-at-home daughter's artistic son. In each novel unlucky events accompany a fatal stroke; in each, there's a disastrous elopement with a travelling salesman. Small variations teasingly occur as well: a botched tooth-extraction in Bennett becomes a botched haircut in Sanghera.

But *Marriage Material* isn't simply an ingenious exercise in updating. While largely shadowing Bennett's narrative, it markedly diverges from his main concerns. Where the great theme of *The Old Wives' Tale* is time and the surprises and sadnesses it brings, Sanghera's central subject, as in his memoir, *The Boy with the Topknot* (2008), is prejudice.

Bigotries of various kinds stand out in *Marriage Material*'s two storylines: thirty-five-year-old Arjan's ruefully funny account of returning from his thriving career as a graphic artist in London to run the newsagent's shop after his father's sudden death, and alternating third-person chapters that chronicle his family's life there from the 1960s to the present day. Enoch Powell's infamous 1968 'Rivers of Blood' speech stirs murky undercurrents to the surface. A Sikh activists' dispute with Wolverhampton Transport Department over a ban on staff wearing turbans on buses inflames hotheads on all sides into threatening to burn themselves alive. More recent modes of racist abuse and graffiti ('Paki pervert', 'Taleban Peedo') are sardonically shrugged off by Arjan ('I am of Punjabi Indian heritage . . . I have a white girlfriend, Freya, my fiancée, she is an adult').

Within the Sikh community, mixed-race marriages provoke as much animosity as they do with white racists. Another type of prejudice persists too. Caste divisions that could be lethal in the Punjab still rear up and can have brutal consequences. One of the novel's achievements is to keep you in mind of all this while maintaining a tone of shrewdly humorous sanity. Sanghera's forte is for wry comedy tinged with pathos. Affectionate irony plays over his scenes of Sikh family life, social etiquette and religious observances, especially his portrayal of Arjan's grandmother, zealously devoted to custom, ritual and superstitions (bad luck to wash hair on Tuesdays or sneeze before setting out on a journey, never leave one shoe lying on another). Half-mockery of the clumsy earnestness of Arjan's awkward, pedantic father, the shop assistant who (like Bennett's Samuel Povey) has married into the family, goes along with respect for his striving to better himself, as he is shown at the end of each long day behind the counter memorising a new word from his dictionary, poring over an entry in his prized *Encyclopaedia Britannica* and perusing the evening paper so as to have something to say, in his halting English, to the next day's customers.

Deftly chosen chapter headings – 'Indian Observer', 'Cosmopolitan', 'Guardian' – highlight the novel's newsagent setting. But, beneath its workaday routines, secrets lurk, as they did in Sanghera's memoir, which recounted his shock at discovering that his father had for decades been suffering from paranoid schizophrenia. In *Marriage Material* there's a horrific concluding twist that's rather like finding a cobra coiled around a box of confectionery in a corner shop. Carefully prepared for, you realise in retrospect, it's an instance of atrocity unleashed by '*izzat*', the toxically persisting code of 'honour'. The unwaveringly humane stance of Sanghera's engaging novel throws it into particularly damning relief.

Re-workings of smaller-scale Edwardian texts came from William Trevor and Joseph O'Connor, each of whom wrote a short story inspired by one of those in James Joyce's collection, *Dubliners* (1914). 'Two Gallants', the story that a puritanically outraged printer in 1905 refused to set (denying *Dubliners* publication for nearly a decade), was revisited by Trevor in 'Two More Gallants' (1986). Showing a humiliating hoax being played on a Joyce scholar, it skilfully reprised the original's themes of callous exploitation and shamed collusion. Joseph O'Connor's 'Two Little Clouds' (2012) deftly updated 'A Little Cloud', Joyce's vignette of a mild family man being demeaned by a swaggering braggart, to the Dublin of 2007 and the post-Celtic-Tiger slump.

Underlying Templates

Smith, Sanghera, Trevor and O'Connor re-worked classic texts overtly. Often, an underlying antecedent was more covert. It's only gradually, for instance, that affinities between Ian McEwan's novel

Saturday (which criss-crosses central London on 15 February 2003, the day of the mass demonstration against the impending war on Iraq) and *Mrs Dalloway* (Virginia Woolf's 1925 novel, which also focuses on a day in central London) become apparent. Shared concerns – sanity shadowed by unreason, intimations of ageing and mortality, the trauma of war, the precariousness of comfortable stability, preparations for a party – increasingly link McEwan's evocation of an early twenty-first-century day in the metropolis with Woolf's early twentieth-century one.

Behind the strenuously up-to-the-minute world of Jay McInerney's novels, the influence of Scott Fitzgerald's fiction was more and more discernible as his career advanced. Themes and character-types Fitzgerald patented were given a modish makeover. Raccoon-coated playboys, flappers with diamante garters doing the Charleston and the smart set dining at Delmonico's are replaced by 1980s Manhattan glitterati, Ivy League preppies and Wall Street yuppies gobbling sushi between big-money deals. McInerney's socialites get their buzz less from highballs and hip flasks than from lines of coke chopped with a Soho House membership card. Status symbols and the names of voguish restaurants are different. Instead of ragtime tinnily emitted from phonographs, rock blasts from high-tech sound systems. But, in essentials, his fictional ambience is the same as Fitzgerald's Jazz Age one. So is the attitude – fascination laced with irony – he brings to it. Some of his novels revamp ones by Fitzgerald: *The Beautiful and Damned* and *Tender Is the Night* in *Brightness Falls* (1992), *The Great Gatsby* in *The Last of the Savages* (1996), his contemporary take on the interplay between puritan and romantic elements in the American psyche. Continuingly, his fiction shows a Fitzgerald-like entrancement with glamour and disenchantment, the casualties of affluence, metropolitan allure, ideals and their dissipation, charm and its tarnishing.

A more widespread phenomenon in modern fiction was the reappearance of figures endowed with prototype-like significance in classic texts. Avatars of Cervantes' Don Quixote and Sancho Panza journeyed on through a number of novels. In Graham Greene's *Monsignor Quixote* (1982), they took the form of an unworldly Spanish parish priest and a Communist ex-mayor travelling around La Mancha, post-Franco, debating politics and theology in an old car named after Quixote's horse Rocinante. In Angus Wilson's *As If by Magic* (1973), they were a haplessly impractical upper-class gay agronomist touring South-East Asia with his savvy, vigorously heterosexual, working-class photographer. Salman Rushdie's *Quichotte* (2019) had as its Quixote a Bombay-born pharmaceutical salesman, impaired by a stroke, driving around America in the company of his (imaginary) son Sancho on a quest to find his Dulcinea, a one-time Bollywood star. Carys Davies' *West* followed a widower on a quixotic trek across 1815 America from Pennsylvania to Kentucky, accompanied by a Shawnee Indian boy.

Robinson Crusoe and Man Friday are another pair of opposites who have lived on in modern literary imaginations. Narrated by a woman who had been a castaway on the island inhabited by Crusoe and a (tongueless) Friday, J.M. Coetzee's *Foe* (1986) opened up – rather as Jean Rhys's *Wide Sargasso Sea* had done with *Jane Eyre* – a feminist and colonial perspective on to *Robinson Crusoe*. J.G. Ballard, whose *Concrete Island* (1974) stranded a motor accident victim on derelict land cut off by surrounding motorways, declared in its preface: 'The Pacific atoll may not be available, but there are other islands far nearer to home, some of them only a few steps from the pavements we tread every day. They are surrounded, not by sea, but by concrete, ringed by chain-mail fences and walled off by bomb-proof glass.' Reversing Defoe's scenario, Ballard's castaway is what his author calls an 'anti-Crusoe' who 'felt no real need to leave the island, and this alone confirmed that he had established dominion over it.' Far from feeling a need to escape, in fact, he welcomes being marooned as in itself an escape from irksome responsibilities.

The footprint on the beach that gave Crusoe his first intimation that he was not alone also reappears in contexts that would have astonished Defoe: as the print of a child's sandal on a shore of New Zealand's South Island in Keri Hulme's *The Bone People*; as a human footprint near the ocean's edge in the devastated North America of Margaret Atwood's *Oryx and Crake* (2003) where it alerts her protagonist that he is not the single survivor of global cataclysm.

Jekyll and Hyde, emblems of the split self, found reincarnation as a bipolar female in Emma Tennant's *Two Women of London: The Strange Case of Ms Jekyll and Mrs Hyde* (1989). More compellingly, they were formative influences on Ian Rankin's novels featuring the Edinburgh-based police detective, Inspector John Rebus. Though it was revealed in the first of them, *Knots and Crosses* (1987), that Rebus's favourite reading is *Crime and Punishment*, it's a nineteenth-century novel closer to home that looms over Rankin's murder mystery series. Robert Louis Stevenson's *The Strange Case of Dr Jekyll and Mr Hyde* (1886) provided the epigraph – 'My devil had long been caged, he came out roaring' – to the second book in the sequence, the punningly entitled *Hide and Seek* (1991). References to it recur in others, for Stevenson's tale epitomises Rankin's view of Edinburgh as a starkly divided city.

Even its architecture displays this, he stresses: on one side, the impeccable regularity of the New Town's Georgian squares and terraces; on the other, the murky, twisty wynds of the medieval Old Town. Behind the handsome picture-postcard façade a criminal underworld festers. John Knox-like righteousness and repression (frequently ripped open in Rankin's novels) camouflage underlying malignity. Another emblematic Edinburgh ghost his fiction harks back to is the notorious Deacon William Brodie, often cited as a model for Jekyll and Hyde (and later claimed as an ancestor by Muriel Spark's Jean Brodie): a gentleman by day, a felon by night.

Brodie gets a mention in one of the best Rebus novels, *The Falls* (2001), which uncovers skeletons and skulduggery behind a veneer of genteel affluence. In it, Rebus's involvement with a woman who is a curator at an Edinburgh museum means that reminders of the city's often dark past are much in evidence. Macabre exhibits – a plaster cast of an executed criminal with the marks of the hangman's noose visible, ancient black coffins – dot the story. Gothic frissons swirl around modern fatalities. Bygone butchery provides the back-cloth to a narrative that incorporates two present-day funerals, several cemetery scenes, a grisly autopsy, three pathologists, a strangled corpse and a dead priest, as well as some long-defunct cadavers. There's talk of nineteenth-century bodysnatchers (and Burke and Hare, the murderers who fast-forwarded supply of corpses for dissection by cutting out the wait for natural death and burial). Further alluded to in the title of *The Falls'* successor, *Resurrection Men* (2002), they provide subliminal metaphors throughout its narrative (at a climactic point of which, Rebus feels that seeing a killer shed his civilised persona was 'like watching Edward Hyde decide he no longer needed Henry Jekyll').

Frankenstein and Dracula

As might be expected in a period when unearthing the past has been a central fictional concern, literature's most famous tale of recycled body parts, Mary Shelley's *Frankenstein* (1818), was creatively exhumed on more than one occasion and in very differing ways. Catering to the appetite for prequels, *Death's Enemy* (2001) by George Rosie supplied Victor Frankenstein's autobiography of his early years in which, after medical studies at Bavaria's University of Ingolstadt, he worked with doctors in Scotland anatomising cadavers purchased from bodysnatchers. Also featuring 'Doomsday men', who raised the dead from their graves, Peter Ackroyd's *The Casebook of Victor Frankenstein* (2008) simultaneously conjured up a fetidly palpable pre-Victorian London and re-cast Mary Shelley's scenario as a psychotic psychodrama.

Ackroyd used Shelley's novel and the circumstances of its writing to explore Romantic ideology at its feverish peak in the early nineteenth century. Jeanette Winterson's bizarrely titled *Frankissstein* (2019) aimed to relate it to an early twenty-first-century milieu of artificial intelligence and gender transition. In its nineteenth-century sections, Mary Shelley retells the familiar story of how she dreamt up her horror-tale *Frankenstein* when staying in Geneva with her poet-husband, her stepsister and their friend Lord Byron during the notoriously wet summer of 1816. In its present-day sections, Ry Shelley, a transgender surgeon ('fully female ... also partly male'), supplies body parts, among them a severed head, to Professor Victor Frankenstein, a would-be pioneer not just of deep-freeze corporeal preservation but of uploading human intelligence into digital storage for later reclamation.

Though *Frankissstein* enthuses about the latter project, it's hard not to feel that it could have its drawbacks. For, downloaded into Winterson's brain, Mary Shelley's ideas find themselves in strange company. Garish grotesques – not least, a lewd manufacturer of sexbots and his unlikely business partner, an evangelical Christian woman devoted to manufacturing 'bots for Jesus' – feature to crudely satiric purpose. Parallels between past and present-day scenes take the form of strained punning (Lord Byron becomes Ron Lord, his physician Dr Polidori reappears as Polly D.). Amid a jumble of researched scientific data that characters reel out, the basic lineaments of Mary Shelley's Gothic fable – science over-reaching itself, hubris hideously punished, malformed loneliness tragically wreaking havoc – get peculiarly garbled.

More enlivening intelligence crackles through Robert Harris's response to *Frankenstein* in his novel *The Fear Index* (2011), which opens in a secluded mansion as a clock strikes midnight. Sitting by a dying fire in his book-lined study, Dr Alexander Hoffmann pores over pages in an antiquarian volume describing the physical effects of fear ('The heart beats quickly and violently ...'). It could be the start of a nineteenth-century terror-tale. But, as is soon made clear by talk of algorithmic trading on the stock exchange and hedge fund managers on astronomic salaries, the time is the present. The brief flicker of ambivalence about the period is stage-setting for a clever exercise in regenerating a classic. Taking a scenario as up-to-the-minute as a news flash from the money markets, *The Fear Index* gives it the features of Mary Shelley's 1818 shocker.

The lakeside dwelling in which Hoffman, an American physicist turned financial wizard, lives with his artist wife Gabrielle is in Cologny, the suburb of Geneva where, almost two centuries earlier, Shelley had dreamt up her Gothic tale of a scientist who unleashes a monster. Characters and establishments in Harris's story have the same names as some of Shelley's companions and haunts during her momentous stay in Geneva. Like *Frankenstein*, his novel is a tale of the catastrophic consequences of galvanising inanimate matter into uncontrollable life.

The book Hoffmann is scrutinising when the story begins is a first edition of Charles Darwin's *The Expression of the Emotions in Man and Animals* sent by a mystery donor, with a bookmark ominously inserted into the section on fear. Increasingly fearful happenings follow its arrival. In the depths of the night, despite the formidable security installations around the Hoffmanns' $60 million residence, an intruder gains entry and, before escaping, is seen sinisterly sharpening knives in their kitchen. Police investigations come up with puzzling finds. As bewildering harassments mount, Hoffmann is tormented by a sense of persecution from a quarter he can't identify. Is he suffering from paranoia, the target of a business rival's plot or being stalked by a psychopath?

What makes Hoffmann's fear-stricken plight cruelly ironic is that, inspired by the VIX 'fear index' which charts nervous volatility on money markets, he has pioneered a system of computer algorithms programmed to search the web for 'incidences of fear-related language' and use the information to run a fabulously profitable hedge fund. 'Fear is historically the strongest emotion in economics', Hoffmann observes. Capitalising on this, he brings phenomenal returns to a select band of wealthy investors.

But, as the story accelerates through its sensation-packed twenty-four-hour span, Hoffmann's top-secret experiment in 'autonomous machine reasoning' extends its purposes. Devised to track and exploit tremors in the market, it starts to do the same thing to human beings, especially its inventor. Thrown into panic by its manoeuvrings, the global money markets plummet towards disaster. As in *Frankenstein*, an over-reaching scientist finds himself desperately battling to destroy what he has created.

Depicting all this, Harris switches the high-tension techniques that give his thrillers their suspense into black comic mode. Mock-Gothic frissons abound as Hoffmann, struggling to stop the fatally spreading software, enters the cold darkness of a computer control room where 'the forest-eyes of a thousand CPUs blinked at his approach' or is attacked by a homicidally malfunctioning lift (not only markets go into lethal free fall in this novel).

Harris had previously shown himself an early fictional adopter of high-tech innovations (his 2007 thriller *The Ghost* was possibly the first novel to use a satnav to telling effect). Adroitly exploiting anxieties about algorithmic trading to update the Frankenstein story, *The Fear Index* is both cutting edge and continuingly conscious of its literary predecessors. Homages to Mary Shelley's tale constantly surface (even Gabrielle's artworks, which trace MRI body scans on to sheets of glass, seem eerie reflections of Victor Frankenstein's assemblings of human lineaments).

The background presence of other novels sometimes seems discernible too. Like Graham Greene's *Doctor Fischer of Geneva* (1980), a scathing fable about avaricious plutocrats toadying to a millionaire in Switzerland, *The Fear Index* satirically parades an unlovely bevy of the super-rich: from a miserly Swiss couple with a fortune dubiously amassed during the Nazi era to the lacquered virago daughter of an Asiatic warlord. As in Joseph Conrad's *Under Western Eyes* (1911), spruce, law-abiding Geneva is presented as a place of cynical tolerance, profiting from mercenary hospitality to the greedy and disreputable. At a time when re-working classic texts has become a large-scale literary industry, Harris's tongue-in-cheek flesh-creeper is a stand-out specimen of what can be achieved by it.

John Polidori, a background figure among the better-known Romantic travellers who whiled away the tedium of their rainy stay on the shores of Lake Geneva by inventing terror-tales, is credited with initiating a new sub-genre of Gothic menace with his contribution: a story called 'The Vampyre'. It was a later writer though, Bram Stoker, who full-bloodedly attached the vampire to the cultural imagination as a spectre of the same persisting horror as Frankenstein's monster.

His novel *Dracula* – with its portrayal of undead past malignity battening on the present – has held enduring, and often imaginatively revamped, fascination. In 2020, J.S. Barnes's *Dracula's Child* disinterred it as what partly seemed a response to Brexit. His period in which Dracula re-emerges and deviously reasserts his reign of terror is the early twentieth century. As its story ends, Transylvanian blood-drinking segues into wholesale European bloodshed with the outbreak of the First World War. But the book's emphasis on the menace of resurgent bloody-minded nationalism also has distinct modern overtones. Satiric bite breaks though Gothic shudders ('It was as though the present were in some fashion the subject of mockery from the past') as attention is drawn – using 'the very strangest of connecting tissue from the past' – to a rebarbative 'reversion to older times'.

The pervading interest in origins sent one novelist, Joseph O'Connor, back to the genesis of Stoker's tale. Previous books had shown that two subjects – Ireland and the theatre – particularly stirred O'Connor's imagination. *Ghost Light* (2010), his novel about an Irish actress's relationship in 1907 Dublin with the Abbey Theatre playwright John Synge, quivered with the allure of the stage and performance.

Shadowplay (2019) put Victorian theatre in the limelight. Resurrecting it in all its colourful wizardry, O'Connor places three figures centre stage: Henry Irving (the greatest actor impresario of the age), Ellen Terry (its best-loved actress) and Bram Stoker (the Dublin clerk and would-be author who became manager of London's Lyceum Theatre, where Irving's sensational productions were staged).

Irving's tempestuous tenure at the Lyceum provides tremendous scope for transmitting O'Connor's enthralment with drama. Sparks flash from clashing swords as Shakespearian duels in Verona and Elsinore are thrillingly galvanised by the new phenomenon of electricity. Backstage, cannonballs are rolled along a wooden track, known as the Thunder Run, to produce 'the rumpus of storms'.

The personalities behind the performances on stage emerge engrossingly. Cruel arrogance intertwines with thespian charisma in Irving. Terry's charm and wit are beautifully caught. Remembering her love of attending London First Nights, especially of tragedies, she explains 'Darling, who wouldn't? Adultery, vengeance, cruelty, lust, betrayal. That was before one got through the foyer.'

Whether making a barnstorming entry as Mephistopheles perched in the eye-socket of a giant skull lowered from the flies and (thanks to a mouthful of gasoline and a match) spitting fire at the stalls, or flamboyant even off stage in a purple velvet fez, organdie scarves and fur-collared cloak, Irving is a vivid presence. So is the shimmeringly attired Terry. But it's Stoker, the soberly garbed factotum at the Lyceum, who attracts O'Connor's keenest interest. Behind his subfusc exterior, it becomes apparent, a lurid imagination seethes.

It was an imagination that found triumphant vent just once: in his deathless 1897 vampire novel, *Dracula* (many of whose fans must have had eager expectations dashed on hunting down *The Lair of the White Worm* and other flaccid follow-ups). Stoker wrote *Dracula* while employed at the Lyceum, and Irving – aristocratic in mien, ruthlessly self-preserving – has often been cited as a model for the predatory Count. Fleshing this out, *Shadowplay* is alive with Stoker's ambivalent feelings towards the man he finds mesmerically compelling as an actor but resents as an exploiter draining his energies. Other factors fuelling his Gothic imaginings are indicated too: a bedridden childhood when leeches applied to treat his mysterious illness gave him a terrified sense of 'losing one's lifeblood', earlier vampire tales he has read (such as Sheridan Le Fanu's 1872 novella *Carmilla*), Jack the Ripper's bloody 1888 reign of terror seeping into his consciousness.

At one point, Irving taunts Stoker with a *Punch* cartoon of 'The Irish Vampire', depicted as a bloodsucker with 'dripping fangs'. Ugly abuse of the Irish, a recurrent theme in O'Connor's fiction, contributes to Stoker's anxiety at being thought alien. Heightening it, O'Connor follows suggestions that Stoker (a friend of Wilde and Walt Whitman) may have been gay and shows him guiltily making furtive forays from his marriage into a homosexual underworld.

A plethora of material is packed into *Shadowplay*, which like Stoker's novel, *Dracula* – and previous books by O'Connor, most notably *Star of the Sea*, his acclaimed 2002 bestseller about the Irish famine – is a collage of fictitious documents. Supposed extracts from Stoker's journals are interleaved with letters, newspaper cuttings, playbills and transcripts of a phonograph recording of Terry. Never a novelist to shirk profusion, O'Connor – whose writing abounds with brilliantly animated lists of everything from members of a rowdy London audience to catastrophes encountered during the Lyceum company's seventy-two-city tour of America – controls it all with superb flair. The panache and subtlety of his prose perfectly match the gusto and creative finesse of the High Victorian world his novel evokes. Engrossingly knowledgeable, it is a richly imagined example of both historical resurrection writing and creative response to an iconic text.

Books of Genesis: Philip Pullman and J.K. Rowling

Far older palimpsests than condition-of-England novels, desert island narratives, picaresque quixotic quests, Gothic shockers and vampire tales could be traced beneath modern fiction too. As we have seen, the Noah's Ark legend repeatedly came back into view, with fresh concerns taken aboard. Other scriptural stories were also commandeered and re-modelled. An outstanding example is Philip Pullman's epic inversion of the Genesis myth of the Fall in his trilogy *His Dark Materials* (begun with *Northern Lights* in 1995), which extended into a further trilogy *The Book of Dust* (begun with *La Belle Sauvage* in 2017) and several associated novels.

Pullman's starting point, he made clear, was a work he venerated but disagreed with: Milton's *Paradise Lost*.

> In my own case, the trilogy I called *His Dark Materials* (stealing that very phrase from Book II, line 916, with due acknowledgement in the epigraph) began partly with my memories of reading the poem aloud at school so many years before. As I talked to my publisher, I discovered that he too remembered studying it in the sixth form, and we sat at the lunch table swapping our favourite lines; and by the time we'd finished, I seemed to have agreed to write a long fantasy for young readers, which would at least partly, we hoped, evoke something of the atmosphere we both loved in *Paradise Lost*.

With its own journeyings in and out of very different worlds, its cosmic sweep, its angels, daemons, rebels and theocrats, Pullman's multi-volume, multi-faceted fiction about his new Eve, Lyra Belacqua, emulates the span, bravura and audacity of Milton's epic. As if 'drawn by the gravitational attraction of a much greater mass', he found he was circling round 'the same story too'. But, with his interest 'most vividly caught by the meaning of the temptation-and-fall theme', he put forward a contrasting view of it to Milton's:

Suppose that the prohibition on the knowledge of good and evil were an expression of jealous cruelty, and that the gaining of such knowledge were an act of virtue? Suppose the Fall should be celebrated and not deplored? As I played with it, my story resolved itself into an account of the necessity of growing up, and a refusal to lament the loss of innocence. The true end of human life, I found myself saying, was not redemption by a non-existent Son of God, but the gaining and transmission of wisdom, and if we are going to do any good in the world, we have to leave childhood behind.

It's an attitude to the Fall emphatically opposed to that proselytised by C.S. Lewis in his sequence of Narnia novels, at whose conclusion, Susan ('a jolly sight too keen on being grown-up') is in effect debarred by puberty from achieving salvation. Written from the perspective of a 'paranoid bigot', in Pullman's view, Lewis's homiletic fiction for children is something his own novels are, in part, devised to challenge and combat. Dominating Lyra's universe is a theocratic tyranny, 'The Magisterium', which harshly enforces the doctrine of the Fall and Original Sin. Mrs Coulter, its most sinister operative, supervises experimental 'intercision' procedures by which children are cruelly severed from the possibility of attaining intellectual maturity and freedom of thought. In contrast to The Magisterium's stunting dogmas and barbarous puberty-blocking is the concept which, in Lyra's world, Pullman calls 'Dust' ('understanding that since the loss of innocence is inevitable, we should welcome and embrace the next stage of our development instead of hiding our eyes from it').

Milton's epic rendering of the Genesis story also imprinted itself on the imagination of the author of another outstanding young adult fantasy fiction sequence: J.K. Rowling. The most immediately obvious literary antecedent helping to shape her seven Harry Potter books is the English boarding school genre. The larger part of the novels – each of which, from *Harry Potter and the Philosopher's Stone* (1997) to *Harry Potter and the Deathly Hallows* (2007), chronicles a year in Harry's career at Hogwarts School of Witchcraft and Wizardry – takes place in an institution fantastically reminiscent of establishments such as Frank Richards's Greyfriars or Enid Blyton's Malory Towers. Hogwarts, with its towers and turrets and 142 staircases (some of which have an Escher-like propensity for leading somewhere different on Fridays), is a milieu of house rivalries, prefects, detentions and dormitories. Chums bond together to thwart threatening or comic teachers but always respect strict but fair ones. Secret passages come in handy for sleuthing. Quaint servants totter around. There are arcane rites and hallowed rituals, and feasts in the Great Hall where ravenous youngsters tuck into lashings of steak-and-kidney pie and treacle tart. Fires crackle merrily in common-room grates. Last-minute-of-the-match dramas thrillingly occur on the sports field (or, to be more accurate, several feet above it since Quidditch is played on flying broomsticks).

As was highlighted by the increasingly feverish speculation as to the contents of each novel prior to publication (recalling the crowds on the New York quays shouting 'Is Little Nell dead?' to ships bringing in the latest instalment of *The Old Curiosity Shop*), Rowling was also working within a format that had strong affinities with nineteenth-century serial fiction. Besides offering a self-contained story, each novel is an instalment in a longer continuing narrative, rife with suspense and surprise, about Harry and his foe Voldemort. The seven Potter novels, she insisted, were parts of what she had, from the start, planned as a single work.

Dickens, the maestro of the serial form, is the greatest influence. Rowling shares his penchant for menaced orphans (Harry is far from the only parentless child in the books). Like him, she loves intricate family ramifications, Christmas jollities, giveaway names (Crabbe, Goyle, Peeves) and surreal streetscapes (Diagon Alley, for instance, with its stalls offering barrels of bat spleen and eels' eyes, and emporiums like Flourish and Blotts, purveyors of wizard stationery). All gaslights, cobwebby chandeliers, begrimed ancestral portraits and heaps of fascinating lumber, the old house that is the HQ of the Order of the Phoenix anti-Voldemort resistance movement could have been air-lifted out of Dickens's pages.

But, as commentators have noted, within the overarching boarding school and serial fiction frameworks, other literary allusions are profuse (right down to an ill-tempered cat, Mrs Norris, having the same name as Jane Austen's spiteful bully in *Mansfield Park*). Conspicuous among them is the increasing resemblance of Voldemort to Milton's Satan. As in *Paradise Lost* where Satan is finally reduced to a hissing 'monstrous serpent', Voldemort, with his red slit-pupilled eyes and hissing utterance, becomes ever-more snake-like as the series proceeds and ultimately, like Milton's Satan, is completely deformed into one.

Ancient Epics

Far older epics than *Paradise Lost* were re-fashioned too. The *Odyssey* – the template for twentieth-century literature's most monumentally inventive feat of fictional updating: James Joyce's *Ulysses* (1922) – served as a background presence to works of feminist revisionism such as Madeline Miller's 2018 novel *Circe* (which, one reviewer enthused, gave Homer's sorceress a 'kickass' modern makeover). Following in Miller's wake, Natalie Haynes's *A Thousand Ships* (2019) had as one of its narrators, Calliope, the muse of epic poetry, who explained 'I have picked up the old stories and . . . shaken them until the hidden women appear in plain sight.' Other mythical Greek female figures received renewed and rewarding attention: Clytemnestra in Colm Tóibín's *House of Names* (2017), Ariadne in Jennifer Saint's 2021 novel of that name. Margaret Atwood's *The Penelopiad* (2005) gave a jauntily satiric slant to events in Ithaca where the emblematically faithful Penelope awaited her husband's long-postponed return. Kamila Shamsie's *Home Fire* (2017) updated Sophocles' *Antigone* to explore the relationship between young British Muslims and the British state.

Homer's *Iliad* – swivelled into a new perspective by Miller's debut novel *The Song of Achilles* (2011) and Pat Barker's *The Silence of the Girls* and its successor, *The Women of Troy* (2021) – was transposed to 1990s South Armagh in Michael Hughes's *Country* (2018). Near the end of a long bitter conflict, Pat, the gay *protégé* of Achill ('The best sniper the IRA ever seen'), is hideously slaughtered by a captain in the SAS. After bloody revenge is taken in this Irish Troubles remake of the Achilles and Patroclus story, the corpse of Pat's killer Henry (an avatar of Homer's Hector) is dragged through the dirt roped to the towbar of Achill's car. Crammed with Homeric parallels (Helen becomes teenage Nellie, the Greek fleet at harbour becomes a pub called The Ships), Hughes's narrative is delivered – in imitation of the Homeric oral tradition – as direct storytelling to an audience. With vernacular immediacy, it heaps up sickening instances of the butchery and sadistic chaos of war. Where *Ulysses*, Joyce's encyclopaedic Irish re-working of the *Odyssey*, was an epic celebration of the democratic virtues of tolerance, forgiveness and pacific coexistence, Hughes's far smaller-scale Irish re-working of an episode from the *Iliad* casts a harsh light on the 'heroic' values at the opposite extreme to them.

Other ancient tales have lived on in metamorphosed modern forms too. As has been seen, largely due to Salman Rushdie's fervent advocacy and adaptation of its stories, the *1001 Nights* extensively infused and inspired postcolonial fiction. Its presence was also apparent elsewhere. John Barth, one of the American authors Tom Wolfe had deplored for retreating into *recherché* fiction, found it of use for his postmodern purposes. In particular, a late addition to the *Arabian Nights*' huge assemblage of stories, 'The Seven Voyages of Sinbad the Sailor', suited his fixated fascination with narrative archetypes.

Throughout the 1980s and early 1990s, Barth's novels were curiously rigged together from tales and sails. *Sabbatical* (1982) charted the voyage around Chesapeake Bay of a couple hot on narratology and adept at spotting analogies between themselves and mythic wanderers. Its follow-up, *The Tidewater Tales* (1987), launched another bookish couple, nudgingly named the Sagamores, aboard a sailing boat called *Story* (another vessel, called *Reprise*, soon anchors alongside them and a Cap'n Donald Quicksoat also hoves into view). In 1991, *The Last Voyage of Somebody the Sailor* extended Barth's joint entrancement with navigation and narration across the globe and back through the centuries. In it, a twentieth-century author of nautical bent, Simon Behler, slips through a time-loop into the realm of the archetypal tale-telling sailor, Sinbad. Time-travel keeps the narrative veering between modern Maryland and medieval Baghdad. But the book itself seems lodged in a time-warp as a prime example of a phenomenon much in vogue during the 1960s and 1970s: the narrative about narrative.

In his 1979 book *Letters*, Barth characterised himself as 'an artist less enamoured of the world than of the language we signify it with, yet less enamoured of the language than of the signifying narration, and yet less enamoured of the narration than of its formal arrangement'. *The Last Voyage of Somebody the Sailor* exemplifies the intricate shallowness this could result in. Pattern is its protagonist; structure, its subject. All its interest is turned inwards on its own procedures.

Everywhere, symmetries clamour for attention. Behler, like Sinbad, makes seven voyages. Cross-references between them burgeon. Sometimes, these look significant: a sexually abused daughter figures in both the modern and medieval stories. More often – as when the America of Behler's youth is ostentatiously littered with condoms called Sheikhs and cigarettes called Camels – they seem scarcely more than authorial doodling.

As is routine in this 'reflexive' mode of fiction, mirrorings are at a premium. From human twins to binary stars, doubleness excites enthusiasm. Puns are a passion. When Behler's daughter takes up with a Muslim marine biologist, it's merely, you feel, so that Barth can disgorge a laborious quip about 'Musalam and Mussulman mussel-man'.

Characters are little more than pliable lumps of semantic stuff that the author plays with as if they were plasticene. 'Behler' gets twisted into 'Bailor', 'Baylor' and 'Bey el-Loor'. Similar stretchy verbal permutations – 'BeeGee-Bijou-Jewel-Jule-Julia' – mutate the name of his twin sister into that of his girlfriend.

Though there are sporadic bursts of narrative verve – mostly in Sinbad's retelling of his fables – the novel is primarily engrossed in archly fondling its own components. Every so often, a pronoun shift from the third to the first person roguishly reminds you of the author's presence in his text. Lest you should overlook its tinkerings with time, the narrative keeps pausing to extol the merits of some character's Rolex, Omega, Longines, Seiko or Bulova watch. The bracelet of one of these time-pieces has some links missing, and the search for them is repeatedly highlighted as an intimation of the corresponding quest for literary connections that Barth elbows the reader into. With concordances and parallels, reflections and refractions, echoes and homophones riddling his novel, linkages between its varying sections aren't hard to locate. But, for all its elaborate internal interrelatedness, Bath's self-referential and self-reverential artefact seems sterilely cut off from contact with anything beyond itself.

Fairy tales: Philip Pullman, J.K. Rowling and Alison Lurie

John Barth could well have been at the forefront of authors the American poet James Merrill had in mind when he wrote at the start of his verse trilogy *The Changing Light at Sandover* (1982):

> Fed/Up so long and variously by
> Our age's fancy narrative concoctions

I yearned for the kind of unseasoned telling found
In legends, fairy tales, a tone licked clean
Over the centuries by mild old tongues,
Grandam to cub, serene, anonymous.

But (as was shown not least by Merrill's friend, Alison Lurie) fairy tales themselves were now receiving retellings far from 'unseasoned' and 'mild'. It wasn't only revered biblical myths and reverberant Hellenic epics that underwent renovation. Humble folk fables and children's fairy stories did so too.

Fascination with them was apparent in anthologies by contemporary writers. Angela Carter edited and translated *The Fairy Tales of Charles Perrault* (1977) and *Sleeping Beauty and Other Favourite Fairy Tales* (1982), as well as editing *The Virago Book of Fairy Tales* (1990) and *The Second Virago Book of Fairy Tales* (1992). Alison Lurie, who taught courses on children's literature at Cornell, edited *The Oxford Book of Modern Fairy Tales* (1975) and *Clever Gretchen and Other Forgotten Folktales* (1980). Philip Pullman's *Grimm Tales* (2012) caught the fast-paced, vivid magic of his fifty favourite Grimm Brothers stories in wonderfully freshened versions that aimed to be 'clear as water'.

The enthralment this displayed also manifested itself in their own writing. Pullman's fictional universe – fanned out across the *His Dark Materials* trilogy and its successors – teems with the fantastical phenomena of the fairy story: a magic knife that can cut open the invisible barrier between the human world and others, flying witches, armoured bears, elf-like beings riding dragonflies. His concept of the 'daemon' – the external representative of a person's inner self that takes animal form: Lyra's white ermine, her mother's vicious golden monkey, her father's snow leopard – sophisticatedly refashions the talking fauna of folk tales.

Elsewhere, Pullman's fable *Clockwork* (1996) – as dextrously constructed as the church clock with revolving automata that dominates its Gothic world – interlocked a story as gripping as any Grimm tale with deftly crafted commentary on narrative and its powers. His jaunty version of *Puss in Boots* (2000) colourfully enlivened Perrault's tale with more comedy and complication. *I Was a Rat!* (1999) offered a sequel to *Cinderella*, in which one of the rodents transformed into a pageboy to accompany the heroine's coach to the ball doesn't make it back by midnight and is left stuck as a human.

While J.K. Rowling didn't remake individual fairy tales, she lavishly plundered them for her Harry Potter novels. Goblins and goblets, wizards, spells, shape-shifters, mermaids, giants, ghosts, pixies, trolls and other fairy-tale familiars tumble out across her pages. Her phenomenal creative verve ensures that none seem stereotyped. When dragons appear, the identifying marks of different breeds are briskly pointed out: the smooth-scaled Common Welsh Green, the bluish-grey Swedish Short-Snout with long pointed horns, the scarlet Chinese Fireball with its distinctive facial fringe of fine gold spikes. Quirky detail revivifies fairy-tale types and tropes. Deepening resonance adds intensity. Rowling's most fearsome ghouls, the Dementors, with their clammy, rotting grey hands and empty eye-sockets, don't merely serve as daunting guards of the wizard prison, Azkaban. Leeching hope and happiness away and leaving only wretched memories, they are grim spectres of depression.

Alison Lurie gained admiration as a writer who had marked affinities with Jane Austen. From her first novel, *Love and Friendship* (1962), which borrowed its title from Austen's juvenile story of the same name, to her last with its Austenish-sounding title, *Truth and Consequences* (2005), she brought a similar sense and sensibility to ironic comedies of domestic and social life, and punctured pride and prejudice with the same satiric zest and flair. But there was a further facet to her fiction. The heroine of her novel *Foreign Affairs* (1985) is an Ivy League professor with 'a well-established reputation in the expanding field of children's literature'. It's a description also applicable to Lurie. Surveyed in her essay collections – *Don't Tell the Grown-Ups* (1990) and *Boys and Girls Forever* (2003) – motifs from such literature increasingly featured in her fiction. Opening with the fairy-tale formula, 'Once upon a time', and ending with the traditional finale, 'lived happily ever after', *Only Children* (1979) was particularly fertile with them. Over a hot July holiday weekend in 1935, two couples and their children stay at the home, deep in the country, of a fairy-godmother-like headmistress of a progressive school. Much play is made with the title's double meaning: single children, merely children. Adult tensions and misbehaviour are counterpointed with imagery from fairy tales. One of the two little girls through whose eyes events are seen – and often misunderstood or only part-understood – thinks of herself as an ugly duckling who will never become a beautiful swan. The other shrinks from reality behind fantasies of being a princess in an inviolable castle. As the two eight-year-olds, wearing paper crowns, perform a play they have written about The Goose Girl, other dramas of untrustworthiness are acted out among the adults, and charms of various kinds come into conflict.

Margaret Atwood: *The Robber Bride*

In the introduction to his *Grimm Tales*, Philip Pullman remarked that: 'There is no psychology in a fairy tale ... The tremors and mysteries of human awareness, the whispers of memory, the promptings of half-understood regret or doubt or desire that are so much part of the subject-matter of the modern novel are absent entirely'. With *The Robber Bride* (1993), Margaret Atwood showed what could be achieved by infusing complexity and nuance of this kind into the scenario of a lesser-known Grimms' tale: 'The Robber Bridegroom'.

A character in the novel who is 'in the renovation business' reflects that 'you never knew which little doodads from the past could be recycled'. It's an attitude Atwood shares. Literary reclamation and recycling – seizing on genres dismissed as trashy and bringing out their latent potential – has been a speciality. *Lady Oracle* (1976) re-worked the bodice-ripper romance. *Bodily Harm* (1981) did the

313

same with the beach-read thriller. Her nineteenth-century historical novel *Alias Grace* (1996) refurbished the penny-dreadful murder ballad. *The Blind Assassin* (1993) put 1930s dime-magazine science fiction stories to new purpose.

The Robber Bride re-works several earlier types of fiction and a modern one not usually held in high critical esteem: its focus on three female friends who regularly meet for lunch, mutual support and catch-up gossip seems a nod towards chick lit of the *Sex and the City* mode (not least as a city, Toronto, is a vibrant presence throughout). But as its title intimates the main blueprint is the fairy tale, something made explicit when two little girls who have 'decided that all the characters in every story had to be female' listen to a version of 'The Robber Bridegroom' obligingly re-gendered into the Robber Bride.

Atwood's re-working likewise replaces the marauding male with a marauding female: Zenia, a *femme fatale* who has malevolently impinged on the lives and loves of three women – Tony, Charis and Roz – and, they believe, perished in violent circumstances some years ago. As they enjoy lunch on a late October day at a favourite restaurant, though, 'Zenia returns from the dead', striding past their table in a waft of perfume that is 'dense and murky, sullen and ominous'. The memorial service they had relievedly attended turns out to have been – like so much about Zenia – an elaborate fraud. Casting a sinister shimmer over scenes, an atmosphere of revenants and the undead now swirls about her, and merges with the novel's themes: the persisting hold of the past, the re-surfacing of banked-down traumas, the risk of falling victim to malign intents.

Zenia, who has gone in for lavish erotic-appeal-enhancing plastic surgery, is several times likened to a seductive version of Frankenstein's monster. Tapping into another vein of Gothic fiction, Atwood also endows her with vampire-like attributes. Caught in headlights, her eyes have a red gleam. At one point, recalling a scene from *Dracula*, she climbs in through a bedroom window. As in classic vampire tales, she can only batten on her prey if they invite her into their home. To beguile them into doing so, she targets their 'point of most vulnerability, and the vulnerable point is the one most prized': Tony's pride in her tough, unflinching intelligence, Charis's desire to offer spiritual healing and restorative calm, Roz's confidence that she is streetwise enough not to be tricked.

'Some of the characters in fairy tales', Pullman noted, 'come in sets of multiples.' Line-ups of twelves and sevens are popular, so are threes. The trio in *The Robber Bride* are contrastingly individualised. Intellectual Tony is an academic specialist in military history, Charis is a hazily pacific New Age drifter, Roz is a wise-cracking, hardheaded businesswoman. What they have in common – besides having been worsted by Zenia – is a traumatic childhood. Each has attained a seemingly secure but precarious maturity by severing herself from her early life and suppressing memories of it: in the case of Charis (once Karen, a molested child) by adopting a new name and persona as an adult.

Like much modern fiction, *The Robber Bride* is long on retrospect. From the vantage point of the first year of the 1990s it looks back at three decades – the 1960s, 1970s and 1980s – and, beyond them, at the impact of the Second World War. The novel's actual time-span is just nineteen days, opening on 23 October 1990 and ending on 11 November of the same year. Both dates are significant. On 23 October, it's pointed out, 'The sun moves into Scorpio', the zodiac's most ominous sign, as Charis is aware. Governed by Mars, the planet of war, it presides over Atwood's tale of aggression and encroachment. Linked also to Pluto, God of the underworld, it is associated with the buried and repressed, hidden truths and their unsettling power: all of which play their part in *The Robber Bride*. Appropriately for this novel of amity and antagonism, Scorpios are traditionally the best of friends and worst of enemies. The date on which the story ends – 11 November – has symbolic resonance too. As Remembrance Day, it highlights the casualties and consequences of war, memory and coming to terms with the past.

With further neatness, the back-story of each woman's falling foul of Zenia is set within the Zeitgeist of a different period. Studious, industrious, conventional, unglamorous, Tony embodies the frugal ethos of the 1950s that persisted into the early 1960s. Charis – mystically inclined, into yoga, meditation, crystals, auras, Tarot readings and theories of reincarnation – is attuned to the spirit of the 1970s. Roz, who has made a thriving career as a businesswoman and property developer, exemplifies that of the 1980s.

The decade that has most affected each, though, is the 1940s. Looking back at damage she suffered as a child, Tony reflects that 'her mother was a war bride, her father was a war husband, she herself was a war baby'. So – also damagingly – were Charis and Roz. Concocting stories about having been a child victim of war herself is Zenia's wiliest strategy for infiltrating their sympathies. As she does so, the male partners of the three women harmed by war become hapless spoils of war.

Tony's academic engagement with the often grisly details of military aggression enables Atwood – who shares her fascination with it and her intellectual bent for knowledge and analysis – to stock the book with historical information about combat. Charis's worldview gives comic scope to Atwood's penchant for imaginatively playing with the colourfully occult. Roz springs from that part of her creativity that revels in sardonic wit and smart, amused awareness of cutting-edge fashions and fads. Merging the frissons of the Gothic with nuances of social and psychological observation, *The Robber Bride* elaborates a fairy-tale prototype into a novel of impressive reach and accomplishment.

Angela Carter

In her survey of classic children's literature, *Boys and Girls Forever*, Alison Lurie remarked that 'the gifted British writer Angela Carter has become famous for her dramatic retellings of well-known fairy tales'. In fact, she was indebted to them for the revitalisation of her writing.

As a junior reporter for a local newspaper, the *Croydon Advertiser*, Carter once recalled, she was 'sent to the cactus shows'. It was a perceptive move by her editor. For spiky exoticism proved a speciality in the fiction she went on to write. Bristling with sharp points – about sex, pain and pleasure, savagery and civilisation – it burgeoned into fantastic forms. Bizarre vegetation – nippled cacti, fanged lilies – sprouted in jungly profusion from her pages. Mutant fauna prowled the pathways of her narratives: centaurs, a jaguar-woman, an alligator-man. In their eerie depths, vampires pallidly recline in mouldering mansions, werewolves' eyes glint through tangled undergrowth.

Bookishness of an out-of-the-ordinary kind fed Carter's imagination. Works by Gothic fantasists, dandified eccentrics, fabulists and pornographers were most influential: Isak Dinesen's haunting tales, the high-camp artificialities of Ronald Firbank, Swift's scathing parables, the novels of the Marquis de Sade. Eighteenth-century literature struck a particularly responsive chord. The picaresque narrative and the philosophic fable – genres that flourished during the period – were ones she also favoured: her characters regularly embark on journeys through symbolic scenery and across landscapes of the mind. She also shared that century's fascination with the Orient.

In the late 1960s, on the proceeds of a Somerset Maugham travel award, this fascination took her to Japan, an irresistible destination for someone with her appetite for the aesthetic and macabre. Her writings enthuse about its kabuki theatre, bunraku puppetry and tattoo parlours. In Tokyo, she found a job turning the English of Japanese translators into native-sounding English but, simultaneously, the country's own imaginative idiom was adding its accent to her work. Her most ornately gruesome pieces date from this period.

Carter's time in Japan had a further effect too. Temporary work as a bar hostess (where she could 'hardly call my breasts my own'), along with noting the popularity of games in which men took pot-shots at statuettes of nude women or tried to ricochet pinballs into imitation female orifices, ratcheted up her feminism. One outcome was *The Passion of New Eve* (1977), a caustic phantasmagoria in which a screen incarnation of idealised femininity is exposed as a male cross-dresser, and a male chauvinist gets reconstructed (via an obsidian gelding knife and plastic surgery) into a model woman.

But, increasingly esoteric, Carter's fiction was decreasingly admired and lapsed, she felt, into 'deep unsuccess'. What rescued her were fairy tales. A commission to translate Charles Perrault's seventeenth-century anthology of them (what she called 'this great Ur-collection – whence sprung the Sleeping Beauty, Puss in Boots, Little Red Riding Hood, Cinderella, Tom Thumb, all the heroes of pantomime') launched her in a rewarding new direction.

In the foreword to the Perrault book, she observed that 'Each century tends to create or re-create fairy tales after its own taste'. As Edmund Gordon's biography *The Invention of Angela Carter* (2016) points out, her own taste was very evident in her retellings, which 'tested the limits between translation and adaptation, converting Perrault's long, elegant sentences into short blunt ones, adding collo-quial phrases to them, and replacing his verse morals with prose homilies, many of which said the precise opposite of what he intended'.

Where Carter more winningly found a voice of her own was in *The Bloody Chamber* (1979). The ten stories based on folk and fairy tales that it contains were not, she insisted, retellings or 'versions'. Her aim was 'to extract the latent content from the traditional stories and to use it as the beginnings of new stories'. Keenly drawn to cultural commentary – Roland Barthes and Michel Foucault had previously seized her attention – she had pored over Bruno Bettelheim's study of folklore and fairy stories, *The Uses of Enchantment* (1976), while working on Perrault's tales. Though often 'quarrelling furiously' with Bettelheim's psychoanalytic interpretations, she was imaginatively stirred by his association of animals in fairy stories with bodily desires.

Carter's response to fairy tales has been hailed as pioneeringly feminist and deplored as insufficiently so, even 'heteronormative' ('She could never imagine Cinderella in bed with the Fairy Godmother', one critic regretted). To inspect *The Bloody Chamber* through the lens of gender politics, though, is to distort what the book focuses on. There are some feminist re-jiggings: the bride of a Bluebeard-like murderer is saved not by her brothers, as in the original, but by her mother who gallops to the rescue, clutching a revolver. But Carter's stories are remote from what A.S. Byatt categorised as 'resolute feminist rewritings of fairy tales, making wilful changes to plots and forms to show messages of female power (often written under the enthusiastic misapprehension that fairy tales in general show powerless females)'.

As in folklore and fairy stories, entrapment and predation are much to the fore. Giving feral physicality to her book's twin concern with 'fear of devourment' and the need to recognise animal aspects of human nature, carnivores of a hybrid kind abound: werewolves, a lion-man, a man who is part-tiger, a female vampire with 'the fangs and talons of a beast of prey'. Undressed by her husband, the young bride in the title story ominously sees herself as 'bare as a lamb chop'. At other times, removing clothes and smoothing down beasts' rough pelts prove salutary. Acceptance of animality brings contentment: Carter's Red Riding Hood sleeps 'sweet and sound ... between the paws of the tender wolf'.

Doubleness suffuses the book in other ways too. Ravishingly written, the stories are simultaneously sumptuous and stark. Sophisticated artistry plays over the primal archetypes of folk tale. Tonal finesse caresses brute actualities. The cultural and the carnal intertwine. Almost neurasthenic aestheticism – swooning responsiveness to the Liebestod from *Tristan and Isolde* or the 'deliquescent harmonies' of Debussy's piano *études* – quivers in narratives of strangling, butchery, fangs and terror. Choice *objets d'art* (Bokhara rugs, a Bechstein grand piano, Sèvres and Limoges porcelain) resplendently intersperse horrors. Epitomising Carter's love of bejewelled gruesomeness, a ruby choker that looks 'like an extraordinarily precious slit throat' is a wedding gift to an imperilled bride. Modern amenities – cars, telephones, electricity – feature alongside atavistic fears and urges. Ambivalence flickers over relationships and emotions ('desirous dread'). Intimacy can rescue or imprison; 'embracements' can crush.

'The Lady of the House of Love', in which a naïvely decent young English soldier bicycles around Transylvania just before the Great War, opens with ironic poise: 'At last the revenants became so troublesome the peasants abandoned the village.' After he has eluded a vampire's deadly bite, it ends with cruel irony: 'Next day, his regiment embarked for France.' In between, Sleeping Beauty motifs merge with a tale of Nosferatu's last descendant. Witty, elegant and allusive, it's a miniature masterpiece that, like Atwood's *The Robber Bride*, displays what could be achieved by renovating fairy tales and folklore.

Another story in *The Bloody Chamber*, 'Puss-in-Boots', initiated the last and liveliest phase of Carter's career. Markedly different in tone and style from the narratives of beasts and baleful beauties she found lurking in the murky warrens of the psyche, it unleashed a rollicking pantomime version of the Don Juan tale. Her next novel, *Nights at the Circus* (1984), heightened this exuberance. The bedazzlement it conjured up was that of the circus ring and music hall. Fevvers, its Cockney *aerialiste* heroine, has wings but is, basically, the archetypal busty blonde: her prototypes, Carter said, included Mae West and 'a friend's grandmother who spent her professional life being shot from a giant bow'.

At the centre of Carter's final novel, *Wise Children* (1991) – a further rumbustious rummage into the property basket of yesteryear – are prodigies of another kind: septuagenarian identical twins and one-time song-and-dance girls, Dora and Nora Chance. The inspiration for these veteran hoofers was, Carter said, close to home: 'I had an aunt, my mother's sister, who probably should have gone on the halls. She didn't have a very good life at all. She was a clerk in a

rather Dickensian office, and she had a most miserable fading away.
I suppose I wanted to give her a happier life.'

The reason this figure split into two is that Carter also wanted to
create a Shakespearean extravaganza and 'Twins are such a feature of
Shakespeare. It seems to me if you wanted to make the relation
between Shakespeare and life, then you'd use twins to do it.' In fact,
it's not so much the relation between Shakespeare and life as that
between Shakespeare and theatrical life that *Wise Children* is
concerned with. As Dora, now living in Bard Road, Brixton,
reminisces about her career and the stage dynasty from which she
has sprung, a gaudy cavalcade of a century or so of show business
streams out.

At its furthest historical reaches are Ranulph Hazard, a surgingly
histrionic Victorian actor-manager, and Estella, the actress who
marries him after playing Cordelia to his Lear. Taking Shakespeare
to far-flung out-posts of the Empire, they periodically encounter
odd overlappings of art and life – most drastically when, after a
rapturously received *Othello*, they are caught in a fatal jealousy
scenario of their own (rave reviews of the play fill the morning papers;
the real-life drama, coming to light slightly later, makes the after-
noon editions).

Their twin sons, Melchior and Peregrine, next move centre stage.
In time, each spawns a brace of female twins: the illegitimate Chance,
and the supposedly legitimate Hazard, girls. From this point on, the
book brims with Shakespearean parallels and parody (Carter prided
herself on having got in allusions to every play except *Titus Andronicus*
and *The Two Noble Kinsmen*). Structured in five chapters on the
model of a five-act drama, it re-works Shakespeare's substitute-
bedmate and swapped-bride tricks. There are usurpations, father–
daughter reunions and attempted food poisonings by a Regan-like
wicked sister, famous as a television cook. A 1920s foray out to
Hollywood – a modern enchanted forest where weird transforma-
tions occur – leads to a triple wedding ceremony. On 23 April (the

birthday of Shakespeare, Dora and Nora, Melchior and Peregrine), an intertangled plot is resolved, as a tempest rages, by a sequence of revelations and reconciliations.

As a euphoric burlesque of Shakespearean properties, *Wise Children* is cleverly entertaining. But its most exhilarating attraction is the vivacious garrulity of its narrator, Dora. Spry and peppy, slapping on the warpaint an inch thick and lipsticking herself a 'Joan Crawford mouth' before sallying forth, she is the irrepressible embodiment of 'illegitimate' theatre – the vaudeville and music hall that she has sadly watched dwindle into glum nude revues and tame TV variety shows. Delivered with much oomph and pizazz, her reminiscences comprise a virtually non-stop review of her and her sister's appearances as everything from Mexican jumping beans in red tights to bulldogs in a wartime morale-raiser, and Mustardseed and Peaseblossom ('our bras and knicks had leaves appliquéed at the stress points') in an ill-starred film of *A Midsummer Night's Dream*.

Besides all this, Dora gives jaunty voice to the spirit of early twentieth-century South London. As she breezily recounts her memories, even a washing line leaps into lively animation: 'Long black stockings stepping out with gents' longjohns, striped shirts doing the Lambeth Walk with flannel nighties.' The atmosphere of an era and an area – 'The lights of Electric Avenue glowing like bad fish through a good old London fog' – is pungently evoked. As Dora (and the novel) go out with high-kicking gusto, the sadistic voluptuaries and impaled brides of Carter's earlier fiction seem to have been left merrily behind. It's a transition she was conscious of, mock-ruefully remarking, not long before her early death at the age of fifty-two: 'All these years, I've been fighting the Falstaff in my soul. All these years, I've had this deep conviction that I was the Prince of Denmark when, really and truly, I was Juliet's nurse.'

There was, though, an underlying continuity: the persisting presence of her personal past. Hers was a family, she once said, in which 'the umbilical cord wasn't terribly well severed'. The repercussions of her mother's excessive protectiveness and possessiveness – which, as Gordon's invaluably informative biography documents, led to anorexia and disturbance in Carter's youth – seem palpable in the qualms about closeness in her earlier fiction. In contrast, another aspect of her family background (especially her 'indomitable' grannies, one with canary yellow hair and magenta lips keen on sipping stout) erupts in the South London working-class ebullience of her final books.

In *Wise Children* 'high' and 'low' culture collide and coalesce. While herself a 'rather booksy person', Carter tended 'to regard all aspects of culture as coming in on the same level'. Tapping into folklore for inspiration, she simultaneously believed 'Our literary heritage is a kind of folklore ... a folklore of the intelligentsia.' Her fiction sent down fruitful roots into both.

A.S. Byatt and *Possession*

No modern writer has been more attached to the literary heritage than A.S. Byatt. It's an attribute shared by her characters, whose appetite for print is prodigious. To call them bookworms would be miserable understatement. They are literary anacondas, ingesting books voraciously and in bulk. One of the two sisters at the centre of her autobiographical early novels, *The Virgin in the Garden* (1978) and *Still Life* (1985), exults after a viva: 'I got all sorts of things in, *Britannicus* and *Henry VIII* and *The Broken Heart* and *The Winter's Tale*.' This was as nothing, though, to what Byatt herself got in: mention of most major English novelists of the eighteenth, nineteenth and early twentieth centuries, copious allusion to numerous Elizabethan, Metaphysical and Romantic poets.

Literary leanings showed themselves on even the most intimate occasions. One character is conceived when his father returns home after a particularly stimulating WEA class on Shakespeare's late plays. Another, while having sex, 'thought, as he often thought in this

323

position, of T.S. Eliot'. A potential lover is rejected as 'unexciting, apart from an encyclopaedic knowledge of Thomas Mann'. Frantically packing her suitcase as her contractions start ('toothbrush, soap, Wordsworth ... *Four Quartets*'), a mother-to-be becomes frenzied when prevented from taking *War and Peace* into the delivery room with her.

In accord with the omnipresent bookishness, an introductory note to *Still Life* acknowledged that 'This novel could not have been written without the help of the London Library'. Taking Byatt's indebtedness to that institution a stage further, her next novel, *Possession* (1990), opened in its reading room where, ensconced at his favourite table, a young academic, Roland Michell, muses on the library's long literary associations.

It's an opening that might cause qualms, given the way characters in Byatt's preceding novels had been half-submerged under a slurry of literary allusiveness. But *Possession* resourcefully extricated itself from this impasse. Pulling loose from the more or less naturalistic mode of its predecessors into what an epigraph from Hawthorne calls the 'latitude' of the romance, it fans out with storytelling brio across a fictional terrain shimmering with myth and legend and haunted by the literary past.

An 'attempt to connect a bygone time with the very present that is flitting away from us' is also spoken of in the Hawthorne epigraph. True to this, *Possession* oscillates between the late 1980s and the Victorian age. Out of a book Roland is perusing for significant marginalia flutter drafts of letters by an eminent nineteenth-century poet, Randolph Ash.

The path on which they propel Roland unwinds through libraries and archives, out to a Victorian Gothic mansion in the Fens, along beaches in North Yorkshire, across rural Brittany and into the innards of a desecrated grave in a storm-tossed churchyard at dead of night. Accompanying him on what becomes a trail strewn with Victorian revelations and modern self-discoveries is Maud, a specialist in

Women's Studies he has joined forces with after finding that the addressee of Ash's letters was an obscure nineteenth-century poet, Christabel LaMotte, the subject of Maud's research.

Previously, no relationship between the two had been known of. Ash, it was believed, led an unimpeachable married life with his slightly ailing spouse. LaMotte – now gaining acclaim in feminist circles – is assumed to have lived in manless felicity with her friend, Blanche Glover, until the latter, in a fit of melancholia, drowned herself in the Thames.

Pulling buried secrets back to light, the novel intertwines the tensions of the detective story with different strands of literary and biographical investigation. Ingeniously, its scholar-sleuths follow a paperchase in which not only Victorian journals and letters but also lines and images embedded in poetry furnish clues to eyes able to decode them. Tightening the suspense, this isn't just a search but a race. Competing with Roland and Maud are rivals such as a predatory American professor, eager to seize any new finds for his affluently endowed college.

With its Victorian sections focusing on literary prodigies and its modern episodes focusing on academics, *Possession* could be seen as setting up an antithesis: in the past, creativity; in the present, criticism. But, though dichotomies of this and other kinds (emotional sophistication/sexual knowingness, imagination/analysis) are brought out by the story's shifts between its two periods, continuities and connections are more to the fore.

Bedecked with fossils, relics, heirlooms and descendants, the novel traces persisting traits and patterns. Its nineteenth-century characters and complications have counterparts, it emerges, in the modern period. Parallels can extend even further back: as his name implies, Roland's quest has analogies with medieval romance.

Medievalism was enthusiastically revived in the Victorian age of course – as literature and architecture in this novel often exhibit. A major preoccupation in *Possession* is the 'persistent shape-shifting life of things long-dead': recuperations and re-workings by succeeding generations of past literary and legendary material. Critics reinterpret the work of Ash and LaMotte in fashions congenial to current orthodoxies. In their poetry, Ash and LaMotte reshaped myths to fit their purposes. Religious uncertainties quiver through Ash's Nordic Edda poem, *Ragnarök*. Sexual ambivalences undulate through LaMotte's retelling of the legend of a snake-woman. Ash's most admired works are Browning-like dramatic monologues which breathe life and voice into long-defunct figures such as Lazarus and a varied array of potentates, theologians, scientists, musicians and artists. At seances frequented by LaMotte, more literal credence is given to communications from beyond the grave. Throughout the novel, the motif of possession by spirits and the spirit of the past hovers.

It manifests itself most remarkably in the pastiche Victorian poems Byatt invents for Ash and LaMotte, which capture with uncanny flair past thought-patterns and the imaginative configurations they assumed. Besides the William Morris-like saga *Ragnarök*, Byatt writes for Ash two superbly Browning-esque monologues: a suave, sarcastic ventriloquial exposure of a fraudulent female medium, and the death-bed ruminations of a seventeenth-century Dutch entomologist ('The one-day flies, I gave my years to them', he reflects in a haunting line). Emily Dickinson-like verses – sly, demure, cryptic, unsettling – are provided for LaMotte, whose serpent-woman poem, *Melusina*, has all the glimmer, glamour and shadowy undercurrents of Victorian romanticism.

'*Possession*', Byatt explained in an essay, 'plays serious games with the variety of possible forms of narrating the past – the detective story, the biography, the medieval verse Romance, the modern romantic novel, and Hawthorne's fantastic historical Romance in between, the campus novel, the Victorian third-person narration, the epistolary novel, the forged manuscript novel, and the primitive fairy tale.' Energised by all these modes, it has an impetus that generously satisfies what Byatt refers to in the book as 'narrative greed'.

Storytelling pace and panache lacking from its predecessors quickened its appeal. Adding excitement to erudition, vitalising scholarship with suspense, it was a triumphant achievement that surmounted the main obstacle always facing Byatt's abundantly intellectual talent: a propensity to congest her pages with an overload of cultural cross-reference.

Continuing to present a challenge, this weighed down much of her ensuing fiction until, with *The Children's Book* (2009), her wide-ranging knowledgeability was again channelled into a novel of compelling power. Where *Possession* opened in the London Library, it opens in another preserve of cultural heritage: the South Kensington Museum (soon to become the Victoria and Albert) in 1895. Amid its riches, Olive Wellwood, a writer in her thirties, consults a curator about a tale of ancient treasure she is planning.

Partly modelled on E. Nesbit, the author of Edwardian classics such as *The Railway Children* (1906), Olive is a writer of children's stories with a large young family of her own. Reactivating the flair for period pastiche that embellished *Possession*, Byatt artfully reproduces several of her fantasy tales as well as portraying the first night of a *Peter Pan*-like play she writes, whose hero is based on her eldest son.

The era her own novel resurrects, Byatt contends, was one when – reflected in an extraordinary outpouring of child-centred fiction – childhood became a subject of unique, intense fascination. Differing aspects of it are surveyed as her novel spreads out from Olive's bohemian *ménage* to other families. Ways in which lives can be shaped or stunted in early years are traced. Exploitation of children – physically, emotionally, psychologically and artistically – is disclosed.

As a backdrop, Byatt unrolls crisp summaries of political and social developments against which her characters' ambitions and activities are seen. Intellectual keenness keeps the novel pulsing with ideas but it is alive with imaginative energy too. Olive, we're told, 'lived most intensely in an imagined world peopled by things and creatures that drew their energy and power from other human imaginings, centuries and centuries of them'; her 'response to any performance, any work of art, was the desire to make another, to make her own'. It's a response her author shares. Byatt has always been stirred into creativity by other people's creations. Elizabethan poetry and painting inspired *The Virgin in the Garden*. Van Gogh's canvases stimulated its sequel, *Still Life*, as the paintings of a later artist did with *The Matisse Stories* (1993). High among the qualities giving *The Children's Book* aesthetic appeal is Byatt's responsiveness to the art and artefacts of the period she chronicles.

Fairy tales are particularly influential. After the publication of Andrew Lang's *Blue Fairy Book* in 1889, it's remarked of Olive that 'The coming – or return – of the fairytale opened some trapdoor in her imagination.' Something similar happened to Byatt, she has said, after reading a fervent advocacy of the fairy story genre by Angela Carter. *The Children's Book* shows the results. Grimm's fairy tales and later works of fantasy for children shape its narrative patterns. Motifs of changelings, locked rooms and underground journeys feature. Images of sleeping beauties sinisterly cling around traumatically arrested girlhoods, as does that of Peter Pan, 'The Boy Who Wouldn't Grow Up', around damaged young males.

A panoramic cavalcade of a novel, *The Children's Book* musters together what Byatt regards as the defining concerns of the quarter century it spans from 1895 to the aftermath of the First World War. It is also compendiously representative of the period during which it was written. Themes that characterise modern fiction fill its pages. Imperial concerns are highlighted by talk of 'Randlord' speculators in the diamond fields and gold mines of the Cape, bulletins about the Boer War, and a scene where the aged Empress of India progresses in her open landau to lay a foundation stone of the Victoria and Albert Museum. Damage that scars children's lives – from incestuous molestation to boarding school abuse and emotional exploitation – becomes growingly evident, as do complicit silences that shroud it. As Edwardian idylls give way to the corpse-spattered trenches of the Somme, the Lost Boys scenario of James Barrie's *Peter Pan* becomes hideously actual. Period resurrection is performed on a wide scale. Criss-crossing Britain and Europe, the novel swarms with a huge cast of late Victorian and Edwardian writers, artists, anarchists, City financiers, imperialists, Fabian progressives, potters, puppeteers, dons, debutantes, New Women, suffragettes, soldiers, philanthropists and philanderers. Real-life figures such as Oscar Wilde or Auguste Rodin appear alongside ones modelled on Eric Gill or D.H. Lawrence and H.G. Wells. Not only fairy-tale patterns and prototypes but hosts of other past fictional influences suffuse and shape the book.

Just one aspect of the modern preoccupation with the past escapes Byatt's omnivorous attention: the way in which it has not only manifested itself through 'the shape-shifting life of things long-dead' but in novels envisaging the shape of things to come. It is to this that we should turn in conclusion.

Part V

Back to the Future: The Impending Past

In a period when the past was paramount, what of the future? Though fiction since 1970 or so has been extensively engaged in looking back, novelists have also looked forward. While varying in how far ahead they peer (anything from a few years to several millennia), their envisionings of what the future holds display a disquieting like-mindedness. The overwhelming message from modern fiction that looks forward is that there's not much to look forward to.

One of the stories in Martin Amis's *Einstein's Monsters* (1987) anticipates a future world in which the days of the week will have grim new names: Shunday, Moansday, Tearsday, Woundsday, Thirstday, Fireday and Shatterday. This comfortless calendar seems well suited to coming times as envisaged by other writers too. The fictional weather forecast, for instance, isn't good – though opinions differ as to whether conditions will be unbearably hot or unbearably cold or (as some authors predict) both. Maggie Gee's *The Ice People* (1998) has the Tropical Time starting in 2005, followed by an ice age two decades later. Doris Lessing's *Mara and Dann* (1999), set thousands of years ahead, opens amid scorching drought and ends on the glacial shores of a frozen Mediterranean.

Other extreme weather events – 'multi-megaton hurricanes', 'gigawatt thunderstorms' – are in the offing according to Amis's *London Fields* (1989). Edwina Currie's *The Ambassador* (1999) foresees cataclysmic flooding: in her 2099 London, Buckingham Palace survives on an island in a vastly enlarged Thames spanned by the Blair Memorial Suspension Bridge which stretches from Holborn to Bermondsey.

In fiction published during the closing decades of the twentieth century the prevailing apprehension is of an imminent ice age. Gee's novel begins with quotations from scientific sources about the inexorable recurrence of ice ages lasting around 100,000 years, between which are warm 'interglacials' of 10,000 to 15,000 years (our own civilisation, it's chillingly pointed out, has flourished during one now nearing its end). In the view of most future-gazing novelists a period of ferocious heat will come first. Paul Johnston's thriller, *Water of Death* (1999), shows Edinburgh in 2025 sweltering amid 'global stewing', with water in such short supply that a dream prize in the state lottery is a five-minute shower every week for a month.

It might be thought that scenarios of inevitable ice ages would depict *Homo sapiens* as the unfortunate casualty of inexorable planetary processes. In fact, in most novels about the future the atmosphere is thick with blame: as evidence of human contribution to global warming and climate change mounts, humanity is portrayed as receiving retribution for ecological fecklessness, arrogance, neglect and greed. Radiation spillages, toxic waste, chemical pollution, pesticides infiltrating the food-chain, and genetic tamperings all become sources of nemesis.

As a result of our species' short-sightedness, gruesome mutations occur. The resulting freak-show is paraded with obvious relish in Amis's pages, where people are born with 'webs and pouches . . . trotters and beaks' or are 'furred or shelled or slippery'. Life-forms around them aren't alluring, either. A monstrous canine (8 foot long and 4 foot high) has a grotesque extra limb instead of a tail, scurvy yellow eyes, a fungoid pelt of hair and slavering jaws which drip venomous crimson acidic saliva. Its carcinogenic teeth infect anyone they even graze with 'anthrax, foul brood, rinderpest, staggers, scours, glanders, hard pad, sheep rot and mange'. Lessing's *Mara and Dann* further swells the future's baleful bestiary: giant 'water stingers' crawl around her pages brandishing people-crushing pincers and poisonous barbs on whip-like tails.

Life in the third millennium AD, it soon becomes apparent, won't lack hazards. Disease is an especial menace. Sinister medical acronyms – RISM, HPV – keep spelling trouble in future fiction. Virulent new strains of TB, AIDS and CJD rage. In Philip Kerr's *The Second Angel* (1998), Human Parvo Virus has infected 80 per cent of the world's surface by the second half of the twenty-first century and wiped out at least 150 million people.

Clinical advances to cope with these crises prove woefully inadequate. Though two free facelifts in a lifetime are available on the NHS in Currie's *The Ambassador*, this hardly seems much solace in view of the epidemic onslaught foreseen by other novels of 'a new kind of haemorrhaging fever' (Jean Hegland's *Into the Forest*, 1996) or 'a new kind of Ebola coinciding with haemorrhagic sleeping sickness' (*The Ice People*).

The most frequently prophesied maladies in future fiction are infertility and sterility. John Updike's *Toward the End of Time* (1998) takes place after 'a catastrophic drop in the world population'. P.D. James's *The Children of Men* (1992) foresees sterility for our species and a society in which, as the population becomes overwhelmingly elderly, euthanasia is covertly enforced by the state. In Margaret Atwood's *The Handmaid's Tale*, secret 'gene-splicing experiments with mumps' have led to a sparsity of fertile sperm. Warpings caused by radiation and chemical contamination mean that 'viable ovaries' are in short supply too. 'Unbabies' – misshaped progeny with snouts or webbed hands and feet – are common. Having a healthy infant is a rare triumph (even more so in James's novel, where it is finally achieved in circumstances suggestive of the Nativity). Gynaecological prospects even thousands of years ahead remain bleak: in *Mara and Dann*, 'it is hard for us to get pregnant', 'something seems to have happened to our eggs'.

Technology proves as much of a let-down as biology. Set around 3700 AD, Peter Ackroyd's *The Plato Papers* (1999) lists the ages through which mankind has evolved. Our own time comes near the end of what future historians call the Age of Mouldwarp (1500–2300), an era which culminates in mass-revulsion against technology, and the smashing of all machines. To judge from other prediction fiction, the Mouldwarpers' reaction is well-advised. Just as much as mutant viruses and malformed creatures, malevolent hardware poses a major threat. This isn't just a matter of alarming new weaponry – air tasers that jam brain messages and scramble neuromuscular systems, particle guns that instantaneously reduce a body to a dripping mist of red droplets. In *The Ice People*, DOVES (robots designed to DO VEry simple things) at first whisk helpfully through household chores, but then start to malfunction and do other very simple things such as scraping off people's faces and eating babies. In *Toward the End of Time*, trouble is obviously brewing when 'metallobioforms' evolve from 'a soup of spilled chemical and petroleum by-products ... energized by low-level leaks of radioactivity'. *The Second Angel* gives a scary twist to the concept of the computer virus – the computer as virus: minuscule slivers of technology invade the human bloodstream, bent on takeover. More pervasive than these techno-gothic nightmares, ruinous hi-tech wars – between China and Russia in *Into the Forest*, between America and China in *Toward the End of Time* – shatter civilisation.

The most notable feature of communities seen as emerging in the future is that, whether the ice caps expand or shrink, societies become polarised. Economic divides between the prosperous and outcasts cruelly widen. In Jay Merrick's *Horse Latitudes* (1999), out beyond the pampered enclaves of the elite, 'degradees' fester amid cellulose and vinyl waste. In *The Ambassador*, a clandestine eugenics programme enhances the IQ of the Euro-Elite but is withheld from the sub-class. Adrian Matthews's *Vienna Blood* (1999) uncovers racist right-wing genetic skulduggery in Austria which leaves hated foreign 'guest-workers' fatally susceptible to pneumonitis.

Racial divides also feature in *The Handmaid's Tale* but gender divides are most to the fore. In its neo-biblical Republic of Gilead, even women's names – Offred, Ofglen – signal their status as men's chattels. The opposite obtains in Amis's imaginings where, under a hefty matri-archy, females with cropped heads, flat chests, bulging muscles and several cowed husbands apiece, have names like Keithette and Kevinia. 'Segging' – sexual segregation – is the norm in *The Ice People*. Women, often fiercely aggressive figures with butch haircuts and sack-like clothes, live in communes with their 'sheroes'. Men, who favour figure-hugging Lycra vests, contour-enhancing calf-length tights and trans-parent boots to show off their elegantly polished toenails, cluster together in cosier quarters. Politics are polarised between Wicca and Manguard, female and male special interest parties.

Recreational options in the future predominantly veer between sadism and synthetic sex. Big get-togethers tend to take the form of public executions – or 'particicutions' as they are called in *The Handmaid's Tale* where 'gender-traitors' and the like are communally battered to death. Time-travelling to 2500 AD, the hero of Ronald Wright's *A Scientific Romance* (1997) finds he is allocated the star-ring role in a very literal public re-enactment of the Crucifixion. Less lethal excitements in futuristic fiction are on offer from the likes of Robo-Dolls or Sexbots, Cyber-sex or (in Currie's novel) a visit to a nightclub called The Toy Shop where cloned replicants of lusted-after celebrities are purchasable. Accurate in every detail, they include Mae West, Marilyn Monroe, and – less expectedly – Margaret Thatcher.

To judge from fiction about the future, fiction itself hasn't much future. Reading is an offence punishable by amputation in *The*

Handmaid's Tale. By 3700 AD, in *The Plato Papers*, literature has become 'a word of unknown provenance, generally attributed to "litter"'. Simplified John Grisham novels are set-books in schools in Updike's future America. Vestigial rememberings of classic texts – Rom and Jul, Mam Bova, Anakrena – are all that survive in *Mara and Dann*.

In another way, though, past fiction continuingly survives in books about the future – not in what their characters read but in the fabric of the novels themselves. Explaining why *Riddley Walker* (1980), his excursion into a 'debased and degraded future', is narrated in 'corrupted English', Russell Hoban observed: 'Language is an archaeological vehicle, full of the remnants of dead and living pasts, lost and buried civilizations and technologies . . . a whole palimpsest of human effort and history.' His novel is a palimpsest not only linguistically but conceptually. In its bare-subsistence 'Inland', devastated two millennia or so earlier by nuclear holocaust – eroded memories linger of long-ago rulers: the 'Puter Leat'. The contrast between this bygone computer elite and the neo-Iron Age primitives in Hoban's post-apocalyptic England seems modelled on the blueprint of Aldous Huxley's 1932 dystopia *Brave New World*, a persisting template for narratives which juxtapose a pampered elite (often scientific or technological, sometimes theological) with 'savages', inferiors, the unorthodox, supposedly sub-standard and less advanced.

A bifurcated 'Brave New World' of this type is starkly on view in Paul Theroux's *O-Zone* (1986), where characters from an AD 2036 Manhattan that is the tightly guarded, enervatingly artificial preserve of high-status plutocrats make a sensation-seeking jet-rotor trip to the Ozarks, only to find that that the territory, sealed off after radiation spillage, has recovered and become a haven for more vigorous ways of life. Before disaster obliterated most of the human race, the solitary protagonist of *Oryx and Crake*, the first book in Margaret Atwood's 'speculative fiction' trilogy, lived within a privileged fortress-like enclave of technocrats fortified against 'the pleeblands', the violently anarchic North America outside it. What she called its 'sibling novel', *The Year of the Flood* (2009), moved out into that seething anarchy. Kazuo Ishiguro's *Klara and the Sun* (2021) gradually disclosed apartheid between an elite and social left-behinds in a dystopia where risky genetic enhancement bestows upper-echelon power and pre-eminence.

Nineteen Eighty-Four (whose first sentence is parodied in the opening line of Kerr's *The Second Angel*) has been another persisting influence. Where Huxley set a pattern for dystopias divided between a devitalised elite and raw outsiders, Orwell provided one for dystopias oppressed by various forms of terror-tyranny. It was in 1984, the year of his novel about political totalitarianism, that Atwood began writing *The Handmaid's Tale*, her novel about theocratic totalitarianism.

One of the best late twentieth-century novels about the future, Wright's *A Scientific Romance*, imaginatively recycled the best late nineteenth-century novel about it: H.G. Wells's *The Time Machine*. Apparently discovering the vehicle in which Wells's narrator journeyed across the centuries, Wright's narrator redeploys it for a journey of his own – to a devastated and depopulated tropic London, half a millennium away, where mynah birds chatter in the long-deserted corridors of Parliament and a puma prowls the jungle-swathed ruins of Canary Wharf.

Humming with the energies of a young writer first realising his powers, *The Time Machine* fused artistic exhilaration with intellectual pessimism. Its journey across future millennia is thrilling but reaches bleak conclusions about human prospects: degeneration, then extinction, it's revealed, await. By AD 802,701, through a process of evolutionary nemesis, *Homo sapiens* has split into two antagonistic species. Morlocks, red-eyed subterranean albino mammals, carnivorously prey upon Eloi, twittering descendants of the Victorian rich who, Wells observes, economically preyed upon the Morlocks' working-class predecessors. Speeding aeons onwards, the Time

Traveller finally alights in an eerily silent, bitterly cold world where all that remains of terrestrial life is the slime of lichens under a dying sun in a jet-black sky.

No novel since has matched this inky futurity. No matter how harsh things turn in fictions about the future, mankind clings on. So does hope. In a coda to *The Handmaid's Tale*, Atwood's theocratic police state Gilead is seen as a long-vanished aberration, the subject of civilised scrutiny at an AD 2195 academic symposium. Her sequel, *The Testaments* (2019), mordantly chronicled the start of its collapse.

The bleakest modern novel set in the future, Cormac McCarthy's *The Road* (2006), follows an unnamed father and son as they struggle across a post-disaster America that is a carbonised hellscape of ashes and cannibalism. An unspecified catastrophe (distantly registered as 'a long sear of light and then a series of low concussions') has incinerated the continent. The countryside is a charred waste of burnt forests, lifeless waterways, fire-blackened fields. Cities are scorched charnel houses: 'The mummified dead everywhere ... Shrivelled and drawn like latterday bogfolk.' Frequently surfacing, as we have seen, in modern fictional contexts of violence and atrocity, the 'bogfolk' image here appears in a world of hideous extremity. With civilisation reduced to cinders, 'bloodcults' have thrived, then destroyed each other. Human flesh – as stomach-turning glimpses convey – is hungrily hunted as a supply of fresh living meat or brutalised sexual prey. The father's most valued possession is a pistol with two bullets: last-ditch means of saving his son and himself from such fates. Yet, against savage odds, persevering humanity pulls through. Though the man dies of an injury, the boy – urged not to lose hope but to 'carry the fire' (an oddly chosen image for redemptive fortitude in a novel black with havoc wreaked by fire) – is last seen joining a family of decent survivors.

After *The Time Machine*, Wells swung away from foreseeings of planetary extinction. With the advent of the twentieth century, his forward-looking books took on hopeful titles like *Anticipations* (1901) and exhibited utopias that fizz with optimistic notions about human betterment. In the decades leading up to and beyond the turn into the twenty-first century, similarly upbeat visions of what's in store have been rare – and almost as disheartening as dire predictions: not all spirits will soar at the prospect of the Disney-like wonder world unrolled in Arthur C. Clarke's *3001: The Final Odyssey* (1997), where genetically boosted gorillas lend a paw with housework, gardening is performed by cutely miniaturised dinosaurs, and a favoured relaxation is clipping on a pair of wings and fluttering around to the strains of *Swan Lake*.

Glimmers of optimism relieve Atwood's dark future worlds. Where the political dystopia of *The Handmaid's Tale* is finally seen not as a terminal but passing period of atrocity, the biological dystopia of her *Oryx and Crake* trilogy is seeded with pockets of hope in which collectives of eco-zealots fight to reverse environmental devastation. Flashbacks showing the paths to disaster are on view as well. The future horrors in her 'speculative fiction', Atwood emphasises, are fabricated from past and present actualities. An afterword to her trilogy's final volume, *Maddaddam*, affirmed that it 'does not include any technologies or bio-beings that do not already exist, are not under construction, or are not possible in theory'. 'My rules for *The Handmaid's Tale*', she said, 'were simple: I would not put into the book anything that humankind had not already done, somewhere, sometime, or for which it did not already have the tools.'

The past is a shaping presence in other authors' novels of the future too: not just in the form of underlying prototypes such as *Brave New World* or *Nineteen Eighty-Four* but in narratives of nemesis, where future catastrophe – particularly ecological calamity and technological meltdown – is presented as the ruinous price paid for past myopia, complacent lack of foresight, blinkered disregard and neglect.

From the 1980s onwards, a vogue for what was sometimes called 'retro-futurism' began to spread. Sci-fi-like novels (some labelled 'Steam Punk') intermingled the past and the future. Pastiche

Victorian or Regency worlds were freakishly shot through with anticipations of scientific breakthroughs still far ahead. Natasha Pulley, a novelist who brought a dandified, almost rococo sensibility to the genre in novels such as *The Watchmaker of Filigree Street* (2015) and its sequel *The Lost Future of Pepperharrow* (2019), added a further element to the temporal mix. As if prompted by the White Queen's observation in *Alice Through the Looking Glass* that 'It's a poor sort of memory that only works backwards', one of her main characters, Keita Mori, has the ability to 'remember' possible futures: 'it was just like ordinary memory, but it worked forwards as well as backwards. If something was about to happen, he knew it clearly – in just the same way anyone else knew what had just happened a minute ago. If something was only a distant, hazy possibility, he remembered it like it had happened twenty years ago, buried under all the more recent, more likely things. The second a thing was no longer possible, he forgot it.'

Mori, a baron of Japanese samurai descent, is first encountered in mid-1880s London where, at one point, Gilbert and Sullivan are seen gathering material for *The Mikado* at the newly opened Japanese Village Exhibition in Knightsbridge. In tune with this, there's a teasing witty buoyancy to Pulley's topsy-turvy toyings with time.

Memory and what's to come coalesce more grimly in fictional scenarios of drastic regression, novels where rebarbative long-gone ages have re-emerged around the shattered remnants of humanity. It wasn't only *Riddley Walker*, with its gruelling neo-Iron Age world, that prophesied a future punitively reclaimed by the past. Jim Crace's *The Pesthouse* (2007) foresaw a Dark Ages America hundreds of years ahead. Seismic convulsions whose lethal repercussions still reverberate have reduced a prosperous industrial society to perilous panoramas of wreckage. Bandits, slave-drivers and crazed religious zealots swarm around what 'used to be America', now a lawless toxic wasteland where a plague known as 'the flux' is rife. Across this nightmare landscape, Crace re-spools the classic storyline of the

American Dream. Where pioneering emigrants from Europe once headed west in search of fabled opportunity and prosperity, desperate survivors now migrate towards the eastern seaboard and a risky, reverse Atlantic passage to a Europe offering safety and hope.

Robert Harris's *The Second Sleep* (2019) effects another kind of reversal. Opening 'in the Year of Our Risen Lord 1468' with a young cleric urging his worn-out horse across wild moorland towards a remote Wessex village as dusk descends, it at first seems a historical novel. The Church holds stern sway. Corpses of felons dangle from gibbets. Peasants share fetid hovels with their meagre livestock. In the middle of the night candles flicker as the custom of having an interval of wakefulness between 'first' and 'second' periods of sleep is observed.

Dispatched by his autocratic bishop to conduct the burial of the village's recently deceased priest, the young cleric Fairfax soon begins to make disorientating discoveries, as does the reader. The novel is set, it's gradually revealed, in a retro-future, 800 years on from a twenty-first-century catastrophe that obliterated technology and its amenities (after which, as the Church reasserted authoritarian control, the calendar was re-wound to start from the year 666, the scriptural 'number of the beast'). In this neo-medieval theocratic England, 'scientism' is heresy and freedom of thought a hanging offence. Historical investigation is prohibited, 'the very word "anti-quarian" forbidden from use'. 'The path of Hell', it's declared, 'begins with too much searching into the past.'

It's a path that Fairfax (like other Harris protagonists) finds himself impelled to take. The dead priest, he discovers, was a 'heretic'. Banned volumes such as 'The Proceedings and Papers of the Society of Antiquaries' line his bookshelves. A cabinet in his study hoards illegal relics: 'plastic banknotes from the Elizabethan era', a plate commemorating a royal wedding and 'one of the devices used by the ancients to communicate ... black and smooth and shiny ... On the back was the ultimate symbol of the ancients' hubris and blasphemy – an apple with a bite taken out of it.'

Hi-tech logo turned sacrilegious icon, the Apple symbol, once a hallmark of technological accomplishment, now signifies forbidden fruit. One of 'six possible catastrophic scenarios that fundamentally threaten the existence of our advanced science-based way of life' listed in a document surviving from 2022 that Fairfax peers at by candlelight is 'A general failure of computer technology due either to cyber warfare, an uncontrollable virus, or solar activity'. Precisely which scenario brought about catastrophe never becomes known in the novel. But warnings about insufficient attention to the dangers of over-dependence on technology recur. As a hazardous archaeological dig unearths shards of sophisticated electronics, someone notes: 'The Romans depended on slaves, the ancients on science. They made their lives too luxurious and in the end rendered themselves helpless.'

The importance of learning from the past is stressed: 'All civilisations consider themselves invulnerable, history warns us that none is.' The fragility of rational, liberal values and the civilisation they nourish is made as apparent as the risks of considering technology's benefits permanently guaranteed. *The Second Sleep*'s title takes on wider resonance in its closing scene as – with the suffocating of Fairfax and other truth-seekers – temporary enlightenment lapses back into darkness.

As Harris's time-twisting scenario suggests, the past in modern fiction looks likely to have an enduring future.

NOTES

All editions referenced are those published in the United Kingdom, unless otherwise stated.

Epigraph

'The past is made of paper': 'In Search of Alias Grace', *Curious Pursuits* (2006)

Introduction

Novels written:

in blank verse: *Genesis*, Frederick Turner (1988); *The Marlowe Papers*, Ros Barber (2012)

in three-line stanzas: *History: The Home Movie*, Craig Raine (1994)

ottava rima: *The Golden Gate*, Vikram Seth (1986); *Bloodlines*, Fred D'Aguiar (2000); *Byrne*, Anthony Burgess (1995)

serial form: *The Heart Goes Last*, Margaret Atwood (2015); *44 Scotland Street*, by Alexander McCall Smith, was first published in daily instalments, starting in January 2004, in *The Scotsman* and initiated an ongoing sequence of more than a dozen novels also written in the same serial form

strip-cartoons: *Gemma Bovery* (1999), *Tamara Drewe* (2007), *Cassandra Darke* (2018), Posy Simmonds

published as podcast: *Corduroy Mansions*, Alexander McCall Smith (2009), first published as daily serial podcast in 100 episodes starting on 15 September 2008

published on Twitter: the first section of David Mitchell's mock-gothic five-part novel *Slade House* (2015) was released as a series of 280 tweets. Jennifer Egan published her 2012 science fiction story, 'Black Box', on Twitter

Novels interleaved with:

    photographs: *The Collected Works of Billy the Kid*, Michael Ondaatje (1976); *The Stone Diaries*, Carol Shields (1993)

    maps: *Intimate Cartographies: A Three-Dimensional Novel*, Lynne Alexander (2000)

    recipes: *The Debt to Pleasure*, John Lanchester (1996); *Cooking with Fernet-Branca* (2004), *Amazing Disgrace* (2006) and *Rancid Pansies* (2008), James Hamilton-Paterson's trilogy, whose foodie narrator, a British expat in Tuscany, offers recipes for memorable dishes of his creation such as Mice Krispies, Vole au Vent and Badger Wellington

    composed of texts and emails: *The Appeal*, Janice Hallett (2012)

    with chapters printed in different colours: *Gould's Book of Fish*, Richard Flanagan (2001)

    that can be read back to front or front to back: *How to Be Both*, Ali Smith (2015)

magic realism and dirty realism on same bookshelf: Angela Carter and Raymond Carver

novels by:

    politicians: many, including Douglas Hurd, Anne Widdecombe, Jeffrey Archer, Nadine Dorries, Edwina Currie, Roy Hattersley, Alastair Campbell

    comedians: Ben Elton, David Baddiel

    chefs and food-writers: Anthony Bourdain, *Bone in the Throat* (1995)

    foreign correspondents: Gerald Seymour, Martin Sixsmith

    catwalk model: Sophie Dahl

    celebrity ballroom dancer: Anton du Beke

    jockey: Dick Francis, John Francombe

    tennis champion: Ilie Nastase, *Break Point* (1987); Martina Navratilova ('and Liz Nickles'), *Breaking Point* (1996), *Killer Instinct* (1997)

    concert pianist: Stephen Hough, *The Final Retreat* (2018)

    TV gardener: Alan Titchmarsh, *Mr MacGregor* (1998)

    quiz show host: Richard Osman, author of the 2020 bestseller *The Thursday Murder Club*, and its 2021 successor, *The Man Who Died Twice*

    South London vicar: Toby Forward, writing as Rahila Shah, *Down the Road, Miles Away* (1987)

novels:

    with variant endings: *Life after Life*, Kate Atkinson (2013); *Should We Stay or Should We Go*, Lionel Shriver (2021)

    in which things happen backwards: *Time's Arrow*, Martin Amis (1991)

    written in second person singular: *A Pagan Place*, Edna O'Brien (1970); *Bright Lights, Big City*, Jay McInerney (1984); *The Reluctant Fundamentalist* (2007) and *How to Get Filthy Rich in Rising Asia* (2013), Mohsin Hamid

    written in first person plural: *Then We Came to the End*, Joshua Ferris (2007)

    consisting entirely of questions: *The Interrogative Mood*, Padgett Powell (2009)

'sourced word for word' from a hundred other books: *Felix Culpa*, Jeremy
    Gavron (2018)
using only words spoken by Ophelia: *Let Me Tell You*, Paul Griffiths (2014)
containing a 13,955-word sentence: *The Rotters' Club*, Jonathan Coe (2001)
eschewing the verb 'to have': *Next*, Christine Brooke-Rose (1990)
narrated by:
    a Sumerian pot: *The Collector Collector*, Tibor Fischer (1997)
    a supermarket trolley: *Scepticism Inc.*, Bo Fowler (1998)
    a fig tree: *The Island of Missing Trees*, Elif Shafak (2021)
    a bottle of wine: *Blackberry Wine*, Joanne Harris (2000)
    a book: *The Pages*, Hugo Hamilton (2021)
    short story narrated by a condom: 'Unprotected', Sam Rich, the *New Yorker*,
      23 July 2012
    homicidal high-rise: *Gridiron*, Philip Kerr (1995)
    lethal hedge-fund algorithm: *The Fear Index*, Robert Harris (2011)
    novels featuring dwarves: *A Prayer for Owen Meany*, John Irving (1989);
      Maybe the Moon, Armistead Maupin (1992); *Mendel's Dwarf*, Simon
      Mawer (1997)
    giant: *The Giant, O'Brien*, Hilary Mantel (1998)
    fiddle-playing foetus: *Spring Sonata*, Bernice Rubens (1979)
    budding Hamlet: *Nutshell*, Ian McEwan (2016)
    139-year-old Australian conman: *Illywhacker*, Peter Carey (1985)
    saxophone-playing bear: *The Bear Comes Home*, Rafi Zabor (1997)
    man who believes he is a bird: *Birdy*, William Wharton (1978)
    rabbits: *Watership Down*, Richard Adams (1972)
    moles: *Duncton Wood*, William Horwood (1980)
    apes, chimpanzees and monkeys: *Great Apes*, Will Self (1997); *Gor Saga*,
      Maureen Duffy (1981); *Congo*, Michael Crichton (1980); *We Are All
      Completely Beside Ourselves*, Karen Joy Fowler (2014)
    black Labrador: *The Last Family in England*, Matt Haig (2004)
    Monroe's Maltese terrier: *The Life and Opinions of Maf the Dog, and of His
      Friend Marilyn Monroe*, Andrew O'Hagan (2010)
    Plantagenet pig: *The Pig Plantagenet*, Allen Andrews (1980)
    woodworm: *A History of the World in 10½ Chapters*, Julian Barnes (1989)
    Time Machine: *A Scientific Romance*, Ronald Wright (1997)
Novels set in:
    Britain as Soviet colony: *Russian Hide and Seek*, Kingsley Amis (1980)
    outpost of the victorious Third Reich: *Fatherland*, Robert Harris (1992);
      Dominion, C.J. Sansom (2012)
    as subject territory of Papacy: *The Alteration*, Kingsley Amis (1976)
Vladimir Nabokov observed: in *Ada* (1969)
'an archaeological dig': 'The Search for a Happy Ending', *The Telegraph
    Magazine*, 2 May 2014
J.G. Ballard remarked: Introduction, *Myths of the Near Future* (1982)
'wasn't respectable': Reith Lecture 1, 'The Day Is for the Living',
    13 June 2017

declared Philip Glazebrook: *Journey to Khiva* (1992), p. 193
'the status of historical fiction': 'Sitting at the Feet of Ghosts', *The Times*,
  23 April 1998

Part I Ends of Empire

'To the British at home': 'Enoch Sahib: A Slight Case of Culture Shock', *My
  Appointment with the Muse, Essays 1961–75* (1986)
'a girl running': ibid. p. 60
'if rape must be used as the metaphor': 'Outside the Whale', in *Imaginary
  Homelands* (1991), p. 89
'the metaphor I have presently chosen': 'After Malabar: Britain and India, a
  Post-Forsterian View', *My Appointment*, p. 115
'the artist's *duende*': 'Liberalism and the Social Conscience: The Novel', in *My
  Appointment*, p. 137
'protection and safety': quoted in Hilary Spurling, *Paul Scott: A Life* (1990),
  p. 113
'My father's family': Spurling, p. 9
'Half close your eyes': ibid., p. 9
'fictional glamour': *Imaginary Homelands*, p. 92
'a very long line': ibid., p. 88
'a multiplicity of commingled faiths': *Imaginary Homelands*, p. 16
'peculiar fusions': *Imaginary Homelands*, p. 125
'a genuine kind of Bombay-talkie': '*Midnight's Children* and *Shame*', *Kunapipi:
  Journal of Postcolonial Writing and Culture*, vol. 7, no. 1, p. 4, University of
  Wollongong (1985)
'what I was trying to do': *Conversations with Salman Rushdie*, ed. Michael
  R. Reder (2000), p. 43
'a migrant's-eye view of the world': 'In Good Faith', *Imaginary Homelands*,
  p. 394
'those other freakish, hybrid, mutant, exceptional beings': 'Is Nothing Sacred?',
  ibid., p. 425
'For the first time an Indian writer': quoted in Ian Hamilton, 'The First Life
  of Salman Rushdie', *The Trouble with Money and Other Essays* (1998),
  p. 122
'Before *Midnight's Children*': 'An Interview with Bharati Mukherjee', *Canadian
  Fiction Magazine*, May 1987, p. 20
'gave us permission': 'My Cultural Firsts', *Sunday Times*, 23 October 2022
'It inspired us': interview with Ellen Peirson-Hagger, *New Statesman*,
  18 October 2022
'needs to be decolonised', *The Times*, 3 July 1988
'the silences of strangled nations', 'Redreaming the World', *Guardian*, 9 August
  1990
'Magic realism': 'Gabriel García Márquez', *Imaginary Homelands*, pp. 301–2
'they will forever consume': 'Power to the Caribbean People', *New York Review
  of Books*, 3 September 1970

'an artificial fragmented colonial society': 'The Corpse at the Iron Gate', *New York Review of Books*, 10 August 1972

'profoundly a colonial people': 'A Country Dying on Its Feet', *New York Review of Books*, 4 April 1974

'the fragmentation of a country': *The Writer and the World* (2002), p. 5

'nonsense name' and 'red-eyed vacancy': 'A New King for the Congo', *New York Review of Books*, 26 June 1975

'the great dereliction': 'The Writer and India', *New York Review of Books*, 4 March 1999

'set in Trinidad': 'Jasmine', *The Times Literary Supplement*, 4 June 1964

'It's like Vienna or Madrid': 'Trading Places', *Sunday Times*, 23 February 1992

'material to strengthen the illusion': ibid.

'Liverpool, Venice, Istanbul': ibid.

'stricken by the sight': *Independent on Sunday*, 23 February 1992

'On 16 September, 1985', *Armageddon?* (1987), p. 115

'cat flap between Europe and Japan': 'The Art of Fiction', No. 204, *Paris Review*, Summer 2010

'delivers a stereo narrative': 'Past, Imperfect', *Daily Telegraph*, 8 May 2010

'What feels like a curse when you're younger': 'David Mitchell: By the Book', *New York Times*, 18 October 2012

'the story of Australia': 'The Art of Fiction', No. 118, *Paris Review*, Summer 2006

'I have the good fortune': ibid.

Part II Scars and Silences

'hideous wound . . . and there was silence': 'The Art of Fiction', No. 243, *Paris Review*, Winter 2018

'all my interest in war': interview with Peter Kemp, *Sunday Times*, 1 July 2007

'What I took away': 'How I Wrote *The Silence of the Girls*', *Guardian*, 7 August 2021

'I think trauma': 'Inheritance', interview with Ian Parker, *New Yorker*, 26 May 2014

'I thought, it's impossible . . . horrified by': ibid.

'planned to be an archaeologist': Sarah Moss website, section on *Cold Earth*

'an archaeologist manquée': *Ammonites and Leaping Fish* (2013), p. 232

'the great sustaining ballast': ibid., p. 4

'What was driving me': 'Toni Morrison and the Ghosts in the House', *New Yorker*, 27 October 2003

'*the bit*': 'The Art of Fiction', No. 134, *Paris Review*, Fall 1993

'a common agenda': 'Is There a Poltergeist Within Me?', *Independent*, 29 May 2009

'changed what could be said': 'The Art of Fiction', No. 214, *Paris Review*, Winter 2011

Part III Resurrection Writing

'The journey of the imagination': 'The Art of Fiction', No. 15, *Paris Review*, Winter 1956

'You may multiply': Henry James, *Letters* (ed. Leon Edel), vol. 4, p. 208, 5 October 1901

'to shift the scene': interview in *Independent on Sunday*, 15 March 1992

'historical novelists face': 'The Day Is for the Living', 2017 Reith Lecture 1

'The task of historical fiction': 'Can These Bones Live?', 2017 Reith Lecture 4

'frees people from the archive': 'The Day Is for the Living'

'your real job as a novelist': ibid.

'It's the novelist's job': 'Can These Bones Live?'

'A quite extraordinary number': 'The Classical Tone', *Daemon Voices: Essays on Storytelling* (2017), p. 241

'Ancient Romans': among numerous fictional appearances, Julius Caesar features with increasing prominence in Robert Harris's *Cicero Trilogy* – *Imperium* (2009), *Lustrum* (2010), *Dictator* (2016), and in Steven Saylor's *Roma Sub Rosa* detective series. Allan Massie has fictionally portrayed various Roman emperors in novels ranging from *Augustus* (1986) to *Tiberius* (1991). Robert Fabbri devoted a nine-novel sequence to Vespasian. Nero, who also appears in it, takes centre stage in Margaret George's *The Confessions of Young Nero* (2017) and, seen through the eyes of Petronius, in David Wishart's *Nero* (1996)

'even the Windsors': *Gone with the Windsors*, Laurie Graham (2005); *The Windsor Faction* (2013), D.J. Taylor's alternative history novel which opens with King Edward VIII attending the funeral of Wallis Simpson, who has died from a botched appendectomy

'British Navy in the age of Nelson': most extensively in Patrick O'Brian's Aubrey/Maturin novel sequence and also in William Golding's *To the Ends of the Earth* trilogy, comprising *Rites of Passage* (1990), *Close Quarters* (1997) and *Fire Down Below* (1989)

Alexander Laing: *Laing*, Ann Schlee (1987)

John Franklin: *The Broken Lands*, Robert Edric (2002)

Captain Scott: *The Birthday Boys*, Beryl Bainbridge (1994)

Jack the Ripper: *Dan Leno and the Limehouse Golem*, Peter Ackroyd (1994); *Pentecost Alley*, Anne Perry (1996)

Yorkshire Ripper: in David Peace's *Red-Riding Quartet* (1999–2002)

Hitler: recurrently in Philip Kerr's Bernie Gunther thrillers and in Jane Thynne's Berlin-based Clara Vine novels, and featuring with Churchill and Stalin in Kerr's alternative history novel, *Hitler's Peace* (2005)

Stalin: *The Noise of Time*, Julian Barnes (2016)

Idi Amin: *The Last King of Scotland*, Giles Foden (1998)

Cleopatra: *The Memoirs of Cleopatra*, Margaret George (1997); Steven Saylor, *The Judgment of Caesar* (2004)

Catherine the Great: *To the Hermitage*, Malcolm Bradbury (2000)

Oliver Cromwell: *The White Horse*, Robert Leeson (1977)

Churchill: perhaps most extensively fictionalised by Michael Dobbs in his novels *Winston's War* (2002), *Never Surrender* (2003), *Churchill's Hour* (2004) and *Churchill's Triumph* (2005)

'In 1997 alone ... Christ's earthly career': *The Gospel According to the Son*, Norman Mailer; *Quarantine*, Jim Crace

'elderly Virgin Mary': *The Testament of Mary*, Colm Tóibín (2012)

'In a 1984 novel': *The Secret Gospel of Mary Magdalene*, Michèle Roberts

'a 2006 novel written by "an ordinary Little League mom"': *The Expected One*, Kathleen McGowan

Helen of Troy: *The Women of Troy*, Pat Barker (2021)

Sappho: *Sappho's Leap*, Erica Jong (2003)

Boudicca: most centrally in a four-volume saga by Manda Scott, extending from *Dreaming the Eagle* (2003) to *Dreaming the Serpent Spear* (2006)

Heloise and Abelard: *Love without End*, Melvyn Bragg (2019)

Saladin: *The Book of Saladin*, Tariq Ali (1998)

Lucrezia and other Borgias: *Blood and Beauty*, Sarah Dunant (2013)

Gutenberg: *The Justification of Johann Gutenberg*, Blake Morrison (2000)

Robespierre: *A Place of Greater Safety*, Hilary Mantel (1993)

Newton: *Dark Matter*, Philip Kerr (2002)

Nelson: *The Volcano Lover*, Susan Sontag (1992)

Copernicus: *Doctor Copernicus*, John Banville (1976)

Casanova: *Casanova*, Andrew Miller (1998)

Kant: *Critique of Criminal Reason*, Michael Gregorio (2006)

Kepler: *Kepler*, John Banville (1981)

Lincoln: *Lincoln*, Gore Vidal (1994); *Lincoln in the Bardo*, George Saunders (2017)

Mason and Dixon: *Mason & Dixon*, Thomas Pynchon (1997)

Cecil Rhodes: *Manly Pursuits*, Ann Harris (1999)

Theodore Roosevelt: *The Perilous Adventure of the Cowboy King*, Jerome Charyn (2019)

Eleanor Roosevelt: *White Houses*, Amy Bloom (2018)

Machiavelli: *In the Name of the Family*, Sarah Dunant (2017)

Mack Sennett and Fatty Arbuckle: *Keystone*, Peter Lovesey (1983)

Freud: *Mortal Mischief*, Frank Tallis (2005)

Alfred Hitchcock: *Fear in the Sunlight*, Nicola Upson (2021)

Lee Harvey Oswald: *Libra*, Don DeLillo (1988); *Oswald's Tale*, Norman Mailer (1995)

Martin Luther King: *The Bishop's Pawn*, Steve Berry (2018)

Richard Nixon: *Our Gang*, Philip Roth (1971); *The Public Burning*, Robert Coover (1977)

Marilyn Monroe: *Blonde*, Joyce Carol Oates (2000); *The Life and Opinions of Maf the Dog, and of His Friend Marilyn Monroe*, Andrew O'Hagan (2010)

Leonardo da Vinci: *Painting Mona Lisa*, Jeanne Kalogridis (2006)

Velázquez: *Painter to the King*, Amy Sackville (2018)

Vermeer: *Girl with a Pearl Earring*, Tracy Chevalier (1999)

Rembrandt: *The Painter*, Will Davenport (2003)

Canaletto: *Canaletto and the Case of Westminster Bridge*, Janet Lawrence (1997)
Géricault: *The Raft*, Arabella Edge (2006)
Watts: *Tennyson's Gift*, Lynne Truss (2010)
Van Gogh: *Leaving Van Gogh*, Carol Wallace (2011)
Monet: *In the Kingdom of Mists*, Jane Jakeman (2003)
Schiele: *The Flames*, Sophie Haydock (2022)
Alfred Wallis: *The Voyages of Alfred Wallis*, Peter Everett (1999)
Byrd: *English Music*, Peter Ackroyd (1992)
Bach: *The Great Passion*, James Runcie (2022)
Beethoven: *Mr Beethoven*, Paul Griffiths (2021)
Berlioz: *Symphony*, Jude Morgan (2006)
Elgar: *Gerontius*, James Hamilton-Paterson (1989)
Mahler: *Death and the Maiden*, Frank Tallis (2011)
Delius: fictionalised as 'Leonard Verity' in 'Interference' in *Cross Channel*, Julian
    Barnes (1996)
Sibelius: 'The Silence', in *The Lemon Table*, Julian Barnes (2004)
Shostakovitch: *The Noise of Time*, Julian Barnes (2016)
Adam and Eve, Cain and Abel: *The Very Model of a Man*, Howard Jacobson
    (1992)
Abraham and Sarah: *Only Human*, Jenny Diski (2018)
David: *God Knows*, Joseph Heller (1995),
David, Saul, Absalom: *King David*, Allan Massie (1995)
Tamar: *The Rape of Tamar*, Dan Jacobson (1970)
Perseus: in the novella 'Bellerophoniad', *Chimera*, John Barth (1972)
Circe: *Circe*, Madeline Miller (2018)
Sinbad: *The Last Voyage of Somebody the Sailor*, John Barth (1991)
Merlin: *Merlin*, Robert Nye (1978); *The Warlord Trilogy*: *The Winter King*
    (1995), *Enemy of God* (1997), *Excalibur* (1998), Bernard Cornwell
'as the zeitgeist': 'The Art of Fiction', No. 204, *Paris Review*, Summer 2010
'DNA has changed the crime novel': *Speaking Volumes: Conversations with
    Remarkable Writers*, Ramona Koval (2010)
'historical fiction comes out of greed for experience': 'The Day Is for the Living'
'the past is a foreign country': epigraph to *The Go-Between*, L.P. Hartley (1953)
'Language in historical fiction is a dilemma': 'Note on Language', *Pilgrims*
    (2020)
'a shadow tongue': 'A Note on Language', *The Wake*, Paul Kingsnorth
'iPads and cappuccinos': ibid.
'The first and most important rule': ibid.
'I wanted a sense of strangeness': interview, *Sunday Times*, 15 September 2019
'Bygonese': interview, *Daily Telegraph*, 8 May 2010
'I began writing fiction': 'The Day Is for the Living'
'I only became a novelist because': ibid.
'I wasn't after quick results': ibid.
'a way of getting a foot in the door': 'The Art of Fiction', No. 226, *Paris Review*,
    Spring 2015

'mountains of research': ibid.

'I decided to march': ibid.

'a distillation': 'My Work Here Is Done', interview with Rosie Kinchen, *Sunday Times Magazine*, 22 February 2020

'from behind his eyes': 'The Art of Fiction', No. 226, *Paris Review*, Spring 2015

'masses and masses of material': ibid.

'terrible years': 'The Years at My School Nearly Killed Me', *Sunday Times*, 6 May 2018

'the moment at which medieval certainties': 'A Life in Books', *Guardian*, 15 November 2010

'It's difficult: ibid.

'Going to Liverpool': interview, 'Trading Places', *Sunday Times*, 23 February 1992

'It chimed in': ibid.

'found the triumphalism': ibid.

'I felt a certain kind of guilt': 'Digging for Truths in the Past', *The Times*, 29 July 1999

'the emergence of America': 'Return of the Romans', *Sunday Times*, 31 August 2003

'The comparison': ibid.

'a revelation': ibid.

'to demonstrate': 'Why I Write Political Fiction', *Guardian*, 9 October 2015

'the characters at that time': 'Hooked on the Classics', *Sunday Times*, 13 August 2006

'the quintessential politician': interview, *Guardian*, 30 June 2018

'the first to approach': 'Hooked on the Classics'

'the whole point of my book': ibid.

'about 20%': 'Trading Places'

'*Bravo Two Zero* meets *Gladiator*': 'Letter to the Reader' at the end of *The Last Hour*

'to bring the dark brooding menace': 'A Letter to the Reader' at the end of *The Return*

'I like to explore': ibid.

'A novelist must know': interview in *New York Times*, 16 May 1993

'There is something': ibid.

'O'Brian wasn't writing': quoted in *Patrick O'Brian: A Very Private Life*, Nikolai Tolstoy, 2019, p. 225 (pb)

'had been reading naval history': 'Black, Choleric & Married?', autobiographical essay written for inclusion in the British Library's 'Patrick O'Brian: Critical Appreciations and a Bibliography' and appended to paperback edition of *The Thirteen-Gun Salute*

'when I describe a fight': Author's Note to *Master and Commander*

'authenticity is a jewel': ibid.

'he frequently emphasised': *Patrick O'Brian: A Very Private Life*

'The tale or narrative': 'Black, Choleric & Married?'

Part IV Post-scripts

authors in fiction:

    Marlowe: *A Dead Man in Deptford*, Anthony Burgess (1993)

    Milton: *Milton in America*, Peter Ackroyd (1986)

    Congreve: *A Mirror for Monkeys*, John Spurling (2021)

    Chatterton: *Chatterton*, Peter Ackroyd (1987)

    Blake: *Burning Bright*, Tracey Chevalier (2007)

    Clare: *The Quickening Maze*, Adam Foulds (2009)

    Austen: Plausibly featuring in Gill Hornby's *Godmersham Park* (2022), which assembles a plot reminiscent of *Mansfield Park* around her

    Byron: *Passion*, Jude Morgan (2004)

    Keats: ibid.; *The Invention of Dr Cake*, Andrew Motion (2003)

    Tennyson: *Tennyson's Gift*, Lynne Truss (1996)

    Ruskin: *Light, Descending*, Octavia Randolph (2014); *Manly Pursuits*, Ann Harries (1999)

    Browning: *A Rich Full Death*, Michael Dibdin (1986)

    Carroll: *The Looking Glass House*, Vanessa Tait (2016)

    Tolstoy: *The Last Station*, Jay Parini (1993)

    Dostoevsky: *The Master of Petersburg*, J.M. Coetzee (1994)

    Chekhov: 'Errand', in *Where I'm Calling From* (2019) Raymond Carver (1993)

    Stoker: *Shadowplay*, Joseph O'Connor

    Wells: *A Man of Parts*, David Lodge (2011)

    Stevenson: *Stevenson Under the Palm Trees*, Albert Manguel (2004); *The Last Bookaneer*, Matthew Pearl (2015)

    Kipling: *The Great Indian Novel*, Shashi Tharoor (1989), *Manly Pursuits*, Ann Harries (1999)

    Mann: *The Magician*, Colm Tóibín (2021)

    Owen: *Regeneration*, Pat Barker (1991)

    Sassoon: ibid.

    Graves: *The Telling*, Miranda Seymour (1998)

    Lawrence: *Darkness at Zennor*, Helen Dunmore (1993)

    Woolf: *The Hours*, Michael Cunningham (1998), *But Nobody Lives in Bloomsbury*, Gillian Freeman (2006)

    Maugham: *The Other Side of Silence*, Philip Kerr (2016), *The House of Doors*, Tan Twan Eng (2023)

as detectives:

    Aristotle: *Aristotle, Detective*, Margaret Doody (1978)

    Chaucer: *Murder on the Canterbury Pilgrimage*, Mary Devlin (2000)

    Shakespeare: *The Spy of Venice* (2016), *The Assassin of Verona* (2019), Benet Brandreth

    Dr Johnson: *The Exploits of Dr. Sam Johnson: Detector*, Lillian de la Torre (1987)

    Twain: *Mark Twain, Detective*, Joseph Peter Theroux (2020)

    Brontës: *The Vanished Bride*, Bella Ellis (2019)

    Henry Adams: *Panama*, Eric Zencey (1995)

NOTES

Conan Doyle: *Arthur & George*, Julian Barnes (2005)
Christie: in Andrew Wilson's series: *A Talent for Murder* (2017), *A Different Kind of Evil* (2018), *Death in a Desert Land* (2019), *I Saw Him Die* (2020)
Tey: in Nicola Upson's ten-novel 'Josephine Tey' series, beginning with *An Expert in Murder* (2008)
Shakespeare's Dark Lady: *The Dark Lady's Mask*, Mary Sharratt (2016)
Pepys's wife: *The Journal of Mrs Pepys*, Sara George (1998)
Newton's niece: *Newton's Niece*, Derek Beaven (1994)
Jane Austen's sisters: Cassandra in *Miss Austen*, Gill Hornby (2020); Mary in *The Other Bennet Sister*, Janice Hadlow (2020); Kitty in *Her Summer at Pemberley*, Sallianne Hines (2020); Lydia in *Lydia Bennet's Story*, Jane Odiwe (2009) and numerous other works, including *Lydia Bennet's Blog*, Valerie Laws (2012)
Elizabeth Barrett Browning's maid: *Lady's Maid*, Margaret Forster (1991)
Einstein's daughter: *Mrs. Einstein*, Anna McGrail (1998)
Proust's mother: *Madame Proust and the Kosher Kitchen*, Kate Taylor (2003)
John Synge's mistress: *Ghost Light*, Joseph O'Connor (2010)
Mrs Gulliver: *The Mistress of Lilliput*, Alison Fell (1999)
Mr Rochester's first wife: *Wide Sargasso Sea*, Jean Rhys (1966)
Anna Karenina's son: *Monsieur Ka*, Vesna Goldsworthy (2018)
Mary Watson and Mrs Hudson: Michelle Birkby's series, *The House at Baker Street* (2016), *The Women of Baker Street* (2017) and their successors
Holmes unmasked as Jack the Ripper: *The Last Sherlock Holmes Story*, Michael Dibdin (1978)
Joanna Trollope's makeover of *Sense and Sensibility* (2013)
Val McDermid's makeover of *Northanger Abbey* (2014)
Alexander McCall Smith's makeover of *Emma* (2015)
Curtis Sittenfeld's makeover of *Pride and Prejudice* – as *Eligible* (2016)
Miss Bates' Alzheimer's: *Emma in Love*, Emma Tennant (1996)
John Knightley as buffoon: ibid.
Frank Churchill propositioning Mr Knightley: *Pride and Promiscuity: The Lost Sex Scenes of Jane Austen*, Arielle Echstut (2001)
Charlotte Lucas flagellating Mr Collins: ibid.
orally pleasured by a harpsichord-tuner: *Charlotte*, Helen Moffett (2020)
Henry Tilney alarming Catherine Morland: *Pride and Promiscuity*
Jane Bennet entangled in threesome: ibid.
Jane Fairfax as jilted bride: *Emma in Love*
Mrs Bennet having problems with the menopause: *Mrs Bennet's Menopause*, Lucy Kate King (2013)
Colonel Brandon mowed down in Spain: *Eliza's Daughter*, Joan Aiken (1994)
Mrs Jennings felled by dropsy: ibid.
Mrs Dashwood suffering from senile dementia: ibid.
Elinor Ferrars almost starving: ibid.

Emma Knightley tempted into lesbian fling: *Emma in Love*
Elizabeth Darcy faced with murder: *Death Comes to Pemberley*, P.D. James (2011)
Jeffrey Deaver Bond novel: *Carte Blanche* (2011)
William Boyd Bond novel: *Solo* (2013)
Ham-fisted 'completions':
    of *Sanditon*: *Sanditon: Jane Austen's Unfinished Masterpiece Completed*, Juliette Shapiro (2009)
    of *The Buccaneers*: Marion Mainwaring (1994)
'full of thieves and crooks': 'Live and Let Spy', interview with Peter Kemp, *Sunday Times*, 25 May 2008
'a pretty straightforward sort of newspaperman's style': ibid.
'not saying I'm possessed by the soul of Henry James': 'On Writing *Mrs Osmond*', talk at University of Chicago, 9 February 2017, YouTube
governess facing new twists: *Miles and Flora*, Hilary Bailey (1997)
Mauberley in 1930s: *Famous Last Words*, Timothy Findley (1981)
Lady Chatterley as Tinder bot: composed by Libby Heaney
Mrs Dalloway in 1990s Greenwich Village: *The Hours*, Michael Cunningham (1998)
Virginia Woolf in twenty-first-century Manhattan: *Virginia Woolf in Manhattan*, Maggie Gee (2014)
pallid sequel to *Rebecca*: *Mrs de Winter*, Susan Hill (1993)
Billy Bunter's adult career: *But for Bunter*, David Hughes (1985)
Variations on:
    Wuthering Heights: *Heathcliff Redux*, Lily Tuck (2020)
    Jane Eyre: *The Wife Upstairs*, Rachel Hawkins (2021)
    A Christmas Carol: *I Am Scrooge*, Adam Roberts (2009)
    Peter Pan: *Peter Pan in Scarlet*, Geraldine McCaughrean
    Henry IV Part One: *The Last Family in England*, Matt Haig (2004)
    'buccaneers and buried gold': 'A tale of buccaneers and buried gold', subtitle to *Treasure Island*
    'nice phrase': *Sunday Times*, 13 October 1996
Emma Tennant extensions to and re-workings of classic novels:
    Sense and Sensibility: *Elinor and Marianne* (1996)
    Pride and Prejudice: *Pemberley* (1993); *An Unequal Marriage* (1994)
    Jane Eyre: *Adèle* (2003)
    Wuthering Heights: *Heathcliff's Tale* (2005)
    Tess of the d'Urbervilles: *Tess* (1993)
    The Aspern Papers: *Felony* (2002)
    The Turn of the Screw: *The Beautiful Child* (2010)
    Dr Jekyll and Mr Hyde: *Two Women of London* (1989)
    Kidnapped: *Seized* (2008)
    Confessions of a Justified Sinner: *The Bad Sister* (1978)
    Faust: *Faustine* (1991)
'equels': 'Philip Pullman launches *La Belle Sauvage*', *Guardian*, 19 October 2017

'a cover version': '*Shakespeare's* canon to be re-worked', *Guardian*, 27 June 2013

Jacobson take on *The Merchant of Venice*: *Shylock Is My Name* (2016)

Tyler retelling of *The Taming of the Shrew*: *Vinegar Girl* (2016)

'in the play we never see her drown': *Shakespeare Unlimited* podcast, episode 124, 'You Speak Like A Green Girl', interview with Barbara Bogaev, Folger Shakespeare Library

Shylock's point of view: *The Merchant*, Arnold Wesker (1976)

Lear's wife and daughters: *Learwife*, J.R. Thorp (2021), *Lear's Daughters*, Elaine Feinstein and Women's Theatre Group (1987)

Rosencrantz and Guildenstern: *Rosencrantz and Guildenstern Are Dead*, Tom Stoppard (1966)

Twelfth Night transposed to Wales: *A Good Voyage*, Katharine Davies (2004)

A Midsummer Night's Dream transposed to 1930s Hollywood: *Wise Children*, Angela Carter (1991)

'boiling detestation': interview with Damian Barr, *Guardian*, 19 September 2014

'shoplifted characters': *Marriage Material*, Acknowledgments

'In my own case': *Daemon Voices*, p. 64

'drawn by the gravitational attraction': ibid., p. 64

'Suppose that': ibid., p. 64

'a paranoid bigot': ibid., p. 450

'understanding': ibid., p. 98

'as commentators have noted': see, especially, *Literary Allusion in Harry Potter*, Beatrice Groves (2017)

'a "kickass" modern makeover': Siobhan Murphy, *The Times*, 21 April 2018

'no psychology in a fairy tale': *Grimm Tales*, Introduction, p. xiii, Philip Pullman (2021)

'Some of the characters in fairy tales': ibid., p. xiv

'sent to the cactus shows': 'Magical Mystery Tour', interview with Peter Kemp, *Sunday Times*, 9 June 1991

'could hardly call my breasts my own': ibid.

'this great Ur-collection': quoted in *The Invention of Angela Carter*, Edmund Gordon (2016), p. 266

'tested the limits': ibid.

'to extract the latent content': *Novelists in Interview*, John Haffenden (1985), p. 84

'could never imagine Cinderella in bed with the Fairy Godmother': *Writing on the Wall*, Patricia Duncker (2002), p. 75

'resolute feminist rewritings': 'Old Tales, New Forms', *On Histories and Stories*, A.S. Byatt (2000), p. 143

'a friend's grandmother': 'Magical Mystery Tour'

'I had an aunt': ibid.

'Twins are such a feature': ibid.

'All these years': ibid.

'the umbilical cord': ibid.

'a rather booksy person': *Novelists in Interview* p. 85

'literary heritage': ibid., p. 82
'plays serious games': 'Forefathers', *On Histories and Stories*, p. 48
'she has said': 'The Art of Fiction' No. 168, *Partisan Review*, Fall 2001

Part V Back to the Future

'Language is an archaeological vehicle': Russell Hoban, *Novelists in Interview*, ed. John Haffenden (1985) p. 138
'My rules for *The Handmaid's Tale*': Margaret Atwood, 'Dire Cartographies', *In Other Worlds* (2011) p. 88

INDEX

Achebe, Chinua, 39, 59–60
Ackroyd, Peter: *The Casebook of Victor Frankenstein* (2008), 297–8; *The Last Testament of Oscar Wilde* (1983), 245; *The Plato Papers* (1999), 336, 338
Adichie, Chimamanda Ngozi, 60–1
Africa, colonial and postcolonial experience, 59–61, 76–8, 105
America, and imperialism, 83–6
Amis, Kingsley: *Russian Hide and Seek* (1980), 79 *see also* Markham, Robert
Amis, Martin: *Einstein's Monsters* (1987), 333, 334–5; *London Fields* (1989), 119, 334; *Money*, 290; *Other People* (1981), 137; *Time's Arrow* (1991), 5
Anholt, Laurence, *Stone Girl Bone Girl* (2006), 133
apartheid, 65–6
apocalyptic novels, 5
archaeology: in fiction, 108–9; and trauma, 126–32, 153
Archer, Jeffrey, *First Among Equals* (1984), 284
Atkins, Ace, 242

Atkins, Jeannine, *Mary Anning and the Sea Dragon* (2012), 133
Atwood, Margaret: 'The Labrador Fiasco' (1996), 137–8; 'Stone Mattress' (2014), 129; *Alias Grace* (1996), 141, 314; *The Blind Assassin* (1993), 314; *Bodily Harm* (1981), 141, 313–14; *Cat's Eye* (1988), 141–4; *The Edible Woman* (1969), 141; *Hag-Seed* (2018), 261–3; *The Handmaid's Tale* (1985), 141, 142, 143, 150, 335, 337–8, 339, 340, 341; *Lady Oracle* (1976), 313; *Life Before Man* (1980), 129, 141; *Oryx and Crake* trilogy, 5, 296, 338–9, 341; *The Penelopiad* (2005), 103–4, 307–8; *The Robber Bride* (1993), 141, 313–16; *The Testaments* (2019), 340; *The Year of the Flood* (2009), 339
Auel, Jean M., *Earth's Children* series, 188–9
Austen, Jane: declines to write Saxe-Coburg historical romance, 169; and Golding's *Rites of Passage* and *Close Quarters*, 223; in the novels of Stephanie Barron, 237;

359